THE

MYSTERY OF MARY STUART

Walker & Cockerell, ph. sc.

Mary Stuart

From the portrait in the collection

of the Earl of Morton.

Reprinted from the edition of 1901, London
First AMS EDITION published 1970
Manufactured in the United States of America

Library of Congress Catalogue Card Number: 78-111771
SBN: 404-03858-1

AMS PRESS, INC.
NEW YORK, N. Y. 10003

THE

MYSTERY OF MARY STUART

BY

ANDREW LANG

WITH ILLUSTRATIONS

AMS PRESS
NEW YORK

INTRODUCTION

MR. CARLYLE not unjustly described the tragedy of Mary Stuart as but a personal incident in the true national History of Scotland. He asked for other and more essential things than these revelations of high life. Yet he himself wrote in great detail the story of the Diamond Necklace of Marie Antoinette. The diamonds of the French, the silver Casket of the Scottish Queen, with all that turned on them, are of real historical interest, for these trifles brought to the surface the characters and principles of men living in an age of religious revolution. Wells were sunk, as it were, deep into human personality, and the inner characteristics of the age leaped upwards into the light.

For this reason the Mystery of Mary Stuart must always fascinate : moreover, curiosity has never ceased to be aroused by this problem of Mary's guilt or innocence. Hume said, a hundred and fifty years ago, that the Scottish Jacobite who believed in the Queen's innocence was beyond the reach of reason or argument. Yet from America, Russia, France, and Germany we receive works in which the guilt of Mary is denied, and the arguments of Hume, Robertson, Laing, Mignet, and Froude are contested. Every inch of the ground has been inspected as if by detectives on the scene of a recent murder; and one might suppose that the Higher Criticism had uttered its last baseless conjecture and that every syllable of the fatal Casket Letters, the only external and documentary testimony to Mary's guilt, must have been weighed, tested, and analysed. But this, as we shall see, is hardly the fact. There are 'points as yet unseized by Germans.' Mary was never tried by a Court of Justice during her lifetime. Her cause has been in process of trial ever since. Each newly discovered manuscript, like the fragmentary biography by her secretary, Nau, and the Declaration of the Earl of Morton, and the newly translated dispatches of the Spanish ambassadors, edited by Major Martin Hume (1894), has brought fresh light, and has modified the tactics of the attack and defence.

As Herr Cardauns remarks, at the close of his 'Der Sturz der Maria Stuart,' we cannot expect finality, and our verdicts or hypotheses may be changed by the emergence of some hitherto unknown piece of evidence. Already we have seen too many ingenious theories overthrown. From the defence of Mary by Goodall (1754) to the triumphant certainties of Chalmers (1818), to the arguments of MM. Philippson and Sepp, of Mr. Hosack, and of Sir John Skelton (1880–1895), increasing knowledge of facts, new emergence of old MSS. have, on the whole, weakened the position of the defence. Mr. Henderson's book 'The Casket Letters and Mary Stuart' (First Edition 1889) is the last word on the matter in this country. Mr. Henderson was the first to publish in full Morton's sworn Declaration as to the discovery, inspection, and safe keeping of the fatal Casket and its contents. Sir John Skelton's reply [1] told chiefly against minor points of criticism and palæography.

The present volume is not a Defence of Mary's innocence. My object is to show, how the whole problem is affected by the discovery of the Lennox Papers, which admit us behind the scenes, and enable us to see how Mary's prosecutors, especially the Earl of Lennox, the father of her murdered husband, got up their case. The result of criticism of these papers is certainly to reinforce Mr. Hosack's argument, that there once existed a forged version of the long and monstrous letter to Bothwell from Glasgow, generally known as ' Letter II.' In this book, as originally written, I had myself concluded that Letter II., as it stands, bears evidence of garbling. The same is the opinion of Dr. Bresslau, who accepts the other Casket Papers as genuine. The internal chronology of Letter II. is certainly quite impossible, and in this I detected unskilled dove-tailing of genuine and forged elements. But I thought it advisable to rewrite the first half of the Letter, in modern English, as if it were my own composition, and while doing this I discovered the simple

---

[1] *Blackwood's Magazine*, December, 1889.

and ordinary kind of accident which may explain the dislocation of the chronology, and remove the evidence to unskilled dove-tailing and garbling. In the same spirit of rather reluctant conscientiousness, I worked out the scheme of dates which makes the Letter capable of being fitted into the actual series of events. Thus I am led, though with diffidence, to infer that, though a forged version of Letter II. probably once existed, the Letter may be, at least in part, a genuine composition by the Queen. The fact, however, does not absolutely compel belief, and, unless new manuscripts are discovered, may always be doubted by admirers of Mary.

Sir John Skelton, in his 'Maitland of Lethington,' regarded the supposed falsification of Letter II. as an argument against all the Casket Letters ('false in one thing, false in all'). But it is clear that forgery may be employed to strengthen the evidence, even of a valid cause. If Mary's enemies deemed that the genuine evidence which they had collected was inadequate, and therefore added evidence which was not genuine, that proves their iniquity, but does not prove Mary's innocence. Portions of the Letter II., and of some of the other Letters, have all the air of authenticity, and suffice to compromise the Queen.

This inquiry, then, if successfully conducted, does not clear Mary, but solves some of the darkest problems connected with her case. I think that a not inadequate theory of the tortuous and unintelligible policy of Maitland of Lethington, and of his real

relations with Mary, is here presented. I also hope
that new light is thrown on Mary's own line of defence, and on the actual forgers or contaminators of
her Letters, if the existence of such forgery or con-
tamination is held to be possible.

By study of dates it is made clear, I think, that
the Lords opposing Mary took action, as regards the
Letters, on the very day of their discovery. This
destroys the argument which had been based on the
tardy appearance of the papers in the dispatches of
the period, an argument already shaken by the revelations of the Spanish Calendar.

Mary's cause has, hitherto, been best served by her
accusers, most injured by her defenders. For political and personal reasons her enemies, her accomplices,
or the conscious allies of her accomplices, perpetually stultified themselves and gave themselves the
lie. Their case was otherwise very badly managed.
Their dates were so carelessly compiled as to make
their case chronologically impossible. Their position,
as stated, probably by George Buchanan and Makgill, in 'The Book of Articles,' and the 'Detection,'
is marred by exaggerations and inconsistencies.
Buchanan was by no means a critical historian, and he
was here writing as an advocate, mainly from briefs
furnished by Lennox, his feudal chief, the father of
the murdered Darnley. These briefs we now possess,
and the generosity of Father Pollen, S.J., has allowed
me to use these hitherto virgin materials.

The Lennox Papers also enable us to add new

and dramatically appropriate anecdotes of Mary and Darnley, while, by giving us some hitherto unknown myths current at the moment, they enable us to explain certain difficulties which have puzzled historians. The whole subject throws a lurid light on the ethics and the persons of the age which followed the Reformation in Scotland. Other novelties may be found to emerge from new combinations of facts and texts which have long been familiar, and particular attention has been paid to the subordinate persons in the play, while a hitherto disregarded theory of the character of Bothwell is offered ; a view already, in part, suggested by Mignet.

The arrangement adopted is as follows :

First, in two preliminary chapters, the characters and the scenes of the events are rapidly and broadly sketched. We try to make the men and women live and move in palaces and castles now ruinous or untenanted.

Next the relations of the characters to each other are described, from Mary's arrival in Scotland to her marriage with Darnley ; the murder of Riccio, the interval of the eleven predicted months that passed ere beside Riccio lay 'a fatter than he,' Darnley : the slaying of Darnley, the marriage with Bothwell, the discovery of the Casket, the imprisonment at Loch Leven, the escape thence, and the flight into England.

Next the External History of the Casket Letters, the first hints of their existence, their production before Elizabeth's Commission at Westminster, and Mary's attitude towards the Letters, with the obscure intrigues of the Commission at York, and the hasty and scuffling examinations at Westminster and Hampton Court, are described and explained.

Next the Internal Evidence of the Letters themselves is criticised.

Finally, the later history of the Letters, with the disappearance of the original alleged autograph texts, closes the subject.

Very minute examination of details and dates has been deemed necessary. The case is really a police case, and investigation cannot be too anxious, but certain points of complex detail are relegated to Appendices.

In writing the book I have followed, as Socrates advises, where the *Logos* led me. Several conclusions or theories which at first beguiled me, and seemed convincing, have been ruined by the occurrence of fresher evidence, and have been withdrawn. I have endeavoured to search for, and have stated, as fully as possible, the objections which may be urged to conclusions which are provisional, and at the mercy of criticism, and of fresh or neglected evidence.

The character of Mary, *son naturel*, as she says, or is made to say in the most incriminating Letter, is full of fascination, excellence and charm. Her terrible expiation has won the pity of gentle hearts, and sentiment has too often clouded reason, while

reaction against sentiment has been no less mis-
chievous. But History, the search for truth, should
be as impersonal as the judge on the bench. I am
not unaccustomed to be blamed for 'destroying
our illusions,' but to cultivate and protect illusion
has never been deemed the duty of the historian.
Mary, at worst, and even admitting her guilt (guilt
monstrous and horrible to contemplate) seems to
have been a nobler nature than any of the persons
most closely associated with her fortunes. She fell,
if fall she did, like the Clytæmnestra to whom a
contemporary poet compares her, under the almost
demoniacal possession of passion; a possession so
sudden, strange and overpowering that even her
enemies attributed it to 'unlawful arts.'

I have again to acknowledge the almost, or quite,
unparalleled kindness of Father Pollen in allowing
me to use his materials. He found transcripts of
what I style the 'Lennox MSS.' among the papers
of the late learned Father Stevenson, S.J. These
he collated with the originals in the University
Library at Cambridge. It is his intention, I understand, to publish the whole collection, which was
probably put together for the use of Dr. Wilson,
when writing, or editing, the 'Actio,' published with
Buchanan's 'Detection.' Father Pollen has also read
most of my proof-sheets, but he is not responsible
for any of my provisional conclusions. I have also
consulted, on various points, Mr. George Neilson
and Dr. Hay Fleming.

Miss Dorothy Alston made reduced drawings, omitting the figures, of the contemporary charts of Edinburgh, and of Kirk o' Field. Mr. F. Compton Price supplied the imitations of Mary's handwriting, and the facsimiles in Plates A B, B A, &c.

For leave to photograph and publish the portrait of Darnley and his brother I have to acknowledge the gracious permission of his Majesty, the King.

The Duke of Hamilton has kindly given permission to publish photographs of the Casket at Hamilton Palace (see Chapter XVIII.).

The Earl of Morton has been good enough to allow his admirable portraits of Mary (perhaps of 1575) and of the Regent Morton to be reproduced.

Mr. Oliphant, of Rossie, has placed at my service his portrait of Mary as a girl, a copy, probably by Sir John Medina, of a contemporary French likeness.

To the kindness of the Right Hon. A. J. Balfour and Miss Balfour we owe the photographs of the famous tree at Whittingham, Mr. Balfour's seat, where Morton, Lethington, and Bothwell conspired to murder Darnley.

The Lennox Papers are in the Cambridge University Library.

The Suppressed Confessions of Hepburn of Bowton

Too late for notice in the body of this book, the following curious piece of evidence was observed by Father Ryan, S.J., in the Cambridge MS. of the deposition of Hepburn of Bowton. This kinsman and accomplice of Bothwell was examined on December 8, 1567, before Moray, Atholl, Kirkcaldy, Lindsay, and Bellenden, Lord Justice Clerk. The version of his confession put in at the Westminster Conference, December 1568, will be found in Anderson, ii. 187 *et seq.*, and in Laing, ii. 256–259. The MS. is in Cotton Caligula, C.I. fol. 325. It is attested as a 'true copy' by Bellenden. But if we follow the Cambridge MS. it is *not* a true copy. A long passage, following ' and lay down with him,' at the end, is omitted. That passage I now cite :

'Farther this deponar sayis that he inquirit at my lord quhat securitie he had for it quhilk wes done, because their wes sic ane brute and murmo^r in the toun And my lord ansuerit that diuerse noblemen had subscrivit the deid with him And schew the same band [1] to the deponar, quhairat wes the subscriptionis of the erles of huntlie, ergile, boithuile altogether, and the secretares subscriptioun far beneth the rest. And insafar as the deponar remembers this was the effect of it, it contenit sum friuose [frivolous ?] and licht caussis aganis the king sic as hys behavio^r contrar the quene, quhilk band wes in ane of twa silver cofferis and wes in dunbar, and the deponar saw the same there the tyme that they wer thare after the quenis revissing And understandis that the band wes with the remanent letters, and putt in the castell be george dalgleis. Inquirit quha

[1] Bond

deuisit that the king suld ludge at the kirk of feild?

'Answeris Sr James balfo^r can better tell nor he And knew better and befoir the deponer yof. And quhen the Quene wes in glasgow my lord Boithuile send the deponar to Sr James balfo^r desiring that he wald cum and meit my lord at the kirk of feild To quhome Schir James ansuerit, "will my lord cum thair? gif he cum it wer gude he war quiet." And yit they met not at that place than nor at natyme thairefter to the deponers knawledge.

'Thair wes xiiii keyis quhilkis this deponer efter the murtho^r keist in the grevvell hoill [? quarrel-hoill, *i.e.* quarry-hole] betuix the abbay and leith. And towardes the makers of the keyis they were maid betuix Leuestoun and Sr James balfo^r and thai twa can tell. Item deponis that Ilk ane that wer of the band and siclike the erle of Morton and Sy^r James balfo^r suld haif send twa men to the committing of the murther. And the erle boithuile declarit to the deponar ane nyt or twa afore the murtho^r falland in talking of thame that wer in the kingis chalmer My lord said that Sandy Durham wes ane gude fallowe and he wald wische that he weir out of the same.

'This is the trew copy, etc.'

Perhaps few will argue that this passage has been fraudulently inserted in the Cambridge MS. If not, Bellenden lied when he attested the mutilated deposition to be a true copy. His own autograph signature

a

attests the Cambridge copy. Moray, who heard
Bowton make his deposition, was a partner to the
fraud. The portion of the evidence burked by Moray
is corroborated, as regards the signatures of the band
for Darnley's murder, by Ormistoun, much later
(Dec. 13, 1573) in Laing, ii. 293. Ormistoun, however, probably by an error of memory, says that he
saw what Bothwell affirmed to be the signature of
Sir James Balfour, in addition to those spoken of by
Bowton, namely Argyll, Bothwell, Huntly, and Lethington. But this statement as to Balfour he withdrew
in his dying confession as published. Bowton's remark that Lethington's signature came 'far beneath
the rest' sounds true. Space would be left above
for the signatures of men of higher rank than the
secretary.

Bowton saw the band at Dunbar (April–May,
1567, during Mary's detention there), 'in one of two
silver coffers.' He only 'understands' that the band
was 'with the remanent letters, and put in the Castle
by George Dalgleish.' If 'the remanent letters' are
the Casket Letters, and if Bowton, at Dunbar, had
seen them with the band, and read them, his evidence
would have been valuable as to the Letters. But as
things are, we have merely his opinion, or 'understanding,' that certain letters were kept with the
band, as Drury, we know, asserted that it was in
the Casket with the other papers, and was destroyed,
while the Letters attributed to Mary 'were kept to be
shown.' Of course, if this be true, Morton lied when

he said that the contents of the Casket had neither been added to nor diminished.

Next, Bowton denied that, to his knowledge, Bothwell and Balfour met at the Kirk o' Field, while Mary was at Glasgow, or at any other time. If Bowton is right, and he was their go-between, Paris lied in his Deposition where he says that Bothwell and Sir James had passed a whole night in Kirk o' Field, while Mary was at Glasgow.[1]

Bowton's confession that Morton ' should have sent two men to the committing of the murder,' explains the presence of Archibald Douglas, Morton's cousin, with Binning, his man. These two represented Morton. Finally, Bowton's confession in the Cambridge MS. joins the copy of his confession put in at Westminster, on the point of the fourteen false keys of Kirk o' Field, thrown by Bowton into a gravel hole. Unless then the Cambridge MS. is rejected, the Lord Justice Clerk and Moray deliberately suppressed evidence which proved that Moray was allied with two of Darnley's murderers in prosecuting his sister for that crime. Such evidence, though extant, Moray, of course, dared not produce, but must burke at Westminster.

I have shown in the text (p. 144) that, even on Bowton's evidence as produced at Westminster, Moray was aware that Bothwell had allies among the nobles, but that, as far as the evidence declares, he asked no questions. But the Cambridge MS. proves

[1] Laing, ii. 284.

his full knowledge, which he deliberately suppressed. The Cambridge MS. must either have been furnished to Lennox, before the sittings at Westminster; or must have been the original, or a copy of the original, later supplied to Dr. Wilson while preparing Buchanan's ' Detection,' the ' Actio,' and other documents for the press in November 1571.[1] It will be observed that when Lethington was accused of Darnley's murder, in September 1569, Moray could not well have prosecuted him to a conviction, as his friends, Atholl and Kirkcaldy, having been present at Bowton's examination, knew that Moray knew of Lethington's guilt, yet continued to be his ally. The Cambridge copy of the deposition of Hay of Tala contains no reference to the guilt of Morton or Lethington; naturally, for Morton was present at Hay's examination. Finally, the evidence of Binning, in 1581, shows that representatives of Lethington and Balfour, as well as of Morton, were present at the murder, as Bowton, in his suppressed testimony, says had been arranged.

It is therefore clear that Moray, in arraigning his sister with the aid of her husband's assassins, could suppress authentic evidence. Mary's apologists will argue that he was also capable of introducing evidence less than authentic.

[1] See Murdin, p. 57.

CONTENTS

APPENDICES

LIST OF ILLUSTRATIONS

PHOTOGRAVURE PLATES

OTHER ILLUSTRATIONS

THE

MYSTERY OF MARY STUART

I

DRAMATIS PERSONÆ

HISTORY is apt to be, and some think that it should be,
a mere series of dry uncoloured statements.   Such an
event occurred, such a word was uttered, such a deed
was done, at this date or the other.   We give references to our authorities, to men who heard of the
events, or even saw them when they happened.   But
we, the writer and the readers, *see* nothing : we only
offer or accept bald and imperfect information.   If
we try to write history on another method, we
become 'picturesque :' we are composing a novel,
not striving painfully to attain the truth.   Yet, when
we know not the details ;—the aspect of dwell-
ings now ruinous ; the hue and cut of garments
long wasted into dust ; the passing frown, or smile,
or tone of the actors and the speakers in these
dramas of life long ago ; the clutch of Bothwell at
his dagger's hilt, when men spoke to him in the
street ; the flush of Darnley's fair face as Mary and

he quarrelled at Stirling before his murder—then
we know not the real history, the real truth. Now
and then such a detail of gesture or of change of
countenance is recorded by an eyewitness, and
brings us, for a moment, into more vivid contact with
the past. But we could only know it, and judge
the actors and their conduct, if we could see the
personages in their costume as they lived, passing
by in some magic mirror from scene to scene. The
stage, as in Schiller's ' Marie Stuart,' comes nearest
to reality, if only the facts given by the poet were
real ; and next in vividness comes the novel, such as
Scott's ' Abbot,' with its picture of Mary at Loch Leven,
when she falls into an hysterical fit at the mention of
Bastian's marriage on the night of Darnley's death.
Far less intimate than these imaginary pictures of
genius are the statements of History, dull when they
are not 'picturesque,' and when they are ' picturesque,'
sometimes prejudiced, inaccurate, and misleading.

We are to betake ourselves to the uninviting
series of contradictory statements and of contested
dates, and of disputable assertions, which are the dry
bones of a tragedy like that of the ' Agamemnon ' of
Æschylus. Let us try first to make mental pictures
of the historic people who play their parts on what is
now a dimly lighted stage, but once was shone upon
by the sun in heaven ; by the stars of darkling nights
on ways dimly discerned ; by the candles of Holyrood,
or of that crowded sick-room in Kirk o' Field, where
Bothwell and the Lords played dice round the fated

Darnley's couch; or by the flare of torches under which Mary rode down the Blackfriars Wynd and on to Holyrood.

The foremost person is the Queen, a tall girl of twenty-four, with brown hair, and sidelong eyes of red brown. Such are her sidelong eyes in the Morton portrait; such she bequeathed to her great-great-grandson, James, 'the King over the Water.' She was half French in temper, one of the proud bold Guises, by her mother's side; and if not beautiful, she was so beguiling that Elizabeth recognised her magic even in the reports of her enemies.[1]

'This lady and Princess is a notable woman,' said Knollys; 'she showeth a disposition to speak much, to be bold, to be pleasant, and to be very familiar. She showeth a great desire to be avenged of her enemies, she showeth a readiness to expose herself to all perils in hope of victory, she delighteth much to hear of

---

[1] Among the mysteries which surround Mary, we should not reckon the colour of her hair! Just after her flight into England, her gaoler, at Carlisle, told Cecil that in Mary Seton the Queen had 'the finest busker of a woman's hair to be seen in any country. Yesterday and this day she did set such a curled hair upon the Queen, that was said to be a perewyke, that showed very delicately, and every other day she hath a new device of head dressing that setteth forth a woman gaily well.' Henceforth Mary varied the colour of her 'perewykes.' She had worn them earlier, but she wore them, at least at her first coming into England, for the good reason that, in her flight from Langside, she had her head shaved, probably for purposes of disguise. So we learn from Nau, her secretary. Mary was flying, in fact, as we elsewhere learn, from the fear of the fiery death at the stake, the punishment of husband-murder. Then, and then only, her nerve broke down, like that of James VIII. at Montrose; of Prince Charles after Culloden; of James VII. when he should have ridden with Dundee to the North and headed the clans.

hardiness and valiance, commending by name all approved hardy men of her country, although they be her enemies, and concealeth no cowardice even in her friends.'

There was something 'divine,' Elizabeth said, in the face and manner which won the hearts of her gaolers in Loch Leven and in England. 'Heaven bless that sweet face!' cried the people in the streets as the Queen rode by, or swept along with the long train, the 'targetted tails' and 'stinking pride of women,' that Knox denounced.

She was gay, as when Randolph met her, in no more state than a burgess's wife might use, in the little house of St. Andrews, hard by the desecrated Cathedral. She could be madly mirthful, dancing, or walking the black midnight streets of Edinburgh, masked, in male apparel, or flitting 'in homely attire,' said her enemies, about the Market Cross in Stirling. She loved, at sea, 'to handle the boisterous cables,' as Buchanan tells. Pursuing her brother, Moray, on a day of storm, or hard on the doomed Huntly's track among the hills and morasses of the North; or galloping through the red bracken of the October moors, and the hills of the robbers, to Hermitage; her energy outwore the picked warriors in her company. At other times, in a fascinating languor, she would lie long abed, receiving company in the French fashion, waited on by her Maries, whose four names 'are four sweet symphonies,' Mary Seton and Mary Beaton, Mary Fleming and Mary Livingstone. To the

Mary at Eighteen.

Council Board she would bring her woman's work, embroidery of silk and gold. She was fabled to have carried pistols at her saddle-bow in war, and she excelled in matches of archery and pall-mall.

Her costumes, when she would be queenly, have left their mark on the memory of men: the ruff from which rose the snowy neck; the brocaded bodice, with puffed and jewelled sleeves and stomacher; the diamonds, gifts of Henri II. or of Diane; the rich pearls that became the spoil of Elizabeth; the brooches enamelled with sacred scenes, or scenes from fable. Many of her jewels—the ruby tortoise given by Riccio; the enamel of the mouse and the ensnared lioness, passed by Lethington as a token into her dungeon of Loch Leven; the diamonds bequeathed by her to one whom she might not name; the red enamelled wedding-ring, the gift of Darnley; the diamond worn in her bosom, the betrothal present of Norfolk—are, to our fancy, like the fabled star-ruby of Helen of Troy, that dripped with blood-gouts which vanished as they fell. Riccio, Darnley, Lethington, Norfolk, the donors of these jewels, they were all to die for her, as Bothwell, too, was to perish, the giver of the diamond carried by Paris, the recipient of the black betrothal ring enamelled with bones and tears. 'Her feet go down to death,' her feet that were so light in the dance, 'her steps take hold on hell. . . . Her lips drop as an honeycomb, and her mouth is smoother than oil. But her end is bitter as wormwood, sharp as a two-edged sword.'

The lips that dropped as honeycomb, the laughing mouth, could wildly threaten, and vainly rage or beseech, when she was entrapped at Carberry; or could waken pity in the sternest Puritan when, half-clad, her bosom bare, her loose hair flowing, she wailed from her window to the crowd of hostile Edinburgh.

She was of a high impatient spirit: we seem to recognise her in an anecdote told by the Black Laird of Ormistoun, one of Darnley's murderers, in prison before his execution. He had been warned by his brother, in a letter, that he was suspected of the crime, and should 'get some good way to purge himself.' He showed the letter to Bothwell, who read it, and gave it to Mary. She glanced at it, handed it to Huntly, 'and thereafter turnit unto me, and turnit her back, and gave *ane thring* with her shoulder, and passit away, and spake nothing to me.' But that 'thring' spoke much of Mary's mood, unrepentant, contemptuous, defiant.

Mary's gratitude was not of the kind proverbial in princes. In September 1571, when the Ridolfi plot collapsed, and Mary's household was reduced, her sorest grief was for Archibald Beaton, her usher, and little Willie Douglas, who rescued her from Loch Leven. They were to be sent to Scotland, which meant death to both, and she pleaded pitifully for them. To her servants she wrote: 'I thank God, who has given me strength to endure, and I pray Him to grant you the like grace. To you will

your loyalty bring the greatest honour, and when-
soever it pleases God to set me free, I will never fail
you, but reward you according to my power. . . .
Pray God that you be true men and constant,
to such He will never deny his grace, and for you,
John Gordon and William Douglas, I pray that He
will inspire your hearts. I can no more. Live in
friendship and holy charity one with another, bearing each other's imperfections. . . . You, William
Douglas, be assured that the life which you hazarded
for me shall never be destitute while I have one
friend alive.'

In a trifling transaction she writes: ' Rather
would I pay twice over, than injure or suspect any
man.'

In the long lament of the letters written during
her twenty years of captivity, but a few moods return
and repeat themselves, like phrases in a fugue.
Vain complaints, vain hopes, vain intrigues with
Spain, France, the Pope, the Guises, the English
Catholics, succeed each other with futile iteration.
But always we hear the note of loyalty even to
her humblest servants, of sleepless memory of their
sacrifices for her, of unstinting and generous gratitude.
Such was the Queen's ' natural,' *mon naturel* : with
this character she faced the world : a lady to live
and die for : and many died.

This woman, sensitive, proud, tameless, fierce,
and kind, was browbeaten by the implacable Knox :
her priests were scourged and pilloried, her creed

was outraged every day; herself scolded, preached at, insulted; her every plan thwarted by Elizabeth. Mary had reason enough for tears even before her servant was slain almost in her sight by her witless husband and the merciless Lords. She could be gay, later, dancing and hunting, but it may well be that, after this last and worst of cruel insults, her heart had now become hard as the diamond; and that she was possessed by the evil spirits of loathing, and hatred, and longing for revenge. It had not been a hard heart, but a tender; capable of sorrow for slaves at the galley oars. After her child's birth, when she was holiday-making at Alloa, according to Buchanan, with Bothwell and his gang of pirates, she wrote to the Laird of Abercairnie, bidding him be merciful to a poor woman and her 'company of puir bairnis' whom he had evicted from their 'kindly rowme,' or little croft.

Her more than masculine courage her enemies have never denied. Her resolution was incapable of despair; 'her last word should be that of a Queen.' Her plighted promise she revered, but, in such an age, a woman's weapon was deceit.

She was the centre and pivot of innumerable intrigues. The fierce nobles looked on her as a means for procuring lands, office, and revenge on their feudal enemies. To the fiercer ministers she was an idolatress, who ought to die the death, and, meanwhile, must be thwarted and insulted. To France, Spain, and Austria she was a piece in the game of diplomatic chess. To the Pope she seemed an instrument that might win back both Scotland and England for the Church, while the English Catholics regarded her as either their lawful or their future Queen. To Elizabeth she was, naturally, and inevitably, and, in part, by her own fault, a deadly rival ; whatever feline caresses might pass between them : gifts of Mary's heart, in a heart-shaped diamond ; Elizabeth's diamond 'like a rock,' a rock in which was no refuge. Yet Mary was of a nature so large and unsuspicious that, on the strength of a ring and a promise, she trusted herself to Elizabeth, contrary to the advice of her staunchest adherents. She was no natural dissembler, and with difficulty came to understand that others could be false. Her sense of honour might become perverted, but she had a strong native sense of honour.

One thing this woman wanted, a master. Even before Darnley and she were wedded, at least publicly, Randolph wrote, ' All honour that may be attributed unto any man by a wife, he hath it wholly and fully.' In her authentic letters to Norfolk, when, a captive in England, she regarded herself as betrothed to him, we find her adopting an attitude of submissive obedience. The same tone pervades the disputed Casket Letters, to Bothwell, and is certainly in singular consonance with the later, and genuine epistles to Norfolk. But the tone—if the Casket Letters are forged—may have been borrowed from what was known of her early submission to Darnley.

The second *dramatis persona* is Darnley, 'The
Young Fool.' Concerning Darnley but little is
recorded in comparison with what we know of Mary.
He was the son, by the Earl of Lennox, a royal
Stewart, of that daughter whom Margaret Tudor,
sister of Henry VIII., and widow of James IV., bore
to her second husband, the Earl of Angus. Darnley's
father regarded himself as next to the Scottish crown,
for the real nearest heir, the head of the Hamiltons,
the Duke of Chatelherault, Lennox chose to consider
as illegitimate. After playing a double and dishonest
part in the troubled years following the death of
James V., Lennox retired to England with his wife, a
victim of the suspicions of Elizabeth.[1] The education
of his son, Henry, Lord Darnley, seems to have been
excellent, as far as the intellect and the body are
concerned. The letter which, as a child of nine, he
wrote to Mary Tudor, speaking of a work of his own,
'The New Utopia,' is in the new 'Roman' hand,
carried to the perfection of copperplate. The
Lennox MSS. say that 'the Queen was stricken
with the dart of love by the comliness of his sweet
behaviour, personage, wit, and vertuous qualities, as
well in languages[2] and lettered sciencies, as also in
the art of music, dancing, and playing on instruments.'
When his murderers had left his room at midnight,
his last midnight, his chamber-child begged him to

---

[1] The papers used by Lennox in getting up his indictment against
Mary are new materials, which we often have occasion to cite.

[2] Mr. Henderson doubts if Darnley knew French.

THES.BE THE SONES OF TE RIGHT HONERABLES FERLE OF LENOXE
TE LADY MARGARETZ GRACE COVNTYES OF LENOXE AD ANGWYSE

1565

318
CHARLES STEWARDE   HENRY STEWARDE LORD DAR
HIS BROTHER ÆTATIS 6   LEY AND DOWGLAS ÆTATIS 17

Darnley at about the age of 18.

play, while a psalm was sung, but his hand, he
replied, was out for the lute, so say the Lennox
Papers. Physically he was ' a comely Prince of a
fair and large stature, pleasant in countenance . . .
well exercised in martial pastimes upon horseback as
any Prince of that age.' The Spanish Ambassador
calls him ' an amiable youth.' But it is plain that
' the long lad,' the *gentil hutaudeau*, with his girlish
bloom, and early tendency to fulness of body, was a
spoiled child. His mother, a passionate intriguer,
kept this before him, that, as great-grandson of
Henry VIII., and as cousin of Mary Stuart, he should
unite the two crowns. There were Catholics enough
in England to flatter the pride of a future king,
though now in exile. This Prince *in partibus*, like
his far-away descendant, Prince Charles Edward,
combined a show of charming manners, when he
chose to charm, with an arrogant and violent
petulance, when he deemed it safe to be insulting.
At his first arrival in Scotland he won golden
opinions, ' his courteous dealing with all men is well
spoken of.' As his favour with Mary waxed he
' dealt blows where he knew that they would be taken;'
he is said to have drawn his dagger on an official who
brought him a disappointing message, and his foolish
freedom of tongue gave Moray the alarm. It was
soon prophesied that he ' could not continue long.'
' To all honest men he is intolerable, and almost
forgetful of her already, that has adventured so much
for his sake. What shall become of her or what life

with him she shall lead, that already taketh so much
upon him as to control and command her, I leave
it to others to think.' So Randolph, the English
Ambassador, wrote as early as May, 1565. She was
'blinded, transported, carried I know not whither or
which way, to her own confusion and destruction:'
words of omen that were fulfilled.

Whether Elizabeth let Darnley go to Scotland
merely for Mary's entanglement, whether Mary fell
in love with the handsome accomplished lad (as
Randolph seems to prove) or not, are questions then,
and now, disputed. The Lennox Papers, declaring
that she was smitten by the arrow of love; and
her own conduct, at first, make it highly probable
that she entertained for the *gentil hutaudeau* a passion,
or a passionate caprice.

Darnley, at least, acted like a new chemical
agent in the development of Mary's character. She
had been singularly long-suffering; she had borne
the insults and outrages of the extreme Protestants;
she had leaned on her brother, Moray, and on
Lethington; following or even leading these advisers
to the ruin of Huntly, her chief coreligionist.
Though constantly professing, openly to Knox, secretly to the Pope, her desire to succour the ancient
Church, she was obviously regarded, in Papal circles,
as slack in the work. She had been pliant, she had
endured the long calculated delays of Elizabeth, as
to her marriage, with patience; but, so soon as
Darnley crossed her path, she became resolute, even

reckless. Despite the opposition, interested, or
religious, or based on the pretext of religion, which
Moray and his allies offered, Mary wedded Darnley.
She found him a petulant, ambitious boy; sullen,
suspicious, resentful, swayed by the ambition to be a
king in earnest, but too indolent in affairs for the
business of a king.

At tennis, with Riccio, or while exercising his
great horses, his favourite amusement, Darnley was
pining to use his jewelled dagger. In the feverish
days before the deed it is probable that he kept his
courage screwed up by the use of stimulants, to
which he was addicted. That he devoted himself to
loose promiscuous intrigue injurious to his health, is
not established, though, when her child was born,
Mary warned Darnley that the babe was 'only too
much his son,' perhaps with a foreboding of heredi-
tary disease. A satirist called Darnley ' the leper :'
leprosy being confounded with ' la grosse vérole.'
Mary, who had fainting fits, was said to be epileptic.

Darnley, according to Lennox, represented himself as pure in this regard, nor have we any valid
evidence to the contrary. But his word was
absolutely worthless.

Outraged and harassed, broken, at last, in health,
in constant pain, expressing herself in hysterical out-
bursts of despair and desire for death, Mary needed
no passion for Bothwell to make her long for freedom
from the young fool. From his sick-bed in Glasgow,
as we shall see, he sent, by a messenger, a cutting

verbal taunt to the Queen; so his own friends
declare, they who call Darnley ' that innocent lamb.'
It is not wonderful if, in an age of treachery and
revenge, the character of Mary now broke down.
' I would not do it to him for my own revenge. My
heart bleeds at it,' she says to Bothwell, in the
Casket Letter II., if that was written by her. But,
whatever her part in it, the deed was done.

Of Bothwell, the third protagonist in the tragedy
of Three, we have no portrait, and but discrepant
descriptions. They who saw his body, not yet
wholly decayed, in Denmark, reported that he must
have been ' an ugly Scot,' with red hair, mixed with
grey before he died. Much such another was the
truculent Morton.[1] Born in 1536 or 1537, Bothwell
was in the flower of his age, about thirty, when
Darnley perished. He was certainly not old enough
to have been Mary's father, as Sir John Skelton
declared, for he was not six years her senior. His
father died in 1556, and Bothwell came young into
the Hepburn inheritance of impoverished estates,
high offices, and wild reckless blood. According to
Buchanan, Bothwell, in early youth, was brought up
at the house of his great-uncle, Patrick Hepburn,
Bishop of Moray, who certainly was a man of profligate
life. It is highly probable that Bothwell was educated in France.

' Blockish ' or not, Bothwell had the taste of a

---

[1] M. Jusserand has recently seen the corpse of Bothwell. Appendix A.

bibliophile. One of two books from his library, well bound, and tooled with his name and arms, is in the collection of the University of Edinburgh. Another was in the Gibson Craig Library. The works are a tract of Valturin, on Military Discipline (Paris, 1555, folio), and French translations of martial treatises attributed to Vegetius, Sextus Julius, and Ælian, with a collection of anecdotes of warlike affairs (Paris, 1556, folio). The possession of books like these, in such excellent condition, is no proof of doltishness. Moreover, Bothwell appears to have read his ' CXX Histoires concernans le faite guerre.' The evidence comes to us from a source which discredits the virulent rhetoric of Buchanan's ally.

It was the cue of Mary's foes to represent Bothwell as an ungainly, stupid, cowardly, vicious monster : because, he being such a man, what a wretch must the Queen be who could love him ! ' Which love, whoever saw not, and yet hath seen him, will perhaps think it incredible. . . . But yet here there want no causes, for there was in them both a likeness, if not of beauty or outward things, nor of virtues, yet of most extream vices.' [1] Buchanan had often celebrated, down to December 1566, Mary's extreme virtues. To be sure his poem, recited shortly before Darnley's death, may have been written almost as early as James's birth, in readiness for the feast 'at his baptism, and before Mary's intrigue with Bothwell

---

[1] *Actio*, probably by Dr. Wilson, appended to Buchanan's *Detection.*

could have begun. In any case, to prove Bothwell's
cowardice, some ally of Buchanan's cites his behaviour
at Carberry Hill, where he wishes us to believe that
Bothwell showed the white feather of Mary's ' pretty
venereous pidgeon.' As a witness, he cites du Croc,
the French Ambassador, an aged and sagacious man.
To du Croc he has appealed, to du Croc he shall go.
That Ambassador writes : ' He ' (Bothwell) ' told me
that there must be no more parley, for he saw that
the enemy was approaching, and had already crossed
the burn. He said that, if I wished to resemble the
man who tried to arrange a treaty between the forces
of Scipio and Hannibal, their armies being ready to
join in battle, like the two now before us, and who
failed, and, wishing to remain neutral, took a point
of vantage, and beheld the best sport that ever he
saw in his life, why then I should act like that man,
and would greatly enjoy the spectacle of a good
fight.' Bothwell's memory was inaccurate, or du
Croc has misreported his anecdote, but he was
certainly both cool and classical on an exciting
occasion.

Du Croc declined the invitation ; he was not
present when Bothwell refused to fight a champion
of the Lords, but he goes on : ' I am obliged to say
that I saw a great leader, speaking with great confidence, and leading his forces boldly, gaily, and skil-
fully. . . . I admired him, for he saw that his foes
were resolute, he could not be sure of the loyalty of
half of his own men, and yet he was quite un-

moved.'[1]   Bothwell, then, was neither dolt, lout, nor
coward, as Buchanan's ally wishes us to believe, for
the purpose of disparaging the taste of a Queen,
Buchanan's pupil, whose praises he had so often sung.

In an age when many gentlemen and ladies could
not sign their names, Bothwell wrote, and wrote
French, in a firm, yet delicate Italic hand, of
singular grace and clearness.[2] His enemies accused
him of studying none but books of Art Magic in his
youth, and he may have shared the taste of the great
contemporary mathematician, Napier of Merchistoun,
the inventor of Logarithms. Both Mary's friends
and enemies, including the hostile Lords in their
proclamations, averred that Bothwell had won her
favour by unlawful means, philtres, witchcraft, or
what we call Hypnotism. Such beliefs were universal: Ruthven, in his account of Riccio's murder,
tells us that he gave Mary a ring, as an antidote
to poison (not that *he* believed in it), and that
both she and Moray took him for a sorcerer.
On a charge of sorcery did Moray later burn the
Lyon Herald, Sir William Stewart, probably basing
the accusation on a letter in which Sir William
confessed to having consulted a prophet, perhaps
Napier of Merchistoun, the father, not the inventor
of Logarithms.[3] Quite possibly Bothwell may really
have studied the Black Art in Cornelius Agrippa

[1] Teulet, ii. p. 176.   Edinburgh, June 17, 1567.
[2] See a facsimile in Teulet, ii. 256.
[3] Appendix B.   'Burning of the Lyon King at Arms.'

and similar authors. In any case it is plain that, as regards culture, the author of *Les Affaires du Comte de Boduel*, the man familiar with the Court of France, where he had held command in the Scots Guards, and had probably known Ronsard and Brantôme, must have been a *rara avis* of culture among the nobles at Holyrood. So far, then, Mary's love for him, if love she entertained, was the reverse of ' incredible.' It did not need to be explained by a common possession of ' extreme vices.' The author, as usual, overstates his case, and proves too much : Lesley admits that Bothwell was handsome, an opinion emphatically contradicted by Brantôme.

Bothwell had the charm of recklessness to an unexampled degree. He was fierce, passionate, unyielding, strong, and, in the darkest of Mary's days, had been loyal. He had won for her what Knollys tells us that she most prized, victory. A greater contrast could not be to the false fleeting Darnley, the bully with ' a heart of wax.' In him Mary had more than enough of bloom and youthful graces : she could master him, and she longed for a master. If then she loved Bothwell, her love, however wicked, was not unnatural or incredible. He had been loved by many women, and had ruined all of them.

Among the other persons of the play, Moray is foremost, Mary's natural brother, the son of her whom James V. loved best, and, it was said, still dreamed of while wooing a bride in France. Moray is an enigma. History sees him, as in Lethington's phrase, 'looking through his fingers,' looking thus at Riccio's and at Darnley's murders. These fingers hide the face. He was undeniably a sound Protestant : only for a brief while, in Mary's early reign, was he sundered from Knox. In war he was, as he aimed at being, 'a Captain in Israel,' cool, courageous, and skilled. That he was extremely acquisitive is certain. Born a royal bastard, and trained for the Church, he clung as 'Commendator' to the Church's property which he held as a layman. His enormous possessions in land, collected partly by means that sailed close to the wind, partly from the grants of Mary, excited the rash words of Darnley, that they were 'too large.'

An early incident in Moray's life seems characteristic. The battle of Pinkie was fought in 1547, when he was sixteen. Among the slain was the Master of Buchan, the heir-apparent of the Earl of Buchan. He left a child, Christian Stewart, who was now heiress of the earldom. In January 1550, young Lord James Stewart, though Prior of St. Andrews, contracted himself in marriage with the little girl. The old earl was extravagant, perhaps more or less insane, and was deep in debt. His lands were mortgaged. In 1556 the Lord James bought and secured from the Regent, Mary of Guise, the right of redemption. In 1562, being all powerful now with Mary, he secured a grant of the 'ward, non-entries, and reliefs of the whole estates of the

earldom of Buchan.' Now, by the proclamation
made, as usual, before Pinkie fight, all these were
left by the Crown, free, to the heirs of such as might
fall in the battle. Therefore they ought to have
appertained to Christian Stewart, whom Moray had not
married, her grandfather being dead. Moray secured
everything to himself, by charters from the Crown.
The unlucky Christian went on living at Loch Leven,
with Moray's mother, Lady Douglas. In February
1562 Moray wedded Agnes Keith, daughter of the
Earl Marischal. His brother, apparently without his
knowledge, then married Christian. Moray wrote a
letter to his own mother complaining of this marriage
as an act of treachery. The Old Man peeps out
through the godly and respectful style of this epistle.
Moray speaks of Christian as 'that innocent;' perhaps she was not remarkable for intellect. He adds
that whoever tries to take from him the lady's
estates will have to pass over 'his belly.' And,
indeed, he retained the possessions. The whole
transaction does seem to savour of worldliness, to be
regretted in so good a man.

Moray continued, after he was pardoned for his
rebellion, to add estate to estate. He was a pensioner
of England; from France he received valuable
presents. His widow endeavoured to retain the
diamonds which Mary had owned, and wished to
leave attached to the Scottish crown. His ambition
was probably more limited than his covetousness,
and the suspicion that he aimed at being king,

though natural, was baseless. While he must have known, at least as well as Mary, the guilt of Morton, Lethington, Balfour, Bothwell, and Argyll, he associated familiarly with them, before he left Scotland prior to Mary's marriage with Bothwell, and he used Bothwell's accomplices, including the Bishop who married Bothwell to Mary, in his attack on the character of his sister. Whether he betrayed Norfolk, or not, was a question between David Hume and Dr. Robertson. If to report Norfolk's private conversation to Elizabeth is to betray,[1] Moray was a traitor, and did what Lethington scorned to do. But Moray's most remarkable quality was caution. He always had an *alibi*. He knew of Riccio's murder—and came to Edinburgh next day. He left Edinburgh in the morning, some sixteen hours before the explosion of Kirk o' Field. He left Edinburgh for England and France, twelve days before the nobles signed the document upholding Bothwell's innocence, and urging him to marry the Queen. He allowed Elizabeth to lie, in his presence, and about her encouragement of his rebellion, to the French Ambassador. His own account of his first interview with his sister, in prison at Loch Leven, shows him as an adept in menace cruelly suspended over her helpless head. The account of Mary's secretary, Nau, is much less unfavourable to Moray than his own, for obvious reasons.

[1] The private report is in the Lennox MSS.

As Regent he was bold, energetic, and ruth-less : the suspicion of his intention to give up a suppliant and fugitive aroused the tolerant ethics of the Border. A strong, patient, cautious man, capable of deep reserve, in his family relations, financial matters apart, austerely moral, Moray would have made an excellent king, but as a Queen's brother he was most dangerous, when not permitted to be all powerful. He could not have rescued Darnley, or saved Mary from herself, without risks which a Knox or a Craig would certainly have faced, but which no secular leader in Scotland would have dreamed of encountering. Did he wish to save the doomed prince ? A precise Puritan, he was by no means like a conscience among the warring members of the body politic. Mary rejoiced at the news of his murder, pensioned the assassin, and, of all people, chose an Archbishop as her confidant.

Reviled by Mary's literary partisans, Moray to Mr. Froude seemed ' noble ' and ' stainless.' He was a man of his time, a time when every traitor or assassin had ' God ' and ' honour ' for ever on his lips. At the hypocrisies and falsehoods of his party, deeds of treachery and blood, Moray ' looked through his fingers.'

Infinitely the most fascinating character in the plot was William Maitland, the younger, of Lething-ton. The charm which he exercised over his con-temporaries, from Mary herself to diplomatists like Randolph, and men of the sword like Kirkcaldy of

Grange, has not yet exhausted itself. Readers of
Sir John Skelton's interesting book, ' Maitland of
Lethington,' must observe, if they know the facts,
that, in presence of Lethington, Sir John is like
' birds whom the charmer serpent draws.' He is an
advocate of Mary, but of Mary as a ' charming
sinner.' By Lethington he is dominated : he will
scarcely admit that there is a stain on his scutcheon,
a scutcheon, alas! smirched and defaced. Could a
man of to-day hold an hour's converse with a man
of that age, he would choose Lethington. He was
behind all the scenes : he held the threads of all the
plots ; he made all the puppets dance at his will.
Yet by birth he was merely the son of the good and
wise poet and essayist, Sir Richard Lethington, laird
of a rugged tower and of lands in Lauderdale, *pastorum
loca vasta*. He was born about 1525, had studied in
France, and was a man of classical culture, without a
touch of pedantry. As early as 1555, we find him
arguing after supper with Knox, on the lawfulness of
bowing down in the House of Rimmon, attending
the Mass. Knox had the last word, for Lethington
was usually tactful ; in argument Knox was a babe
in the hands of the amateur theologian. Appointed
Secretary to Mary of Guise, in the troubled years of
the Congregation, Lethington deserted her and joined
the Lords. He negotiated for them with Cecil and
Elizabeth, and almost to the last he was true to one
idea, the union of the crowns of England and Scotland in peace and amity.

Through all the windings of his policy that idea governed him if not thwarted by personal considerations, as at the last. Before Mary's arrival in Scotland he hastened to make his peace with her, and her peace and trust she readily granted. Lethington was the spoiled child of the political world, ' the flower of the wits of Scotland,' as Elizabeth styled him ; was reckoned indispensable, was petted, caressed, and forgiven. He not only withstood Knox, in the interests of religious toleration, but he met him with a smile, with the weapons of *persiflage*, which riddled and rankled in the vanity of the Reformer. Lethington was modern to the finger-tips, a man of to-day, moving among the bravos, and using the poisoned tools, of an age of violence and perfidy.

Allied by marriage to the Earl of Atholl, in hours of peril he placed the Tay and the Pass of Killiecrankie between himself and the Law.

From the time of his restoration to Mary's favour after Riccio's murder, his part in the obscure intrigue of Darnley's murder, indeed all his future course, is a mystery. Being now over forty he had long wooed and just before the murder had won the beautiful Mary Fleming, of all the Four Maries the dearest to the Queen. His letter to Cecil on his love affair is a charming interlude. ' He is no more fit for her than I to be a page,' says the brawny, grizzled, Kirkcaldy of Grange. His devotion is often ridiculed by perhaps envious acquaintances. But, from September 20, 1556, Lethington was deep in every scheme against Darnley. He certainly signed the murder 'band.' He was with Mary at Stirling (April 22–23, 1567) when, if he did not know that Bothwell meant to carry her off (and perhaps he really did not know), he was alone in his ignorance among the inner circle of politicians. Yet he disliked the marriage, and was hated by Bothwell. On the day of Mary's *enlèvement*, Bothwell took Lethington, threatened him, and, but for Mary, would probably have slain him. Passive as to herself, she defended the Secretary with royal courage. Days darkened round the Queen, the nobles rose in arms. Lethington, about June 7, fled first to Livingstone's house of Callendar, then joined Atholl and the enemies of the Queen. We shall later attempt to unfold the secret springs of his tortuous and fatal policy.

Lethington had been the Ahithophel of the age. ' And the counsel of Ahithophel, which he counselled in those days, was as if a man had enquired at the oracle of God.' But the Lord ' turned the counsel of Ahithophel into foolishness.' He wrought against Mary, just after she saved his life from the dagger of Bothwell, some secret inexpiable offence, besides public injuries. Fear of her vengeance, for she knew something fatal to him, drove him into her party when her cause was desperate. He escaped the gallows by a natural death; he had long been smitten by creeping paralysis. Mary hated him dead, as after his betrayal of her she had loathed him living.

Mary was sorely bested, then, between the Young Fool, the Furious Man, the Puritan brother, and Michael Wylie (Machiavelli) as the Scots nick-named Lethington. She was absolutely alone. There was no man whom she could trust. On every hand were known rebels, half pardoned, half recon-ciled. Feuds, above all that of her husband and his clan, the Lennox Stewarts, with the nearest heirs of the crown, the Hamiltons, broke out eternally. The Protestants hated her : the Preachers longed to drag her down : the English Ambassadors were hostile spies. France was far away, the Queen Mother was her enemy : her kindred, the Guises, were cold or powerless. She saw only one strong man who had been loyal, one protector who had served her mother, and saved herself. That man was Bothwell.

Most inscrutable of the persons in the play is Bothwell's wife, Lady Jane Gordon, a daughter of Huntly, the dead and ruined Cock of the North. If we may accept the Casket Sonnets, Lady Jane, a girl of twenty, resisted her brother's scheme to wed her to Bothwell. She preferred some one whom the sonnet calls ' a troublesome fool,' and a note, in the Lennox Papers, informs us that her first love was Ogilvy of Boyne, who consoled himself with Mary Beaton. Still following the sonnets, we learn that the young Lady Bothwell dressed ill, but won her wild husband's heart by literary love letters plagia-rised from ' some illustrious author.' The existing letters of the lady, written after the years of storm,

are businesslike, and deal with business. She consented to her divorce for a valuable consideration in
lands which she held till her death, in the reign of
Charles I. According to general opinion, Bothwell,
as we shall see, greatly preferred her to the Queen,
and continued to live with her after the divorce.
Lady Bothwell kept the dispensation which enabled
her to marry Bothwell, though he was divorced from
her for the want of it. She married the Earl of
Sutherland in 1573, and, after his death, returned
à ses premiers amours, wedding her old true love
who had wooed her in her girlhood, Ogilvy of Boyne.
Their conversation must have been rich in curious
reminiscences. The loves and hatreds of their youth
were extinct; the wild hearts of Bothwell, Mary,
Mary Beaton, Lethington, Darnley, and the rest,
had long ceased to beat, and these two were left,
Darby and Joan, alone in a new world.

II

THE MINOR CHARACTERS

HAVING sketched the chief actors in this tragedy, we may glance at the players of subordinate parts. They were such men as are apt to be bred when a religious and social Revolution has shaken the bases of morality, when acquiescence in theological party cries confers the title of ' godly : ' when the wealth of a Church is to be won by cunning or force, and when feudal or clan loyalty to a chief is infinitely more potent than fidelity to king, country, and the fundamental laws of morality.   The Protestants, the ' godly,' accused the Idolaters (the Catholics) of throwing their sins off their shoulders in the confessional, and beginning anew.   But the godly, if naturally ruffians, consoled and cleared themselves by repentances on the scaffold, and one felt assured, after a life of crime, that he ' should sup with God that night.'

The Earl of Morton is no minor character in the history of Scotland, but his part is relatively subordinate in that of Mary Stuart.   The son of the most accomplished and perfidious scoundrel of the

past generation, Sir George Douglas, brother of
Angus the brother-in-law of Henry VIII., Morton had
treachery in his blood. His father had alternately
betrayed England of which he was a pensioner, and
Scotland of which he was a subject. By a perverse
ingenuity of shame, he had used the sacred Douglas
Heart, the cognisance of the House, the achievement
granted to the descendants of the Good Lord James,
as a mark to indicate what passages in his treasonable letters might be relied on by his English
employers. In Morton's father and uncle had lived
on the ancient inappeasable feud between Douglases
and Stewarts, between the Nobles and the Crown.
It was a feud stained by murder under trust, by
betrayal in the field, and perfidy in the closet.
Morton was heir to the feud of his family, and to the
falseness. When the Reformation broke out, and
the Wars of the Congregation against Idolatry,
Morton wavered long, but at length joined the
Protestants when they were certain of English assistance. Henceforth he was one of Mr. Froude's 'small
gallant band' of Reformers, and, as such, was hostile
to Mary. His sanctimonious snuffle is audible still,
in his remark to Throckmorton at the time when the
Englishman probably saved the life of the Queen
from the Lords. Throckmorton asked to be allowed
to visit Mary in prison : 'The Earl Morton answered
me that shortly I should hear from them, but the
day being destined, as I did see, to the Communion,
continual preaching, and common prayer, they could

not be absent, nor attend matters of the world, but first they must seek the matters of God, and take counsel of Him who could best direct them.'

A red-handed murderer, living in open adultery with the widow of Captain Cullen, whom he had hanged, and daily consorting with murderers like his kinsman, Archibald Douglas, the Parson of Glasgow, Morton approached the Divine Mysteries. His private life was notoriously profligate ; he added avarice to his other and more genial peccadilloes. He intruded on the Kirk the Tulchan Bishops, who were mere filters, or conduits, through which ecclesiastical wealth flowed into his hands. Yet he was godly : he was the foe of Idolaters, and the Kirk, while deploring his excesses, cast on him no unfavourable eye. He held the office of Chancellor, and, during the raids and risings which were protests against Darnley's marriage with Mary, he was in touch with both parties, but did not commit himself. About February, 1566, there seems to have been a purpose to deprive him of the Seals. He seized the moment to join hands with Darnley in antagonism to Riccio : he and his Douglases, George and Archibald, helped to organise the murder of the favourite : he was then driven into England. At Christmas, 1566, after signing a band, not involving murder, against Darnley, he was pardoned, returned, was made acquainted with the scheme for killing Darnley, but, he declared, declined to join without Mary's written warrant. His friend and retainer, Archibald Douglas, was present at the laying of gun-

The Regent Morton
From the portrait in the collection
of the Earl of Morton.

powder in Kirk o' Field. Morton presently signed a band promising to aid and abet Bothwell, but instantly joined the nobles who overthrew him. His retainers discovered the fatal Casket full of Mary's alleged letters to Bothwell, and he was one of the most ardent of her prosecutors. Vengeance came upon him, fourteen years later, from Stewart, the brother-in-law of John Knox.

In person, Morton was indeed one of the Red Douglases. A good portrait at Dalmahoy represents him with a common but grim set of features, and reddish tawny hair, under a tall black Puritanic hat.

A jackal constantly attendant on Morton was his kinsman, Archibald Douglas, a son of Douglas of Whittingham. In Archibald we see the ' strugfor-lifeur ' (as M. Daudet renders Darwin) of the period. A younger son, he was apparently educated for the priesthood, before the Reformation. In 1565, he was made ' Parson of Douglas,' drawing the revenues, and also was an Extraordinary Lord of Session. Involved in Riccio's murder, he fled to France (where he may have been educated), but returned to negotiate Morton's pardon. He was go-between to Morton, Bothwell, and Lethington, in the affair of Darnley's murder, and was present at, or just before, the explosion, losing one of his embroidered velvet dress shoes, in which he had perhaps been dancing at Bastian's marriage masque. He was also a spectator of the opening of the Casket (June 21, 1567), and so zealous and useful against Mary, that, after her defeat at Langside, he received the forfeited lands of the Laird of Corstorphine, near Edinburgh. In 1568 he became an Ordinary, or regular Judge of the Court of Session, and, later obtained the parish of Glasgow. The messenger of the Kirk, who came to bid him prepare his first sermon, found him playing cards with the Laird of Bargany. He had previously been plucked in the examination for the ministry : this was his second chance. Being examined he declined to attempt the Greek Testament ; and requested another minister to pray for him, 'for I am not used to pray.' His sermon was not thought savoury. After Morton became Regent, Archibald, for money, took the Queen's side, and is accused of an ungrateful and unclerical scheme to murder his cousin, Morton. Just for the devilry of it, and a little money, he was intriguing, a traitor to Morton, his benefactor, with Mary's party, and also acting as a spy for Drury and the English. He was, later, restored to his place on the Bench of Scottish Themis, crowded as it was with assassins, but he fled to England when Morton was accused and dragged down by Stewart of Ochiltree (1581). Morton, in his dying declaration, remembered his grudge against Archibald or for some other reason freely confessed *his* iniquities. Archibald now distinguished himself as a forger of letters intended to injure Stewart, but was denounced by his own brother, also a judge, Douglas of Whittingham. The later career of this accomplished gentleman was a series of treacherous betrayals of Mary. In England his charm and accomplishments recommended him to the friendship of Fulke Greville, who did not penetrate his character. His letters reveal a polished irony. He was for some time ambassador of James VI. to Elizabeth, was again accused of forgery, and, probably, ended his active career in rural retirement. History sees Archibald in the pulpit, a Stickit Minister : on the Bench administering justice : hobbling hurriedly from Kirk o' Field in one shoe ; watching the bursting open of the silver Casket ; playing cards, spying, dancing, and winning hearts, and forging letters : a versatile man of considerable charm and knowledge of the world. His life, after 1581, is a varied but always sordid chapter of romance.

A grimmer and a godlier man is Mr. John Wood, secretary of Moray, with whom he had been in France, an austere person, a rebuker of Mary's dances and frivolity. He, too, was a Lord of Session, and was wont to spur Moray on against Idolaters. We shall find him very busy in managing the Casket Letters. He was slain by Forbes of Reres, husband, or son, of the corpulent Lady Reres, rumoured to have been the complacent confidant of Mary's amour with Bothwell. Reres had certainly no reason to love Mr. John Wood. George Buchanan, too, is on the scene, the Latin poet, the Latin historian, who sang of and libelled his Queen, his pupil. Old now, and a devoted partisan of the Lennoxes, no man contributed

D

more to the cause of Mary's innocence than Buchanan, so grossly inaccurate and amusingly inconsistent are his various indictments of her behaviour. 'He spak and wret as they that wer about him for the tym infourmed him,' says Sir James Melville, 'for he was becom sleprie and cairles.' Melville speaks of a later date, but George's invectives against Mary are 'careless' in all conscience.

Besides these there is a pell-mell of men and women; crafty courteous diplomatists like the two Melvilles; burly Kirkcaldy of Grange, a murderer of the Cardinal, a spy of England when he was in French service, a secret agent of Cecil, a brave man and good captain, but accused of forgery, and by no means 'the second Wallace of Scotland,' the frank, manly, open-hearted Greysteil of historical tradition. Huntly and Argyll make little mark on the imagination: both astute, both full of promise, both barren of accomplishment. The Hamiltons have a lofty position, but are destitute of brains as of scruples; even the Archbishop, most unscrupulous of all, is no substitute for Cardinal Beaton.

There is a crowd of squires; loyal, gallant Arthur Erskine, Willie Douglas, who drew Mary forth of prison, the two Standens, English equerries of Darnley, whose lives are unwritten romances (what one of them did write is picturesque but untrustworthy), Lennox Lairds, busy Minto, Provost of Glasgow, and Houstoun, and valiant dubious Thomas

Crawford, called 'Gauntlets,' and shifty Drumquhassel;
spies like Rokeby, assassins if need or opportunity
arise; copper captains like Captain Cullen; and most
truculent of all, Bothwell's Lambs, young Tala, who
ceased reading the Bible when he came to Court; and
the Black Laird of Ormistoun, he who, on the day of
his hanging, said ' With God I hope this night to sup.'
Said he, ' Of all men on the earth I have been one of
the proudest and (sic) high-minded, and most filthy of
my body. But specially I have shed innocent blood
of one Michael Hunter with my own hands. Alas
therefore, because the said Michael, having me lying
on my back, having a pitchfork in his hand, might
have slain me if he pleased, but did it not, which
of all things grieves me most in conscience. . . .
Within these seven years I never saw two good men,
nor one good deed, but all kind of wickedness; and
yet my God would not suffer me to be lost, and has
drawn me from them as out of Hell . . . . for the
which I thank him, and I am assured that I am one
of his Elect.' This devotee used to hang about Mary
in Carlisle, when she had fled into England. 'Not
two good men, nor one good deed,' saw Ormistoun,
in seven long years of riding the Border, and following Bothwell to Court or Warden's Raid. Few are the
good men, rare are the good deeds, that meet us in
this tragic History. ' There is none that doeth good,
no, not one.'

But behind the men and the time are the
Preachers of Righteousness, grim, indeed, as their

Geneva gowns, not gentle and easily entreated, crying out on the Murderess, Adulteress, Idolatress, to be led to block or stake, but yet bold to rebuke Bothwell when he had cowed all the nobles of the land. The future was with these men, with the smaller barons or lairds, and with sober burgesses, like the discreet author of the 'Diurnal of Occurrents,' and with honest hinds, like Michael Hunter, whom Ormistoun slew in cold blood. The social and religious cataclysm withdrew its waves : a new Creed grew into the hearts of the people : intercourse with England slowly abated the ruffianism of the Lords : slowly the Law extended to the Border : swiftly the bonds of feudal duty were broken : but not in Mary's time.

One strange feature of the time we must not forget : the universal belief in sorcery. Mary and Moray (she declares) both believed that Ruthven had given her a ring of baneful magical properties. Foes and friends alike alleged that Bothwell had bewitched Mary ' by unleasom means,' philtres, ' sweet waters,' hypnotism. The preachers, when Mary fled, urged Moray to burn witches, and the cliffs of St. Andrews flared with the flames wherein they perished. The Lyon King at Arms, as has been said, died by fire, apparently for confessed dealings with a wizard, who foretold the events of the year, and for treasure hunting with the divining rod. A Napier of Merchistoun did foretell Mary's escape (according to Nau) ; this man, *ayant réputation de grand*

magicien, may have been the soothsayer : his son
sought for hidden treasure by divination. Buchanan
tells how a dying gentleman beheld Darnley's fate in
a clairvoyant vision : and how a dim shapeless thing
smote and awoke, successively, four Atholl men in
Edinburgh, on the night of the crime of Kirk o'
Field. Old rhyming prophecies were circulated and
believed. Knox himself was credited with winning
his sixteen-year-old bride by witchcraft, as Bothwell
won Mary. Men listened to his reports of his own
' premonitions.'

When Huntly, one of the band for Darnley's
murder, died, his death was strange. He had hunted,
and taken three hares and a fox, after dinner he
played football, fell into a fit, and expired, crying
' never a word save one, looking up broad with his
eyes, and that word was this, " Look, Look, Look ! " '
Unlike the dying murderer of Riccio, Ruthven, he
perhaps did not behold the Angel Choir. His coffers
were locked up in a chamber, with candles burning.
Next day a rough fellow, banished by Lochinvar, and
received by Huntly, fell into unconsciousness for
twenty-four hours, and on waking, cried ' *Cauld, cauld,
cauld!*' John Hamilton, opening one of the dead
Earl's coffers, fell down with the same exclamation.
Men carried him away, and, returning, found a third
man fallen senseless on the coffer. ' All wrought as
the Earl of Huntly wrought in the death thraw.' The
chamber was haunted by strange sounds : the word
went about that the Earl was rising again. Says

Knox's secretary, Bannatyne, who tells this tale, 'I maun praise the Lord my God, and bless his holy name for ever, when I behold the five that was in the conspiracy, not only of the King's [Darnley's] and the second Regent's murder, but also of the first Regent's murder. Four is past with small provision, to wit, Lethington, Argyll, Bothwell, and last of all Huntly. I hope in God the fifth [Morton] shall die more perfectly, and declare his life's deeds with his own mouth, making his repentance at the gallows foot.' Part of his life's deeds Morton did declare on his dying day.

In such a mist of dark beliefs and dreads was the world living, beliefs shared by Queen, preacher, and Earl, scholar, poet, historian, and the simple secretary of Knox : while the sun shone fair on St. Leonard's gardens, and boys like little James Melville were playing tennis and golf. The scenes in which the wild deeds were done are scarcely recognisable in modern Scotland. Holyrood is altered by buildings of the Restoration ; the lovely chapel is a ruin, where Mary prayed, and the priests at the altar were buffeted. The Queen's chamber is empty, swept and garnished, as is the little cabinet whereinto came the livid face of Ruthven, clad in armour, and Darnley, half afraid, and Standen, later to boast, with different circumstances, that he saved the Queen from the dirk of Patrick Ballantyne. The blood of Riccio, outside the door of the state chamber, is washed away : there are only a tourist or two in the long hall where Mary leaned on Chastelard's breast in the dance called 'The Purpose' or 'talking dance.' The tombs of the kings through which Mary stole, stopping, says Lennox, to threaten Darnley above the new mould of Riccio's grave, have long been desecrated.

At Jedburgh we may still see the tall old house, with crow-stepped gables, and winding stairs, and the little chambers where Mary tried to make so good an end, and where the wounded Bothwell was tended. In the long gallery above, Lethington, and Moray, and du Croc must have held anxious converse, while physicians came and went, proposing uncouth remedies, and the Confessor flitted through, and the ladies in waiting wept. But least changed are the hills of the robbers, sweeping slopes of rough pasturage, broken by marshes, and the foaming burns of October, through which Mary rode to the wounded Bothwell in Hermitage Castle, now a huge shell of grey stone, in the pastoral wastes.

Most changed of all is Glasgow, then a pretty village, among trees, between the burn and the clear water of Clyde. The houses clustered about the Cathedral, the ruined abodes of the religious, and the Castle where Lennox and Darnley both lay sick. while Mary abode, it would seem, in the palace then empty of its Archbishop. We see the little town full of armed Hamiltons, and their feudal foes, the Stewarts of Lennox, who anxiously attend her with suspicious glances, as she goes to comfort their young chief.

In thinking of old Edinburgh, as Mary knew it, our fancy naturally but erroneously dwells on the narrow wynds of the old town, cabined between grimy slate-roofed houses of some twelve or fifteen stories in height, ' piled black and massy steep and high,' and darkened with centuries of smoke, squalid, sunless, without a green tree in the near view, so we are apt to conceive the Edinburgh of Queen Mary. But we do the good town injustice : we are conceiving the Edinburgh of Queen Mary under the colours and in the forms of the Edinburgh of Prince Charles and of Robert Burns.

There exists a bird's-eye view of the city, probably done by an English hand, in 1544. It looks a bright, red-roofed, sparkling little town, in contour much resembling St. Andrews. At St. Andrews the cathedral forms, as it were, the handle of a fan, from which radiate, like the ribs of the fan, North Street, Market Street, and South Street, with the houses and lanes between them. At Edinburgh the Castle Rock was the handle of the fan. Thence diverged two spokes or ribs of streets, High Street and Cowgate, lined with houses with red-tiled roofs Quaint wooden galleries were suspended outside the first floor, in which, not in the ground floor, the front door usually was, approached by an outer staircase. Quaintness, irregularity, broken outlines, nooks, odd stone staircases, were everywhere. The inner stairs

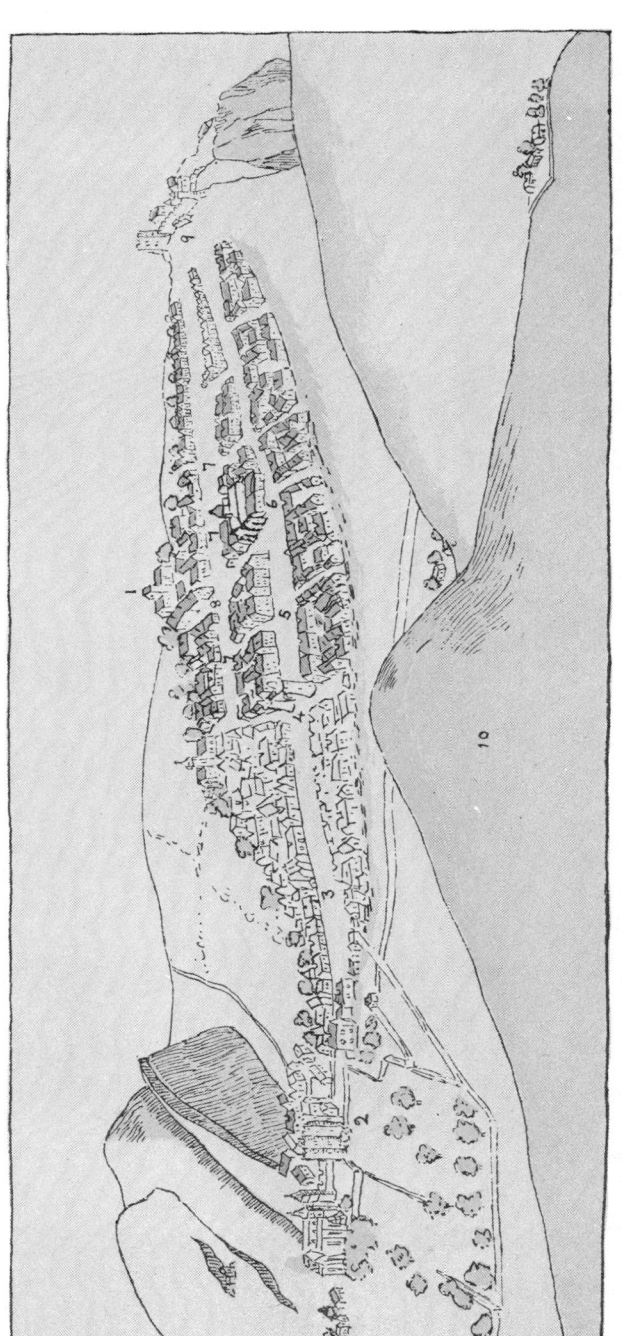

1. Kirk o'Field Church
2. Holyrood
3. Canongate
4. Netherbow Port
5. Netherbow
6. St. Giles's Church
7. Cowgate
8. Wynd leading to Kirk o'Field
9. Castle
10. Calton Hill

or turnpikes were within semicircular towers, and these, with the tall crow-stepped gables, high-pitched roofs, and dormer windows, made up picturesque clumps of buildings, perforated by wynds. St. Giles's Church occupied, of course, its present site, and the 'ports,' or gates which closed the High Street towards Holyrood, had turrets for supporters. Through the gate, the Nether Bow, the Court suburb of the Canongate ran down to Holyrood, with gardens, and groves, and green fields behind the houses. The towers of the beautiful Abbey of Holyrood, partly burned by the English in 1544, ended the line of buildings from the Castle eastward.

Far to the left of the town, on a wooded height, the highest and central point of the landscape, we mark a tall rectangular church tower, crowned with a crow-stepped high-pitched roof. It is the church of Kirk o' Field, soon to be so famous as the scene of Darnley's death.

The blocks of buildings are intersected, we said, by narrow wynds, not yet black, though, from Dunbar's poem, we know that Edinburgh was conspicuously dirty and insanitary. But the narrow, compact, bright little town running down the spine of rock from the Castle to Holyrood, was on every side surrounded by green fields, and there were still trout in the Norloch beneath the base of the Castle cliff, where now the railway runs. New town, of course, there was none. Most of the town of Mary's

age was embraced by the ruinous wall, hastily
constructed after the defeat and death of James IV.
Such was the city: of the houses we may gain an
idea from the fine old building traditionally called
John Knox's house: if we suppose it neat, clean,
its roof scarlet, its walls not grimy with centuries
of reek. The houses stood among green gardens,
hedges, and trees, and on the grassy hills between
the city and the sea, and to the east and west, were
châteaux and peel-towers of lords and lairds.

Such was Queen Mary's Edinburgh : long, narrow,
and mightily unlike the picturesque but stony,
and begrimed, and smoke-hidden capital of to-day.[1]

'There were fertile soil, pleasant meadows, woods,
lakes, and burns, all around,' where now is nothing
but stone, noisy pavement, and slate. The monas-
teries of the Franciscans and Dominicans lay on
either side of St. Mary in the Fields, or Kirk of Field,
with its college quadrangle and wide gardens.[2] But,
in Mary's day, the monastic buildings and several
churches lay in ruins, owing to the recent reform of
the Christian religion, and to English invaders.

The palaces of the Cowgate and of the Canongate
were the homes of the nobles ; the wynds were
crowded with burgesses, tradesmen, prentices, and
the throng of artisans. These were less godly than
the burgesses, were a fickle and fiery mob, ready to

---

[1] See the sketch, coloured, in Bannatyne *Miscellany*, vol. i. p. 184.

[2] See description by Alesius, about 1550, in Bannatyne *Miscellany*,
i. 185–188.

run for spears, or use their tools to defend their May-day sport of Robin Hood against the preachers and the Bible-loving middle classes. Brawls were common, the artisans besieging the magistrates in the Tolbooth, or the rival followings of two lairds or lords coming to pistol-shots and sword-strokes on the causeway, while burgesses handed spears to their friends from the windows. Among popular pleasures were the stake, at which witches and murderesses of masters or husbands were burned; and the pillory, where every one might throw what came handy at a Catholic priest, and the pits in the Norloch where fornicators were ducked. The town gates were adorned with spikes, on which were impaled the heads of sinners against the Law.

Mary rode through a land of new-made ruins, black with fire, not yet green with ivy. On every side, wherever monks had lived, and laboured, and dealt alms, and written manuscripts, desolation met Mary's eyes. The altars were desecrated, the illumined manuscripts were burned, the religious skulked in lay dress, or had fled to France, or stood under the showers of missiles on the pillory. It was a land of fallen fanes, and of stubborn blind keeps with scarce a window, that she passed through, with horse and litter, lace, and gold, and velvet, and troops of gallants and girls. In the black tall Tolbooth lurked the engines of torture, that were to strain or crush the limbs of Bothwell's Lambs. Often must Mary have seen, on the skyline, the gallows tree, and the fruits which that tree bore, and the flocking ravens; one of that company followed Darnley and her from Glasgow, and perched ominous on the roof of Kirk o' Field, croaking loudly on the day of the murder. So writes Nau, Mary's secretary, informed, probably, by one of her attendants.

III

THE CHARACTERS BEFORE RICCIO'S MURDER

AFTER sketching the characters and scenes of the tragedy, we must show how destiny interwove the life-threads of Bothwell and Mary. They were fated to come together. She was a woman looking for a master, he was a masterful and, in the old sense of the word, a 'masterless' man, seeking what he might devour. In the phrase of Aristotle, 'Nature *wishes*' to produce this or that result. It almost seems as if Nature had long 'wished' to throw a Scottish Queen into the hands of a Hepburn. The Hepburns were not of ancient *noblesse*. From their first appearance in Scottish history they are seen to be prone to piratical adventure, and to courting widowed queens. The unhappy Jane Beaufort, widow of James I., and of the Black Knight of Lorne, died in the stronghold of a Hepburn freebooter. A Hepburn was reputed to be the lover of Mary of Gueldres, the beautiful and not inconsolable widow of James II. This Hepburn, had he succeeded in securing the person of Mary's son, the boy James III., might have played Bothwell's part. The name rose to power and rank

on the ruin of the murdered James III., and of
Ramsay, his favourite, who had worn, but forfeited to
the Hepburn of the day, the title of Bothwell. The
name was strong in the most lawless dales of the
Border, chiefly in Liddesdale, where the clans
alternately wore the cross of St. Andrew and of
St. George, and impartially plundered both countries.
The more profitable Hepburn estates, however, were
in the richer bounds of Lothian.

The attitude and position of James Hepburn, our
Bothwell, were, from the first, unique. He was at
once a Protestant, ' the stoutest and the worst
thought of,' and also an inveterate enemy of
England, a resolute partisan of Mary's mother, Mary
of Guise, the Regent, in her wars against the Protestant rebels, 'the Lords of the Congregation.'
From this curious and illogical position, adopted in
his early youth, Bothwell never wandered. He was
to end by making Mary wed him with Protestant
rites, while she assured her confessor that she only
did so in the hope of restoring the Catholic Church!
We must briefly trace the early career of Bothwell.

While Darnley was being educated in England,
with occasional visits to France, and while Mary was
residing there as the bride of the Dauphin: while
Moray was becoming the leader of the Protestant
opposition to Mary of Guise ('the Lords of the Congregation'), while Maitland was entering on his
career of diplomacy, Bothwell was active in the
field. In 1558, after Mary of Guise had been

deserted by her nobles at Kelso, as her husband had been at Fala, young Bothwell, being now Lieutenant-General on the Border, made a raid into England. In the war between Mary of Guise, as Regent, and the Protestant Lords of the Congregation, Bothwell fought on her side. A Diary of the Siege of Leith (among the Lennox MSS.) describes his activity in intercepting and robbing poor peaceful tradesmen. From another unpublished source we learn that he, among others, condemned the Earl of Arran (in absence) as the cause of the Protestant rebellion.[1] On October 5, 1559, Bothwell seized, near Haddington, Cockburn of Ormiston, who was carrying English gold to the Lords.[2] They, in reprisal, sacked his castle of Crichton, and nearly caught him. He later in vain challenged the Earl of Arran (the son of the chief of the Hamiltons, the Duke of Châtelherault) to single combat. A feud of far-reaching results now began between Arran and Cockburn on one side, and Bothwell on the other. When Leith, held for Mary of Guise, in 1560, was besieged by the Scots and English, Bothwell (whose estates had been sold) was sent to ask aid from France. He went thither by way of Denmark, and now, probably, he was more or less legally betrothed to a Norwegian lady, Anne Throndssön, whom he carried from her home, and presently deserted. Already, in 1559, he

---

[1] Information from Father Pollen, S.J.

[2] This gentleman must not be confused with Ormistoun of Ormistoun, in Teviotdale, '.The Black Laird,' a retainer of Bothwell.

was said to be ' quietly married or handfasted ' to
Janet Beaton, niece of Cardinal Beaton, and widow
of Sir Walter Scott of Buccleugh, the wizard Lady of
Branksome in Scott's ' Lay of the Last Minstrel.' [1]
She was sister of Lady Reres, wife of Forbes of
Reres, the lady said to have aided Bothwell in his
amour with Mary.   In 1567 one of the libels issued
after Darnley's murder charged the Lady of Branksome with helping Bothwell to win Mary's heart by
magic.

Anne Throndssön, later, accused Bothwell of
breach of promise of marriage, given to her and her
family ' by hand and mouth and letters.'   In 1560
the Lady of Branksome circulated a report that
Bothwell had wedded a rich wife in Denmark : she
does not seem to have been jealous.[2]   An anonymous
writer represents Bothwell as having three simul-
taneous wives, probably Anne, the Branksome lady,
and his actual spouse, Lady Jane Gordon, sister of
Huntly.   But the arrangements in the first two cases
were probably not legally valid.   There is no doubt
that Bothwell, ugly or not, was a great conqueror
of hearts.   He may have been *un beau laid*, and he
possessed, as we have said, the qualities, so attractive
to many women, of utter recklessness, of a bullying
manner, of great physical strength, and of a repu-

[1] Riddell, *Inquiry into the Law and Practice of the Scottish
Peerage*, i. 427.   Joseph Robertson, *Inventories*, xcii., xciii.   Schiern,
Life of Bothwell, p. 53.
[2] Randolph to Cecil, Edinburgh, Sept. 23, 1560.   Foreign Calendar.
1560-61, p. 311.

Le Dueil Blanc

Sketch by Janet 1561.

tation for *bonnes fortunes*. That Bothwell was extravagant and a gambler is probably true: and, in short, he was, to many women, a most attractive character. To the virtuous, like Lady Jane Gordon, he would appear as an agreeable brand to be snatched from the burning.

Dropping poor Anne Throndssön in the Netherlands, on his way from Denmark, Bothwell, in 1560, went to the French Court, where he was made Gentilhomme de la Chambre, but could not procure aid for Mary of Guise. He acquired more French polish, and (so his enemies and his valet, Paris, said) he learned certain infamous vices. Mary Stuart became a widow, and Dowager of France, in December 1560 : it is not certain whether or not Bothwell was in her train at Joinville in April 1561.[1] After Mary's return to Scotland the old feud between Arran and Bothwell broke out afresh. Bothwell and d'Elbœuf paid a noisy visit to the handsome daughter of a burgess, said to be Arran's mistress. There were brawls, and presently Bothwell attacked Cockburn of Ormiston, the man he had robbed, Arran's ally, and carried off his son to Crichton Castle. This occurred in March, 1562, and, as early as February 21, Randolph, the English minister at Holyrood, had 'marked something strange' in Arran.[2] His feeble ambitious mind was already tottering, which casts doubt on what followed. On

---

[1] Hay Fleming, *Mary Queen of Scots*, p. 236, note 32.
[2] Cal. For. Eliz. 1561–62, iv. 531–539.

E

March 25, Bothwell visited Knox (whose ancestors
had been retainers of the House of Hepburn), and
invited the Reformer to reconcile him with Arran.
The feud, Bothwell said, was expensive : he dared
not move without a company of armed men.   Knox
contrived a meeting at the Hamilton house near the
fatal Kirk o' Field.   The enemies were reconciled,
and next day went together to ' the Sermon,' a
spiritual privilege of which Bothwell was only too
neglectful.   Knox had done a good stroke for the
Anti-Marian Protestant party, of whose left wing
Arran was the leader.[1]

But alas for Knox's hopes !   Only three days
after the sermon, on March 29, Arran (who had
been wont to confide his love-sorrows to Knox)
came to the Reformer with a strange tale.   Bothwell had opened to him, in the effusions of their
new friendship, his design to seize Mary, and put
her in Arran's keeping, in Dumbarton Castle.
He would slay Mar (that is Lord James Stuart,
later Moray) and Lethington, whom he detested,
' and he and I would rule all,' said Arran, who
knew very well what sort of share he would be
permitted to enjoy in the dual control.   I have very
little doubt that the impoverished, more or less
disgraced Bothwell did make this proposal.   He was
safe in doing so.   If Arran accused him, Arran
would, first, be incarcerated, till he proved his
charge (which he could not do), or, secondly, Both-

---

[1] Knox, Laing's edition, ii. 322–327.   Randolph to Cecil *ut supra*.

well would appeal to Trial by Combat, for which he knew that Arran had no taste. In his opinion, Bothwell merely meant to entrap him, and his idea was to write to Mary and her brother. Whether Knox already perceived that Arran was insane, or not, he gave him what was perhaps the best advice— to be silent. Arran's position was perilous. If the plot came to be known, if Bothwell confessed all, then he would be guilty of concealing his fore-knowledge of it; like Morton in the case of Darnley's murder.

Arran did not listen to Knox's counsel. He wrote to Mary and Mar, partly implicating his own father; he then fled from his father's castle of Keneil, hurried to Fife, and was brought by Mar (Moray) to Mary at Falkland, whither Bothwell also came, perhaps warned by Knox, who had a family feudal attach-ment to the Hepburns. Arran now was, or affected to be, distraught. He persisted, however, in his charge against Bothwell, who was warded in Edinburgh Castle, while Arran's father was deprived of Dumbarton Castle.

The truth of Arran's charge is uncertain. In any case, 'the Queen both honestly and stoutly behaves herself,' Randolph wrote. While Bothwell lay, a prisoner on suspicion, in Edinburgh Castle, Mary was come to a crisis in her reign. Her political position, hitherto, may be stated in broad outline. The strains of European tendencies, political and theological, were dragging Scotland in opposite directions. Was the country to remain Protestant, and in alliance with England, or was it to return to the ancient league with France, and to the Church of Rome ?

During Mary's first years in Scotland, she and the governing politicians, her brother Moray and Maitland of Lethington, were fairly well agreed as to general policy. With all her affection for her Church and her French kinsmen, Mary could not hope, at present, for much more than a certain measure of toleration for Catholics. As to the choice of the French or English alliance, her ambitions appeared to see their best hope in an understanding with Elizabeth, under which Mary and her issue should be recognised as heirs of the English throne. So far the ruling politicians, Moray, Lethington, and Morton, were sufficiently in accord with their Queen. A restoration of the Church they would not endure. Not only their theological tenets (sincerely held by Moray) opposed any such restoration, but their hold of Church property was what they would not abandon save with life. The Queen and her chief advisers, therefore, for years enjoyed a *modus vivendi* : a pacific kind of compromise. Mary was so far from being ardently Catholic in politics, that, while Bothwell was confined in Edinburgh Castle, she accompanied Moray to the North, and overthrew her chief Catholic supporter, Huntly, ' the Cock of the North,' and all but the king of the Northern Catholics. Before she set foot in Scotland, he had offered to restore her by force, and with her, the Church. She preferred the alliance of her brother, of Lethington, and of *les politiques*, the moderate Protestants. Huntly died in battle against his Queen ; his family, for the hour, was ruined ; but Huntly's son and successor in the title represented the discontents and ambitions of the warlike North, as Bothwell represented those of the warlike Borderers. Similarity of fortunes and of desires soon united these two ruined and reckless men, Huntly and Bothwell, in a league equally dangerous to Moray, to amity with England, and, finally, to Mary herself.

To restore his family to land and power, Huntly was ready to sacrifice not only faith and honour, but natural affection. Twice he was to sell his sister, Lady Jane, once when he married her to Bothwell against her will : once when, Bothwell having won her love, Huntly compelled or induced her to divorce him. But these things lay in the future. For the moment, the autumn of 1562, the Huntlys were ruined, and Bothwell (August 28, 1562), in the confusion, escaped from prison in Edinburgh Castle. ' Some whispered that he got easy passage by the gates,' says Knox. ' One thing,' he adds, ' is certain, to wit, the Queen was little offended at his escaping.' [1] He was, at least, her mother's faithful servant.

We begin to see that the Protestant party henceforward suspected the Queen of regarding Bothwell as, to Mary, a useful man in case of trouble. Both-

---

[1] Knox, ii. 347.

well first fled to Hermitage Castle in Liddesdale.
As Lieutenant-General on the Border he commanded
the reckless broken clans, the 'Lambs,' his own Hepburns, Hays, Ormistouns of Ormistoun, and others
who aided him in his most desperate enterprises;
while, as Admiral, he had the dare-devils of the sea
to back him.

Lord James now became Earl of Moray, and all-
powerful; and Bothwell, flying to France, was storm-
stayed at Holy Island, and held prisoner by Elizabeth.
His kinsfolk made interest for him with Mary, and,
on February 5, 1564, she begged Elizabeth to allow
him to go abroad. In England, Bothwell is said to
have behaved with unlooked-for propriety. 'He is
very wise, and not the man he was reported to be,'
that is, not 'rash, glorious, and hazardous,' Sir Harry
Percy wrote to Cecil. 'His behaviour has been
courteous and honourable, keeping his promise.' Sir
John Forster corroborated this evidence. Bothwell,
then, was not loutish, but, when he pleased, could act
like a gentleman. He sailed to France, and says himself that he became Captain of the Scottish Guards,
a post which Arran had once held. In France he is
said to have accused Mary of incestuous relations with
her uncle, the Cardinal.

During Bothwell's residence in England, and in
France, the equipoise of Mary's political position had
been disturbed. She had held her ground, against
the extreme Protestants, who clamoured for the
death of all idolaters, by her alliance with *les politiques*,

led by Moray and Lethington.   Their ambition, like
hers, was to see the crowns of England and Scotland
united in her, or in her issue.   Therefore they maintained a perilous amity with England, and with Elizabeth, while plans for a meeting of the Queens, and
for the recognition of Mary as Elizabeth's heir, were
being negotiated.   But this caused ceaseless fretfulness
to Elizabeth, who believed, perhaps correctly, that to
name her successor was to seal her death-warrant.
The Catholics of England would have hurried her to
the grave, she feared, that they might welcome Mary.
In the same way, no conceivable marriage for Mary
could be welcome to Elizabeth, who hated the very
name of wedlock.   Yet, while Bothwell was abroad,
and while negotiations lasted, there was a kind of
repose, despite the anxieties of the godly and their
outrages on Catholics.   Mary endured much and endured with some patience.   One chronic trouble was
at rest.   The feud between the Hamiltons, the nearest heirs of the crown, and the rival claimants, the
Lennox Stewarts, was quiescent.

The interval of peace soon ended.   Lennox, the
head of the House hateful to the Hamiltons, was, at
the end of 1564, allowed to return to Scotland, and
was reinstated in the lands which his treason had
forfeited long ago.   In the early spring of 1565,
Lennox's son, Darnley, followed his father to the
North, was seen and admired by Mary, and the peace
of Scotland was shattered.   As a Catholic by education, though really of no creed in particular, Darnley

excited the terrors of the godly. His marriage with Mary meant, to Moray, loss of power ; to Lethington, a fresh policy ; to the Hamiltons, the ruin of their hopes of royalty, while, by most men, Darnley soon came to be personally detested.

Before it was certain that Mary would marry Darnley, but while the friends and foes of the match were banding into parties, early in March 1565, Bothwell returned unbidden to Scotland, and lurked in his Border fastness. According to Knox, Moray told Mary that either he or Bothwell must leave the country. Mary replied that, considering Bothwell's past services, ' she could not hate him,' neither could she do anything prejudicial to Moray.[1] ' A day of law ' was set for Bothwell, for May 2, but, as Moray gathered an overpowering armed force, he sent in a protest, by his comparatively respectable friend, Hepburn of Riccartoun, and went abroad. Mary, according to Randolph, had said that she ' altogether misliked his home-coming without a licence,' but Bedford feared that she secretly abetted him. He was condemned in absence, but Mary was thought to have prevented the process of outlawry. Dr. Hay Fleming, however, cites Pitcairn's ' Criminal Trials,' i. 462,[2] as proof that Bothwell actually was outlawed, or put to the horn. Knox's continuator, however, says that Bothwell ' was not put to the horn, for the Queen continually bore a great favour to him, and

---

[1] Knox, ii. 473.
[2] Hay Fleming, p. 359, note 29.

kept him to be a soldier.'[1] The Protestants ever feared that Mary would 'shake Bothwell out of her pocket,' against them.[2]

Presently, her temper outworn by the perpetual thwartings which checked her every movement, and regardless of the opposition of Moray, of the Hamiltons, of Argyll, and of the whole Protestant community, Mary wedded Darnley (July 29, 1565). Her adversaries assembled in arms, secretly encouraged by Elizabeth, and what Kirkcaldy of Grange had prophesied occurred : Mary ' shook Bothwell out of her pocket' at her opponents. In July, she sent Hepburn of Riccartoun to summon him back from France. Riccartoun was captured by the English, but Bothwell, after a narrow escape, presented himself before Mary on September 20. By October, Moray, the Hamiltons, and Argyll were driven into England or rendered harmless. Randolph now reported that Bothwell and Atholl were all-powerful. The result was ill feeling between Darnley and Bothwell. Darnley wished his father, Lennox, to govern on the Border, but Mary gave the post to Bothwell.[3] Her estrangement from Darnley had already begun. Jealousy of Mary's new secretary, Riccio, was added.

The relations between Darnley, Bothwell, Mary, and Riccio, between the crushing of Moray's revolt, in October 1565, and the murder of the Italian

---

[1] Knox, ii. 479.

[2] See Cal. For. Eliz. 1565, 306, 312, 314, 319, 320, 327, 340, 341, 347, 351.

[3] Calendar, Bain, ii. 223.

Secretary, in March 1566, are still obscure. Was
Riccio Mary's lover ? What were the exact causes of
the estrangement from Darnley, which was later used
as the spring to discharge on Riccio, and on Mary,
the wrath of the discontented nobles and Puritans ?
The Lennox Papers inform us, as to Mary and
Darnley, that 'their love never decayed till their
return from Dumfries,' whence they had pursued
Moray into England.

Mary had come back to Edinburgh from Dumfries
by October 18, 1565. Riccio was already, indeed by
September 22, complained of as a foreign upstart,
but not as a lover of Mary, by the rebel Lords.[1] The
Lennox Papers attribute the estrangement of Mary
and Darnley to her pardoning without the consent of
the King, her husband, ' sundry rebels,' namely the
Hamiltons. The pardon implied humiliation and
five years of exile. It was granted about December 3.[2]
The measure was deeply distasteful to Darnley and
Lennox, who had long been at mortal feud, over the
heirship to the crown, with the Lennox Stewarts.
The pardon is attributed to the influence of ' Wicked
David,' Riccio. But to pardon perpetually was the
function of a Scottish prince. Soon we find Darnley
intriguing for the pardon of Moray, Ruthven, and
others, who were not Hamiltons. Next, Lennox
complains of Mary for ' using the said David more
like a lover than a husband, forsaking her husband's
bed and board very often.' But this was not before

[1] Bain, ii. 213.   [2] *Ibid.* ii. 242, 243.

November. The 'Book of Articles' put in against
Mary by her accusers is often based on Lennox's
papers. It says 'she suddenly altered the same'
(her 'vehement love' of Darnley) 'about November,
for she removed and secluded him from the counsel
and knowledge of all Council affairs.'[1] The 'Book
of Articles,' like Lennox's own papers, omits every
reference to Riccio that can be avoided. The 'Book
of Articles,' indeed, never hints at his existence.
The reason is obvious: Darnley had not shone in the
Riccio affair. Moreover the Lennox party could not
accuse Mary of a guilty amour before mid November,
1565, for James VI. was born on June 19, 1566. It
would not do to discredit his legitimacy. But, as
early as September 1565, Bedford had written to
Cecil that 'of the countenance which Mary gave to
David he would not write, for the honour due to the
person of a Queen.'[2] Thus, a bride of six weeks,
Mary was reported to be already a wanton! Moreover, on October 13, 1565, Randolph wrote from
Edinburgh that Mary's anger against Moray (who
had really enraged her by rising to prevent her from
marrying Darnley) came from some dishonourable
secret in Moray's keeping, 'not to be named for
reverence sake.' He 'has a thing more strange' even
than the fact that Mary 'places Bothwell in honour
above every subject that she hath.' As the 'thing'
is *not* a nascent passion for Bothwell, it may be an
amour with Riccio.[3] Indeed, on October 18, 1565,

[1] Hosack, i. 524.   [2] Cal. For. Eliz. 1564-5, 464.   [3] Bain, ii. 222-223.

he will not speak of the cause of mischief, but hints at 'a stranger and a varlet,' Riccio.[1] Randolph and the English diplomatists were then infuriated against Mary, who had expelled their allies, Moray and the rest, discredited Elizabeth, their paymistress, and won over her a diplomatic victory. Consequently this talk of her early amour with Riccio, an ugly Milanese musician, need not be credited. For their own reasons, the Lennox faction dared not assert so early a scandal.

They, however, insisted that Mary, in November, 'removed and secluded' Darnley from her Council. To prevent his knowing what letters were written, when he signed them with her, she had his name printed on an iron stamp, 'and used the same *in all things*,' in place of his subscription. This stamp was employed in affixing his signature to the 'remission' to the Hamiltons.[2]

In fact, Darnley's ambitions were royal, but he had an objection to the business which kings are well paid for transacting. Knox says that he 'passed his time in hunting and hawking, and such other pleasures as were agreeable to his appetite, having in his company gentlemen willing to satisfy his will and affections.' He had the two Anthony Standens, wild young English Catholics. While Darnley hunted

---

[1] Bain, ii. 225. Cal. For. Eliz. 1564–5, 464, 495. Hay Fleming, pp. 380, 381.

[2] Miss Strickland avers that 'existing documents afford abundant proof, that whenever Darnley and the Queen were together, his name was written by his own hand.'

and hawked, Lennox ' lies at Glasgow ' (where he had a castle near the Cathedral), and ' takes, I hear, what he likes from all men,' says Randolph.[1] He writes (November 6) that Mary ' above all things desires her husband to be called King.'[2] Yet it is hinted that she is in love with Riccio ! On the same date ' oaths and bands are taken of all that . . . acknowledge Darnley king, and liberty to live as they list in religion.' On November 19, Mary was suffering from ' her old disease that commonly takes her this time of year in her side.' It was a chronic malady : we read of it in the Casket Letters. From November 14 to December 1, she was ill, but Darnley hunted and hawked in Fife, from Falkland probably, and was not expected to return till December 4.[3] Lennox was being accused of ' extortions ' at Glasgow, complained of ' to the Council.' Châtelherault was ' like to speed well enough in his suit to be restored,' after his share in Moray's rebellion.

Darnley was better engaged, perhaps, in Fife, than in advocating his needy and extortionate father before the Council, or in opposing the limited pardon to old Châtelherault. In such circumstances, Darnley was often absent, either for pleasure, or because his father was not allowed to despoil the West ; while the Hamilton chief, the heir presumptive of the throne, was treated as a repentant rebel, rather than as a feudal enemy. He was an exile, and lost his

[1] October 31, 1565. Bain, ii. 232.　　[2] Bain, ii. 234.
[3] Randolph to Cecil, Nov. 19, Dec. 1, 1565. Bain, ii. 241, 242.

'moveables' and all his castles, so he told Elizabeth.[1]
During, or after, these absences of Darnley, that 'iron
stamp,' of which Buchanan complains, was made
and used.

The Young Fool had brought this on himself.
Mary already, according to Randolph, had been
heard to say that she wished Lennox had never
entered Scotland 'in her days.' Lennox, the father-
in-law of the Queen, was really a competitor for the
crown. If Mary had no issue, he and Darnley
desired the crown to be entailed on them, passing
over the rightful heirs, the House of Hamilton. A
father and son, with such preoccupations, could not
safely be allowed to exercise power. The father
would have lived on robbery, the son would have
shielded him. Yet, so occupied was Darnley with
distant field sports, that, says Buchanan, he took the
affair of the iron stamp easily.[2] Next comes a
terrible grievance. Darnley was driven out, in the
depth of winter, to Peebles. There was so much
snow, the roads were so choked, the country so bare,
that Darnley might conceivably have been reduced to
'halesome parritch.' Luckily the Bishop of Orkney,
the jovial scoundrel, 'Bishop Turpy,' who married
Mary to Bothwell, and then denounced her to
Elizabeth, had brought wine and delicacies. This is
Buchanan's tale. A letter from Lennox to Darnley,
of December 20, 1565, represents the father as
anxious to wait on 'Your Majesty' at Peebles, but

[1] Bain, ii. 242.   [2] Buchanan, *Historia*, 1582, fol. 210.

scarcely expecting him in such stormy weather. Darnley, doubtless, really went for the sake of the deer: which, in Scotland, were pursued at that season. He had been making exaggerated show of Catholicism, at matins on Christmas Eve, while Mary sat up playing cards.[1] Presently he was to be the ally of the extreme Protestants, the expelled rebels. Moray was said not to have two hundred crowns in the world, and was ready for anything, in his English retreat. Randolph (Dec. 25) reported 'private disorders' between Darnley and Mary, 'but these may be but *amantium iræ*,' lovers' quarrels.[2] Yet, two months before he had hinted broadly that Riccio was the object of Mary's passion.

On this important point of Mary's guilt with Riccio, we have no affirmative evidence, save Darnley's word, when he was most anxious to destroy the Italian for political reasons. Randolph, who, as we have seen, had apparently turned his back on his old slanders, now accepted, or feigned to accept, Darnley's anecdotes of his discoveries.

It is strange that Mary at the end of 1565, and the beginning of 1566, seems to have had no idea of the perils of her position. On January 31, 1565, she wrote ' to the most holy lord, the Lord Pope Pius V.,' saying: 'Already some of our enemies are in exile,

---

[1] Bain, ii. 247.

[2] The Foreign Calendar cites Randolph up to the place where *amantium iræ* is quoted, but omits that. The point is important, if it indicates that Randolph had ceased to believe in Mary's amour with Riccio. Cf. Bain, ii. 248.

and some of them are in our hands, but their fury, and the great necessity in which they are placed, urge them on to attempt extreme measures.' [1]   But, ungallant as the criticism may seem, I fear that this was only a begging letter *in excelsis*, and that Mary wanted the papal ducats, without entertaining any great hope or intention of aiding the papal cause, or any real apprehension of ' extreme measures ' on the side of her rebels.   Her intention was to forfeit and ruin Moray and his allies, in the Parliament of the coming March.   She also wished to do something ' tending to ' the restoration of the Church, by reintroducing the spiritual lords.   But that she actually joined the Catholic League, as she was certainly requested to do, seems most improbable.[2]   Having arranged a marriage between Bothwell and Huntly's sister, Lady Jane Gordon, she probably relied on the united strength of the two nobles in the North and the South.   But this was a frail reed to lean upon. Mary's position, though she does not seem to have realised it, was desperate.   She had incurred the feud of the Lennox Stewarts, Lennox and Darnley, by her neglect of both, and by Darnley's jealousy of Riccio. The chiefs of the Hamiltons, who could always be trusted to counterbalance the Lennox faction, were in exile.   Moray was desperate.   Lethington was secretly estranged.   The Protestants were at once

---

[1] Nau, p. 192.

[2] The subject is discussed, with all the evidence, in Hay Fleming, pp. 379, 380, note 33.

angry and terrified : ready for extremes. Finally,
Morton was threatened with loss of the seals, and
almost all the nobles loathed the power of the low-
born foreign favourite, Riccio.

Even now the exact nature of the intrigues which
culminated in Riccio's murder are obscure. We
cannot entirely trust the well-known 'Relation'
which, after the murder, on April 2, Morton and
Ruthven sent to Cecil. He was given leave to
amend it, and it is, at best, a partisan report. Its
object was to throw the blame on Darnley, who had
deserted the conspirators, and betrayed them.
According to Ruthven, it was on February 10 that
Darnley sent to him George Douglas, a notorious
assassin, akin both to Darnley and Morton. Darnley,
it is averred, had proof of Mary's guilt with Riccio,
and desired to disgrace Mary by slaying Riccio in
her presence. The negotiation, then, began with
Darnley, on February 10.[1] But on February 5
Randolph had written to Cecil that Mary 'hath said
openly that she will have mass free for all men that
will hear it,' and that Darnley, Lennox, and Atholl
daily resort to it. 'The Protestants are in great fear
and doubt what shall become of them. The wisest
so much dislike this state and government, that they
design nothing more than the return of the Lords,
either to be put into their own rooms, or once again
to put all in hazard.'[2] 'The wisest' is a phrase apt

---

[1] *Ruthven's Narrative.* Keith, iii. 260. There are various forms
of this Narrative; one is in the Lennox MSS. [2] Goodall, i. 274.

to mean Lethington. Now, on February 9, before
Darnley's motion to Ruthven, Lethington wrote to
Cecil: 'Mary! I see no certain way unless we chop
at the very root; you know where it lieth.' [1] When
Mary, later, was a prisoner in England, Knox,
writing to Cecil, used this very phrase, 'If ye strike
not at the root, the branches that appear to be
broken will bud again' (Jan. 2, 1570). When
Lethington meant to 'chop at the very root,' on
February 9, 1560, he undoubtedly intended the death
of Riccio, if not of Mary.

In four days (February 13) Randolph informed
Leicester of Darnley's jealousy, and adds, 'I know
that there are practices in hand, contrived between
the father and son' (Lennox and Darnley), 'to come
by the crown against her will.' 'The crown' may
only mean 'the Crown Matrimonial,' which would,
apparently, give Darnley regal power for his lifetime.
'I know that, if that take effect which is intended,
David, with the consent of the King, shall have his
throat cut within these ten days. Many things
grievouser and worse than these are brought to
my ears: yea, of things intended against her own
person . . . ' [2]

The conspiracy seems to have been political and
theological in its beginnings. Mary was certainly
making more open show of Catholicism : very possibly

---

[1] Bain, ii. 255.

[2] Printed in a scarce volume, *Maitland's Narrative*, and in Tytler
iii. 215. 1864.

to impress the French envoys who had come to con-
gratulate her on her marriage, and to strengthen her
claim on the Pope for money. But Lennox and
Darnley were parading their Catholic devoutness : they
had no quarrel with Mary on this head. The Protestants, however, took alarm. Darnley was, perhaps,
induced to believe in Mary's misconduct with Riccio
after ' the wisest,' and Lethington, had decided ' to
chop at the very root.' Ruthven and Morton then won
Darnley's aid : he consented to secure Protestantism,
and, by a formal band, to restore Moray and the
exiles : who, in turn, recognised him as their sovereign.
Randolph, banished by Mary for aiding her rebels,
conspired with Bedford at Berwick, and sent copies
to Cecil of the ' bands ' between Darnley and the
nobles (March 6).[1]

Darnley himself, said Randolph, was determined
to be present at Riccio's slaying. Moray was
to arrive in Edinburgh immediately after the deed.
Lethington, Argyll, Morton, Boyd, and Ruthven
were privy to the murder, also Moray, Rothes,
Kirkcaldy, in England, with Randolph and Bedford.
It is probable that others besides Riccio were
threatened. There is a ' Band of Assurance for
the Murder.'[2] Darnley says that he has enlisted
' lords, barons, freeholders, gentlemen, merchants, and
craftsmen to assist us in this enterprise, which cannot
be finished without great hazard. And because it
may chance that there be certain great personages

---

[1] Bain, ii. 259–261.   [2] Goodall, i. 266–268.

present, who may make them to withstand our enterprise, wherethrough certain of them may be slain,' Darnley guarantees his allies against the blood feud of the 'great persons.' These, doubtless, are Bothwell, Atholl, and Huntly. The deed ' may chance to be done in presence of the Queen's Majesty, or within her palace of Holyrood House.' The band is dated March 1, in other texts, March 5. The indications point to a design of killing Mary's nobles, while she, in her condition, might die of the shock. She was to be morally disgraced. So unscrupulous were Mary's foes that Cecil told de Foix, the French Ambassador in London, how Riccio had been slain in Mary's arms, *reginam nefario stupro polluens*.[1] Cecil well knew that this was a lie : and it is natural to disbelieve every statement of a convicted liar and traitor like Darnley.

Just before the explosion of the anti-Riccio conspiracy, Bothwell *se rangea*. Mary herself made a match for him (the contract is of February 9, 1566) with Lady Jane Gordon, a Catholic, a sister of Huntly, and a daughter of that Huntly who fell at Corrichie burn. The lady was only in her twentieth year. The parties being akin, a dispensation was necessary, and was granted by the Pope, and issued by the Archbishop of St. Andrews.[2] The marriage took place in the Protestant Kirk of the Canongate, though

[1] Hosack, ii. 78, note 3.
[2] See Dr. Stewart, *A Lost Chapter in the History of Mary Queen of Scots*, pp. 93, 94.

the bride was a Catholic, and Mary gave the wedding dress (February 24). The honeymoon was interrupted, on March 9, by the murder of Riccio.

The conspirators made the fatal error of not securing Bothwell and Huntly before they broke into Mary's room and slew Riccio. While Bothwell, Huntly, and Atholl were at large, the forces of the Queen's party had powerful friends in the North and on the Border. When the tumult of the murderers was heard, these nobles tried to fight their way to Mary's assistance, but were overpowered by numbers, and compelled to seek their apartments. An attempt was made to reconcile them to the situation, but they escaped under cloud of night. In her letter to the French Court (May 1567) excusing her marriage with Bothwell, Mary speaks of his 'dexterity' in escaping, 'and how suddenly by his prudence not only were we delivered out of prison,' after Riccio's death, 'but also that whole company of conspirators dissolved . . .' 'We could never forget it,' Mary adds, and Bothwell's favour had a natural and legitimate basis in the gratitude of the Queen. Very soon after the outrage she had secretly communicated with Bothwell and Huntly, 'who, taking no regard to hazard their lives,' arranged a plan for her flight by means of ropes let down from the windows.[1] Mary preferred the passage through the basement into the royal tombs, and, by aid of Arthur Erskine and Stewart of Traquair, she made her way to Dunbar.

[1] This is alleged by Mary, and by Claude Nau, her secretary.

Here Huntly, Atholl, and Bothwell rallied to her standard: Knox fled from Edinburgh, Morton and Ruthven with their allies found refuge in England: the lately exiled Lords were allowed to remain in Scotland: Darnley betrayed his accomplices, they communicated to Mary their treaties with him, and the Queen was left to reconcile Moray and Argyll to Huntly, Bothwell, and Atholl.

IV

BEFORE THE BAPTISM OF THE PRINCE

MARY'S task was ' to quieten the country,' a task perhaps impossible. Her defenders might probably make a better case for her conduct and prudence, at this time, than they have usually presented. Her policy was, if possible, to return to the state of balance which existed before her marriage. She must allay the Protestants' anxieties, and lean on their trusted Moray and on the wisdom of Lethington. But gratitude for the highest services compelled her to employ Huntly and Bothwell, who equally detested Lethington and Moray. Darnley was an impossible and disturbing factor in the problem. He had, publicly, on March 20, and privately, declared his innocence, which we find him still protesting in the Casket Letters. He had informed against his associates, and insisted on dragging into the tale of conspirators, Lethington, who had retired to Atholl. Moreover Mary must have despised and hated the wretch. Perhaps her hatred had already found expression.

The Lennox MSS. aver that Darnley secured Mary's escape to Dunbar ' with great hazard and danger of his life.' Claude Nau reports, on the other hand, that he fled at full speed, brutally taunting Mary, who, in her condition, could not keep the pace with him. Nau tells us that, as the pair escaped out of Holyrood, Darnley uttered remorseful words over Riccio's new-made grave. The Lennox MSS. aver that Mary, seeing the grave, said 'it should go very hard with her but a fatter than Riccio should lie anear him ere one twelvemonth was at an end.' In Edinburgh, on the return from Dunbar, Lennox accuses Mary of threatening to take revenge with her own hands. 'That innocent lamb' (Darnley) 'had but an unquiet life' (Lennox MSS.).

Once more, Mary had to meet, on many sides, the demand for the pardon of the Lords who had just insulted and injured her by the murder of her servant. On April 2, from Berwick, Morton and Ruthven told Throckmorton that they were in trouble 'for the relief of our brethren and the religion,' and expected 'to be relieved by the help of our brethren, which we hope in God shall be shortly.'[1] Moray was eager for their restoration, which must be fatal to their betrayer, Darnley. On the other side, Bothwell and Darnley, we shall see, were presently intriguing for the ruin of Moray, and of Lethington, who, still unpardoned, dared not take to the seas lest Bothwell should intercept him.[2] Bothwell and Darnley had been on ill terms in April,

---

[1] Goodall, i. 264, 265.   [2] Bain, ii. 289.

according to Drury.[1] But common hatreds soon drew them together, as is to be shown.

Randolph's desire was 'to have my Lord of Moray again in Court' (April 4), and to Court Moray came.

Out of policy or affection, Mary certainly did protect and befriend Moray, despite her alleged nascent passion for his enemy, Bothwell. By April 25, Moray with Argyll and Glencairn had been received by Mary, who had forbidden Darnley to meet them on their progress.[2] With a prudence which cannot be called unreasonable, Mary tried to keep the nobles apart from her husband. She suspected an intrigue whenever he conversed with them, and she had abundant cause of suspicion. She herself had taken refuge in the Castle, awaiting the birth of her child.

Mary and Moray now wished to pardon Lord Boyd, with whom Darnley had a private quarrel, and whom he accused of being a party to Riccio's murder.[3] On May 13, Randolph tells Cecil that 'Moray and Argyll have such misliking of their King (Darnley) as never was more of man.'[4] Moray, at this date, was most anxious for the recall of Morton, who (May 24) reports, as news from Scotland, that Darnley 'is minded to depart to Flanders,' or some other place, to complain of Mary's unkindness.[5] Darnley was an obstacle to Mary's efforts at general

---

[1] Cal. For. Eliz. viii. 51.   [2] Bain, ii. 276.   Cal. For. Eliz. viii. 52.
[3] Cal. For. Eliz. viii. 62.   [4] Bain ii. 278.   [5] Ibid. ii. 281.

conciliation, apart from the horror of the man which she probably entertained. In England Morton and his gang had orders, never obeyed, to leave the country: Ruthven had died, beholding a Choir of Angels, on May 16.

At this time, when Mary was within three weeks of her confinement, the Lennox Papers tell a curious tale, adopted, with a bewildering confusion of dates, by Buchanan in his 'Detection.' Lennox represents Mary as trying to induce Darnley to make love to the wife of Moray, while 'Bothwell alone was all in all.' This anecdote is told by Lennox himself, on Darnley's own authority. The MS. is headed, 'Some part of the talk between the late King of Scotland and me, the Earl of Lennox, riding between Dundas and Lythkoo (Linlithgow) in a dark night, taking upon him to be the guide that night, the rest of his company being in doubt of the highway.' Darnley said he had often ridden that road, and Lennox replied that it was no wonder, he riding to meet his wife, 'a paragon and a Queen.' Darnley answered that they were not happy. As an instance of Mary's ways, he reported that, just before their child's birth, Mary had advised him to take a mistress, and if possible 'to make my Lord ——' (Moray) 'wear horns, and I assure you I shall never love you the worse.' Lennox liked not the saying, but merely advised Darnley never to be unfaithful to the Queen. Darnley replied, 'I never offended the Queen, my wife, in meddling with any woman in thought, let be

in deed.' Darnley also told the story of 'horning'
Moray to a servant of his, which Moray 'is privy
unto.'

. The tale of Darnley's then keeping a mistress arose,
says Lennox, from the fact that one of two Englishmen in his service, brothers, each called Anthony
Standen, brought a girl into the Castle. The sinner
was, when Lennox wrote, in France. Nearly forty
years after James VI. imprisoned him in the Tower,
and he wrote a romantic memoir of which there is a
manuscript copy at Hatfield.

Whatever Mary's feelings towards Darnley, when
making an inventory of her jewels for bequests,
in case she and her child both died, she left her
husband a number of beautiful objects, including the
red enamel ring with which he wedded her.[1] Whatever her feelings towards Moray, she lodged him and
Argyll in the Castle during her labour : 'Huntly and
Bothwell would also have lodged there, but were
refused.'[2] Sir James Melville (writing in old age)
declares that Huntly and Lesley, Bishop of Ross,
' envied the favour that the Queen showed unto the
Earl of Moray,' and wished her to ' put him in ward,'
as dangerous. Melville dissuaded Mary from this
course, and she admitted Moray to the Castle, while
rejecting Huntly and Bothwell.[3]

James VI. and I. was born on June 19. Killigrew carried Elizabeth's congratulations, and found

---

[1] See Joseph Robertson's *Inventories*, 112.   [2] Bain, ii. 283.
[3] Melville, pp. 154, 155.

that Argyll, Moray, Mar, and Atholl were 'linked together' at Court. Bothwell had tried to prejudice Mary against Moray, as likely to 'bring in Morton during her child-bed,' but Bothwell had failed, and gone to the Border. 'He would not gladly be in the danger of the four that lie in the Castle.' Yet he was thought to be 'more in credit' with Mary than all the rest. If so, Mary certainly 'dissembled her love,' to the proverbial extent. Darnley was in the Castle, but little regarded.[1] Moray complained that his own 'credit was yet but small:' he was with the Privy Council, Bothwell was not.[2] By July 11, Moray told Cecil that his favour 'stands now in good case.'[3]

He had good reason to thank God, as he did. According to Nau, Huntly and Bothwell had long been urging Darnley to ruin Moray and Lethington, and Darnley had a high regard for George Douglas, now in exile, his agent with Ruthven for Riccio's murder.[4] This is confirmed by a letter from Morton in exile to Sir John Forster in July. Morton had heard from Scotland that Bothwell and Darnley were urging Mary to recall the said George Douglas, whom they expected to denounce Moray and Lethington as 'the devisers of the slaughter of Davy.' 'I now find,' says Morton, 'that the King and Bothwell are not likely to speed, as was written, for the Queen likes nothing of their desire.'[5]

---

[1] Bain, ii. 288, 289.   [2] Bain, ii. 290.   [3] Bain, ii. 294.
[4] Nau, 20, 22.   [5] Bain, ii. 296.

Thus Mary was protecting Moray from the grotesque combination of Bothwell and Darnley. This is at a time when 'Bothwell was all in all,' according to Lennox, and when she had just tried to embroil Moray and her husband by bidding Darnley seduce Lady Moray. By Moray's and Morton's own showing, Moray's favour was 'in good case,' and he was guarded from Darnley's intrigues.

However, Buchanan makes Mary try to drive Darnley and Moray to dagger strokes after her 'deliverance.'[1] We need not credit his tale of Mary's informing Darnley that Moray meant to kill him, and then calling Moray out of bed, half-naked, to hear that he was to be killed by Darnley. All that is known of this affair of the hurried Moray speeding through the corridors in his dressing-gown, comes from certain notes of news sent by Bedford to Cecil on August 15. 'The Queen declared to Moray that the King had told her he was determined to kill him, finding fault that she bears him so much company. The King confessed that reports were made to him that Moray was not his friend, which made him speak that of which he repented. The Queen said that she could not be content that either he or any else should be unfriend to Moray.' 'Any else' included Bothwell. 'Moray and Bothwell have been at evil words for Lethington. The King has departed; he cannot bear that the Queen should use familiarity with man or woman.'[2] This may

---

[1] *Detection*, 1689, pp. 2, 3. [2] Cal. For. Eliz. viii. 118.

be the basis of Buchanan's legend. Moray and
Darnley hated each other. On the historical evidence of documents as against the partisan legends
of Lennox and Buchanan, Mary, before and after
her delivery, was leaning on Moray, whatever may
have been her private affection for Bothwell. She
even confided to him 'that money had been sent
from the Pope.' Moray was thus deep in her
confidence. That she should distrust Darnley,
ever weaving new intrigues, was no more than
just. His wicked folly was the chief obstacle to
peace.

Peace, while Darnley lived, there could not be.
Morton was certain to be pardoned, and of all feuds
the deadliest was that between Morton and Darnley,
who had betrayed him. Meanwhile Mary's dislike of
Darnley must have increased, after her fear of dying
in child-birth had disappeared. When once the
nobles were knitted into a combination, with
Lethington restored to the Secretaryship (for which
Moray laboured successfully against Bothwell), with
Morton and the Douglases brought home, Darnley
was certain to perish. Lennox was disgraced, and
his Stewarts were powerless, and Darnley's own
Douglas kinsmen were, of all men, most likely to
put their hands in his blood : as they did. Mary
was his only possible shelter. Nothing was more to
be dreaded by the Lords than the reconciliation of
the royal pair ; whom Darnley threatened with the
vengeance he would take if once his foot was on

their necks. But of a sincere reconciliation there was no danger.

A difficult problem is to account for the rise of Mary's passion for Bothwell. In February, she had given him into the arms of a beautiful bride. In March, he had won her sincerest gratitude and confidence. She had, Lennox says, bestowed on him the command of her new Guard of harquebus men, a wild crew of mercenaries under dare-devil captains. But though, according to her accusers, her gratitude and confidence turned to love, and though that love, they say, was shameless and notorious, there are no contemporary hints of it in all the gossip of scandalous diplomatists. We have to fall back on what Buchanan, inspired by Lennox, wrote after Darnley's murder, and on what Lennox wrote himself in language more becoming a gentleman than that of Buchanan. If Lennox speaks truth, improper relations between Mary and Bothwell began as soon as she recovered from the birth of her child. He avers that Mary wrote a letter to Bothwell shortly after her recovery from child-bed, and just when she was resisting Bothwell's and Darnley's plot against Moray and Lethington. Bothwell, reading the letter among his friends, exclaimed, 'Gyf any faith might be given to a princess, they' (Darnley and Mary) 'should never be togidder in bed agane.' A version in English (the other paper is in Scots) makes Mary promise this to Bothwell when he entered her room, and found her washing her hands. Buchanan's tale of

Mary's secret flight to Alloa, shortly after James's birth, and her revels there in company with Bothwell and his crew of pirates, are well known. Lennox, however, represents her as departing to Stirling, 'before her month,' when even women of low degree keep the house, and as 'taking her pleasure in most uncomely manner, arraied in homely sort, dancing about the market cross of the town.'

According to Nau, Mary and her ladies really resided at Alloa as guests of Lord Mar, one of the least treacherous and abandoned of her nobles. Bedford, in a letter of August 3, 1567, mentions Mary's secret departure from Edinburgh, her intended meeting with Lethington (who had been exiled from Court since Riccio's death), at Alloa, on August 2, and her disdainful words about Darnley. He adds that Bothwell is the most hated man in Scotland : 'his insolence is such that David [Riccio] was never more abhorred than he is now,' but Bedford says nothing of a love intrigue between Bothwell and Mary.[1] The visit to Alloa, with occasional returns to Edinburgh, is of July–August.

In August, Mary, Bothwell, Moray, and Darnley hunted in Meggatdale, the moorland region between the stripling Yarrow and the Tweed.   They had poor sport : poachers had been busy among the deer. Charles IX., in France, now learned that the royal pair were on the best terms ;[2] and Mary's Inventories

---

[1] Stevenson, *Selections*, pp. 163–165.
[2] Cheruel, *Marie Stuart et Catherine de Médicis*, p. 47.

prove that, in August, she had presented Darnley
with a magnificent bed; by no means 'the second-
best bed.'   In September she also gave him a
quantity of cloth of gold, to make a caparison for his
horse.[1] Claude Nau reports, however, various
brutal remarks of Darnley to his wife while they
were in Meggatdale. By September 20, Mary,
according to Lethington, reconciled Bothwell and
himself. This was a very important event. The
reconciliation, Lethington says, was quietly managed
at the house of a friend of his own, Argyll, Moray,
and Bothwell alone being present. Moray says:
'Lethington is restored to favour, wherein I trust he
shall increase.' [2] This step was hostile to Darnley's
interests, for he had attempted to ruin Lethington.
It is certain, as we shall see, that all parties were
now united in a band to resist Darnley's authority,
and maintain that of the Queen, though, probably,
nothing was said about violence.

At this very point Buchanan, supported and
probably inspired by Lennox, makes the guilty
intimacy of Mary and Bothwell begin in earnest. In
September, 1566, Mary certainly was in Edinburgh,
reconciling Lethington to Bothwell, and also working
at the budget and finance in the Exchequer House.
It 'was large and had pleasant gardens to it, and
next to the gardens, all along, a solitary vacant
room,' says Buchanan. But the real charm, he
declares, was in the neighbourhood of the house of

[1] Robertson, *Inventories*, p. 167.   [2] Bain, ii. 300.

David Chalmers, a man of learning, and a friend of Bothwell. The back door of Chalmers's house opened on the garden of the Exchequer House, and according to Buchanan, Bothwell thence passed, through the garden, to Mary's chamber, where he overcame her virtue by force. She was betrayed into his hands by Lady Reres.

This lady, who has been mentioned already, was the wife of Arthur Forbes of Reres. His castle, on a hill above the north shore of the Firth of Forth, is now but a grassy mound, near Lord Crawford's house of Balcarres. The lady was a niece of Cardinal Beaton, a sister of the magic lady of Branksome, and aunt of one of the Four Maries, Mary Beaton. Buchanan describes her as an old love of Bothwell, ' a woman very heavy, both by unwieldy age and massy substance ; ' her gay days, then, must long have been over. She was also the mother of a fairly large family. Cecil absurdly avers that Bothwell obtained his divorce by accusing himself of an amour with this fat old lady.[1]   Knox's silly secretary, Bannatyne, tells us that the Reformer, dining at Falsyde, was regaled with a witch story by a Mr. Lundie. He said that when Lady Atholl and Mary were both in labour, in Edinburgh Castle, he came there on business, and found Lady Reres lying abed. ' He asking her of her disease, she answered that she was never so troubled with no bairn that ever she bare, for the Lady Atholl had cast all the pain of her child-birth upon

[1] Bain, ii. 440.

her.'[1] It was a case of Telepathy. Lady Reres had been married long enough to have a grown-up son, the young Laird of Reres, who was in Mary's service at Carberry Hill (June, 1567). According to Dr. Joseph Robertson, Lady Reres was wet-nurse to Mary's baby. But, if we trust Buchanan, she was always wandering about with Mary, while the nurseling was elsewhere. The name of Lady Reres does not occur among those of Mary's household in her *Etat* of February 1567. We only hear of her, then, from Buchanan, as a veteran procuress of vast bulk who, at some remote period, had herself been the mistress of Bothwell.

A few days after the treasonable and infamous action of Bothwell in violating his Queen, we are to believe that Mary, still in the Exchequer House, sent Lady Reres for that hero. Though it would have been simple and easy to send a girl like Margaret Carwood, Mary and Margaret must needs let old Lady Reres 'down by a string, over an old wall, into the next garden.' Still easier would it have been for Lady Reres to use the key of the back door, as when she first admitted Bothwell. But these methods were not romantic enough: ' Behold, the string suddenly broke, and down with a great noise fell Lady Reres.' However, she returned with Bothwell, and so began these tragic loves.

[1] Bannatyne, *Journal*, p. 238. This transference of disease, as from Archbishop Adamson to a pony, was believed in by the preachers.

This legend is backed, according to Buchanan, by
the confession of Bothwell's valet, George Dalgleish,
'which still remaineth upon record,' but is nowhere
to be found.   In Dalgleish's confession, printed in
the 'Detection,' nothing of the kind occurs.   But a
passage in the Casket Sonnet IX. is taken as referring
to the condoned rape :

> Pour luy aussi j'ai jeté mainte larme,
> Premier, quand il se fist de ce corps possesseur,
> Duquel alors il n'avoit pas le cœur.

In the Lennox MSS. Lennox himself dates the
beginning of the intrigue with Bothwell about
September, 1566.   But he and Buchanan are practically but one witness.   There is no other.

As regards this critical period, we have abundant
contemporary information.   The Privy Council,
writing to Catherine de' Medici, from Edinburgh, on
October 8, make Mary, ten or twelve days before
(say September 26), leave Stirling for Edinburgh, on
affairs of the Exchequer.   She offered to bring
Darnley, but he insisted on remaining at Stirling,
where Lennox visited him for two or three days,
returning to Glasgow.   Thence he wrote to Mary,
warning her that Darnley had a vessel in readiness,
to fly the country.   The letter reached Mary on
September 29, and Darnley arrived on the same day.
He rode to Mary, but refused to enter the palace,
because three or four of the Lords were in attendance.
Mary actually went out to see her husband, apparently dismissed the Lords, and brought him to her

chamber, where he passed the night.   On the following day, the Council, with du Croc, met Darnley.
He was invited, by Mary and the rest, to declare his
grievances : his attention was directed to the 'wise
and virtuous' conduct of his wife.   Nothing could
be extracted from Darnley, who sulkily withdrew,
warning Mary, by a letter, that he still thought of
leaving the country.   His letter hinted that he was
deprived of regal authority, and was abandoned by
the nobles.   To this they reply that he must be
aimable before he can be *aimé*, and that they will
never consent to his having the disposal of affairs.[1]

A similar account was given by du Croc to
Archbishop Beaton, and, on October 17, to Catherine
de' Medici, no friend of Mary, also by Mary to
Lennox.[2]

We have not Darnley's version of what occurred.
He knew that all the powerful Lords were now united
against him.   Du Croc, however, had frequent inter-
views with Darnley, who stated his grievance.   It
was not that Bothwell injured his honour.   Darnley
kept spies on Mary, and had such a noisy and bur-
lesque set of incidents occurred in the garden of
Exchequer House as Buchanan reports, Darnley
should have had the news.   But he merely complained
to du Croc that he did not enjoy the same share of
power and trust as was his in the early weeks of his

[1] Teulet, *Papiers d'État*, ii. 139–146, 147, 151.   See also Keith, ii.
448–459.
[2] Frazer, *The Lennox*, ii. 350, 351.

wedding. Du Croc replied this fortune could never
again be his. The 'Book of Articles' entirely omits
Darnley's offence in the slaying of Riccio. Du Croc
was more explicit. He told Darnley that the Queen
had been personally offended, and would never restore
him to his authority. 'He ought to be well content
with the honour and good cheer which she gave him,
honouring and treating him as the King her husband,
and supplying his household with all manner of good
things.' This goes ill with Buchanan's story about
Mary's stinginess to Darnley. It is admitted by the
Lennox MSS. that she did not keep her alleged promise to Bothwell, that she and Darnley should never
meet in the marriage bed.

When Mary had gone to Jedburgh, to hold a
court (about October 8), du Croc was asked to meet
Darnley at some place, apparently Dundas, 'three
leagues from Edinburgh.' Du Croc thought that
Darnley wished Mary to ask him to return. But
Darnley, du Croc believed, intended to hang off till
after the baptism of James, and did not mean to be
present on that occasion (*pour ne s'y trouver point*).
He had, in du Croc's opinion, but two causes of un-
happiness : one, the reconciliation of the Lords with
the Queen, and their favour ; the other, a fear lest
Elizabeth's envoy to the baptism might decline to
recognise him (*ne fera compte de luy*). The night-
ride from Dundas to Linlithgow, in which (according
to Lennox) Darnley told the tale of Mary's advice to
him to seduce Lady Moray, must have occurred at

this very time, perhaps after the meeting with du
Croc, three leagues from Edinburgh. In his paper
about the night-ride, Lennox avers that Mary yielded
to Bothwell's love, before this ride and conversation.
But he does not say that he himself was already aware
of the amour, and his whole narrative leaves the impression that he was not. We are to suppose that, if
Buchanan's account is true, the adventures of the
Exchequer House and of Lady Reres were only known
to the world later. Certainly no suspicion of Mary
had crossed the mind of du Croc, who says that
he never saw her so much loved and respected ;
and, in short, there is no known contemporary hint
of the beginning of the guilty amour, flagrant as
were its alleged circumstances. This point has,
naturally, been much insisted upon by the defenders
of Mary.

It must not escape us that, about this time, almost
every Lord, from Moray downwards, was probably
united in a signed 'band' against Darnley. The
precise nature of its stipulations is uncertain, but
that a hostile band existed, I think can be demonstrated. The Lords, in their letter of October 8 to
Catherine, declare that they will never consent to
let Darnley manage affairs. The evidence as to a
band comes from four sources : Randolph, Archibald
Douglas, a cousin and ally of Morton, Claude Nau,
Mary's secretary, and Moray himself.

First, on October 15, 1570, Randolph, being in
Edinburgh after the death of the Regent Moray,

writes : 'Divers, since the Regent's death, either to cover their own doings or to advance their cause, have sought to make him odious to the world. The universal bruit runs upon three or four persons ' (Bothwell, Lethington, Balfour (?), Huntly, and Argyll) ' who subscribed upon a bond promising to concur and assist one another in the late King's death. This bond was kept in the Castle, in a little coffer covered with green, and, after the apprehension of the Scottish Queen at Carberry Hill, was taken out of the place where it lay by the Laird of Lethington, in presence of Mr. James Balfour. . . . This being a thing so notoriously known, as well by Mr. James Balfour's own report, as testimony of other who have seen the thing, is utterly denied to be true, *and another bond produced which they allege to be it, containing no such matter, at the which, with divers other noblemen's hands, the Regent's was also made, a long time before the bond of the King's murder was made,* and now they say that if it can be proved by any bond that they consented to the King's death, the late Regent is as guilty as they, and for testimony thereof (as Randolph is credibly informed) have sent a bond to be seen in England, which is either some new bond made among themselves, and the late Regent's hand counterfeited at the same (which in some cases he knows has been done), or the old bond at which his hand is, containing no such matter.' Randolph adds, as an example of forgery of Moray's hand, the order for Lethington's release by Kirkcaldy, to whom

Robert Melville attributed the forgery.[1] Thus both
sides could deal in charges of forging hands.

But what is 'the old band,' *signed by Moray*
'a long time before the bond of the King's murder
was made'? To this question we probably find a
reply in the long letter written by Archibald Douglas
to Mary, in April, 1583, when he (one of Darnley's
murderers) was an exile, and was seeking, and
winning, Mary's favour. Douglas had fled to France
after Riccio's murder, but was allowed to return to
Scotland, 'to deal with Earls Murray, Athol, Bodvel,
Arguile, and Secretary Ledington,' in the interests of
a pardon for Morton, Ruthven, and Lindsay. This
must have been just after September 20, when the
return of Lethington to favour occurred. But
Murray, Atholl, Bothwell, Argyll, and Lethington
told Douglas that they had made a band, with other
noblemen, to this effect : that they 'were resolved to
obey your Majesty as their natural sovereign, *and
have nothing to do with your husband's command whatsoever.*' So the Lords also told Catherine de' Medici.
They wished to know, before interfering in Morton's
favour, whether he would also sign this anti-Darnley
band, which Morton and his accomplices did. Archibald Douglas then returned, with their signatures,
to Stirling, at the time of James's baptism, in mid
December, 1566. Morton and his friends were then
pardoned on December 24.[2] This anti-Darnley band,
which does not allude to *murder*, must be that pro-

[1] Cal. For. Eliz. ix. 354, 355.   [2] Laing, ii. 331, 334.

duced in 1570, according to Randolph, by 'divers, since Moray's death, either to cover their own doings, or to advance their own cause, seeking to make him odious to the world.' We thus find Moray, and all the most powerful nobles, banded against Darnley, some time between September and December 1567.

Now, Claude Nau, inspired by Mary, attributes Darnley's murder to a band 'written by Alexander Hay, at that time one of the clerks of the Council, and signed by the Earls of Moray, Huntly, Bothwell, and Morton, by Lethington, James Balfour, and others.' Moray certainly did not sign the murderous band kept in the green-covered coffer, nor, as he alleged at his death, did Morton. But Nau seems to be confusing *that* band with the band of older date, to which, as Randolph admits, and as Archibald Douglas insists, Moray, Morton, and others put their hands, Morton signing as late as December 1567.

Nau says : 'They protested that they were acting for the public good of the realm, pretending that they were freeing the Queen from the bondage and misery into which she had been reduced by the King's behaviour. They promised to support each other, and to avouch that the act was done justly, licitly, and lawfully by the leading men of the Council. They had done it in defence of their lives, which would be in danger, they said, if the King should get the upper hand and secure the government of the realm, at which he was aiming.' [1]

[1] Nau, p. 35.

Randolph denies that there was any hint of murder in the band signed by Moray. Archibald Douglas makes the gist of it 'that they would have nothing to do with your husband's command whatsoever.' Nau speaks of ' the act,' but does not name murder explicitly as part of the band. Almost certainly, then, there did exist, in autumn 1567, a band hostile to Darnley, and signed by Moray and Morton. It seems highly probable that the old band, made long before the King's murder, and of a character hostile to Darnley's influence, and menacing to him, is that which Moray himself declares that he did sign, ' at the beginning of October,' 1566. When Moray, in London, on January 19, 1569, was replying to an account (the so-called 'Protestation of Argyll and Huntly') of the conference at Craigmillar, in November 1566, he denied (what was not alleged) that he signed any band *there* : at Craigmillar. 'This far the subscriptioun of bandes be me is trew, that indeed I subscrivit ane band with the Erlis of Huntlie, Ergile, and Boithvile in Edinburgh, at the begynning of October the same yeir, 1566 : quhilk was devisit in signe of our reconciliatioun, in respect of the former grudgis and displesouris that had been amang us. Whereunto I wes constreinit to mak promis, before I culd be admittit to the Quenis presence or haif ony shew of hir faveur. . .' [1]

Now Moray had been admitted to Mary's presence two days after the death of Riccio, before her flight

---

[1] Bain, ii. 599, 600.

to Dunbar. On April 25, 1566, Randolph writes
from Berwick to Cecil: 'Murray, Argyll, and Glencairn are come to Court. I hear his (Moray's) credit
shall be good. The Queen wills that all controversies
shall be taken up, in especial that between Murray
and Bothwell.' [1] On April 21, 1566, Moray, Argyll,
Glencairn, and others were received by Mary in the
Castle, and a Proclamation was made to soothe 'the
enmity that was betwixt the Earls of Huntly, Bothwell, and Murray.' [2] Thenceforward, as we have
proved in detail, Moray was ostensibly in Mary's
favour. Moray would have us believe that he only
obtained this grace by virtue of his promise to sign a
band with Huntly, Bothwell, and Argyll: the last
had been on his own side in his rebellion. But the
band, he alleges, was not signed till October, 1566,
though the promise must have been given, at least
his 'favour' with Mary was obtained, in April. And
Moray signed the band precisely at the moment when
Darnley was giving most notorious trouble, and had
just been approached and implored by Mary, the
Council, and the French ambassador. That was
the moment when the Privy Council assured Catherine that they 'would never consent' to Darnley's
sovereignty. Why was that moment selected by
Moray to fulfil a promise more than four months
old? Was the band not that mentioned by Randolph,
Archibald Douglas, and Nau, and therefore, in some
sense, an anti-Darnley band, not a mere 'sign of

[1] Bain, ii. 276.   [2] *Diurnal*, p. 99.

reconciliation'? The inference appears legitimate, and this old band signed by Moray seems to have been confused, by his enemies, with a later band for Darnley's murder, which we may be sure that he never signed. He only 'looked through his fingers.'

On October 7, or 8, or 9, Mary left Edinburgh to hold a Border session at Jedburgh. She appears to have been in Jedburgh by the 9th.[1] On October 7, Bothwell was severely wounded, in Liddesdale, by a Border thief. On October 15, Mary rode to visit him at Hermitage.[2] Moray, says Sir John Forster to Cecil (October 15), was with her, and other nobles. Yet Buchanan says that she rode 'with such a company as no man of any honest degree would have adventured his life and his goods among them.' Life, indeed, was not safe with the nobles, but how Buchanan errs ! Du Croc, writing from Jedburgh on October 17, reports that Bothwell is out of danger : 'the Queen is well pleased, his loss to her would have been great.'[3] Buchanan's account of this affair is, that Mary heard at Borthwick of Bothwell's wound, whereon ' she flingeth away like a mad woman, by great journeys in post, in the sharp time of winter' (early October !), 'first to Melrose, then to Jedburgh. There, though she heard sure news of his life, yet her affection, impatient of delay, could not temper itself; but needs she must bewray her outrageous lust, and in an inconvenient time of the

---

[1] See the evidence in Hay Fleming, 414, note 61.
[2] Cal. For. Eliz. viii. 139. *Diurnal*, 101.   [3] Teulet, ii. 150

year, despising all incommodities of the way and
weather, and all dangers of thieves, she betook herself headlong to her journey.' The 'Book of Articles'
merely says that, after hearing of Bothwell's wound,
she 'took na kindly rest' till she saw him—a
prolonged *insomnia*. On returning to Jedburgh, she
prepared for Bothwell's arrival, and, when he was
once brought thither, then perhaps by their excessive
indulgence in their passion, Buchanan avers, Mary
nearly died.

All this is false. Mary stayed at least five days
in Jedburgh before she rode to Hermitage, whither,
says Nau, corroborated by Forster, Moray accompanied her. She fell ill on October 17, a week before Bothwell's arrival at Jedburgh. On October 25,
she was despaired of, and some thought she had
passed away. Bothwell arrived, in a litter, about
October 25. Forster says October 15, wrongly.
These were no fit circumstances for 'their old pastime,' which they took 'so openly, as they seemed to
fear nothing more than lest their wickedness should
be unknown.' 'I never saw her Majesty so much
beloved, esteemed, and honoured,' du Croc had
written on October 17.

Buchanan's tale is here so manifestly false, that it
throws doubt on his scandal about the Exchequer
House. That Mary abhorred Darnley, and was
wretched, is certain. 'How to be free of him she
sees no outgait,' writes Lethington on October 24.
He saw no chance of reconciliation.[1] That she and

---

[1] Laing, ii. 72.

House occupied by Queen Mary at Jedburgh.

Bothwell acted profligately together while he was ill at Hermitage, and she almost dead at Jedburgh, is a grotesquely malevolent falsehood. Darnley now visited Jedburgh : it is uncertain whether or not he delayed his visit long after he knew of Mary's illness. Buchanan says that he was received with cruel contempt.[1] In some pious remarks of hers when she expected death, she only asks Heaven to 'mend' Darnley, whose misconduct is the cause of her malady.[2] On November 20, Mary arrived at Craigmillar Castle, hard by Edinburgh. Du Croc mentions her frequent exclamation, ' I could wish to be dead,' and, from Darnley, and his own observation, gathered that Darnley would never humble himself, while Mary was full of suspicions when she saw him converse with any noble. For disbelieving that reconciliation was possible du Croc had several reasons, he says ; he may have detected the passion for Bothwell, but makes no allusion to that subject ; and, when Darnley in December behaved sullenly, his sympathy was with the Queen. In the ' Book of Articles' exhibited against Mary in 1568, it is alleged that, at Kelso, on her return from Jedburgh, she received a letter from Darnley, wept, told Lethington and Moray that she could never have a happy day while united to her husband, and spoke of suicide. Possibly Darnley wrote about his letter against her to the Pope, and the Catholic Powers. But the

---

[1] Hay Fleming, 418, 419.
[2] *Queen Mary at Jedburgh*, p. 23.

anecdote is dubious.   She proceeded to Craigmillar
Castle.

Then came the famous conference at Craigmillar.
Buchanan says (in the ' Detection') that, in presence of
Moray, Huntly, Argyll, and Lethington, she spoke of
a divorce, on grounds of consanguinity, the Dispensation ' being conveyed away.'   One of the party said
that her son's legitimacy would be imperilled.   So
far the ' Book of Articles' agrees with the ' Detection.'
Not daring to ' disclose her purpose to make away
her son' (the ' Book of Articles' omits this), she
determined to murder her husband, and her son.   A
very different story is told in a document sent by
Mary to Huntly and Argyll, for their signatures, on
January 5, 1569.   This purports to be a statement
of what Huntly had told Bishop Lesley.   He and
Argyll were asked to revise, omit, or add, as their
recollection served, sign, and return, the paper
which was to be part of Mary's counter-accusations
against her accusers.[1]   The document was intercepted, and was never seen nor signed by Huntly and
Argyll.   The statement, whatever its value (it is
merely Lesley's recollection of remarks by Huntly),
declares that Moray and Lethington roused Argyll
from bed, and suggested that, to induce Mary to
recall Morton (banished for Riccio's murder), it would
be advisable to oblige Mary by ridding her of
Darnley.   Huntly was next brought in, and, last,
Bothwell.   They went to Mary's rooms, and proposed

---

[1] Bain, ii. 597–599.   Anderson, iv. pt. ii. 186.   Keith, iii. 290–294.

a divorce. She objected that this would, or might, invalidate her son's legitimacy, and proposed to retire to France. Lethington said that a way would be found, and that Moray would 'look through his fingers.' Mary replied that nothing must be done which would stain her honour and conscience. Lethington answered that, if they were allowed to guide the matter, 'Your Grace shall see nothing but good, and approved by Parliament.'

Though Huntly and Argyll never saw this piece, they signed, in September, 1568, another, to like purpose. Starting from the same point, the desire to win Morton's pardon, they say that they promised to secure a divorce, either because the dispensation for Mary's marriage was not published (conceivably the marriage occurred before the dispensation was granted) or for adultery : or to bring a charge of treason against Darnley, 'or quhat other wayis to dispeche him ; quhilk altogidder hir Grace refusit, as is manifestlie knawin.' [1] It is plain, therefore, that Huntly and Argyll would have made no difficulty about signing the Protestation which never reached them.

While Buchanan's tale yields no reason for Mary's consent to pardon the Riccio murderers (whom of all men she loathed), Huntly and Argyll supply a partial explanation. In Buchanan's History, it is casually mentioned, later, that Mary wished to involve Moray and Morton in the guilt of Darnley's

[1] Goodall, ii. 359.

H

murder. But how had Morton returned to Scotland?
Of *that*, not a word.[1] In truth, both French and
English influence had been used ; Bothwell, acting
'like a very friend,' says Bedford, and others had
openly added their intercessions. James's baptism
was an occasion for an amnesty, and this was granted
on Christmas Eve. The pardon might well have been
given, even had no divorce or murder of Darnley
been intended, but the step was most threatening to
Darnley's safety, as the exiles hated him with a deadly
hatred. On the whole, taking the unsigned 'Protestation' of Huntly and Argyll with the document
which they did sign, it seems probable, or certain,
that a conference as to getting rid of Darnley, in
some way, was held at Craigmillar, where Moray
certainly was.

Moray, in London, was shown the intercepted
'Protestation,' and denied that anything was said, at
Craigmillar, in his hearing 'tending to ony unlawfull
or dishonourable end.'[2] But, if the Protestation can
be trusted, nothing positively unlawful was proposed.
Lethington promised 'nothing but good, and approved by Parliament.' Moray also denied having
signed a 'band,' except that of October 1567,
but about a 'band' the Protestation says nothing.
Moray *may* have referred to what (according to the
'Diurnal,' pp. 127, 128) Hay of Talla said at his
execution (January 3, 1567). He had seen a 'band'
signed by Bothwell, Huntly, Argyll, Lethington, and

---

[1] *Historia*, fol. 214.   [2] Keith, iii. 294. Bain, ii. 600.

Sir James Balfour. The first four, at least, were at Craigmillar. Buchanan, in the ' Detection,' gives Hay's confession, but not this part of it. Much later, on December 13, 1573, Ormistoun confessed that, about Easter, after the murder, Bothwell tried to reassure him by showing him a ' contract subscryvit be four or fyve handwrittes, quhilk he affirmit to me was the subscription of the erle of Huntlie, Argyll, the Secretar Maitland, and Sir James Balfour.' The contract or band stated that Darnley must be got rid off ' by ane way or uther,' and that all who signed should defend any who did the deed. It was subscribed a quarter of a year before the murder, that is, taking the phrase widely, after the Craigmillar conference.[1]

What did Lethington mean, at Craigmillar, by speaking of a method of dealing with Darnley which Parliament would approve ? He may have meant to arrest him, for treason, and kill him if he resisted. That this was contemplated, at Craigmillar, we proceed to adduce the evidence of Lennox.

This hitherto unknown testimony exists, in inconsistent forms, among the several indictments which Lennox, between July and December, 1568, drew up to show to the English Commissioners who, at York and Westminster, examined the charges against Mary. In the evidence which we have hitherto seen, the plans of Mary's Council at Craigmillar are left vague, and Mary's objections, as described by

[1] Laing, ii. 293, 294.

Huntly and Argyll, are spoken of as final. Mention is made of only one conference, without any sequel. But Lennox asserts that there was at least one other meeting, at Craigmillar, between Mary and her advisers. His information is obviously vague, but he first makes the following assertions.

'In this mean time' (namely in December 1566, when the Court was at Stirling for James's baptism), 'his father, being advertised ['credibly informed'] [1] that at Craigmillar the Queen and certain of her Council *had concluded* upon an enterprise to the great peril and danger of his ['Majesty's'] person, which was that he should have been *apprehended and put in ward*, which rested' (was postponed) 'but only on the finishing of the christening and the departure of the said ambassadors, which thing being not a little grievous unto his father's heart, did give him warning thereof; whereupon he, by the advice of sundry that loved him, departed from her shortly after the christening, and came to his father to Glasgow, being fully resolved with himself to have taken ship shortly after, and to have passed beyond the seas, but that sickness prevented him, which was the cause of his stay.'

In this version, Lennox is warned, by whom he does not say, of a plan, formed at Craigmillar, to arrest Darnley. The plan is not refused by the Queen, but is 'concluded upon,' yet postponed till

[1] The original MS. has been corrected by Lennox, in the passages within brackets. The italics are my own.

the christening festivities are over. *Nothing is said about the design to kill Darnley if he resists.* The scheme is communicated to Darnley by Lennox himself.

Next comes what seems to be the second of Lennox's attempts at producing a 'discourse.' This can be dated. It ends with the remark that, after Langside fight, Mary spoke with Ormistoun and Hob Ormistoun, ' who were of the chiefest murderers of the King, her husband.' These men now live with the Laird of Whithaugh, in Liddesdale, ' who keepeth in his house a prisoner, one Andrew Carre, of Fawdonside, by her commandment.' This was Andrew Ker of Faldonside, the most brutal of the murderers of Riccio. Now on October 4, 1568, in a list of ' offences committed by the Queen's party,' a list perhaps in John Wood's hand, we read that Whithaugh, and other Elliots, ' took ane honest and trew gentleman, Ker of Faldonside, and keep him prisoner by Mary's command ; ' while Whithaugh cherishes the two Ormistouns.[1] This discourse of Lennox, then, is of, or about, October 4, 1568, and was prepared for the York Conference to inquire into Mary's case, where it was not delivered.

He says : ' How she used him (Darnley) at Craig-millar, my said Lord Regent (Moray), who was there present, can witness. One thing I am constrainit to declare, which came to my knowledge by credible persons, which was that certain of her familiar and

[1] Bain, ii. 516, 517.

privy counsellors, of her faction and Bothwell's, should present her a letter at that house, subscribed with their hands, the effect of which letter was to apprehend the King my son's person, and to put him in ward, and, *if he happened to resist them, to kill him :* she answered that the ambassadors were come,[1] and the christening drew near, so that the time would not then serve well for that purpose, till the triumph was done, and the ambassadors departed to their country. . . Also I, being at Glasgow about the same time, and having intelligence of the foresaid device for his apprehension at Craigmillar, did give him warning thereof ; ' consequently, as he was also ill-treated at Stirling, Darnley went to Glasgow, ' where he was not long till he fell sick.' Lennox here adds the plot to kill Darnley if he resisted arrest. His reference to certain of Mary's Privy Council, who laid the plot, cannot have been grateful to Lethington, who was at York, where Lennox meant to deliver his speech.

The final form taken by Lennox's account of what occurred at Craigmillar looks as if it were a Scots draft for the ' Brief Discourse ' which he actually put in, in English, at Westminster, on November 29, 1568. He addresses Norfolk and the rest in his opening sentences. The Privy Council who made the plot are they ' *of thay dayis,*' which included Moray, Argyll, Huntly, Lethington, and Bothwell. These Lords, or some of them, either

---

[1] De Brienne came to Craigmillar on November 21, 1568, *Diurnal.*

subscribe ' a lettre ' of warrant for Darnley's capture alive or dead, or ask Mary to sign one; Lennox is not certain which view is correct. She answered that they must delay till the ambassadors departed. ' But seeing in the mean time this purpose divulgate,' she arrested the ' reportaris,' namely Hiegait, Walker, the Laird of Minto (we do not elsewhere learn that he was examined), and Alexander Cauldwell. Perceiving ' that the truth was like to come to light, she left off further inquisition.'

This version does not state that Lennox, or any one else, revealed the Craigmillar plot for his arrest to Darnley. It later describes a quarrel of his with Mary at Stirling, and adds, ' Being thus handled, at the end of the christening he came to me to Glasgow.' This tale of a plot to arrest, and, if he resisted, to kill Darnley, corresponds with Paris's statement that Bothwell told him, ' We were much inclined to do it lately, when we were at Craigmillar.'

This evidence of Lennox, then, avers that, after the known conference at Craigmillar, which Lethington ended by saying that ' you shall see nothing but good, and approved of by Parliament,' there was another conference. On this second occasion some of the Privy Council suggested the arrest of Darnley, who, perhaps, was to be slain if he resisted. Parliament might approve of this measure, for there were reasons for charging Darnley with high treason. Mary, says Lennox, accepted the scheme, but post-

poned it till after the Baptism.   Within two or three
weeks Lennox heard of the plan, and gave Darnley
warning.   But Lennox's three versions are hesitating
and inconsistent : nor does he cite his authority for
the conspiracy to kill Darnley.

V

BETWEEN THE BAPTISM AND THE MURDER

MARY passed from Craigmillar and Edinburgh to the baptism of her son James at Stirling. The 17th December, 1566, was the crowning triumph of her life, and the last. To the cradle came the Ambassadors of France and England bearing gifts : Elizabeth, the child's godmother, sent a font of enamelled gold. There were pageants and triumphs, fireworks, festivals, and the chanting of George Buchanan's Latin elegiacs on Mary, the *Nympha Caledoniæ*, with her crowns of Virtue and of Royalty. Above all, Mary had won, or taken, permission to baptize the child by the Catholic rite, and Scotland saw, for the last time, the ecclesiastics in their splendid vestments. Mary busied herself with hospitable kindnesses, a charming hostess in that dark hold where her remote ancestor had dirked his guest between the table and the hearth. But there was a strange gap in the throng of nobles. The child's father, though in the Castle, did not attend the baptism, was not among the guests, while the grandfather, Lennox, remained apart at his castle in Glasgow.

According to du Croc, who was at Stirling, Darnley announced his intention to depart, two days before the christening, but remained and sulked.

A month before the ceremony, du Croc had expected Darnley to sulk and stay away. At Stirling he declined to meet Darnley, so bad had his conduct been, and said that, if Darnley entered by one door of his house, he would go out by the other. It has been averred by Camden, writing in the reign and under the influence of James I., when King of England, that the English ambassador, Bedford, warned his suite not to acknowledge Darnley as King, and punished one of them, who, having known him in England, saluted him. Nau says that Darnley refused to associate with the English, unless they would acknowledge his title of King, and to do this they had been forbidden by the Queen of England, their mistress,[1] who knew that Darnley kept up a more or less treasonable set of intrigues with the English Catholics.[2] Bedford, a sturdy Protestant, could not be a *persona grata* to Darnley: and, as to Darnley's kingship, his own father, in 1568, rather represented him as an English subject. On the other side we have only the evidence of Sir James Melville, gossiping long after the event, to the effect that Bedford, when leaving Stirling, charged him with a message to Mary. He bade her ' entertain Darnley as she had done at the beginning, for her own honour and advancement of her affairs,' which

---

[1] Nau, p. 33.   [2] Bain, ii. 293, 310.

warning Melville repeated to her.[1] But there was an
awkwardness as between ' the King ' and the English,
nor do we hear that Bedford made any advance to
Darnley, whose natural sulkiness is vouched for by
all witnesses.

As to what occurred at Stirling in regard to Darnley's
ill-treatment, the Lennox MSS. are copious. Mary,
' after an amiable and gentle manner,' induced him to
go to Stirling before her, without seeing the ambassadors. At Stirling, ' she feigned to be in a great
choler against the King's tailors, that had not made
such apparel as she had devised for him against the
triumph.' Darnley, to please her, kept out of the
way of the ambassadors. She dismissed his guards,
Lennox sent men of his own, and this caused a
quarrel.[2] Darnley flushed with anger, and Mary said,
' If he were a little daggered, and had bled as much
as my Lord Bothwell had lately done, it would make
him look the fairer.' This anecdote (about which,
in June 1568, while getting up his case, Lennox made
inquiries in Scotland) is given both in English and
Scots, in different versions. The ' Book of Articles '
avers that Bothwell himself was in fear, and was
strongly guarded.

While all at Stirling seemed gay, while Mary
played the hostess admirably, du Croc found her
once weeping and in pain, and warned his Govern-

[1] Melville, p. 172. (1827.)
[2] Crawford, in his deposition against Mary, says that she spoke
sharp words of Lennox, at Stirling, to his servant, Robert Cunningham.

ment that 'she would give them trouble yet'
(December 23).[1]   Mary had causes for anxiety of
which du Croc was not aware.   Strange rumours
filled Court and town.   A man named Walker, a retainer of her ambassador at Paris, Archbishop Beaton,
reported that the Town Clerk of Glasgow, William
Hiegait, was circulating a tale to the effect that Darnley
meant to seize the child prince, crown him, and rule
in his name.   Now for months Darnley had been full
of mad projects ; to seize Scarborough, to seize the
Scilly Islands, and the scheme for kidnapping
James had precedents enough.

Darnley was in frequent communication with the
discontented Catholics of the North and West of
England, and his retainers, the Standens, were young
men yearning for adventures.   'Knowing I am an
offender of the laws, they professed great friendship,'
wrote William Rogers to Cecil, with some humour.[2]

A rumour of some attempt against Mary reached
Archbishop Beaton, in Paris, at the end of 1566,
through the Spanish Ambassador there, who may

---

[1] Keith, i. xcviii.

[2] Bain, ii. 293.   This Rogers it was who, on July 5, 1567, informed
Cecil that 'gentlemen of the west country' had sent to Darnley a chart
of the Scilly Isles.   If Darnley, among other dreams, thought of a
descent on them, as he did on Scarborough, he made no bad choice.
Mr. A. E. W. Mason points out to me that the isles 'commanded the
Channel, and all the ships from the north of England,' which passed
between Scilly and the mainland, twenty-five miles off.   The harbours
being perilous, and only known to the islesmen, a small fleet at Scilly
could do great damage, and would only have to run back to be quite safe.
Darnley, in his moods, was capable of picturing himself as a pirate
chief.

have heard of it from the Spanish Ambassador in London, with whom the English Catholics were perpetually intriguing. There is a good deal of evidence that Darnley had been complaining of Mary to the Pope and the Catholic Powers, as insufficiently zealous for the Church. Darnley, not Mary, was the Scottish royal person on whom the Church ought to rely,[1] and Mary, says Knox's continuator, saw his letters, by treachery. Consumed with anger at his degraded position, so unlike the royalty for which he hungered, and addicted to day dreams about descents on Western England, and similar wild projects, Darnley may possibly, at this time, have communicated to the English Catholics a project for restoring himself to power by carrying off and crowning his child. This fantasy would drift through the secret channels of Catholic diplomacy to the Spanish Ambassador in Paris, who gave Beaton a hint, but declined to be explicit. Mary thanked Beaton for his warning, from Seton, on February 18, nine days after Darnley's death.[2] 'But alas! it came too late.' Mary added that the Spanish ambassador in London had also given her warning.

There may, then, have been this amount of foundation for the report which, according to Walker, at Stirling, Hiegait was circulating about mid-December 1566. Stirling was then full of 'honest men of the Lennox,' sent thither by Lennox himself (as he says in one of his manuscript discourses), because

[1] Hay Fleming, p. 415, note 63.　　　[2] Labanoff, ii.

Darnley's usual guard had been withdrawn. Mary objected to the presence of so many of Lennox's retainers, and there arose that furious quarrel between her and her husband. Possibly Mary, having heard Walker's story of Darnley's project, thought that his Lennox men were intended to bear a hand in it.

In any case Walker filled Mary's ears, at Stirling —as she wrote to Archbishop Beaton, her ambassador in France, on January 20, 1567—with rumours of ' utheris attemptatis and purposis tending to this fyne.' He named Hiegait 'for his chief author,' ' quha,' he said, ' had communicat the mater to hym, as apperyt, of mynd to gratify us; sayand to Walcar, " gif I had the moyen and crydet with the Quenis Majestie that ze have, I wald not omitt to mak hir previe of sic purposis and bruitis that passes in the cuntrie." ' Hiegait also said that Darnley could not endure some of the Lords, but that he or they must leave the country. Mary then sent for Hiegait, before the Council, and questioned *him*. He (probably in fear of Lennox) denied that he had told Walker the story of Darnley's project, but he had heard, from Cauldwell, a retainer of Eglintoun's, that Darnley himself was to be 'put in ward.' Eglintoun, ' a rank Papist,' was described by Randolph as never a trustworthy Lennoxite, 'never good Levenax.' His retainer, Cauldwell, being summoned, expressly denied that he ever told the rumour about the idea of imprisoning Darnley, to Hiegait. But Hiegait informed the Laird of Minto (a Stewart and a Lennoxite), who again told Lennox, who told Darnley, by whose desire Cauldwell again spoke to Hiegait. The trail of the gossip runs from Cauldwell (the estate of that name is in Eglintoun's country, Ayrshire) to Hiegait, from him to Stewart of Minto, from him to Lennox, and from Lennox to Darnley. Possibly Eglintoun (the cautious Lord who slipped away when Ainslie's band was being signed, and hid under straw, after the battle of Langside) was the original source of the rumour of Darnley's intended arrest. This is a mere guess. If there was a very secret plot, at Craigmillar, to arrest Darnley, we cannot tell how it reached Hiegait. Mary 'found no manner of concordance' in their answers, and she rebuked Walker and Hiegait in her own name, and that of their master, Beaton himself.[1] These men, with Minto, were allied with Lennox, and one of them may have been his authority for the story of the second Craigmillar conference.

We now see why it was that, in the height of her final triumph, the christening festival at Stirling Mary wept and was ill at ease. Her husband's conduct was intolerable: now he threatened to leave before the ceremony, next he stayed on, a dismal figure behind the scenes. His guard of Lennox men might aim at slaying Bothwell, or Mary might think, on Walker's evidence, that they intended to kidnap her child. Worse followed, when she and her Council examined Walker. Out came the tale of Hiegait, and

---

[1] Labanoff, i. 396-398. Mary to Beaton, Jan. 20, 1567.

Queen and Council, if they had really plotted to arrest Darnley, knew that their scheme was discovered and was abortive. Finally, on December 24, either in consequence of Lennox's warning, or because Morton, Lindsay, and the other Riccio conspirators whom he betrayed were pardoned, Darnley rode off to his father at Glasgow. There he fell ill, soon after his arrival, but Lennox's MSS. never hint that he was poisoned at Stirling (as Buchanan declares), or that he fell sick when he had ridden but a mile from the town. That they deny.

After Darnley's departure, Moray, with Bedford, the English Ambassador, went to St. Andrews, and other places in Fife. Till January 2, 1567, when she returned to Stirling, Mary was at Drummond Castle, and at Tullibardine, where, says Buchanan, she and Bothwell made love in corners 'so that all were highly offended.' After January 13, she visited Calendar House, and then went to Holyrood.

It is said that she never wrote to Darnley till after January 14, when she took her child to Edinburgh, with the worst purposes, Buchanan declares. Then she wrote to Darnley, the Lennox Papers inform us, excusing herself, and offering to visit him in his sickness at Glasgow. Darnley told her messenger verbally, say the Lennox MSS., that the Queen must judge herself as to the visit to him. 'But this much ye shall declare unto her, that I wish Stirling to be Jedburgh, and Glasgow to be the Hermitage, and I the Earl of Bothwell as I lie here, and then I doubt

not but she would be quickly with me undesired.'
This was a tactless verbal message, and, if given,
must have proved to Mary that Darnley suspected
her amour. Moreover, this Lennoxian story, that
Mary offered the visit, and that Darnley replied with
reserve, and with an insult to be verbally delivered,
agrees ill with what is said in the deposition
(December, 1568) of Lennox's retainer, Thomas
Crawford. According to Crawford, 'after theire
metinge and shorte spekinge together she asked hym
of hys lettres, wherein he complained of the crueletye
of som.' 'He answered that he complained not
without cause . . .' 'Ye asked me what I ment bye
the crueltye specified in my lettres, yt procedeth of
you onelye that wille not accept mye *offres* and
repentance.' Now, in the Lennox Papers this
'innocent lamb' has nothing to repent of, and
has made no offers. These came from Mary's
side.[1]

The Lennox account goes on to say that later
Mary sent 'very loving messages and letters unto him
to drive all suspicions out of his mind,' a passage
copied by Buchanan in his History. Darnley, therefore, after Mary's visit to Glasgow, returned with her
to Edinburgh, 'contrary to his father's will and
consent.' Lennox, however, here emphatically denies
that either he or Darnley suspected any murderous
design on the part of the Queen. Yet, in Letter II.,
she is made to say that he 'fearit his liff,' as the

[1] Hosack, ii. 580. Crawford's deposition.

I

passage is quoted in the 'Book of Articles.' [1]   As to
the story that Darnley's illness at Glasgow was caused
by poison ; poison, of course, was suspected, but, if
the Casket Letters are genuine, Mary therein calls
him 'this pocky man,' and Bedford says that he had
small-pox : a disease from which Mary had suffered
in early life.[2]   He also reports that Mary sent to
Darnley her own physician, though Buchanan says
'All this while the Queen would not suffer so much
as a physician to come at him.'   In the 'Book of
Articles' she refuses to send her apothecary.   Bedford never hints at scandalous doings of Mary and
Bothwell at Stirling.

On January 20, from Edinburgh, Mary wrote that
letter to Archbishop Beaton in Paris, as to the
Hiegait and Walker affair, which we have already
cited.   She also expressed her desire that her son
should receive the titular captaincy of the Scots
Guard in France, though, according to Buchanan,
she determined at Craigmillar to 'make away with'
her child.   Nothing in Mary's letter of January 20,
to Beaton, hints at her desire of a reconciliation with
Darnley.   Yet, on or about the very day when she
wrote it, she set forth towards Glasgow.

The date was January 20, as given by the Diary
of Birrel, and in the 'Diurnal.'   The undesigned
coincidence of diaries kept by two Edinburgh citizens
is fairly good evidence.[3]   Drury makes her arrive at

---

[1] Hosack, i. 534.   [2] Cal. For. Eliz. viii. 163, 164. January 9, 1567.
[3] See Appendix C, ' The date of Mary's visit to Glasgow.'

Glasgow on January 22. What occurred between Mary and her husband at Glasgow is said to be revealed in two of her Casket Letters written to Bothwell. Their evidence, and authenticity, are to be discussed later : other evidence to the point we have none, and can only say, here, that, at the end of January, Mary brought Darnley, his face covered with taffeta, to the house of Kirk o' Field, just beside the wall of Edinburgh, where the University buildings now stand.

Here he was in an insecure and dangerous house, close to a palace of his feudal foes, the Hamiltons. The Lennox MSS. declare that ' the place was already prepared with [undermining and] trains of powder therein.' [1] We return to this point, which was later abandoned by the prosecution.

Darnley, say the Lennox MSS., wished to occupy the Hamilton House, near Kirk o' Field, but Mary persuaded him that ' there passed a privy way [to] between the palace and it,' Kirk o' Field, ' which she could take without going through the streets.' The Lennox author adds that, on the night of the murder, Bothwell and his gang ' came the secret way which she herself was wont to come to the King her husband.' The story of the secret way recurs in Lennox MSS., and, of course, is nonsense, and was dropped. There was no subterranean passage from

---

[1] The ' undermining and ' are words added by Lennox himself to the MS. They are important.

Holyrood to Kirk o' Field. Bothwell and the murderers, in their attack on the Kirk o' Field, had no such convenience for the carriage of themselves and their gunpowder. It is strange that Lennox and his agents, having access to several of the servants of Darnley, including Nelson who survived the explosion, accepted at one time, or expected others to accept, this legend of a secret passage. Edinburgh tradition holds that there was such a tunnel between Holyrood and the Castle, which may be the basis of this fairy-tale.

The tale of the secret passage, then, is told, in the Lennox MSS., as the excuse given by Mary to Darnley for lodging him in Kirk o' Field, not in the neighbouring house of the Hamiltons. But, in the 'Book of Articles,' we read that the Archbishop of St. Andrews was then living in the Hamilton House 'onely to debar the King fra it.' The fable of the secret way, therefore, was dropped in the final version prepared by the accusers.

Mary, whether she wrote the Casket Letters or not, was, demonstrably, aware that there was a plot against Darnley, before she brought him to a house accessible to his enemies. It is certain that, hating and desiring to be delivered from Darnley, she winked at a conspiracy of which she was conscious, and let events take their course. This was, to all appearance, the policy of her brother James, 'the Good Regent Moray;' and one of Mary's apologists, Sir John Skelton, is inclined to hold that this *was* Mary's

THE OLD TOWER, WHITTINGHAM

attitude. He states the hypothesis thus : ' that Mary was not entirely unaware of the measures which were being taken by the nobility to secure in one way or other the removal of Darnley ; that, if she did not expressly sanction the enterprise, she failed, firmly and promptly, to forbid its execution.' Hence she was in ' an equivocal position,' could not act with firmness and dignity, and in accepting Bothwell could not be accounted a free agent, yielded to force, and, with a heavy heart, ' submitted to the inevitable.' [1]

That Mary knew of the existence of a plot is proved by a letter to her from Morton's cousin, Archibald Douglas, whose character and career are described in the second chapter, ' Minor Characters.' In a letter of 1583, written by Douglas to win (as he did win) favour and support from Mary, during his exile in England, he says that, in January, 1567, about the 18th or 19th, Bothwell and Lethington visited Morton at Whittingham, his own brother's place, now the seat of Mr. A. J. Balfour. The fact of the visit is corroborated by Drury's contemporary letter of January 23, 1567.[2] After they had conferred together, Morton sent Archibald Douglas with Bothwell and Lethington to Edinburgh, to learn what answer Mary would make to a proposal of a nature unknown to Archibald, so he says. ' Which' (answer) ' being given to me by the said persons, as God shall be my judge, was no other than these

[1] *Maitland of Lethington.*   [2] Cal. For. Eliz. viii. 167–168.

words, " Schaw to the Earl Morton that the Queen
will hear no speech of the matter appointed to him,"
i.e. arranged with him.   Now Morton's confession,
made before his execution, was to the effect that
Bothwell, at Whittingham, asked him to join the conspiracy to kill Darnley, but that he refused, unless
Bothwell could procure for him a written warrant
from the Queen.   Obviously it was to get this
warrant that Archibald Douglas accompanied Lethington and Bothwell to Edinburgh.   But Bothwell
and Lethington (manifestly after consulting Mary)
told Douglas that ' the Queen will hear no speech of
that matter.'   Douglas, though an infamous ruffian,
could not have reported to Mary, when attempting,
successfully, to win her favour, a compromising fact
which she, alone of living people, must have known
to be false.   Mary was not offended.[1]   Taking, then,
Morton's statement that he asked Bothwell, at
Whittingham, for Mary's warrant, with Douglas's
statement to Mary herself, that he accompanied
Lethington and Bothwell from Whittingham to
Edinburgh, and was informed by them that the
Queen ' would hear no speech of the matter,' we
cannot but believe that ' the matter ' was mooted to
her.   Therefore, in January, 1567, she was well

---

[1] On July 16, 1583, she wrote from Sheffield to Mauvissière, the
French Ambassador, bidding him ask the King of France to give
Archibald Douglas a pension, ' because he is a man of good under-
standing and serviceable where he chooses to serve, as you know.'
She intended to procure his pardon from James (Labanoff, v. 351, 368).
She employed him, and he betrayed her.

THE WHITTINGHAM TREE
(After a Drawing by Richard Doyle)

aware that *something* was intended against Darnley by Bothwell, Lethington, and others.[1]

Yet her next step was to seek Darnley in Glasgow, where he was safe among the retainers of Lennox, and thence to bring him back to Edinburgh, where his deadly foes awaited him.

Now this act of Mary's cannot be regarded as merely indiscreet, or as a half-measure, or as a measure of passive acquiescence. Had she not brought Darnley from Glasgow to Edinburgh, under a semblance of a cordial reconciliation, he might, in one way or another, have escaped from his enemies. The one measure which made his destruction certain was the measure that Mary executed, though she was well aware that a conspiracy had been framed against the unhappy lad. Even if he wished to come to Edinburgh, uninvited by her, she ought to have refused to bring him.

We can only escape from these conclusions by supposing that Archibald Douglas, destitute and in exile, hoped to enter into Mary's good graces by telling her what she well knew to be a lie; namely that Bothwell and her Secretary had declared that she would not hear of the matter proposed to her. Douglas tells us even more. While seeking to conciliate Mary, in his letter already cited, he speaks of ' the evil disposed minds of the most part of your nobility against your said husband . . . which I am assured was sufficiently known to himself, *and to all*

[1] Laing, ii. 223–236.

that had judgment never so little in that realm.'
Mary had judgment enough, and, according to the
signed declaration of her friends, Huntly and Argyll
(Sept. 12, 1568), knew that the scheme was, either to
divorce Darnley, or convict him of treason, ' or in
what other ways to *dispatch him.'* These means,
say Huntly and Argyll, she ' altogether refused.'
Yet she brought Darnley to Kirk o' Field !

Shall we argue that, pitying his illness, and returning to her old love, she deemed him safest in her
society ?   In that case she might have carried him
from Glasgow to Dumbarton Castle, or dwelt with
him in the hold where she gave birth to James VI.
—in Edinburgh Castle.   But she brought him to an
insecure house, among his known foes.

Mary's conduct towards Darnley, after Craigmillar,
and before his murder, and her behaviour later as
regards Bothwell, are always capable of being covered
by one or other special and specious excuse.   On
this occasion she brings Darnley to Edinburgh that a
tender mother may be near her child ; that a loving
wife may attend a repentant husband, who cannot
be so safe anywhere as under the ægis of her royal
presence.   In each and every case there is a special,
and not an incredible explanation.   But one cause,
if it existed, would explain every item of her conduct
throughout, from Craigmillar to Kirk o' Field : she
hated Darnley.   On the hypothesis of her innocence,
and accepting the special pleas for each act, Mary
was a weak, ailing, timid, and silly woman, with ' a

THE WHITTINGHAM TREE

(*External view*)

heart of wax.'   On the hypothesis of her guilt, though
ailing, worn, wretched, she had ' a heart of diamond,'
strong to scheme and act a Clytæmnestra's part, even
contre son naturel.   The *naturel* of Clytæmnestra, too,
was good, says Zeus in the Odyssey.   But in her case,
' Love was a great master.'

Still, we have seen no contemporary evidence, or
hint of evidence, that love for Bothwell was Mary's
master.   Her conduct, from her recovery of power,
after Riccio's murder, to her reconciliation of Lethington with Bothwell, is, on the face of it, in accordance
with the interests and wishes of her brother, Moray,
who hated Bothwell.   As the English envoy, Randolph, had desired, she brought Moray to Court.
She permitted him to attend in the Castle while she
was in child-bed, and ' refused Bothwell.'   She pro-
tected Moray from Bothwell's and Darnley's intrigues.
She took Moray's side, as to the readmission of
Lethington to favour, though Bothwell stormed.
She even made Moray her confidant as to money received from the Pope : perhaps Moray had his share !
Lethington and Moray, not Bothwell, seem to have
had her confidence.   At Moray's request she annulled
her restoration of consistorial jurisdiction to Archbishop Hamilton.   Moray and Lethington, not Bothwell, opened the proposals at Craigmillar.   Such is
the evidence of history.   On the other side are the
scandals reported by Buchanan, and, in details,
Buchanan erred : for example, as to the ride to
Hermitage.

If Mary knew too much, how much was known by 'the noble, stainless Moray'?

As to Moray's foreknowledge of Darnley's murder, can it be denied? He did not deny that he was at Craigmillar during the conference as to 'dispatching' Darnley. If the news of the plan for arresting or killing him reached underlings like Hiegait and Walker, could it be hidden from Moray, the man most in Mary's confidence, and likely to be best served by spies? He glosses over his signature to the band of early October, 1566—the anti-Darnley band—as if it were a mere 'sign of reconciliation' which he promised to subscribe 'before I could be admitted to the Queen's presence, or have any show of her favour.' But, when he did sign, he had possessed Mary's favour for more than three months, and she had even saved him from a joint intrigue of Bothwell and Darnley. In January, 1569, Moray declared that, except the band of early October, 1566, 'no other band was proposed to me in any wise,' either before or after Darnley's murder. And next he says that he would never subscribe any band, 'howbeit I was earnestly urged and pressed thereto by the Queen's commandment.'[1] Does he mean that no band was proposed to him, and yet that the Queen did press him to sign a band? Or does he mean that he would never have signed, even if the Queen had asked him to do so? We can never see this man's face; the fingers through which he looks on at murder hide his shifty eyes.

[1] Bain, ii. 599, 600.

VI

THE MURDER OF DARNLEY

I<small>T</small> is not easy for those who know modern Edinburgh to make a mental picture of the Kirk o' Field. To the site of that unhappy dwelling the Professors now daily march, walking up beneath the frowning Castle, from modern miles of stone and mortar which were green fields in Mary's day. The students congregate from every side, the omnibuses and cabs roll by through smoky, crowded, and rather uninteresting streets of shops : the solid murky buildings of the University look down on a thronged and busy populace which at every step treads on history, as Cicero says men do at Athens. On every side are houses neither new enough to seem clean, nor old enough to be interesting : there is not within view a patch of grass, a garden, or a green tree. The University buildings cover the site of Kirk o' Field, but the ghosts of those who perished there would be sadly at a loss could they return to the scene.

In Mary's time whoever stood on the grassy crest of the Calton Hill, gazing south and west, beheld,

as he still does, Holyrood at his feet, and, crowning
the highest point of the central left of the town, the
tall square tower of the church of St. Mary in the
Fields, on the limit of the landscape. In going, as
Mary often went, from Holyrood to Kirk o' Field,
you walked straight out of the palace, and up the
Canongate, through streets of Court suburb, with
gardens behind the houses. You then reached the
gate of the town wall, called the Nether Port, and
entered the street of the Nether Bow, which was a
continuation of the High Street. By any one of the
lanes, or wynds, which cut the Nether Bow at right
angles on the left, you reached the Cowgate (the street
of palaces, as Alesius, the Reformer, calls it), running
from the Castle parallel to the High Street and its
continuation, the Nether Bow. From the Cowgate,
you struck into one or other of the wynds which led
to the grounds of what were, in Mary's time, the
ruined church and houses of the Dominican monastery, or Black Friars, and to Kirk o' Field.

Beyond this, all is very difficult to explain and
understand. The church of Kirk o' Field, and the
quadrangle of houses tenanted, just as in Oxford or
Cambridge, by the Prebendaries and Provost of that
collegiate church, lay, at an early date, *outside* of the
walls of Edinburgh. This is proved by the very
name of the collegiate church, ' St. Mary in the Fields.'
But by 1531, a royal charter speaks of ' the College
Church of the Blessed Virgin Mary in the Fields,
within the walls of the burgh of Edinburgh,' the city

wall having been recently extended in that direction.[1]
The monastery of the Black Friars, close to Kirk o'
Field, was also included, by 1531, within the walls
of the burgh. But the town wall which encircled
Kirk o' Field and the Black Friars on the south, was
always in a ruinous condition. In 1541, we find the
Town Council demanding that 'ane honest substantious
wall' shall be made in another quarter.[2] In 1554,
the Provost and Prebendaries of Kirk o' Field granted
part of their grounds to the Duke of Châtelherault,
because their own houses had been 'burned down
and destroyed by their auld enemies of England,' in
the invasions of 1544–1547.[3] In 1544–1547, the town
wall encircling Kirk o' Field on the south must also
have been partially ruined. Châtelherault built on
the ground thus acquired, quite close to Kirk o'
Field, a large new house or château from which,
according to George Buchanan, Archbishop Hamilton
sent forth ruffians to aid in Darnley's murder.

By 1557, we find that the town wall, at the point
where it encircled the Black Friars, just west and
north of Kirk o' Field, was ' fallen down,' and was to be
' reedified and mended.'[4] By August, 1559, the Town
Council protest against a common passage through the
' slap,' or ' slop,' the broken gap, in the Black Friars
'yard dyke' (garden wall) ' at the east end of the block-
house.' This gap, therefore, is to be built up again,

---

[1] *Registrum de Soltre*, p. xxxv, Bannatyne Club, 1861.
[2] Records of the Burgh of Edinburgh, March 14, 1541.
[3] *Registrum de Soltre*, xxxvii.
[4] Burgh Records, Nov. 5, 1557.

'conform in work to the town wall next adjacent,' but it appears that this was never done. When Bothwell went to the murder, he got into the Black Friars grounds, whence he made his way into Darnley's garden, either by climbing through a 'slap' or gap in the wall, or by sending an accomplice through, who opened the Black Friars gate. This ruinous condition of the town wall was partly due to the habitual negligence of the citizens : partly to the destruction which fell, in 1559–1560, on the religious houses and collegiate churches. So, in February, 1560, we find the town treasurer ordered to pull down the walls of the Black Friars, and use the stones to 'build the town walls therewith.' [1]   On August 11, 1564, we again hear of repairing slaps, or gaps, 'and in especial *the new wall at the college,* so that no part thereof be climbable.' The college may be Kirk o' Field, where the burgesses already desired to build a college, the parent of Edinburgh University. On the day after Darnley's murder (Feb. 11, 1567) the treasurer was ordered ' to take away the hewen work of the back door of the Provost's lodging of the Kirk o' Field, and to build up the same door with lime and sand.' Conceivably this 'back door,' now to be built up and closed, was that door in Darnley's house which opened through the town wall. Finally, on May 7, 1567, the Treasurer was bidden ' to build *the wall of the town decayed and fallen down on the south side* of the Provost of the Kirk o' Field's

---

[1] Burgh Records, Feb. 19, 1560, March 12, 1560.

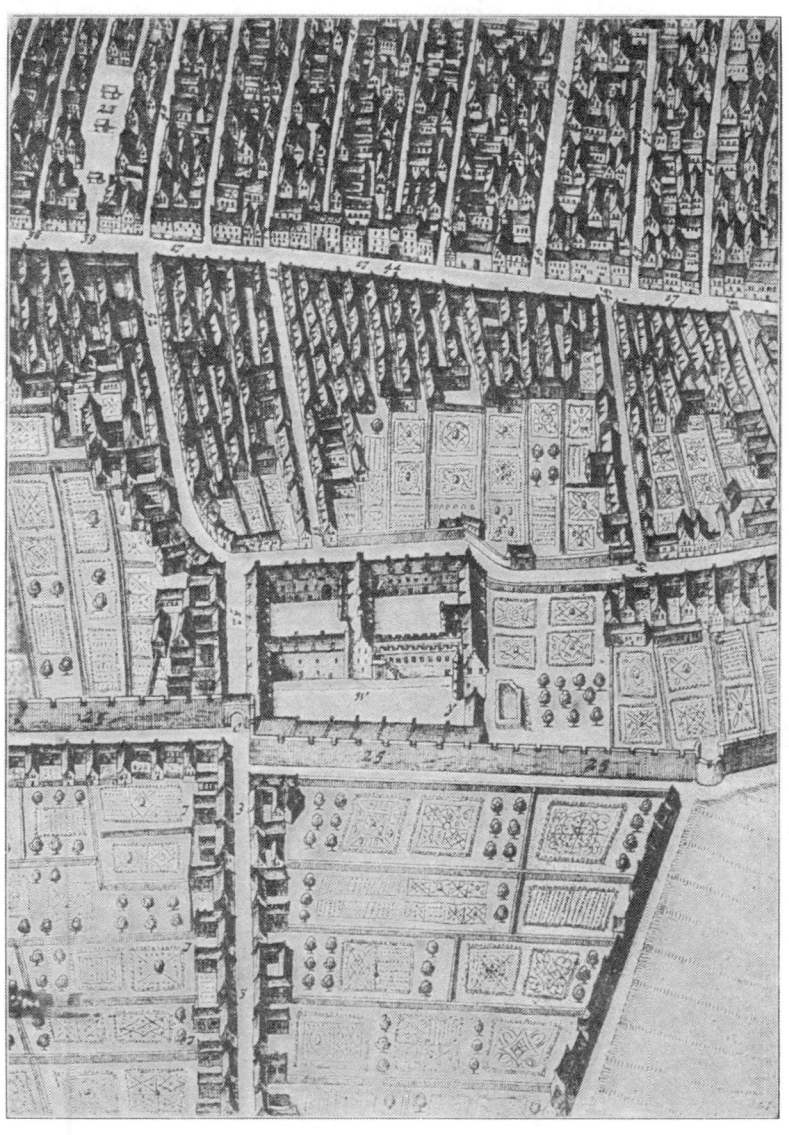

KIRK O'FIELD SITE IN 1646

25 is the Town Wall.   *W* indicates the University, including Hamilton House

lodging, to be built up of lime and stone, conform to
the height and thickness of the *new wall* elsewhere
[ellis] builded, and to pass lineally with the same to
the wall of the church yard of the said church, and
to leave no door nor entry in the said new wall.'[1]

All these facts prove that the old wall which
enclosed Kirk o' Field and the Black Friars on the
south had fallen into disrepair, and that new walls
had for some time before the murder been in course
of building. Now, in the map of 1647, we find a
very neat and regular wall, to the south of the site
that had been occupied by Kirk o' Field. Whereas,
in Darnley's time, there had been a gate called Kirk
o' Field Port to the right, or east, of the Kirk o' Field,
by 1647 there was no such gate, but, instead, Potter
Row Port, to the left, or west, of the University
buildings; by 1647 these included Hamilton House,
and the ground covered by Kirk o' Field. This wall,
extant in 1647, I take to be 'the new wall,' passing
lineally ' to the wall of the church yard ' of Kirk o'
Field. It supplied the place of the old ruinous wall
that is so often referred to as enclosing Kirk o' Field
on the south.

Thus Kirk o' Field, in February, 1567, had, to
the south of it, an old decayed town wall, much
fallen down, and was thus *within* that town wall.
But 'it is traditionally said,' writes the editor of
Keith, Mr. Parker Lawson, in 1845, ' that the house
of the Provost of Kirk o' Field ' (in which house, or

[1] Burgh Records.

the one next to it, Darnley was blown up) ' stood as
near as possible *without* the then city walls.' [1] Scott
follows this opinion in ' The Abbot.' Yet certainly
Kirk o' Field was not without, but within, the
ruinous town wall mentioned in the Burgh Records
of May 7. How are we to understand this discrepancy ?

On looking at the accompanying chart, drawn
from an original coloured design sent to the English
Government in February, 1567, we find the scene represented thus. We are facing Kirk o' Field, and are
looking from south to north. At our right hand, or
eastward, is the gate or port in the town wall, called
' the Kirk o' Field Port.' If we pass through it,
if the chart be right we are in Potter Row. Just
from the Port of Kirk o' Field, the town wall runs
due north, for a few yards : then runs due west,
enclosing the church yard of Kirk o' Field, on the
north, and the church itself, shown in ruins, the
church, as usual, running from east to west.
After running east to west for some fifty yards, the
town wall, battlemented and loopholed, turns at a
right angle, and runs due south to north, being thus
continued till it reaches the northern limit of the
plan. Now this wall, here running due south to
north, is not the ' wall of the town decayed and
fallen down on the south side of the Provost of Kirk
o' Field's lodgings,' as described in the Burgh
Records of May 7, 1567. This wall, on the other

[1] Keith, ii. 151, 152. Editor's note.

hand, leaves the collegiate quadrangle of Kirk o'
Field outside it, on the *west*, and the ruined gable of
Darnley's house, a gable running from west to east,
abuts on this wall, having a door through the wall
into the Thieves' Row. It is true that one of
Darnley's servants, Nelson, who escaped from the
explosion, declared that the gallery of Darnley's
house, and the gable which had a window ' through
the town wall,' ran *south*.

But, by the contemporary chart, the only part of
Darnley's house which was in contact with the town
wall ran west to east, and impinged on the town wall,
which here ran south to north. Again, in the map
of 1647, the wall of that date no longer runs south
to north, but is continued ' lineally ' from that short
part of the town wall, in the chart of 1567, which
did run east to west, forming there the northern
wall of the church yard of Kirk o' Field. This
continuation was ordered to be made by the Town
Council on May 7, 1567, three months after
Darnley's murder. Further, in 1646, Professor
Crawford wrote that the lodgings of the Provost
of Kirk o' Field, in 1567, ' had a garden on the
south, betwixt it and the *present* town wall.' [1]

Now the ruins of Darnley's house, in the map of
1647, have a space of garden between them and ' the
present town wall,' the wall of 1647. But, in 1567,
the gable of Darnley's house actually impinged on,

[1] *Registrum de Soltre*, p. xli.

K

and had a window and a door through the town wall
on, the *east* according to the chart.

The chart, then, shows the whole position thus.
On our right, the east, is the ruined Kirk o' Field
church, the church yard being bordered, on the north,
by the town wall, here running, for a short way, east
and west. After the town wall turns at a right angle
and runs south to north, it is continued east and
west by a short prolongation of some ten yards,
having a gate in it. Next, running east to west, are
two tall houses, forming the south side of a quadrangle. These Crawford (1646) seems to have
regarded as the Provost's lodgings. The west side of
the quadrangle consists of four small houses, as does
the north side. The east side of the quadrangle was
Darnley's house. It was in the shape of an inverted
L, thus ⌐. The long limb faced the quadrangle, the
short limb touched the town wall, and had a door
through it, into the Thieves' Row. Beyond the
Thieves' Row were gardens, in one of which Darnley's
body and that of his servant, Taylor, were found after
the explosion. Mary's room in the short limb of the
⌐ had a garden door, opening into Darnley's garden. Behind Darnley's garden were the grounds
of the Black Friars monastery. On the night of
the murder Bothwell conveyed the gunpowder into
the Black Friars grounds, entering by the gate or
through the broken Black Friars wall to the north-
west of the quadrangle, and thence into Darnley's
garden, and so, by Mary's garden door, into Mary's

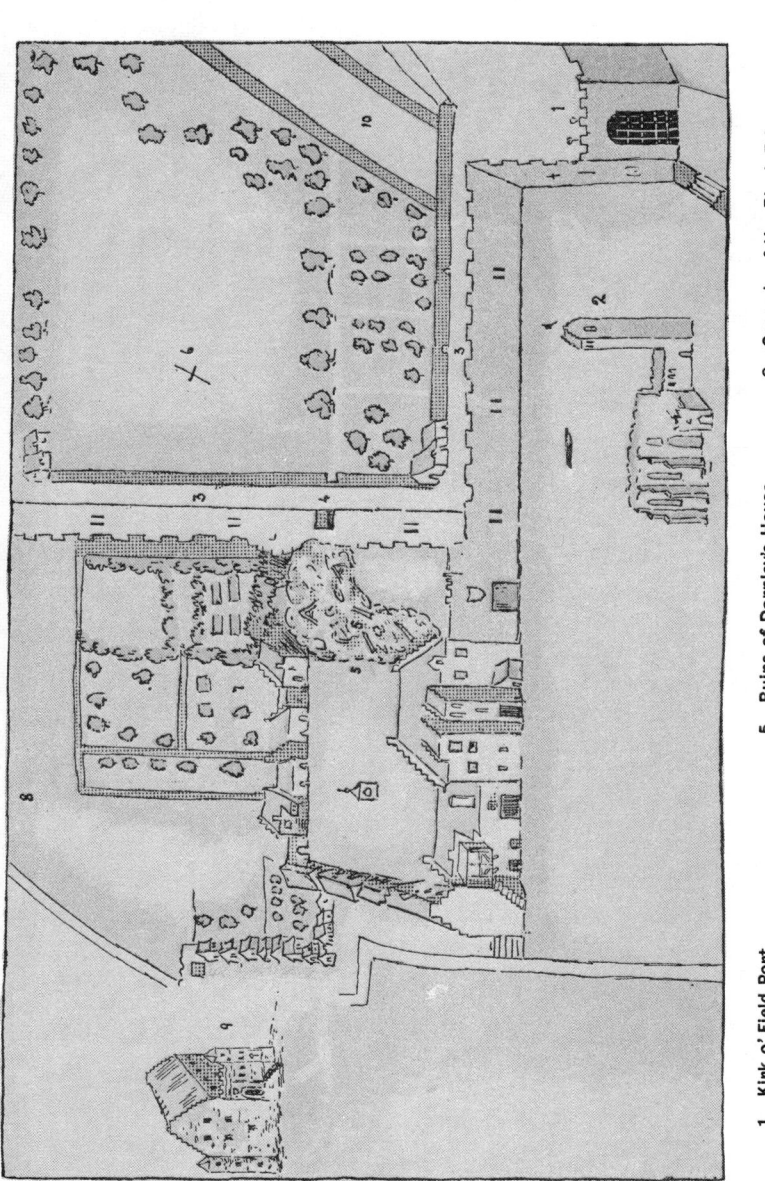

1. Kirk o' Field Port
2. Church of St. Mary-in-the-Fields
3. Thieves' Row
4. Door from Darnley's House into
   Thieves' Row
5. Ruins of Darnley's House
6. Darnley's Body
7. Darnley's Garden
8. Grounds of the Black Friars
9. Hamilton House
10. Potter Row
11. Town Wall

chamber: as the depositions of the accomplices declare.

The whole quadrangle lay amidst wide waste spaces of gardens and trees, with scattered cottages, and with Hamilton House hard by, to the west. Such was the situation of Kirk o' Field, Church and College quadrangle, as shown by the contemporary plan. The difficulties are caused by the wall, in the chart, running south to north, having Darnley's house abutting on it at right angles. The old ruined wall, on the other hand, was to the south of the quadrangle, as was the wall of 1647. When or why the wall running from south to north was built, I do not know, possibly after 1559, out of the stones of the Black Friars.[1] The new work was done under James Lindsay, treasurer in 1559, and Luke Wilson, treasurer in 1560. Perhaps the wall running south to north was the work of these two treasurers. At all events, there the wall was, or there it is in the contemporary design, to the confusion of antiquaries, bewildered between the old ruined wall to the south of Kirk o' Field, and the new wall seen in the map of 1647, a wall which was also to the south of Kirk o' Field, while, in the map of 1647, there is no trace of the south to north wall of the chart of 1567.

Having located Darnley's house, as forming the east side of a small college quadrangle among

<hr>

[1] Burgh Records, Feb. 19, March 12, 1560.

gardens and trees, we now examine the interior of
his far from palatial lodgings.

The two-storied house (the arched vaults on
which it probably stood not counting as a story?)
was just large enough for the invalid, his servants,
and his royal nurse. There was a 'hall,' probably
long and not wide, there was a lower chamber, used
by Mary, which could be entered either from the
garden, or from the passage, opened into by the
front door, from the quadrangle. Mary's room had
two keys, and one must have locked the door from
the passage; the other, the door into the garden.
If the former was kept locked, so that no one could
enter the room by the usual way, the powder could
be introduced, without exciting much attention, by
the door opening on the garden. In the chamber
above Mary's, where Darnley lay, there were also a
cabinet and a garderobe. There was a cellar, probably the kind of vaulted crypt on which houses of
the period were built, like Queen Mary's House in
St. Andrews. From the 'cellar' the door, which
we have mentioned, led through the town wall into
the Thieves' Row. Whoever has seen Queen Mary's
House at Jedburgh (much larger than Kirk o'
Field), or the Queen's room at St. Andrews, knows
that royal persons, in Scotland, were then content
with very small apartments. A servant named
Taylor used to share Darnley's sleeping-room, as
was usual; three others, including Nelson, slept in a
'little gallery,' which apparently ran at right angles

from Darnley's chamber to the town wall. He had neither his own guard, nor a guard of Lennox men, as at Stirling.

If the rooms were small, the tapestries and velvet were magnificent, and in odd contrast with Mary's alleged economic plan of taking a door from the hinges and using it as a bath-cover. This last anecdote, by Nelson, appears to be contradicted by Hay of Tala. 'Paris locked the door that passes up the turnpike to the King's chamber.'[1] The keys appear to have wandered into a bewildering variety of hands: a superfluous jugglery, if Bothwell, as was said, had duplicate keys.

Mary often visited Darnley, and the Lennox documents give us copious, if untrustworthy, information as to his manner of life. They do not tell us, as Buchanan does, that Mary and the vast unwieldy Lady Reres used to play music and sing in the garden of Kirk o' Field, in the balmy nights of a Scotch February! But they do contain a copy of a letter, referred to by Buchanan, which Darnley wrote to Lennox three days before his death.

'My Lord,—I have thought good to write to you by this bearer of my good health, I thank God, which is the sooner come through the good treatment of such as hath this good while concealed their good will; I mean of my love the Queen, which I assure you hath all this while, and yet doth, use

---

[1] Laing, ii. 254.

herself like a natural and loving wife. I hope yet
that God will lighten our hearts with joy that have
so long been afflicted with trouble. As I in this
letter do write unto your Lordship, so I trust this
bearer can satisfy you the like. Thus thanking
almighty God of our good hap, I commend your
Lordship into his protection.

'From Edinburgh the vii of February,
'Your loving and obedient son,
'HENRY REX.'

The Queen, we are told, came in while Darnley
was writing, read the letter, and 'kissed him as
Judas did the Lord his Master.'

'The day before his death she caused the rich
bed to be taken down, and a meaner set up in its
place, saying unto him that that rich bed they should
both lie in the next night, but her meanings were to
save the bed from the blowing up of the fire of
powder.'[1] There has been a good deal of controversy
about this odd piece of economy, reported also by
Thomas Nelson, Darnley's surviving servant. Where
was the bed to be placed for the marriage couch?
Obviously not in Holyrood, and Mary's own bed in
the room below Darnley's is reported by Buchanan
to have been removed.[2] The lost bed which was
blown up was of velvet, 'violet brown,' with gold,
had belonged to Mary of Guise, and had been given
to Darnley, by Mary, in September.

[1] Lennox MSS.   [2] See Hay Fleming, p. 434.

Mary's enemies insist that, apparently on the night of Friday, February 7, she wrote one of the Casket Letters to Bothwell. The Letter is obscure, as we shall see, but is interpreted to mean that her brother, Lord Robert Stuart, had warned Darnley of his danger, that Darnley had confided this to Mary, that Mary now asked Bothwell to bring Lord Robert to Kirk o' Field, where she would confront him with Darnley. The pair might come to blows, Darnley might fall, and the gunpowder plot would be super-fluous. This tale, about which the evidence is inconsistent, is discussed elsewhere. But, in his MSS., Lennox tells the story, and adds, 'The Lord Regent' (Moray) 'can declare it, who was there present.' Buchanan avers that Mary called in Moray to sever the pair, in hopes that he would be slain or compromised: not a plausible theory, and not put forward in the 'Book of Articles.'

Mary twice slept in the room under Darnley's, probably on the 5th and 7th of February. In the Lennox MSS. the description of Darnley's last night varies from the ordinary versions. 'The present night of his death she tarried with him till eleven of the clock, which night she gave him a goodly ring,' the usual token of loyalty. This ring is mentioned in a contemporary English ballad, and by Moray to de Silva (August 3, 1567), also in the 'Book of Articles.' Mary is usually said to have urged, as a reason for not sleeping at Kirk o' Field on the fatal night, her sudden recollection of a

promise to be present at Holyrood, at the marriage
of her servant, Sebastian. This, indeed, is her own
story, or Lethington's, in a letter written in Scots to
her ambassador in France, on February 10, or 11,
1567. But, in the Lennox MSS., it is asserted that
Bothwell and others reminded her of her intention to
ride to Seton, early next morning. Darnley then
'commanded that his great horses should have been
in a readiness by 5 o'clock in the morning, for that
he minded to ride them at the same hour.' After Mary
had gone, he remembered, says Lennox, a word she
had dropped to the effect that nearly a year had passed
since the murder of Riccio, a theme on which she had
long been silent. She was keeping her promise, given
over Riccio's newly dug grave, that 'a fatter than
he should lie anear him' ere the twelvemonth was out.
His servant comforted him, and here the narrator
regrets that Darnley did not 'consider and mark such
cruel and strange words as she had said unto him,' for
example, at Riccio's grave. He also gives a *précis* of
'her letter written to Bothwell from Glasgow before
her departure thence.' This is the mysterious letter
which was never produced or published: it will be
considered under 'External Evidence as to the Casket
Letters.'

After singing, with his servants, Psalm V., Darnley
drank to them, and went to bed. Fifty men, says the
Lennox author, now environed the house, sixteen,
under Bothwell, 'came the secret way by which she
herself was wont to come to the King her husband'

(a mere fairy tale), used the duplicate keys, 'opened the doors of the garden and house,' and so entered his chamber, and suffocated him 'with a wet napkin stipt in vinegar.' They handled Taylor, a servant, in the same way, and laid Darnley in a garden at some distance with 'his night gown of purple velvet furred with sables.' None of the captured murderers, in their confessions, knew anything of the strangling, which was universally believed in, but cannot easily be reconciled with the narratives of the assassins. But had they confessed to the strangling, others besides Bothwell would have been implicated, and the confessions are not worthy of entire confidence.[1]

The following curious anecdote is given by the Lennox MSS. After Mary's visit to Bothwell at Hermitage (October, 1566) her servants were wondering at her energy. She replied : 'Troth it was she was a woman, but yet was she more than a woman, in that she could find in her heart to see and behold that which any man durst do, and also could find in her heart to do anything that a man durst do, if her strength would serve her thereto. Which appeared to be true, for that some say she was present at the murder of the King, her husband, in man's apparel, which apparel she loved oftentimes to be in, in dancing secretly with the King her husband, and going in

---

[1] Lennox's sources must have been Nelson and the younger Standen, to whom Bothwell gave a horse immediately after the murder. Standen returned to England four months later.

masks by night through the streets.' These are
examples of the sayings and reports of her servants,
which, on June 11, 1568, Lennox urged his friends to
collect. This romantic tale proved too great for the
belief of Buchanan, if he knew it. But Lethington
told Throckmorton in July, 1568, that the Lords had
proof against Mary not only in her handwriting, but
by ' sufficient witnesses.' Doubtless they saw her on
the scene in male costume! Naturally they were
never produced.

If an historical event could be discredited, like a
ghost story, by discrepancies in the evidence, we
might maintain that Darnley never was murdered at
all. The chief varieties of statement are concerned
(1) with the nature of his death. Was he (a) taken
out of the house and strangled, or (b) strangled in
trying to escape from the house, or (c) strangled in
the house, and carried outside, or (d) destroyed by the
explosion and the fall? Next (2), accepting any of
the statements which represent Darnley as being
strangled (and they are, so far, unanimous at the time
of the event), who were the stranglers? Were they
(a) some of Bothwell's men, (b) men of Balfour's or
Huntly's, or (c) servants of Archbishop Hamilton, as
the Lennox faction aver, or (d) Douglases under
Archibald Douglas? Finally (3) was Kirk o' Field (a)
undermined by the murderers, in readiness for the
deed, before Darnley's arrival from Glasgow, or (b)
was the powder placed in the Queen's bedroom, under
Darnley's, on the night of the crime; or (c) was it then

placed in the vaults under the room on the first floor
which was occupied by the Queen?

The reader will find that each of these theories
was in turn adopted by the accusers, and that selections were made, later, by the accusers of Morton,
and Archibald Douglas, and Archbishop Hamilton,
just as happened to suit the purpose of the several
prosecutors at the moment.   Moreover it is not certain that the miscreants who blew up the house
themselves knew the whole details of the crime.

Our plan must be, first, to compare the contemporary descriptions of the incident.   Taking, first, the
'Diurnal of Occurrents,' we find that the explosion
took place at 10 A.M., 'two hours before noon;'
which is absurd if correctly read from the MS.   The
murderers opened the door with false keys, and
strangled Darnley, and his servant, Taylor, 'in their
naked beds,' then threw the bodies into a garden,
'beyond the Thief Row' (see the sketch, p. 131), returned, and blew up the house, 'so that there remained
not one stone upon another undestroyed.'   The names
of the miscreants are given, 'as alleged,' Bothwell,
Ormistoun of that ilk; Hob Ormistoun his uncle;
Hepburn of Bowton, and young Hay of Tala.   All
these underlings were later taken, confessed, and were
executed.   The part of the entry in the 'Diurnal'
which deals with them, at least, is probably not contemporary.   The men named professed to know
nothing of the strangling.   For what it is worth the
entry corroborates the entire destruction of the house,

which would imply a mine, or powder in the vaulted cellars. The contemporary drawing shows the whole house utterly levelled with the ground.[1]

Birrel, in his Diary, says, 'The house was raised from the ground with powder, and the King, if he had not been cruelly strangled, after he fell out of the air, with his garters, he had lived.' An official account says, ' Of the whole lodging, walls and other, there is nothing remaining, no, not one stone above another, but all either carried far away, or dung in dross to the very groundstone.'[2]   This could only be done by a mine, but the escape of Nelson proves exaggeration. This version is also in Mary's letter to Archbishop Beaton (February 10, or 11), written in Scots, probably by Lethington, and he, of course, may have exaggerated, as may the Privy Council in their report to the same effect.[3]   Clernault, a Frenchman who carried the news, averred that a mine was employed. Sir James Melville says that Bothwell ' made a train of powder, or had one made before, which came under the house,' but Darnley was first strangled ' in a low stable,' by a napkin thrust into his mouth.[4]   The Lennox MSS. say that Darnley was suffocated ' with a wet napkin steeped in vinegar.' The Savoyard Ambassador, Moretta, on returning to France, expressed the opinion that Darnley fled from the house, when he heard the key of the murderers

---

[1] *Diurnal*, 105, 106.
[2] Keith, i. cii.   [3] Register Privy Council, i. 498.
[4] Melville, p. 174, Bannatyne Club.

grate in the keyhole, that he was in his shirt, carrying his dressing gown, that he was followed, dragged into a little garden outside his own garden wall (the garden across the Thieves' Row), and there strangled. Some women heard him exclaim, ' Pity me, kinsmen, for the love of him who pitied all the world.'[1] His kinsmen were Archibald and other Douglases. Buchanan, in his ' Detection,' speaks of ' the King's lodging, *even from the very foundation*, blown up.' In the ' Actio,' or Oration, printed with the ' Detection,' the writer, whoever he was, says, ' they had *undermined the wall*,' and that Mary slept under Darnley's room, lest the servants should hear ' the noise of the underminers working.'

The ' Detection' and ' Actio' were published to discredit Mary, long after the murderers had confessed that there was no mine at all, that the powder was laid in Mary's room. In the ' Book of Articles,' the powder is placed ' in the laich house,' whether that means the arched ground floor, or Mary's chamber ; apparently the latter, as we read, ' she lay in the house under the King, where also thereafter the powder was placed.'[2] This is made into conformity with the confessions of Bothwell's men, according to whom but nine or ten were concerned in the deed. But Moray himself, two months after the murder, told de Silva that ' it is undoubted that over thirty or forty persons were concerned ' (the fifty of the Lennox Paper) ' and *the house . . . was entirely*

[1] Labanoff, vii. 108, 109, Paris, March 16, 1567.
[2] Hosack, i. 536, 537.

undermined.'[1]   When Morton, long afterwards, was accused of and executed for the deed, the dittay ran that the powder was under the 'angular stones and within the vaults.' In the mysterious letter, attributed to Mary, and cited by Moray and the Lennox Papers, the 'preparation' of the Kirk o' Field is at least hinted at. The 'Book of Articles' avers that, 'from Glasgow, by her letters and otherwise,' Mary 'held him' (Bothwell) 'continually in remembrance of the said house,' which she *did*, in the letter never produced, but not in any of the Casket Letters, unless it be in a note, among other suspicious notes, 'Of the ludgeing in Edinburgh.'[2]   The Lennox MSS., as we saw, say 'the place was already prepared with " undermining and " trains of powder therein.' The whole of the narratives, confirmed by Moray, and by the descriptions of the ruin of the house, prove that the theory of a prepared mine was entertained, till Powrie, Tala, and Bowton made their depositions, and, in the 'Actio,' an appendix to Buchanan's 'Detection,' and the indictment of Morton, even after that. But when the accusers, of whom some were guilty themselves, came to plead against Mary, they naturally wished to restrict the conspiracy to Bothwell and Mary. The strangling disappears. The murderers are no longer thirty, or forty, or fifty. The powder

---

[1] Spanish Calendar, i. 635, April 23.

[2] Hosack, i. 534. The 'Book of Articles,' of 1568, was obviously written under the impression left by a forged letter of Mary's, or by the reports of such a letter, as we shall show later. Yet the author cites a Casket Letter as we possess it.

is placed in Mary's own room, not in a mine. All this altered theory rests on examinations of prisoners.

What are they worth? They were taken in the following order : Powrie, June 23, Dalgleish, June 26, before the Privy Council. Powrie was again examined on July 6 before the Privy Council, and Hay of Tala on September 13. A note of news says that Tala was taken in Fife on September 6, 1567 (annotated ' 7th (Nicolas and Bond).' [1] Tala ' can *bleke* [blacken] some great men with it '—the murder. But as Mr. Hosack cites Bedford to Cecil, September 5, 1567, Hay of Tala ' opened the whole device of the murder, . . . and went so far as to touch a great many not of the smallest,' such as Huntly, Argyll, Lethington, and others, no doubt.[2] Even Laing, however, admits that ' the evidence against Huntly was suppressed carefully in Hay's deposition.' [3] In January, 1568, anonymous writings say that, if the Lords keep Tala and Bowton alive, they could tell them who subscribed the murder bond, and pray the Lords not to seem to lay all the weight on Mary's back. A paper of Questions to the Lords of the Articles asks why Tala and Bowton ' are not compelled openly to declare the manner of the King's slaughter, and who consented thereunto.' [4]

The authors of these Questions had absolute

---

[1] Bain, ii. 393.

[2] This is not, I think, a letter of September 5, but of September 16, but in Foreign Calendar Elizabeth, viii. p. 342, most of the passage quoted by Mr. Hosack is omitted.

[3] Laing, ii. 23. [4] Cal. For. Eliz. viii. p. 392.

right on their side. Moray no more prosecuted the
quest for all murderers of Darnley than Mary had
done. To prove this we need no anonymous pamphlets or placards, no contradictory tattle about
secret examinations and dying confessions. When
Mary's case was inquired into at Westminster
(December, 1568), Moray put in as evidence the
deposition of Bowton, made in December, 1567.
Bothwell, said Bowton, had assured him that the
crime was devised ' by some of the noblemen,' ' other
noblemen had entrance as far as he in that matter.' [1]
This was declared by Bowton in Moray's own
presence. The noble and stainless Moray is not said
to ask ' What noblemen do you mean ? '   No
torture would have been needed to extract their
names from Bowton, and Moray should at once have
arrested the sinners.   But some were his own allies,
united with him in accusing his sister. So no questions were asked. The papers which, at the end of
1567, did ask disagreeable questions must have been
prior to January 3, 1568, when Tala, Bowton, Dalgleish, and Powrie, after being ' put to the knowledge
of an assize,' were executed ; their legs and arms
were carried about the country by boys in baskets !
According to the ' Diurnal,' Tala incriminated, before
the whole people round the scaffold, Bothwell, Huntly,
Argyll, Lethington, and Balfour, with divers other
nobles, and the Queen. On January 7, Drury gave
the same news to Cecil, making Bowton the confessor,

Laing, ii. 256

and omitting the charge against Mary. The incriminated noblemen at once left Edinburgh, 'which,'
says the 'Diurnal,' 'makes the matter . . . the more
probable.'[1] Meanwhile Moray 'looked through his
fingers,' and carried the incriminated Lethington
with him, later, as one of Mary's accusers, while he
enriched Sir James Balfour!

What, we ask once more, in these circumstances,
are the examinations of the murderers worth, after
passing through the hands of the accomplices? On
December 8, 1568, Moray gave in the written records
of the examinations to the English Commissioners.
We have, first, Bothwell's servant, Powrie, examined
before the Lords of the Secret Council (June 23,
July 3, 1567). He helped to carry the powder to
Kirk o' Field on February 9, but did not see what
was done with it. Dalgleish, examined at Edinburgh
on June 26, 1567, before Morton, Atholl, the Provost
of Dundee, and Kirkcaldy, said nothing about the
powder. Tala was examined, on September 13, at
Edinburgh, before Moray, Morton, Atholl, the Lairds
of Loch Leven and Pitarro, James Makgill, and the
Justice Clerk, Bellenden. No man implicated, except Morton, was present. Tala said that Bothwell
arranged to lay the powder in Mary's room, under
Darnley's. This was done; the powder was placed
in 'the nether house, under the King's chamber,' the
plotters entering by the back door, from the garden,
of which Paris had the key. Thus there would be no

---

[1] *Diurnal*, 127, 128. Cal. For. Eliz. viii. 393.

show at the front door, in the quadrangle, of men coming and going : they were in Mary's room, but did not enter by the front door. Next, on December 8, Bowton was examined at Edinburgh before Moray, Atholl, Lindsay, Kirkcaldy of Grange, and Bellenden. He implicated Morton, Lethington, and Balfour, but, at Westminster, Moray suppressed the evidence utterly. (See Introduction, pp. xiii–xviii, for the suppressions). Next we have the trial of Bowton, Tala, Powrie, and Dalgleish, on January 3, 1568, before Sir Thomas Craig and a jury of burgesses and gentlemen. The accused confessed to their previous depositions. The jury found them guilty on the depositions alone, found that ' the whole lodging was raised and blown in the air, and his Grace [Darnley] was murdered treasonably, and most cruelly slain and destroyed by them therein.' When Mr. Hosack asserts that these depositions ' were taken before the Lords of the Secret Council, namely Morton, Huntly, Argyll, Maitland, and Balfour,' he errs, according to the documents cited. Only Powrie is described as having been examined ' before the Lords of the Secret Council.' Mr. Hosack must have known that Huntly and Argyll were not in Edinburgh on June 23, when Powrie was examined.[1] We can only say that Powrie's depositions, made before Lords of the Secret Council unnamed, struck the keynote, to which all later confessions, including that of Both-

[1] Hosack, ii. 245.

well's valet, Paris, correspond.[1]   Thus vanish, for the
moment, the mine and the strangling, while the deed
is done by powder in Mary's own chamber.   Nobody
is now left in the actual crime save Bothwell, Bowton,
Tala, Powrie, Dalgleish, Wilson, Paris, Ormistoun,
and Hob Ormistoun.   They knew of no strangling.[2]

But on February 11, 1567, two women, examined
by a number of persons, including Huntly, stated
thus : Barbara Mertine *heard* thirteen men, and *saw*
eleven, pass up the Cowgate, and *saw* eleven pass
down the Black Friars wynd, after the explosion.
She called them traitors.   May Crokat (by marriage
Mrs. Stirling), in the service of the Archbishop of St.
Andrews (whose house was adjacent to Kirk o' Field),
heard the explosion, thought it was in ' the house
above,' ran out, saw eleven men, caught one by his
silk coat, and ' asked where the crack was.'   They
fled.[3]   The avenging ghost of Darnley pursued his
murderers for twenty years, and, in their cases, we
have later depositions, and letters.   Thus, as to the
men employed, Archibald Douglas, that reverend
parson and learned Lord of Session, informed Morton
that he himself ' was at the deed doing, and came to
the Kirk o' Field yard with the Earls of Bothwell *and*

---

[1] This was obvious to Laing.   Replying to Goodall's criticism of
verbal coincidences in the confessions, Laing says, ' as if in any subse-
quent evidence concerning the same fact, the same words were not
often dictated by the same Commissioner, or recorded by the Clerk,
from the first deposition which they hold in their hands.'   It does not
seem quite a scientific way of taking evidence.

[2] See the Confessions, Laing, ii. 264.

[3] Bain, ii. 312, 313.

Huntly.'   Douglas, at this time (June, 1581), had
fled from justice to England : Morton was underlying
the law.   Morton's confession was made, in 1581, on
the day of his execution, to the Rev. John Durie and
the Rev. Walter Balcanquell, who wrote down and
made known the declaration.   On June 3, 1581,
Archibald Douglas's servant, Binning, was also
executed.   He confessed that Archibald lost one of
his velvet mules (dress shoes) on the scene, or on
the way from the murder.   Powrie had ' deponed '
that three of Bothwell's company wore ' mulis,'
whether for quiet in walking, or because they were
in evening dress, having been at Bastian's wedding
masque and dance.   Douglas, in a collusive trial
before a jury of his kinsmen, in 1586, was acquitted,
and showed a great deal of forensic ability.[1]

It is thus abundantly evident that the depositions
of the murderers put in by Mary's accusers did not
tell the whole truth, whatever amount of truth they
may have told.   We cannot, therefore, perhaps
accept their story of placing the powder in Mary's
room, where it could hardly have caused the amount
of damage described : but that point may be left
open.   We know that Bothwell's men were not alone
in the affair, and the strangling of Darnley, and the
removal of his body, with his purple velvet sable-lined
dressing gown (attested by the Lennox MSS.), may
have been done by the men of Douglas and Huntly.

The treatment of the whole topic by George

---

[1] Arnott and Pitcairn, *Criminal Trials.*

Buchanan is remarkable. In the ' Book of Articles,'
levelled at Mary, in 1568, Darnley is blown up by
powder placed in Mary's room. In the ' Detection,'
of which the first draft (in the Lennox MSS.) is of
1568, reference for the method of the deed is made
to the depositions of Powrie and the others. In the
' History,' there are *three* gangs, those with Bothwell,
and two others, advancing by separate routes. They
strangle Darnley and Taylor, and carry their bodies
into an adjacent garden; the house is then blown up
' from the very foundations.' Buchanan thus returns
to the strangling, omitted, for reasons, in the ' Detection.' Darnley's body is unbruised, and his dressing-
gown, lying near him, is neither scorched nor smirched
with dust. A light burned, Buchanan says, in the
Hamilton House till the explosion, and was then
extinguished; the Archbishop, contrary to custom,
was lodging there, with ' Gloade,' says a Lennox
MS. ' Gloade ' is—Lord Claude Hamilton ![1] While
Buchanan was helping to prosecute Mary, he had
not a word to say about the strangling of Darnley,
and about the dressing-gown and slippers laid beside
the corpse, though all this was in the papers of
Lennox, his chief. Not a word had he to say about
the three bands of men who moved on Kirk o' Field,
or the fifty men of the Lennox MS. The crime was
to be limited to Bothwell, his gang, and the Queen,
as was convenient to the accusers. Later Buchanan
brought into his ' History ' what he kept out of the

[1] Buchanan, *History* (1582), fol. 215.

'Detection' and 'Book of Articles,' adding a slur on Archbishop Hamilton.

Finally, when telling, in his 'History,' how the Archbishop was caught at Dumbarton, and hanged by Lennox, without trial, Buchanan has quite a fresh version. The Archbishop sent six or eight of his bravoes, with false keys of the doors (what becomes of Bothwell's false keys?) to Kirk o' Field. They strangle Darnley, and lay him in a garden, and then, on a given signal, other conspirators blow up the house. Where is Bothwell? The leader of the Archbishop's gang told this, under seal of confession, to a priest, a very respectable man (*viro minime malo*). This respectable priest first blabbed in conversation, and then, when the Archbishop was arrested, gave evidence derived from the disclosure of a Hamilton under seal of confession. The Archbishop mildly remarked that such conduct was condemned by the Church. Later, the priest was executed for celebrating the Mass (this being his third conviction), and he repeated the story openly and fully. The tale of the priest was of rather old standing. When collecting his evidence for the York Commission of October, 1568, Lennox wrote to his retainers to ask, among other things, for the deposition of the priest of Paisley, ' that heard and testified the last exclamation of one Hamilton, which the Laird of Minto showed to Mr. John Wood,' who was then helping Lennox to get up his case (July 11, 1568).[1]

---

[1] *Maitland Miscellany*, iv. i. p. 119.

Buchanan has yet another version, in his ' Admonition to the Trew Lordis : ' here the Archbishop sends only four of his rogues to the murder.

Buchanan's plan clearly was to accuse the persons whom it was convenient to accuse, at any given time ; and to alter his account of the method of the murder so as to suit each new accusation. Probably he was not dishonest. The facts ' were to him ministered,' by the Lords, in 1568, and also by Lennox. Later, different sets of facts were 'ministered' to him, as occasion served, and he published them without heeding his inconsistencies. He was old, was a Lennox man, and an advanced Liberal.

Of one examination, which ought to have been important, we have found no record. There was a certain Captain James Cullen, who wrote letters in July 13 to July 18, 1560, from Edinburgh Castle, to the Cardinal of Lorraine. He was then an officer of Mary of Guise, during the siege of Leith.[1] In the end of 1565, and the beginning of 1566, Captain Cullen was in the service of Frederic II. of Denmark, and was trying to enlist English sailors for him.[2] Elizabeth refused to permit this, and Captain Cullen appears to have returned to his native Scotland, where he became, under Bothwell, an officer of the Guard put about Mary's person, after Riccio's murder. On February 28, 1567, eighteen days after Darnley's murder, Drury writes that 'Captain Cullen

[1] French Foreign Office, *Registre de Depesches d'Ecosse*, 1560–1562, fol. 112.

[2] Cal. For. Eliz. viii. p. 7, No. 31.

with his company have the credit nearest her ' (Mary's)
' person.' On May 13, Drury remarks, 'It was
Captain Cullen's persuasion, for more surety, to have
the King strangled, and not only to trust to the
powder,' the Captain having observed, in his military
experience, that the effects of explosions were not
always satisfactory.   ' The King was long of dying,
and to his strength made debate for his life.' [1]

To return to honest Captain Cullen : after Bothwell was acquitted, and had issued a cartel offering
Trial by Combat to any impugner of his honour, some
anonymous champion promised, under certain conditions, to fight.   This hero placarded the names of
three Balfours, black John Spens, and others, as
conspirators ; as ' doers ' he mentioned, with some
companions, Tala, Bowton, Pat Wilson, and James
Cullen.   On April 25, the Captain was named as a
murderer in Elizabeth's Instructions to Lord Grey.[2]
On May 8, Kirkcaldy told Bedford that Tullibardine
had offered, with five others, to fight Ormistoun,
' Beynston,' Bowton, Tala, Captain Cullen, and James
Edmonstone, who, says Tullibardine, were at the
murder.   On June 16, 1567, the day after Mary's
capture at Carberry, Drury writes, ' The Lords have

---

[1] Cal. For. Eliz. viii. 229.   Drury does not here add to our confidence by saying that ' Sir Andrew Ker ' (of Faldonside) ' with others
were on horseback near to the place for aid to the cruel enterprize if
need had been.'   Ker, a pitiless wretch, was conspicuous in the Riccio
murder, threatened Mary, and had but lately been pardoned.   After
Langside, he was kept prisoner, in accordance with Mary's orders, by
Whythaugh.   He is not likely to have been concerned in Darnley's
death.   [2] Bain, ii. 321, 325.

taken Captain Cullen, who, after some strict dealing [torture], has revealed the King's murder with the whole matter thereof.'[1] Drury was mistaken. He had probably heard of the capture of Blackader, who was hanged on June 24, denying his guilt. He had no more chance than had James Stewart of the Glens with a Campbell jury. His jury was composed of Lennox men, Darnley's clansmen. Our Captain had not been taken, but on September 15 Moray told Throckmorton that Kirkcaldy, in Shetland, had captured Cullen, ' one of the very executors, he may clear the whole action.'[2]

Did Captain Cullen clear the whole action? We hear no more of his embarrassing revelations. But we do know that he was released and returned to the crimping trade : he fought for the Castle in 1573, was taken in a cupboard and executed. He had a pretty wife, the poor Captain, coveted and secured by Morton.

[1] Cal. For. Eliz. viii. 252.
[2] Bain, ii. 394. Cullen is spelled ' Callan,' and is described as Bothwell's ' chalmer-chiel.'

VII

THE CONFESSIONS OF PARIS

FATAL depositions, if trustworthy, are those of the
valet lent by Bothwell to Mary, on her road to
Glasgow, in January, 1567. The case of Paris is
peculiar.   He had escaped with Bothwell, in autumn,
1567, to Denmark, and, on October 30, 1568, he was
extradited to a Captain Clark, a notorious character.
On July 16, 1567, the Captain had killed one Wilson,
a seaman 'much esteemed by the Lords,' of Moray's
faction.   They had quarrelled about a ship that was
ordered to pursue Bothwell.[1]   Nevertheless, in July,
1568, Clark was Captain of the Scots in Danish service,
and was corresponding with Moray.[2]   Clark could
easily have sent Paris to England in time for the
meetings of Commissioners to judge on Mary's case,
in December–January, 1568–1569.   But Paris was not
wanted : he might have proved an awkward witness.
About August 30, 1569, Elizabeth wrote to Moray
asking that Paris might be spared till his evidence
could be taken.   That, alas ! was now impossible :

[1] Bain, ii. 355.
[2] Cal. For. Eliz. viii. 500.   Hosack, i. 350, note 2, and Schiern's
Bothwell.

Paris was no more. He had arrived from Denmark in June, 1569, when Moray was in the North. Why had he not arrived in December, 1568, when Mary's case was being heard at Westminster? He had been examined on August 9, 10, 1569, and was executed on August 16 at St. Andrews. A copy of his deposition was sent to Cecil, and Moray hoped it would be satisfactory to Elizabeth and to Lennox.[1]

In plain truth, the deposition of Paris was not wanted, when it might have been given, at the end of 1568, while Moray and Lethington and Morton were all working against Mary, before the same Commission. Later, differences among themselves had grown marked. Moray and Lethington had taken opposed lines as to Mary's marriage with Norfolk in 1569, and the terms of an honourable settlement of her affairs. Lethington desired; Moray, in his own interest as Regent, opposed the marriage. A charge of guilt in Darnley's murder was now hanging over Lethington, based on Paris's deposition. The cloud broke in storm, he was accused by the useful Crawford, Lennox's man, in the first week of September, 1569. Three weeks earlier, Moray had conveniently strengthened himself by taking the so long deferred evidence of Paris. Throughout the whole affair the witnesses were very well managed, so as to produce just what was needed, and no more. While Lethington and other sinners were working with Moray, then only evidence to the guilt of Bothwell

[1] Laing, ii. 269.

and Mary was available. When Lethington became inconvenient, witness against him was produced. When Morton, much later (1581), was 'put at,' new evidence of *his* guilt was not lacking. Captain Cullen's tale did not fit into the political combinations of September, 1567, when the poor Captain was taken. It therefore was not adduced at Westminster or Hampton Court. It was judiciously burked.

Moray did not send the 'authentick' record of Paris's deposition to Cecil till October, 1569, though it was taken at St. Andrews on August 9 and 10.[1] When Moray at last sent it, he had found that Lethington definitely refused to aid him in betraying Norfolk. The day of reconciliation was ended. So Moray sent the 'authentick' deposition of Paris, which he had kept back for two months, in hopes that Lethington (whom it implicated) might join him in denouncing Norfolk after all.

Paris, we said, was examined (there is no record showing that he ever was tried) at St. Andrews. On the day of his death, Moray caused Sir William Stewart, Lyon King at Arms, by his own appointment, to be burned for sorcery. Of *his* trial no record exists. He had been accused of a conspiracy against Moray, whom he certainly did not admire, no proof had been found, and he was burned as a wizard, or consulter of wizards.[2] The deposition of Paris on August 10 is in the Record Office, and is signed at

---

[1] Bain, ii. 698.
[2] See Appendix B, 'The Burning of the Lyon King at Arms.'

the end of each page with his mark. *We are not told who heard the depositions made.* We are only told that when it was read to him before George Buchanan, John Wood (Moray's man), and Robert Ramsay, he acknowledged its truth : Ramsay being the writer of ' this declaration,' that is of the deposition. He wrote French very well, and was a servant of Moray. There is another copy with a docquet asserting its authenticity, witnessed by Alexander Hay, Clerk of the Privy Council, who, according to Nau, wrote the old band against Darnley (October, 1566), and who was a correspondent of Knox.[1] Hay does not seem to mean that the deposition of Paris was taken in his presence, but that II. is a correct copy of Number I. If so, he is not ' guilty of a double fraud,' as Mr. Hosack declares. Though he omits the names of the witnesses, Wood, Ramsay, and Buchanan, he does not represent himself as the sole witness to the declaration. He only attests the accuracy of the copy of Number I. Whether Ramsay, Wood, and Buchanan examined Paris, we can only infer : whether they alone did so, we know not : that he was hanged and quartered merely on the strength of his own deposition, we think highly probable. It was a great day for St. Andrews : a herald was burned, a Frenchman was hanged, and a fourth of his mortal remains was fixed on a spike in a public place.

Paris said, when examined in August, 1569, that

[1] Bain, ii. 667, 668.

on Wednesday or Thursday of the week of Darnley's death, Bothwell told him in Mary's room at Kirk o' Field, Mary being in Darnley's, that ' *we Lords* ' mean to blow up the King and this house with powder. But Bowton says, that till the Friday, Bothwell meant to kill Darnley ' in the fields.' [1] Bothwell took Paris aside for a particular purpose: he was suffering from dysentery, and said, ' Ne sçais-tu point quelque lieu là où je pouray aller . . . ? ' ' I never was here in my life before,' said Paris.

Now as Bothwell, by Paris's own account (derived from Bothwell himself), had passed an entire night in examining the little house of Kirk o' Field, how could he fail to know his way about in so tiny a dwelling? Finally, Paris found *ung coing ou trou entre deux portes*, whither he conducted Bothwell, who revealed his whole design.

Robertson, cited by Laing, remarks that the narrative of Paris ' abounds with a number of minute facts and particularities which the most dexterous forger could not have easily assembled and connected together with any appearance of probability.' The most bungling witness who ever perjured himself could not have brought more impossible inconsistencies than Paris brings into a few sentences, and he was just as rich in new details, when, in a second confession, he contradicted his first. In the insanitary, and, as far as listeners were concerned, insecure retreat ' between two doors,' Bothwell bluntly told

[1] Laing, ii. 256, 257.

Paris that Darnley was to be blown up, because, if
ever he got his feet on the Lords' necks, he would be
tyrannical. The motive was political. Paris pointed
out the moral and social inconveniences of Bothwell's
idea. 'You fool!' Bothwell answered, 'do you think
I am alone in this affair? I have Lethington, who is
reckoned one of our finest wits, and is the chief under-
taker in this business; I have Argyll, Huntly, Morton,
Ruthven, and Lindsay. These three last will never
fail me, for I spoke in favour of their pardon, and I
have the signatures of all those whom I have
mentioned, and we were inclined to do it lately when
we were at Craigmillar; but you are a dullard, not fit
to hear a matter of weight.' If Bothwell said that
Morton, Ruthven, and Lindsay signed the band, he, in
all probability, lied. But does any one believe that
the untrussed Bothwell, between two doors, held all
this talk with a wretched valet, arguing with him
seriously, counting his allies, real or not, and so
forth? Paris next (obviously enlightened by later
events) observed that the Lords would make Bothwell
manage the affair, 'but, when it is once done, they
may lay the whole weight of it on you' (which, when
making his deposition, he knew they had done), 'and
will be the first to cry *Haro!* on you, and pursue
you to death.' Prophetic Paris! He next asked,
What about a man dearly beloved by the populace,
and the French? 'No troubles in the country when *he*
governed for two or three years, all was well, money
was cheap; look at the difference now,' and so forth.

'Who is the man?' asked Bothwell. 'Monsieur de Moray; pray what side does he take?'

'He won't meddle.'

'Sir, he is wise.'

'Monsieur de Moray, Monsieur de Moray! He will neither help nor hinder, but it is all one.'

Bothwell, by a series of arguments, then tried to make Paris steal the key of Mary's room. He declined, and Bothwell left the appropriate scene of this prolonged political conversation. It occupies more than three closely printed pages of small type.

Paris then devotes a page and a half to an account of a walk, and of his reflections. On Friday, Bothwell met him, asked him for the key, and said that *Sunday* was the day for the explosion. Now, in fact, *Saturday* had been fixed upon, as Tala declared.[1] Paris took another walk, thought of looking for a ship to escape in, but compromised matters by saying his prayers. On Saturday, after dinner, Bothwell again asked for the key: adding that Balfour had already given him a complete set of false keys, and that they two had passed a whole night in examining the house. So Paris stole the key, though Bothwell had told him that he need not, if he had not the heart for it. After he gave it to Bothwell, Marguerite (Carwood?) sent him back for a coverlet of fur: Sandy Durham asked him for the key, and he referred Sandy to the *huissier*, Archibald Beaton. This Sandy is said in the Lennox MSS. to have been warned by Mary to leave the house.

[1] Laing, ii. 253.

He was later arrested, but does not seem to have been punished.

On Sunday morning, Paris heard that Moray had left Edinburgh, and said within himself, ' O Monsieur de Moray, you are indeed a worthy man!' The wretch wished, of course, to ingratiate himself with Moray, but his want of tact must have made that worthy man wince. Indeed Paris's tactless disclosures about Moray, who ' would neither help nor hinder,' and did sneak off, may be' one of the excellent reasons which prevented Cecil from adding Paris's deposition, when he was asked for it, to the English edition of Buchanan's 'Detection.'[1] When the Queen was at supper, on the night of the crime, with Argyll (it really was with the Bishop of Argyll) and was washing her hands after supper, Paris came in. She asked Paris whether he had brought the fur coverlet from Kirk o' Field. Bothwell then took Paris out, and they acted as in the depositions of Powrie and the rest, introducing the powder. Bothwell rebuked Tala and Bowton for making so much noise, which was heard above, as they stored the powder in Mary's room. Paris next accompanied Bothwell to Darnley's room, and Argyll, silently, gave him a caressing dig in the ribs. After some loose babble, Paris ends, ' And that is all I know about the matter.'

This deposition was made ' without constraint or interrogation.' But it was necessary that he should know more about the matter. Next day he was

[1] Murdin, i. 57.

M

interrogué, doubtless in the boot or the pilniewinks, or under threat of these. He *must* incriminate the Queen. He gave evidence now as to carrying a letter (probably Letter II. is intended) to Bothwell, from Mary at Glasgow, in January, 1567. His story may be true, as we shall see, if the dates put in by the accusers are incorrect : and if another set of dates, which we shall suggest, are correct.

Asked as to familiarities between Bothwell and Mary, he said, on Bothwell's information, that Lady Reres used to bring him, late at night, to Mary's room ; and that Bothwell bade him never let Mary know that Lady Bothwell was with him in Holyrood ! Paris now remembered that, in the long conversation in the hole between two doors, Bothwell had told him not to put Mary's bed beneath Darnley's, 'for that is where I mean to put the powder.' He disobeyed. Mary made him move her bed, and he saw that she was in the plot. Thereon he said to her, 'Madame, Monsieur de Boiduel told me to bring him the keys of your door, and that he has an inclination to do something, namely to blow the King into the air with powder, which he will place here.'

This piece of evidence has, by some, been received with scepticism, which is hardly surprising. Paris places the carrying of a letter (about the plot to make Lord Robert kill Darnley ?) on Thursday night. It ought to be Friday, if it is to agree with 'Cecil's Journal:' 'Fryday. She ludged and lay all

nycht agane in the foresaid chalmer, and frome
thence wrayt, that same nycht, the letter concerning
the purpose of the abbott of Halyrudhouse.' On
the same night, Bothwell told Paris to inform Mary
that he would not sleep till he achieved his purpose,
' were I to trail a pike all my life for love of her.'
This means that the murder was to be on Friday,
which is absurd, unless Bothwell means to wake for
several nights. Let us examine the stories told by
Paris about the key, or keys, of Mary's room. In
the first statement, Paris was asked by Bothwell at
the Conference between Two Doors, for the *key* of
Mary's room. This was on Wednesday or Thursday.
On Friday, Bothwell asked again for the *key*, and
said the murder was fixed for Sunday, which it was
not, but for Saturday. On Saturday, Bothwell again
demands *that key*, after dinner. He says that he has
duplicates, from James Balfour, of all the keys.
Paris takes the *key*, remaining last in Mary's room at
Kirk o' Field, as she leaves it to go to Holyrood.
Paris keeps the *key*, and returns to Kirk o' Field. Sandy
Durham, Darnley's servant, asks for the key. Paris
replies that keys are the affair of the Usher. ' Well,'
says Durham, ' since you don't want to give it to me ! '
So, clearly, Paris kept it. On Sunday night, Bothwell
bade Paris go to the Queen's room in Kirk o' Field, 'and
when Bowton, Tala, and Ormistoun shall have entered,
and done what they want to do, you are to leave the
room, and come to the King's room and thence go
where you like. . . . The rest can do without you '

M 2

(in answer to a remonstrance), 'for they have keys enough.' Paris then went into the kitchen of Kirk o' Field, and borrowed and lit a candle : meanwhile Bowton and Tala entered the Queen's room, and deposited the powder. Paris does not *say* that he let them in with the *key*, which he had kept all the time ; at least he never mentions making any use of it, though of course he did.

In the second statement, Paris avers that he took the *keys* (the number becomes plural, or dual) on Friday, not on Saturday, as in the first statement, and *not* after the Queen had left the room (as in the first statement), but while she was dressing. He carried them to Bothwell, who compared them with other, new, false keys, examined them, and said 'They are all right ! take back these others.' During the absence of Paris, the keys were missed by the Usher, Archibald Beaton, who wanted to let Mary out into the garden, and Mary questioned Paris *aloud*, on his return. This is not probable, as, by his own second statement, he had already told her, on Wednesday or Thursday, that Bothwell had asked him for the keys, as he wanted to blow Darnley sky high. She would, therefore, know why Paris had the keys of her room, and would ask no questions.[1] On Saturday, after dinner, Bothwell bade him take the *key* of Mary's room, and Mary also told him to do so. He took it. Thus, in statement II., he has his usual De Foe-like details, different from those equally

[1] Laing, ii. 286, 287.

minute in statement I. He takes the keys, or key, at a different time, goes back with them in different circumstances, is asked for them by different persons, and takes a key *twice*, once on Friday, once on Saturday, though Bothwell, having duplicates that were 'all right' (*elles sont bien*), did not need the originals. As to these duplicates, Bowton declared that, after the murder, he threw them all into a quarry hole between Holyrood and Leith.[1] Tala declared that Paris had a key of the back door.[2] Nelson says that Beaton, Mary's usher, kept the keys: he and Paris.[3]

Paris, of course under torture or fear of torture, said whatever might implicate Mary. On Friday night, in the second statement, Paris again carried letters to Bothwell; if he carried them both on Thursday and Friday, are both notes in the Casket Letters? The Letter of Friday was supposed to be that about the affair of Lord Robert and Darnley. On Saturday Mary told Paris to bid Bothwell send Lord Robert and William Blackadder to Darnley's chamber 'to do what Bothwell knows, and to speak to Lord Robert about it, for it is better thus than otherwise, and he will only have a few days' prison in the Castle for the same.' Bothwell replied to Paris that he would speak to Lord Robert, and visit the Queen. This was on Saturday *evening* (*au soyr*), after the scene, whatever it was or was not, between Darnley and Lord Robert on Saturday

---

[1] Laing, ii. 259.   [2] Laing, ii. 254.   [3] Laing, ii. 267, 268.

morning.[1] As to *that,* Mary 'told her people in her
chamber that Lord Robert had enjoyed a good
chance to kill the King, because there was only
herself to part them.'   Lennox in his MSS. avers
that Moray was present, and 'can declare it.'
Buchanan says that Mary called in Moray to separate
her wrangling husband and brother, hoping that
Moray too would be slain! Though the explosion
was for Sunday night, Mary, according to Paris, was
still urging the plan of murder by Lord Robert on
Saturday night, and Bothwell was acquiescing.

The absurd contradictions which pervade the
statements of Paris are conspicuous.   Hume says:
'It is in vain at present to seek improbabilities in
Nicholas Hubert's dying confession, and to magnify
the smallest difficulty into a contradiction.   It was
certainly a regular judicial paper, given in regularly
and judicially, and ought to have been canvassed at
the time, if the persons whom it concerned had been
assured of their own innocence.'   They never saw
it: it was authenticated by no judicial authority: it
was not 'given in regularly and judicially,' but was
first held back, and then sent by Moray, when it
suited his policy, out of revenge on Lethington.
Finally, it was not 'a dying confession.' Dying confessions are made in prison, or on the scaffold, on the
day of death.   That of Paris 'took God to record,
at the time of his death' (August 16), 'that this
murder was by your' (the Lords') 'counsel, invention,

[1] Laing, ii. 287.

and drift committed,' and also declared that he ' never knew the Queen to be participant or ware thereof.' So says Lesley, but we have slight faith in him.[1] He speaks in the same sentence of similar dying confessions by Tala, Powrie, and Dalgleish.

I omit the many discrepant accounts of dying confessions accusing or absolving the Queen. Buchanan says that Dalgleish, in the Tolbooth, confessed the Exchequer House *fabliau*, and that this is duly recorded, but it does not appear in his Dying Confession printed in the ' Detection.' In his, Bowton says that ' the Queen's mind was acknowledged thereto.' The Jesuits, in 1568, were informed that Bowton, at his trial, impeached Morton and Balfour, and told Moray that he spared to accuse him, ' because of your dignity.' [2] These statements about dying confessions were bandied, in contradictory sort, by both sides. The confession of Morton, attested, and certainly not exaggerated, by two sympathetic Protestant ministers, is of another species, and, as far as it goes, is evidence, though Morton obviously does not tell all he knew. The part of Paris's statement about the crime ends by saying that Huntly came to Bothwell at Holyrood, late on the fatal night, and whispered with him, as Bothwell changed his evening dress, after the dance at Holyrood, for a cavalry cloak and other clothes. Both-

---

[1] Anderson, 1, part II., 76, 77.

[2] Nau, Appendix ii. 151, 152. The Jesuits' evidence was from letters to Archbishop Beaton.

well told Paris that Huntly had offered to accompany him, but that he would not take him. Morton, in his dying confession, declared that Archibald Douglas confessed that he and Huntly were both present : contradicting Paris as to Huntly.

The declarations of Paris were never published at the time. On November 8, 1571, Dr. Wilson, who was apparently translating something—the 'Detection' of Buchanan, or the accompanying Oration ('Actio'), into sham Scots—wrote to Cecil, 'desiring you to send unto me "Paris" closely sealed, and it shall not be known from whence it cometh.' Cecil was secretly circulating libels on Mary, but 'Paris' was not used. His declarations would have clashed with the 'Detection' as written when only Bothwell and Mary were to be implicated. The truth, that there was a great *political* conspiracy, including some of Mary's accusers, and perhaps Morton, Lindsay, and Ruthven (for so Paris makes Bothwell say), would have come out. The fact that Moray 'would neither help nor hinder,' and sneaked off, would have been uttered to the world. The glaring discrepancies would have been patent to criticism. So Cecil withheld documents unsuited to his purpose of discrediting Mary.[1]

The one valuable part of Paris's declarations concerns the carrying of a Glasgow letter. And that is only valuable if we supply the accusers with possible dates, in place of their own impossible

[1] Murdin, p. 57.

chronology, and if we treat as false their tale [1] that
Bothwell 'lodged in the town' when he returned
from Calendar to Edinburgh. The earlier confessions, especially those of Tala, were certainly
mutilated, as we have seen, and only what suited
the Lords came out. That of Paris was a tool to
use against Lethington, but, as it also implicated
Morton, Lindsay, and Ruthven, with Argyll and
Huntly, who might become friends of Morton and
Moray, Paris's declaration was a two-edged sword,
and, probably, was little known in Scotland. In
England it was judiciously withheld from the public
eye. Goodall writes (1754) : 'I well remember that
one of our late criminal judges, of high character
for knowledge and integrity, was, by reading it
[Paris's statement], induced to believe every scandal
that had been thrown out against the Queen.' A
criminal judge ought to be a good judge of evidence, yet the statements of Paris rather fail, when
closely inspected, to carry conviction.

Darnley, in fact, was probably strangled by
murderers of the Douglas and Lethington branches
of the conspiracy. On the whole, it seems more
probable that the powder was placed in Mary's
room than not, though all contemporary accounts of
its effects make against this theory. As touching
Mary, the confessions are of the very slightest value.
The published statements, under examination, of

---

[1] In the 'Book of Articles,' and in the series of dated events called
'Cecil's Journal.'

Powrie, Dalgleish, Tala, and Bowton do not implicate
her.   That of Bowton rather clears her than otherwise.   Thus : the theory of the accusers, supported
by the declaration of Paris, was that, when the
powder was 'fair in field,' properly lodged in Mary's
room, under that of Darnley, Paris was to enter
Darnley's room as a signal that all was prepared.
Mary then left the room, in the time required 'to
say a paternoster.'   But Bowton affirmed that, as he
and his fellows stored the powder, Bothwell 'bade
them make haste, before the Queen came forth of
the King's house, for if she came forth before they
were ready, they would not find such commodity.'
This, for what it is worth, implies that no signal,
such as the entrance of Paris, had been arranged for
the Queen's departure.   The self-contradictory statements of Paris can be torn to shreds in cross-examination, whatever element of truth they may contain.
The 'dying confessions' are contradictorily reported,
and all the reports are worthless.   The guilt of some
Lords, and their alliance with the other accusers,
made it impossible for the Prosecution to produce a
sound case.   As their case stands, as it is presented
by them, a jury, however convinced, on other grounds,
of Mary's guilt, would feel constrained to acquit the
Queen of Scots.

VIII

MARY'S CONDUCT AFTER THE MURDER

NOTHING has damaged Mary's reputation more than
her conduct after the murder of Darnley. Her first
apologist, Queen Elizabeth, adopted the line of
argument which her defenders have ever since
pursued. On March 24, 1567, Elizabeth discussed
the matter with de Silva. Her emissary to spy into
the problem, Killigrew, had dined in Edinburgh at
Moray's house with Bothwell, Lethington, Huntly, and
Argyll. All, except Moray, were concerned in the
crime, and this circumstance certainly gave force to
Elizabeth's reasoning. She told de Silva, on Killigrew's report, that grave suspicions existed 'against
Bothwell, and others who are with the Queen,' the
members, in fact, of Moray's little dinner party to
Killigrew. Mary, said Elizabeth, 'did not dare to
proceed against them, in consequence of the influence
and strength of Bothwell,' who was Admiral, and
Captain of the Guard of 500 Musketeers. Elizabeth
added that, after Killigrew left Scotland, Mary had
attempted to take refuge in the Castle, but had been
refused entry by the Keeper, who feared that Both-

well would accompany Mary and take possession.
This anecdote is the more improbable as Killigrew
was in London by March 24, and the Earl of Mar
was deprived of the command of the Castle on
March 19.[1] To have retired to the Castle, as on other
occasions of danger, and to have remained there,
would have been Mary's natural conduct, had the
slaying of Darnley alarmed and distressed her.
Those who defend her, however, can always fall back,
like Elizabeth, on the theory that Bothwell, Argyll,
Huntly, and Lethington overawed her ; that she
could not urge the finding of the murderers, or even
avoid their familiar society, any more than Moray
could rescue or avenge Darnley, or abstain from
sharing his salt with Bothwell.[2] De Silva inferred
from Moray's talk, that he believed Bothwell to be
guilty.[3]

The first efforts of Mary and the Council were to
throw dust in the eyes of France and Europe. The
Council met on the day of Darnley's death. There
were present Hamilton, Archbishop of St. Andrews,
Atholl, Caithness, Livingstone, Cassilis, Sutherland,
the Bishop of Galloway (Protestant), the Bishop of
Ross, the treasurer, Flemyng, Bellenden, Bothwell,
Argyll, Huntly, and Lethington. Of these the last
four were far the most powerful, and were in the
plot. They must have dictated the note sent by

[1] Hay Fleming, .444.
[2] Spanish Calendar, i. 628. For Moray's dinner party, cf. Bain,
i. 317.   [3] Spanish Calendar, i. 635.

express to France with the news. The line of defence was that the authors of the explosion had just failed to destroy 'the Queen and most of the nobles and lords in her suite, who were with the King till near midnight.' This was said though confessedly the explosion did not occur till about two in the morning. The Council add that Mary escaped by not staying all night at Kirk o' Field. God preserved her to take revenge. Yet all the Court knew that Mary had promised to be at Holyrood for the night, and the conspirators must have seen her escort returning thither with torches burning.[1] The Lennox MSS., in a set of memoranda, insist that Mary caused a hagbut to be fired, as she went down the Canongate, for a signal to Bothwell and his gang. They knew that she was safe from any explosion at Kirk o' Field.

On the same day, February 10 (11 ?), Mary, or rather Lethington for Mary, wrote, in Scots, the same tale as that of her Council, to Beaton, her ambassador in Paris. She had just received his letter of January 27, containing a vague warning of rumoured dangers to herself. The warning she found 'over true' (it probably arose from the rumour that Darnley and Lennox meant to seize the infant Prince). The explosion had been aimed at her destruction; so the letter said. 'It wes dressit alsweill for us as for the King:' she only escaped by chance, or rather because 'God put it in

[1] Laing, ii. 244.

our hede' to go to the masque. Now all the world
concerned knew that Mary was not in Kirk o' Field
at two in the morning, and Mary knew that all the
world knew.[1] To be sure she did not actually write
this letter. Who had an interest in this supposed
plot of general destruction by gunpowder? Not
Lennox and Darnley, of course; not the Hamiltons,
not Mary and the Lords who were to be exploded.
Only the extreme Protestants, whose leader, Moray,
left on the morning of the affair, could have benefited
by the gunpowder plot. In Paris, on February 21,
the deed was commonly regarded as the work of 'the
heretics, who desire to do the same by the Queen.'[2]

This was the inference—namely, that the Protestants were guilty—which the letters of Mary and the
Council were meant to suggest. To defend Mary we
must suppose that she, and the innocent members of
Council, were constrained by the guilty members
to approve of what was written, or were wholly
without guile. The secret was open enough.
According to Nau, Mary's secretary, she had remarked, as she left Kirk o' Field at midnight, 'Jesu,
Paris, how begrimed you are!' The story was
current. Blackwood makes Mary ask 'why Paris
smelled so of gunpowder.' Had Mary wished to

---

[1] Labanoff, ii. 2–4.

[2] Venetian Calendar, vii. 388, 389. There were rumours that
Lennox had been blown up with Darnley, and, later, that he was
attacked at Glasgow, on February 9, by armed men, and owed his
escape to Lord Semple. It is incredible that this fact should be un-
mentioned, if it occurred, by Lennox and Buchanan.

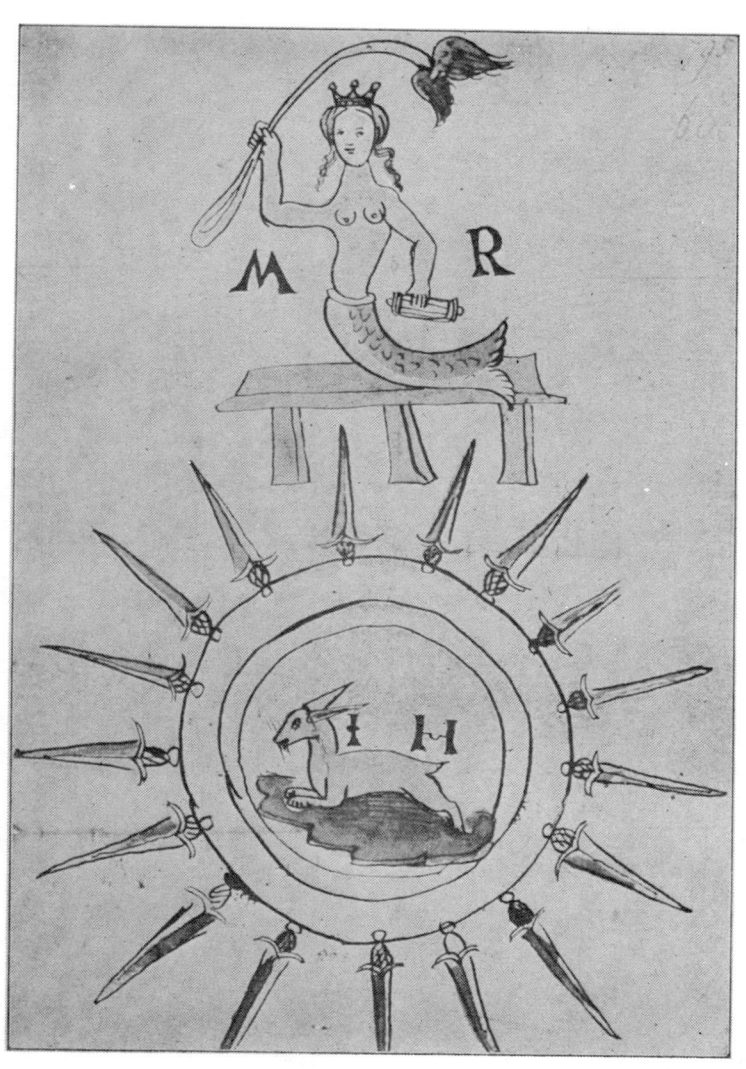

PLACARD OF MARCH 1567. MARY AS A MERMAID

find the guilty, the begrimed Paris would have
been put to the torture at once. The sentinels at
the palace would have been asked who went in and
out after midnight. Conceivably, Mary was unable
to act, but, if her secretary tells truth as to the
begrimed Paris, she could have no shadow of doubt
as to Bothwell's guilt. A few women were interro-
gated, as was Nelson, Darnley's servant, but the
inquiry was stopped when Nelson said that Mary's
servants had the keys. Rewards were offered for the
discovery of the guilty, but produced only anonymous
placards, denouncing some who were guilty, as Bothwell, and others, like 'Black Mr. James Spens,'
against whom nothing was ever proved.

It were tedious and bewildering to examine the
gossip as to Mary's private demeanour. If she had
Darnley buried beside Riccio, she fulfilled the pro-
phecy which, Lennox tells us, she made over Riccio's
new-made grave, when she fled from Holyrood
after the murder of the Italian : 'ere a twelvemonth was over, a fatter than he should lie beside
him.' What she did at Seton and when (Lennox says
that, at Seton, she called for the tune *Well is me
Since I am free*), whether she prosecuted her amour
with Bothwell, played golf, indulged in the unseason-
able sport of archery or not, is matter of gossip.
Nor need we ask how long she sat under candle-light,
in darkened, black-hung chambers.[1] She assuredly
made no effort to avenge her husband. Neither the

[1] Hay Fleming, pp. 442-443.

strong and faithful remonstrances of her ambassador
in France, nor the menace of Catherine de Medicis,
nor the plain speaking of Elizabeth, nor a petition of
the godly, who put this claim for justice last in
a list of their own demands, and late (April 18),
could move Mary.   Bothwell 'ruled all:' Lethington,
according to Sir James Melville, fell into the back-
ground of the Court.   He had taken nothing by the
crime, for which he had signed the band, and it is
quite conceivable that Bothwell, who hated him, had
bullied him into signing.   He may even have had no
more direct knowledge of what was intended, or
when, than Moray himself.   He can never have
approved of the Queen's marriage with Bothwell,
which was fatal to his interests.   He was newly
married, and was still, at least, on terms with Mary
which warranted him in urging her to establish
Protestantism—or so he told Cecil.   But to Bothwell, Mary was making grants in money, in privileges,
and in beautiful old ecclesiastical fripperies : chasu-
bles and tunicles all of cloth of gold, figured with
white, and red, and yellow.[1]   Lennox avers, in the
Lennox Papers, that the armour, horses, and other
effects of Darnley were presented by Mary to Bothwell.   Late in March Drury reported that, in the
popular belief, Mary was likely to marry him.

From the first Lennox had pleaded for the arrest
and trial of Bothwell and others whom he named, but
who never were tried.   Writers like Goodall have

[1] Robertson, *Inventories*, p. 53.

defended, Laing and Hill Burton have attacked, the manner of Bothwell's Trial (April 12). Neither for Lennox nor for Elizabeth, would Mary delay the process. As usual in Scotland, as when Bothwell himself, years before, or when John Knox still earlier, or when, later, Lethington, was tried, either the accused or the accuser made an overwhelming show of armed force. It was 'the custom of the country,' and Bothwell, looking dejected and wretched, says his friend, Ormistoun, was 'cleansed' in the promptest manner, Lennox merely entering a protest. The Parliament of April 19 restored Huntly and others to forfeited lands, ratified the tenures of Moray, and offended Mary's Catholic friends by practically establishing the Kirk. On the same night, apparently after a supper at Ainslie's tavern, many nobles and ecclesiastics signed a band ('Ainslie's band'). It ran thus : Bothwell is, and has been judicially found, innocent of Darnley's death. The signers therefore bind themselves, 'as they will answer to God,' to defend Bothwell to the uttermost, and to advance his marriage with Mary. If they fail, may they lose every shred of honour, and 'be accounted unworthy and faithless Traytors.'

A copy of the names of the signatories, as given to Cecil by John Read, George Buchanan's secretary, 'so far as John Read might remember,' exists. The names are Murray (who was not in Scotland), Argyll, Huntly, Cassilis, Morton, Sutherland, Rothes, Glencairn, Caithness, Boyd, Seton, Sinclair, Semple,

N

Oliphant, Ogilvy, Ross-Halkett, Carlyle, Herries, Home, Invermeath. 'Eglintoun subscribed not, but slipped away.'[1] Names of ecclesiastics, as Lesley, Bishop of Ross, appear in copies where Moray's name does not.[2] It is argued that Moray may have signed before leaving Scotland, that this may have been a condition of his license to depart. Mary's confessor told de Silva that Moray did not sign.[3] That the Lords received a warrant for their signatures from Mary, they asserted at York (October, 1568), but the document was not mentioned later at Westminster. That they were coerced by armed force, was averred later, but not in Kirkcaldy's account of the affair, written on the day following. No Hamilton signs, at least if we except the Archbishop ; and Lethington, with his friend Atholl, seems not even to have been present at the Parliament.

On April 21 (Monday), Mary went to Stirling to see her son, and try to poison him, according to a Lennox memorandum. On the 23rd, she went to

---

[1] Anderson, i. 112. Bain, ii. 322.

[2] Keith knew a copy in the Scots College at Paris, attested by Sir James Balfour as ' the authentick copy of the principall band.' This, or a similar copy, he sent to Mary, in January, 1581, after Morton's arrest. The names of laymen are Huntly, Argyll, Morton, Cassilis, Sutherland, Errol, Crawford, Caithness, Rothes, Boyd, Glamis, Ruthven, Semple, Herries, Ogilvy, Fleming. John Read's memory must have been fallacious. There are eight prelates in Balfour's band, including Archbishop Hamilton, the Bishop of Orkney, who joined in prosecuting Mary, and Lesley, Bishop of Ross (Keith, ii. 562–569). On the whole subject see a discussion by Mr. Bain and Mr. Hay Fleming, in *The Genealogist*, 1900–1901. Some copies are dated April 20. See Fraser, *The Melvilles*, i. 89.

[3] Spanish Calendar, i. 662.

Linlithgow; on the 24th, Bothwell, with a large force, seized her, Huntly, and Lethington, at a disputed place not far from Edinburgh. He then carried her to his stronghold of Dunbar. Was Mary playing a collusive part? had she arranged with Bothwell to carry her off? The Casket Letters were adduced by her enemies to prove that she was a party to the plot. As we shall see when examining the Letters if we accept them they leave no doubt on this point. But precisely here the darkness is yet more obscured by the enigmatic nature of Mary's relations with Lethington, who, as Secretary, was in attendance on her at Stirling and Linlithgow. It will presently be shown that, as to Lethington's policy at this moment, and for two years later, two contradictory accounts are given, and on the view we take of his actions turns our interpretation of the whole web of intrigue.

Whether Mary did or did not know that she was to be carried off, did Lethington know? If he did, it was his interest to ride from Stirling, by night, to his usual refuge, through the pass of Killiecrankie, to the safe and hospitable house of Atholl, before the abduction was consummated. Bothwell's success in wedding Mary would mean ruin to Lethington's favourite project of uniting the crowns on the head of Mary or her child. It would also mean Lethington's own destruction, for Bothwell loathed him. To this point was he brought by his accession to the band for Darnley's murder. His natural action,

then, if he knew of the intended abduction, was to
take refuge with Atholl, who, like himself, had not
signed Ainslie's band.   If Lethington was ignorant,
others were not.   Bothwell had chosen his opportunity with skill.   He had an excellent excuse for
collecting his forces.   The Liddesdale reivers had
just spoiled the town of Biggar, 'and got much substance of coin (corn ?), silks, and horses,' so wrote Sir
John Forster to Cecil on April 24.[1]   On the pretext of
punishing this outrage, Bothwell mustered his forces ;
but politicians less wary than Lethington, and more
remote from the capital, were not deceived.   They
knew what Bothwell intended.   Lennox was flying
for his life, and was aboard ship on the west coast,
but, as early as April 23, he wrote to tell his wife
that Bothwell was to seize Mary.   A spy in Edinburgh (Kirkcaldy, by the handwriting), and Drury in
Berwick, knew of the scheme on April 24, the day
of the abduction.   If Mary did not suspect what
Lennox knew before the event, she was curiously
ignorant, but, if Lethington was ignorant, so may
she have been.[2]

What were the exact place and circumstances of
Mary's arrest by Bothwell, whether he did or did not
offer violence to her at Dunbar, whether she asked
succour from Edinburgh, we know not precisely.   At
all events, she was so far compromised, actually
violated, says Melville,[3] that, not being a Clarissa

[1] Cal. For. Eliz. viii. 213.   [2] Bain, ii. 323, 324.
[3] Melville, p. 177.

Harlowe, she might represent herself as bound to marry Bothwell. Meanwhile Lethington was at Dunbar with her, a prisoner 'under guard,' so Drury reports (May 2). By that date, many of the nobles, including Atholl, had met at Stirling, and, despite their agreement to defend Bothwell, in Ainslie's band, Argyll and Morton, as well as Atholl and Mar, had confederated against him, Atholl probably acting under advice secretly sent by Lethington. 'The Earl Bothwell thought to have slain him in the Queen's chamber, had not her Majesty come between and saved him,' says Sir James Melville, who had been released on the day after his capture between Linlithgow and Edinburgh.[1] Different rumours prevailed as to Lethington's own intentions. He was sometimes thought to be no unwilling prisoner, and even to have warned Atholl not to head the confederacy against Bothwell (May 4).[2] Mary wrote to quiet the banded Lords at Stirling (about May 3), and Lethington succeeded in getting a letter delivered in which he expressed his desire to speak with Cecil, declared that Mary meant to marry Bothwell, and that he had only been rescued from Bothwell's fury by Mary, who said that, 'if a hair of Lethington's head perished, she would cause Bothwell to forfeit lands, goods, and life.'[3] Could the Queen who said that be in love with Bothwell?

Mary, then, was, in one respect at least, no

---

[1] Melville, p. 178.   [2] Drury to Cecil, Cal For. Eliz. viii. 222.
[3] Cal. For. Eliz. viii. 223–224.

passive victim, at Dunbar, and Lethington owed
his life to her. He explained that his letters,
apparently in Bothwell's interest, were extorted from
him, ' but immediately by a trusty messenger he
advertised not to give credit to them.' [1] Meantime
he had arranged to escape, as he did, later. ' He
will come out to shoot with others, and between the
marks he will ride upon a good nag to a place where
both a fresh horse and company tarries for him.' [2]
Lethington made his escape, but not till weeks later,
when he fled first to Callendar, then to the protection
of Atholl ; he joined the Lords, and from this
moment the question is, was he, under a pretext of
secret friendship, Mary's most deadly foe (as she
herself, Morton, and Randolph declared) or her loyal
servant, working cautiously in her interests, as he
persuaded Throckmorton and Sir James Melville to
believe ?

My own impression is that Mary, Morton, and
Randolph were right in their opinion. Lethington,
under a mask of gratitude and loyalty, was urging,
after his escape, the strongest measures against Mary,
till circumstances led him to advise ' a dulce manner,'
because (as he later confessed to Morton) [3] Mary was
likely to be restored, and to avenge herself on him.
Mary, he knew, could ruin him by proving his
accession to Darnley's murder. His hold over her

---

[1] May 6, Drury to Cecil.
[2] Drury to Cecil, May 6.   Cal. For. Eliz. viii. 223, 224.
[3] Undated letter in Bannatyne, of 1570-1572.

would be gone, as soon as the Casket Letters were produced before the English nobles : he had then no more that he could do, but she kept her reserve of strength, her proof against him. His bolt was shot, hers was in her quiver. This view of the relations (later to be proved) between Lethington and the woman whose courage saved his life, explains the later mysteries of Mary's career, and part of the problem of the Casket Letters.

Meanwhile, in the first days of May, the Queen rushed on her doom. Despite the protestations of her confessor, who urged that a marriage with Bothwell was illegal : despite the remonstrances of du Croc, who had been sent from France to advise and threaten, despite the courageous denunciation of Craig, the Protestant preacher, Mary hurried through a collusive double process of divorce, proclaimed herself a free agent, created Bothwell Duke of Orkney, and, on May 15, 1567, wedded him by Protestant rites, the treacherous Bishop of Orkney, later one of her official prosecutors, performing the ceremony.[1] To her or to Lethington's own letter of excuse to the French Court, we return later.

Mary, even on the wedding-day, was miserable. Du Croc, James Melville, and Lethington, who had not yet escaped, were witnesses of her wretchedness. She called out for a knife to slay herself.[2] Mary

---

[1] See Stewart's *Lost Chapter in the History of Queen Mary* for the illegalities of the divorce. The best Catholic opinion is agreed on the subject.

[2] Melville, 182. Teulet, ii. 153, 170.

was ' the most changed woman of face that in so little time without extremity of sickness they have seen.' A Highland second-sighted woman prophesied that she should have five husbands. ' In the fifth husband's time *she shall be burned*, which death divers speak of to happen to her, and it is said she fears the same.' This dreadful death was the legal punishment of women who killed their husbands. The fires of the stake shone through Mary's dreams when a prisoner in Loch Leven. Even Lady Reres, now supplanted by a sister of Bothwell's, and the Lady of Branxholme, ' both in their speech and writing marvellously rail, both of the Queen and Bothwell.' [1]

A merry bridal!

Mary's defenders have attributed her sorrow to the gloom of a captive, forced into a hated wedlock. De Silva assigned her misery to a galling conscience. We see the real reasons of her wretchedness, and to these we must add the most poignant, Bothwell's continued relations with his wife, who remained in his Castle of Crichton. He, too, was ' beastly suspicious and jealous.' No wonder that she called for a knife to end her days, and told du Croc that she never could be happy again.

Meanwhile the Lords, from the first urged on by Kirkcaldy, who said (April 26) that he must avenge Darnley or leave the country, were banded, and were appealing to Elizabeth for help, which she, a Queen,

[1] Cal. For. Eliz. viii. 235.

hesitated to lend to subjects confederated against a sister Queen. Kirkcaldy was the dealer with Bedford, who encouraged him, but desired that the Prince should be brought to England. Robert Melville dealt with Killigrew (May 27). Bothwell, to soothe the preachers, attended sermons, Mary invited herself to dinner with her reluctant subjects; the golden font, the christening gift of Elizabeth, was melted down and coined for pay to the guard of musketeers (May 31). Huntly asked for leave to go to the north. Mary replied bitterly that he meant to turn traitor, like his father. This distrust of Huntly is clearly expressed in the Casket Letters.[1] On May 30, Mary summoned an armed muster of her subjects. On June 6, Lethington carried out his deferred scheme, and fled to the Lords. On the 7th, Mary and Bothwell retired to Borthwick Castle. On June 11, the Lords advanced to Borthwick. Bothwell fled to Dunbar.[2] The Lords then retired to Dalkeith, and thence, on the same night, to Edinburgh Thither Mary had sent a proclamation, still extant in manuscript, bidding the citizens to arm and free her, not from Bothwell, but from the Lords. An unwilling captive would have hurried to their protection. The burgesses permitted the Lords to enter the town. Mary at once, on hearing of this, sent the son of Lady Reres to the commander of Edinburgh Castle, bidding him fire his guns on the Lords. He

[1] Drury to Cecil, Cal. For. Eliz. viii. 240.
[2] Dates from James Beaton's letter of June 17. Laing, ii. 106, 115.

disobeyed.   She then fled in male apparel to Dunbar,
Bothwell meeting her a mile from Borthwick (June 11).
On June 12, the Lords seized the remains of the
golden font, and the coin already struck.   On the
13th, James Beaton joined Mary and Bothwell at
Dunbar, and found them mustering their forces.   He
returned, with orders to encourage the Captain of the
Castle, but was stopped.

Next day (14th) the Lords made a reconnaissance
towards Haddington, and Atholl, with Lethington,
rode into Edinburgh, at the head of 200 horse.
Lethington then for three hours dealt with the
Keeper of the Castle, Sir James Balfour, his associate
in the band for Darnley's murder.   Later, according
to Randolph, they opened a little coffer of Bothwell's
which had a covering of green cloth, and was
deposited in the Castle, and took out the band.
Was this coffer the Casket?   Such coffers had
usually velvet covers, embroidered.   Lethington won
over Balfour, who surrendered the Castle presently.
This was the deadliest stroke at Mary, and it was
dealt by him whose life she had just preserved.

Next day the Lords marched to encounter Bothwell,
met him posted on Carberry Hill, and, after many
hours of manœuvres and negotiations, very variously
reported, the Lords allowed Bothwell to slip away to
Dunbar (he was a compromising captive), and took
Mary, clad unqueenly in a ' red petticoat, sleeves
tied with points, a velvet hat and muffler.'   She
surrendered to Kirkcaldy of Grange : on what terms,

if on any, is not to be ascertained. She herself
in Nau's MS. maintains that she promised to join in
pursuing Darnley's murderers, and 'claimed that
justice should be done upon certain persons of their
party now present, who were guilty of the said murder,
and were much astonished to find themselves discovered.' But, by Nau's own arrangement of his
matter, Mary can only have thus accused the Lords
(there is other evidence that she did so) *after* Bothwell,
at parting from her, denounced to her Morton, Balfour,
and Lethington, giving her a copy of the murder band,
signed by them, and bidding her 'take good care of
that paper.' She did 'take good care' of some paper,
as we shall see, though almost certainly not the band,
and not obtained at Carberry Hill.[1] She asked for an
interview with Lethington and Atholl, both of whom,
though present, denied that they were of the Lords'
party. Finally, after parting from Bothwell, assuring
him that, if found innocent in the coming Parliament,
she would remain his loyal wife, she surrendered to
Kirkcaldy, 'relying upon his word and assurance,
which the Lords, in full Council, as he said, had
solemnly warranted him to make.' So writes Nau.
James Beaton (whose narrative we have followed)
merely says that she made terms, which were granted,
that none of her party should be 'invaded or pursued.'[2]
Sir James Melville makes the Lords' promise depend
on her abandonment of Bothwell.[3]

[1] Nau, 46–48.   [2] Laing, i. 113.   June 17, 1567.
                    [3] Melville, p. 183.

Whatever be the truth as to Mary's surrender, the Lords later excused their treatment of her not on the ground that they had given no pledge, but on that of her adhesion to the man they had asked her to marry.   According to Nau, Lethington persuaded the Lords to place her in the house then occupied by Preston, the Laird of Craigmillar, Provost of Edinburgh   She asked, at night, for an interview with Lethington, but she received no answer.   Next morning she called piteously to Lethington, as he passed the window of her room : he crushed his hat over his face, and did not even look up. The mob were angry with Lethington, and Mary's guards dragged her from the window.   On the other hand, du Croc says that Lethington, on hearing her cries, entered her room, and spoke with her, while the mob was made to move on.[1]   Lethington told du Croc that, when Mary called to him, and he went to her, she complained of being parted from Bothwell.   He, with little tact, told her that Bothwell much preferred his wife.   She clamoured to be placed in a ship with Bothwell, and allowed to drift at the wind's will.[2]   Du Croc said to Lethington that he hoped the pair would drift to France, ' where the king would judge righteously, for the unhappy facts are only too well proved.'   This is a very strong opinion against Mary.   Years later, when Lethington was holding Edinburgh Castle for Mary, he told Craig that, after Carberry ' I myself made the offer to her

[1] Teulet, ii. 179.   [2] Teulet, ii. 169, 170.   June 17.

that, if she would abandon my Lord Bothwell, she should have as thankful obedience as ever she had since she came to Scotland. But no ways would she consent to leave my Lord Bothwell.'[1] Lethington's word is of slight value.

To return to Nau, or to Mary speaking through Nau, on June 16 Lethington did go to see her: 'but in such shame and fear that he never dared to lift his eyes to her face while he spoke with her.' He showed great hatred of Bothwell, and said that she could not be allowed to return to him: Mary, marvelling at his 'impudence,' replied that she was ready to join in the pursuit of Darnley's murderers: who had acted chiefly on Lethington's advice. She then told him plainly that he, Morton, and Balfour had chiefly prevented inquiry into the murder. *They* were the culprits, as Bothwell had told her, showing her the signatures to the murder band, when parting from her at Carberry. She reminded Lethington that she had saved his life. If Lethington persecuted her, she would tell what she knew of him. He replied, angrily, that she would drive him to extremities to save his own life, whereas, if matters were allowed to grow quiet, he might one day be of service to her. If he were kept talking, and so incurred the suspicion of the Lords, her life would be in peril. To 'hedge,' Lethington used to encourage Mary, when she was in Loch Leven. But he had, then, no 'assurance' from her, and, on a false alarm of her

[1] Bannatyne's *Memorials*, p. 126.

escape, mounted his horse to fly from Edinburgh.[1] Thus greatly do the stories of Mary and of Lethington differ, concerning their interview after Carberry. Perhaps Mary is the more trustworthy.

On June 17, 1567, James Beaton wrote to his brother, Mary's ambassador in Paris. He says that no man was allowed to speak to Mary on June 16, but that, in the evening, she asked a girl to speak to Lethington, and pray him to have compassion on her, ' and not to show himself so extremely opposed to her as he does.' Beaton's evidence, being written the day after the occurrences, is excellent, and leaves us to believe that, in the darkest of her dark hours in Scotland, insulted by the populace, with guards placed in her chamber, destitute of all earthly aid, Mary found in extreme opposition to her the man who owed to her his lands and his life.

And why was Lethington thus ' extremely opposed ' ? First, Mary, if free, would join Bothwell, his deadly foe. Secondly, he knew from her own lips that Mary knew his share in Darnley's murder, and had proof. While she lived, the sword hung over Lethington. He, therefore, insisted on her imprisonment in a place whence escape should have been impossible. He is even said to have advised that she should be secretly strangled. Years later, when time had brought in his revenges, and Lethington and Kirkcaldy were holding the Castle for Mary, her last hope, Lethington explained his change of sides in a

---

[1] Nau, 50–54.   [2] Laing, ii, 115.

letter to his opponent, Morton. Does Morton hate him because he has returned to the party of the Queen? He had advised Morton to take the same course, 'being assured that, with time, she would recover her liberty (as yet I have no doubt but she will). I deemed it neither wisdom for him nor me to deserve particular ill will at her hands.' This was a frank enough explanation of his own change of factions. If ever Mary came to her own, Lethington dreaded her feud. We shall see that as soon as she was imprisoned, Lethington affected to be her secret ally. Morton replied that 'it was vain in Lethington to think that he could deserve more particular evil will at Mary's hands than he had deserved already.' [1]

Lethington could not be deeper in guilt towards Mary than he was, despite his appearance of friendship. The 'evil will' which he had incurred was 'particular.' We have another proof. In the same revolution of factions (1570–73) Randolph also wrote to Lethington and Kirkcaldy asking them why they had deserted their old allies, Morton and the rest, for the Queen's party. 'You yourselves wrote against her, and were the chiefest causes of her apprehension, and imprisonment' (at Loch Leven), 'and dimission of her crown. . . . So that you two were her chiefest occasion of all the calamities, *as she hath said*, that she is fallen into. You, Lord of Lethington, *by your persuasion and counsel to*

[1] Bannatyne, *Journal*, 477, 482.

apprehend her, to imprison her, yea, to have taken presently the life from her.' [1]   To this we shall return.

When we add to this testimony Mary's hatred of Lethington, revealed in Nau's MS., a hatred which his death could not abate, though he died in her service, we begin to understand. Sir James Melville and Throckmorton were (as we shall see) deluded by the 'dulce manner' of Lethington. But, in truth, he was Mary's worst enemy, till his bolt was shot, while hers remained in her hands. Then Lethington, in 1569, went over to her party, as a charge of Darnley's murder, urged by his old partisans, was hanging over his head.

Meanwhile, after Mary's surrender at Carberry, the counsel of Lethington prevailed. She was hurried to Loch Leven, after two dreadful days of tears and frenzied threats and entreaties, and was locked up in the Castle on the little isle, the Castle of her ancestral enemies, the Douglases. There she awaited her doom, ' the fiery death.'

[1] Chalmers, *Life of Mary, Queen of Scots* (1818), i. 486, 487, note.

IX

THE EMERGENCE OF THE CASKET LETTERS

I. FIRST HINTS OF THE EXISTENCE OF THE LETTERS

THE Lords, as we have seen, nominally rose in arms to punish Bothwell (whom they had acquitted), to protect their infant Prince, and to rescue Mary, whom they represented as Bothwell's reluctant captive. Yet their first success, at Carberry Hill, induced them, not to make Bothwell prisoner, but to give him facilities of escape. Their second proceeding was, not to release Mary, but to expose her to the insults of the populace, and then to immure her, destitute and desperate, in the island fortress of the Douglases.

These contradictions between their conduct and their avowed intentions needed excuse. They could not say, 'We let Bothwell escape because he knew too much about ourselves: we imprisoned the Queen for the same good reason.' They had to protect themselves, first against Elizabeth, who bitterly resented the idea that subjects might judge princes: next, against the possible anger of the rulers of

o

France and Spain; next, against the pity of the
mobile populace. There was also a chance that
Moray, who was hastening home from France, might
espouse his sister's cause, as, indeed, at this moment
he professed to do. Finally, in the changes of
things, Mary, or her son, might recover power, and
exact vengeance for the treasonable imprisonment of
a Queen.

The Lords, therefore, first excused themselves
(as in Lethington's discourses with du Croc) by
alleging that Mary refused to abandon Bothwell.
This was, no doubt, true, though we cannot accept
Lethington's word for the details of her passionate
behaviour.   Her defenders can fall back on the
report of Drury, that she was at this time with child,
as she herself informed Throckmorton, while Nau
declares that, in Loch Leven, she prematurely gave
birth to twins. Mary always had a plausible and
possible excuse : in this case she could not dissolve
her marriage with Bothwell without destroying the
legitimacy of her expected offspring.   Later, in 1569,
when she wished her marriage with Bothwell to be
annulled, the Lords refused assent.   In the present
juncture, of June, 1567, with their Queen a captive
in their hands, the Lords needed some better excuse
than her obstinate adherence to the husband whom
they had selected for her.   They needed a reason for
their conduct that would have a retro-active effect :
namely, positive proof of her guilt of murder.

No sooner was the proof wanted than it was

found. Mary was imprisoned on June 16 : her
guilty letters to Bothwell, the Casket Letters, with
their instigations to Darnley's murder and her own
abduction, were secured on June 19, and were
inspected, and entrusted to Morton's keeping, on
June 21. To Morton's declaration about the
discovery and inspection of the Casket and Letters,
we return in chronological order : it was made in
December, 1568, before the English Commissioners
who examined Mary's case.

The Lords were now, with these letters to justify
them, in a relatively secure position. They could,
and did, play off France against England : both of
these countries were anxious to secure the person of
the baby Prince, both were obliged to treat with the
Lords who had the alliance of Scotland to bestow.
Elizabeth wavered between her desire, as a Queen,
to help a sister Queen, and her anxiety not to break
with the dominant Scottish party. The Lords had
hanged a retainer of Bothwell, Blackader, taken
after Carberry, who denied his guilt, and against
whom nothing was proved : but he had a Lennox
jury. Two other underlings of Bothwell, his porter
Powrie and his 'chamber-child' Dalgleish, were
taken and examined, but their depositions, as reported
by the Lords themselves, neither implicated Mary,
nor threw any light on the date at which the idea of
an explosion was conceived. It was then believed
to have been projected before Mary went to bring
Darnley from Glasgow. This opinion reflected itself

in what we shall assume to be the earlier forged draught, never publicly produced, of the long ' Glasgow Letter ' (II.) Later information may have caused that long letter to be modified into its present shape, or, as probably, induced the Lords to fall back on a partly genuine letter, our Letter II.

The Lords did by no means make public use, at first, of the Letters which they had found, and were possibly garbling.   We shall later make it clear, it is a new point, that, on the very day of the reading, the Lords sent Robert Melville post haste to Elizabeth, doubtless with verbal information about their discovery.   Leaving Edinburgh on June 21, the day of the discovery, Melville was in London on June 23 or 24, dispatched his business, and was in Berwick again on June 28.   He carried letters for Moray in France, but, for some reason, perhaps because the letters were delayed or intercepted, Moray had to be summoned again.   Meanwhile the Lords, otherwise, kept their own counsel.[1]   For reasons of policy they let their good fortune ooze out by degrees.

On June 25, Drury, writing from Berwick, reports that ' the Queen has had a *box*,' containing

---

[1] Mr. Froude has observed that the Lords, ' uncertain what to do, sent one of their number in haste to Paris, to the Earl of Moray, to inform him of the discovery of the Letters, and to entreat him to return immediately.'   Mr. Hosack says that Mr. Froude owes this circumstance ' entirely to his imagination.'   This is too severe.   The Lords did not send ' one of their number ' to Moray, but they sent letters which Robert Melville carried as far as London, and, seventeen days later, they did send a man who, if not ' one of their number,' was probably Moray's agent, John Wood (Hosack, i. 352).

papers about her intrigues with France. ' It is promised Drury to have his part of it.' This rumour of a ' box ' *may* refer to the capture of the Casket.[1] On June 29, Drury again wrote about the ' box,' and the MSS. in it, ' part in cipher deciphered.' Whether this ' box ' was the Casket, a false account of its contents being given to Drury, is uncertain. We hear no more of it, nor of any of Mary's own papers and letters to her : no letters to her from Bothwell are reported.

The earliest known decided reference to the Letters is that of the Spanish Ambassador, de Silva, writing from London on July 12, 1567. He says that du Croc, the French Ambassador to Mary, has passed through town on his return from Scotland. The French Ambassador in London, La Forest, reports to de Silva that Mary's ' adversaries assert positively that they know she had been concerned in the murder of her husband, which was proved by letters under her own hand, copies of which were in his [whose ?] possession.'[2] Major Martin Hume writes, in his Preface to the Calendar, ' The many arguments against their genuineness, founded upon the long delay in their production, thus disappear.'

It does not necessarily follow, however, that the letters of which du Croc probably carried copies (unless La Forest merely bragged falsely, to vex his Spanish fellow diplomatist) were either wholly genuine, or were identical with the letters later

[1] Cal. For. Eliz. viii. p. 261. [2] Spanish Calendar, i. 657.

produced.   It is by no means certain that Lethington
and Sir James Balfour had not access, before June 21,
to the Casket, which was in Balfour's keeping, within
Edinburgh Castle.   Randolph later wrote (as we have
already seen) that the pair had opened a little ' coffer,'
with a green cloth cover, and taken out the band
(which the pair had signed) for Darnley's murder.[1]
Whether the Casket was thus early tampered with is
uncertain.   But, as to du Croc's copies of the Letters,
the strong point, for the accusers, is, that, when the
Letters were published, in Scots, Latin, and French,
four years later, we do not hear that any holders of
du Croc's copies made any stir, or alleged that the
copies did not tally with those now printed, in 1571–
1573, by Mary's enemies.   This point must be kept
steadily in mind, as it is perhaps the chief objection
to the theory which we are about to offer.   But, on
November 29, 1568, when Mary's accusers were
gathered in London to attack her at the Westminster
Conference, La Forest's successor, La Mothe Fénelon,
writes to Charles IX. that they pretend to possess incriminating letters ' *escriptes et signées de sa main ;* '
written and *signed* by her hand.   Our *copies* are certainly not signed, which, in itself, proves little or
nothing, but Mary's contemporary defenders, Lesley
and Blackwood, urge that there was not even a pre-
tence that the Letters were signed, and this plea of
theirs was not answered.

My point, however, is that though La Forest,

[1] Cal. For. Eliz. ix. pp. 354, 355.

according to de Silva, had copies in July 1567, his successor at the English Court, doubtless well instructed, knows nothing about them, as far as his despatch shows. But he does say that the accusers are in search of evidence to prove the Letters authentic, not forged.[1] He says (November 28) to Catherine de' Medici, that he thinks the proofs of Mary's accusers 'very slender and extremely impertinent,' and he has been consulted by Mary's Commissioners.[2]

Of course it is possible that La Mothe Fénelon was not made acquainted with what his predecessor, La Forest, knew : but this course of secretiveness would not have been judicious. For the rest, the Court of France was not in the habit of replying to pamphlets, like that which contained copies of the Letters. It is unlikely that the copies given to La Forest were destroyed, but we have no hint or trace of them in France. Conceivably even if they differed (as we are to argue that they perhaps did) from the Letters later produced, the differences, though proof of tampering, did not redound to Mary's glory. At the time when France was negotiating Alençon's marriage with Elizabeth, and a Franco-English alliance (January–July, 1572), in a wild maze of international, personal, and religious intrigue, while Catherine de' Medici was wavering between massacre of the Huguenots and alliance with them, it is far

---

[1] Fénelon, *Dépêches* (1838), i. 19, 20.
[2] Fénelon, i. 22. To this point we shall return.

from inconceivable that La Forest's copies of the Letters were either overlooked, or not critically and studiously compared with the copies now published. To vex Elizabeth by criticism of two sets of copies of Letters was certainly not then the obvious policy of France : though the published Letters were thrust on the French statesmen.

The letters of La Mothe Fénelon, and of Charles IX., on the subject of Buchanan's ' Detection,' contain no hint that they thought the Letters, therein published, spurious.   They only resent their publication against a crowned Queen.[1]   The reader, then, must decide for himself whether La Forest's copies, if extant, were likely to be critically scanned and compared with the published Letters, in 1571, or in the imbroglio of 1572; and whether it is likely that, if this was done, and if the two copies did not tally, French statesmen thought that, in the circumstances, when Elizabeth was to be propitiated, and the Huguenots were not to be offended, it was worth while to raise a critical question.   If any one thinks that this course of conduct—the critical comparison of La Forest's copies with the published copies, and the remonstrance founded on any discrepancies detected— was the natural inevitable course of French statecraft, at the juncture—then he must discredit my hypothesis. For my hypothesis is, that the Letters extant in June and July, 1567, were not wholly identical with the Letters produced in December, 1568, and later

[1] La Mothe Fénelon, vii. 275-276.

published. It is hazarded without much confidence, but certain circumstances suggest that it may possibly be correct.

To return to the management of the Letters in June–July, 1567. The Lords, Mary's enemies, while perpetually protesting their extreme reluctance to publish Letters to Mary's discredit, had now sent the rumour of them all through Europe. Spain, and de Silva, were at that time far from friendly to Mary. On July 21, 1567, de Silva writes : ' I mentioned to the Queen [Elizabeth] that I had been told that the Lords held certain letters proving that the Queen [Mary] had been cognisant of the murder of her husband.' (The Letters, if they prove anything, prove more than that.) ' She told me it was not true, *although Lethington had acted badly in the matter*, and if she saw him she would say something that would not be at all to his taste.' Thus Elizabeth had heard the story about Letters (from Robert Melville, as we indicate later) and—what had she heard about Lethington ?[1] On June 21, the very day of the first inspection of the Letters, Lethington had written to Cecil.[2] On June 28, Lethington tells Cecil that, by Robert Melville's letters, he under-stands Cecil's ' good acceptance of these noblemen's quarrel ' for punishment of Darnley's murder and preservation of the Prince, ' and her Majesty's ' (Elizabeth's) ' gentle answer by Cecil's furtherance.'[3] Yet, to de Silva, Elizabeth presently denounced the

[1] Cal. Span. i. 659. Bain, ii. 336 [3] Bain, ii. 338.

ill behaviour of Lethington in the matter, and, appearing to desire Mary's safety, she sent Throckmorton to act in her cause. To the Lords and Lethington, by Robert Melville, she sent a gentle answer : Melville acting for the Lords. To Mary she averred (June 30) that Melville ' used much earnest speech on your behalf' (probably accusing Lethington of fraud as to the Letters), 'yet such is the general report of you to the contrary . . . that we could not be satisfied by him.' [1] Melville, we must remember, was acting for the Lords, but he is described as ' heart and soul Mary's.' He carried the Lords' verbal report of the Letters—but he also discredited it, blaming Lethington. Why did he not do so publicly ? At the time it was unsafe : later he and Lethington were allies in the last stand of Mary's party.

We do not know how much Elizabeth knew, or had been told ; or how much she believed, or what she meant, by her denunciation of Lethington, as regards his conduct in the affair of the Letters. But we do know that, on June 30, the Lords gave the lie, as in later proclamations they repeatedly did, to their own story that they had learned the whole secret of Mary's guilt on June 21. On June 30, they issued, under Mary's name, and under her signet, a summons against Bothwell, for Darnley's murder, and ' for taking the Queen's most noble person by force to her Castle of Dunbar, detaining her, *and for fear of her life making her promise to marry him.*' [2] The Lords

[1] Bain, ii. 339.   [2] Bain, ii. 341.

of Council in Edinburgh, at this time, were Morton (confessedly privy to the murder, and confessedly banded with Bothwell to enable him to marry Mary), Lethington, a signer of the band for Darnley's murder ; Balfour, who knew all ; Atholl, Home, James Makgill, and the Justice Clerk, Bellenden—who had been in trouble for Riccio's murder.[1] The same men, several guilty, were spreading *privately* the rumour of Mary's wicked Letters : and, at the same hour, were *publicly* absolving her, in their summons to Bothwell.   As late as July 14, they spoke to Throckmorton of Mary, ' with respect and reverence,' while alleging that ' for the Lord Bothwell she would leave her kingdom and dignity to live as a simple damsel with him.'   Who can believe one word that such men spoke ?

They assured Throckmorton that du Croc ' carried with him matter little to the Queen's ' (Mary's) ' advantage : ' possibly, though not certainly, an allusion to his copies of the Letters of her whom they spoke of ' with respect and reverence,' and promised ' to restore to her estate'—if she would abandon Bothwell.[2]

' I never saw greater confusion among men,' says Throckmorton, ' for often they change their opinions.'   They were engaged in ' continual preaching and common prayer.'   On July 21, they assured Elizabeth that Mary was forced to be Bothwell's wife

---

[1] Melville to Cecil, July 1.   Bain, ii. 343.
[2] Bain, ii. 350, 351.

' by fear and other unlawful means,' and that he kept
his former wife in his house, and would not have
allowed Mary to live with him for half a year.   Yet
Mary was so infatuated that, after her surrender, 'she
offered to give up realm and all, so she might enjoy
him.'   This formula, we shall see later, the Lords
placed thrice in Mary's mouth, first in a reported letter
of January, 1567 (never produced), next in a letter
of Kirkcaldy to Cecil (April 20), and now (July 21).[1]

At this time of Throckmorton's mission, Lethington
posed to him thus.   ' Do you not see that it does not
lie in my power to do that I would fainest do, which
is to save the Queen, my mistress, in estate, person,
and in honour ? '   He declared that the preachers,
the populace, and the chief nobles wished to take
Mary's life.[2]   Lethington thus drove his bargain with
Throckmorton.   ' If Elizabeth interferes,' he said in
sum, ' Mary dies, despite my poor efforts, and Elizabeth loses the Scottish Alliance.'   But Throckmorton
believed that Lethington really laboured to secure
Mary's life and honour.   His true object was to keep
her immured.   Randolph, as we saw, accuses him to
his face of advising Mary's execution, or assassination.
By his present course with Throckmorton he kept
Elizabeth's favour : he gave himself out as Mary's
friend.

The Lords at last made up their minds.   On
July 25, Lindsay was sent to Loch Leven to extort
Mary's abdication, consent to the coronation of her

[1] Bain, ii. 322, 360.   [2] *Ibid.* 358.

son, and appointment of Moray, or failing him, other nobles, to the Regency. ' If they cannot by fair means induce the Queen to their purpose, they mean to charge her with tyranny for breach of those statutes which were enacted in her absence. Secondly they mean to charge her with incontinence with Bothwell, and others. Thirdly, they mean to charge her with the murder of her husband, *whereof they say they have proof by the testimony of her own handwriting,* which they have recovered, as also by sufficient *witnesses.*' The witnesses were dropped. Probably they were ready to swear that Mary was at the murder in male costume, as in a legend of the Lennox Papers ! Lethington brought this news to Throckmorton between ten and eleven at night.[1] It was the friendly Lethington who told Throckmorton about the guilty Letters.

The Lords had, at last, decided to make use of the Letters attributed to Mary, and of the 'witnesses,' and by these, or other modes of coercion, they extorted her assent (valueless, so Throckmorton and Robert Melville let her know, because she was a prisoner) to their proposals.[2] Despite their know-

[1] Cal. For. Eliz. viii. 297, 298. Keith, ii. 694, 700.

[2] Already, on July 16, Mary had offered verbally, by Robert Melville, to the Lords, to make Moray Regent : or, failing him, to appoint a Council of Regency, Châtelherault, Huntly, Argyll, Atholl, Lennox, and, ' with much ado,' Morton, Moray, Mar, and Glencairn. But she would not abandon Bothwell, as she was pregnant. Throckmorton does not say that she now promised to sign an *abdication.* A letter of Mary's, to Bothwell's captain in Dunbar, was intercepted ' containing matter little to her advantage.' It never was produced by her prosecutors (Throckmorton, July 18. Bain, ii. 355, 356). Robert

ledge of the Letters, the Lords, in proclamations, continued to aver that Bothwell had ravished her by fear, force, and other unlawful means, the very means of coercing Mary which they themselves were employing.   The brutality, hypocrisy, and low vacillating cunning of the Lords, must not blind us to the fact that they certainly, since late in June, held new cards, genuine or packed.

It is undeniable that the first notices of the Letters, by de Silva, prove that the Lords, about the date assigned by Morton, did actually possess themselves of useful documents.   Their vacillations as to how and when they would play these cards are easily explained.   Their first care was to prejudice the Courts of France, Spain, and Elizabeth against Mary by circulating the tale of their discovery.   If they had published the papers at once, they might then have proceeded to try and to execute, perhaps (as the Highland seeress predicted) to *burn* Mary. The preachers urged them to severity, but Lethington and others were too politic to proceed to extremes, which might bring in Elizabeth and France as avengers.   But, if Mary was to be spared in life, to publish the Letters at once would ruin their value as an ' awe-bond.' They could only be used as a means of coercing Mary, while they were unknown to the world at large.   If the worst was known, Mary would face it boldly.   Only while the worst was not

Melville, visiting her, declined to carry such a letter to Bothwell.   See his examination, in Addit. MSS. British Museum,   3531, fol. 119 *et seq.*

generally known could the Letters be used to 'black-mail' her. Whether the Letters were, in fact, employed to extort Mary's abdication is uncertain. She was advised, as we said, by Throckmorton and Robert Melville, that her signature, while a captive, was legally invalid, so she signed the deeds of abdication, regency, and permission to crown her son. For the moment, till Moray arrived, and a Parliament was held, the Lords needed no more. Throckmorton believed that he had saved Mary's life : and Robert Melville plainly told Elizabeth so.[1]

Thus it is clear that the Lords held documents, genuine, or forged, or in part authentic, in part falsified. Their evasive use of the papers, their self-contradictions in their proclamations, do not disprove this fact. But were the documents those which they finally published ? This question, on which we may have new light to throw, demands a separate investigation.

[1] Bain, ii. 367.

X

THE CASKET LETTERS

II. A POSSIBLY FORGED LETTER

WERE the documents in the possession of the Lords, after June 21, those which they later exhibited before Elizabeth's Commissioners at Westminster (December, 1568)? Here we reach perhaps the most critical point in the whole inquiry. A Letter to Bothwell, attributed to Mary, was apparently in the hands .of the Lords (1567–1568), a Letter which was highly compromising, *but never was publicly produced*. We first hear of this Letter by a report of Moray to de Silva, repeated by de Silva to Philip of Spain (July, 1567).

Before going further we must examine Moray's probable sources of information as to Mary's correspondence. From April 7, to the beginning of July, he had been out of Scotland: first in England; later on the Continent. As early as May 8, Kirkcaldy desired Bedford to forward a letter to Moray, bidding him come to Normandy, in readiness to return, (and aid the Lords,) now banding against

Bothwell.[1] 'He will haste him after he has seen it.'
Moray did not 'haste him,' his hour had not come.
He was, however, in touch with his party. On
July 8, a fortnight after the discovery of the
Casket, Robert Melville, at 'Kernye' in Fife, sends
'Jhone a Forret' to Cecil. John is to go on to
Moray, and (Lethington adds, on July 9) a packet
of letters for Moray is to be forwarded 'with the
greatest diligence that may be.' Melville says, as to
'Jhone a Forret' (whom Cecil, in his endorsement,
calls 'Jhon of Forrest'), 'Credit the bearer, who
knows all occurrents.' Can 'Jhone a Forret' be a
cant punning name for John Wood, sometimes
called 'John a Wood,' by the English, a man whom
Cecil knew as Moray's secretary? John Wood was
a Fifeshire man, a son of Sir Andrew Wood of Largo,
and from Fife Melville was writing. Jhone a Forret
is, at all events, a bearer whom, as he 'knows all
occurents,' Cecil is to credit.[2] This Wood is the
very centre of the secret dealings of Mary's enemies,
of the Lords, and Lennox. Cecil, Elizabeth, and
Leicester are asked to 'credit' him, later, as Cecil
'credited' 'Jhone a Forret.'

Up to this date (July 8) when letters were sent
by the Lords to Moray, he was, or feigned to be,
friendly to his sister. On that day a messenger of
his, from France, was with Elizabeth, who told Cecil
that Moray was vexed by Mary's captivity in Loch
Leven, and that he would be 'her true servant in all

---

[1] Bain, ii. 328.　　　　　[2] *Ibd.* i. 346–34 8.

fortunes.' He was sending letters to Mary, which
the Lords were not to see.[1] His messenger was
Nicholas Elphinstone, who was not allowed to give
Mary his letters.[2] After receiving the letters sent to
him from Scotland on July 8, Moray turned his back
on his promises of service to Mary. But, before he
received these letters, Archbishop Beaton had told
Alava that Moray was his sister's mortal enemy and
by him mistrusted.[3] Moray's professions to Elizabeth
may have been a blind, but his letters for Mary's
private eye have a more genuine air.

Moray arrived in England on July 23.

About July 22, Mary's confessor, Roche Mameret,
a Dominican, had come to London. He was much
grieved, he said to de Silva, by Mary's marriage with
Bothwell, which, as he had told her, was illegal. ' He
swore to me solemnly that, till the question of the
marriage with Bothwell was raised, he never saw a
woman of greater virtue, courage, and uprightness.
. . .' Apparently he knew nothing of the guilty
loves, and the Exchequer House scandal. ' She swore
to him that she had contracted the marriage ' with the
object of settling religion by that means, though
Bothwell was so stout a Protestant that he had twice
married Catholic brides by Protestant rites ! ' As regarded the King's murder, her confessor has told me '
(de Silva) ' that she had no knowledge whatever of it.'
Now de Silva imparted this fact to Moray, when he

---

[1] Bain, ii. 346.   [2] *Ibid.* 354.   July 16.
[3] Alava to Philip, July 17   Teulet, v. 29.

visited London, as we saw, in the end of July, 1567, and after Moray had seen Elizabeth. He gave de Silva the impression that 'although he always returned to his desire to help the Queen, this is not altogether his intention.' Finally, Moray told de Silva 'something that he had not even told this Queen, although she had given him many remote hints upon the subject.' The secret was that Mary had been cognisant of Darnley's murder. 'This had been proved beyond doubt by a letter which the Queen had written to Bothwell, containing more than three double sheets (*pliegos*) of paper, written with her own hand and *signed* with her name; in which she says in substance that he is not to delay putting into execution that which he had been ordered (*tenia ordenado*), because her husband used such fair words to deceive her, and bring her to his will, that she might be moved by them if the other thing were not done quickly. She said that she herself would go and fetch him [Darnley], and would stop at a house on the road where she would try to give him a draught; but if this could not be done, she would put him in the house *where the explosion was arranged for the night upon which one of her servants was to be married.* He, Bothwell, was to try to get rid of his wife either by putting her away or poisoning her, since he knew that she, the Queen, had risked all for him, her honour, her kingdom, her wealth, *which she had in France,* and her God; contenting herself with his person alone. . . . . Moray said he had heard of this letter from a man who had read it. . . . '[1]

As to 'hearing of' this epistle, the reader may judge whether, when the Lords sent 'Jhone a Forret' (probably John Wood) to Moray, and also sent a packet of letters, they did not enclose copies of the Casket Letters as they then existed. Is it probable that they put Moray off with the mere hearsay of Jhone a Forret, who 'knows all occurrents'? If so, Jhone, and Moray, and de Silva, as we shall prove, had wonderfully good verbal memories, like Chicot when he carried in his head the Latin letter of Henri III. to Henri of Navarre.

Mr. Froude first quoted de Silva's report of Moray's report of this bloodthirsty letter of Mary's: and declared that Moray described accurately the long Glasgow Letter (Letter II.).[2] But Moray, as Mr. Hosack proved, described a letter totally and essentially different from Letter II. That epistle, unlike the one described by Moray, is *not* signed. We could not with certainty infer this from the want of signatures to our copies; their absence might be due to a common custom by which copyists did not add the writer's signature, when the letter was otherwise described. But Mary's defenders, Lesley and Blackwood, publicly complained of the absence of signatures, and were not answered. This

---

[1] De Silva, July 26, August 2. Spanish Calendar, i. 662, 665. I have occasionally preferred the Spanish text to Major Hume's translations. See also Hosack, i. 215, 216.

[2] Froude, iii. 118. 1866.

point is not very important, but in the actual Casket
Letter II. Mary does not say, as in Moray's account,
that there is danger of Darnley's 'bringing her round
to his will.' She says the reverse, 'The place will
hold,' and, therefore, she does not, as in Moray's
report, indicate the consequent need of hurry. She
does not say that ' she herself will go and fetch him ; '
she was there already : this must be an error of
reporting. She does not speak of 'giving him a
draught' in a house on the road. She says nothing
of a house where ' the explosion was arranged.' No
explosion had been arranged, though some of the
earlier indictments drawn up by Lennox for the
prosecution declare that this was the case : ' The
place was already prepared with [undermining and]
trains of powder therein.' [1] This, however, was the
early theory, later abandoned, and it occurs in a
Lennox document which contains a letter of Darnley
to the Queen, written three days before his death.
The Casket Letter II. says nothing about poisoning or
divorcing Lady Bothwell, nor much, in detail, about
Mary's abandonment of her God, her wealth *in
France*, and her realm, for her lover. On the other
hand she regards God as on her side. In short, the
letter described by Moray to de Silva agrees in no one
point with any of the Letters later produced and
published : except in certain points provocative of
suspicion. Mr. Froude thought that it did harmonise, but the opinion is untenable.

[1] Lennox MSS.

De Silva's account, however, is only at third hand. He merely reports what Moray told him that *he* had heard, from 'a man who had read the letter.' We might therefore argue that the whole reference is to the long Casket Letter II., but is distorted out of all knowledge by passing through three mouths. This natural theory is no longer tenable.

In the Lennox Papers the writer, Lennox, breaks off in his account of Darnley's murder to say, 'And before we proceed any further, I cannot omit to declare and call to remembrance her Letter written to Bothwell from Glasgow before her departure thence, together with such cruel and strange words " unto " him, which he her husband should have better considered and marked, but that " the " hope " he " had to win her " love " now did blind him ; together that it lieth not in the power of man to prevent that which the suffering will of God determineth. The contents of her letter to the said Bothwell was to let him understand that, although the flattering and sweet words of him with whom she was then presently, the King her husband, has almost overcome her, yet the remembering the great affection which she bore unto him [Bothwell] there should no such sweet baits dissuade her, or cool her said affection from him, but would continue therein, yea though she should thereby abandon her God, put in adventure the loss of her dowry in France, " hazard " such titles as she had to the crown of England, as heir apparent thereof, and also the crown of the realm; wishing him then present in her arms therefore bid him go forward with all things, according to their enterprize, and that the place and everything might be finished as they had devised, against her coming to Edinburgh, which should be shortly. And for the time of execution thereof she thought it best to be the time of Bastian's marriage, which indeed was the night of the King her husband's murder. She wrote also in her letter that the said Bothwell should " in no wise fail " in the meantime to dispatch his wife, and to give her the drink as they had devised before.' [1]

Except as regards the draught to be given to Darnley, in a house by the way, and Mary's promise ' to go herself and fetch him,' this report of the letter closely tallies, not with Casket Letter II., but with what the man who had read it told Moray, and with what Moray told de Silva. Did there exist, then, such a compromising letter accepted by Moray's informant, the ' man who read the letter,' and recorded by Lennox in a document containing copy of a letter from Darnley to himself?

This appears a natural inference, but it is suggested to me that the brief reports by Moray and Lennox are ' after all not so very different ' from Letter II. 'If we postulate a Scots translation' (used by Moray and Lennox) ' *with the allusions explained by a hostile hand in the margin*, then those who professed

---

[1] The words within inverted commas are autograph additions by Lennox himself.

to give a summary of its "more than three double pages" in half a dozen lines' (there are thirty-seven lines of Lennox's version in my hand, and Mary wrote large) 'would easily take the striking points, not from the Letter, though it was before their eyes, but from the explanations; which were, of course, much more impressive than that extraordinary congeries of inconsequences,' our Letter II.

To this we reply that, in Moray's and Lennox's versions, we have expansions and additions to the materials of Letter II. All the tale about poisoning Darnley in a house on the way is not a hostile 'explanation,' but an addition. All the matter about poisoning or divorcing Lady Bothwell is not an explanation, but an addition. Marginal notes are brief summaries, but if Moray and Lennox quoted marginal notes, these were so expansive that they may have been longer than the Letter itself.

Take the case of what Mary, as described in the Letter, is to forfeit for Bothwell's sake. Lennox is in his catalogue of these goods more copious than Moray : and Letter II., in place of these catalogues, merely says 'honour, conscience, hazard, nor greatness.' Could a marginal annotator expand this into the talk about God, her French dowry, her various titles and pretensions? Marginal notes always abbreviate : Moray and Lennox expand; and they clearly, to my mind, cite a common text. Lennox has in his autograph corrected this passage and others.

Moray's and Lennox's statements about the poisoning, about the divorce or poisoning for Lady Bothwell, about Bastian (whose marriage Letter II. mentions as a proof of Darnley's knowledge of Mary's affairs), about the 'finishing and preparing of the place' (Kirk o' Field), about ' the house on the way,'—can all these be taken from marginal glosses, containing mere gossip certainly erroneous? If so, never did men display greater stupidity than Lennox and Moray. Where it was important to quote a letter, both (according to the theory which has been suggested) neglect the Letter and cite, not marginal abbreviations, but marginal *scholia* containing mere tattle. If Moray truly said that he had only ' heard of the Letter from a " man who had read it," ' is it conceivable that the man merely cited the marginal glosses to Moray, while Lennox also selected almost nothing but the same glosses? But, of all impossibilities, the greatest is that the author of the glosses expanded ' honour, conscience, hazard, and greatness ' (as in Letter II.) into the catalogue beginning with God, in which Moray and Lennox abound. ' Honour, conscience, hazard, and greatness,' explain themselves. They need no such long elaborate explanation as the supposed scholiast adds on the margin. Where we do find such contemporary marginal notes, as on the Lennox manuscript copy of the Casket Sonnets, they are brief and simply explain allusions. Thus Sonnet IV. has, in the Lennox MSS.,

' un fascheux sot qu'elle aymoit cherement : '

elle being Lady Bothwell.

The marginal note is 'This is written of the Lord of Boyn, who was alleged to be the first lover of the Earl of Bothwell's wife.' [1]   We must remember that Lennox was preparing a formal indictment, when he reported the same Letter as Moray talked of to de Silva; and that, when the Casket Letters were produced, his discrepancies from Letter II. might perhaps be noticed even in an uncritical age. He would not, therefore, quote the *scholia* and neglect the Letter.

The passage about Lady Bothwell's poison or divorce is perhaps mirrored in, or perhaps originated, the legend that she was offered a writing of divorce to sign, with a bowl of poison to drink if she refused. In fact, she received a valuable consideration in land, which she held for some forty years, as Countess of Sutherland.[2]   Suppose that the annotator recorded this gossip about the poisoning of Lady Bothwell on the margin. Could a man like Moray be so foolish as to recite it *viva voce* as part of the text of a letter ?

Once more, the hypothetical marginal notes of explanation explain nothing—to Moray and Lennox. They knew from the first about Bastian's marriage, and the explosion. The passage about poisoning Darnley ' in a house by the way ' does not explain, but contradicts, the passage in Letter II., where Mary

----

[1] Ogilvy of Boyne, who married his old love, Lady Bothwell, after the death of her second husband, the Earl of Sutherland. See pp. 26, 27, *supra*.

[2] *A Lost Chapter in the History of Mary Stuart.*

does not say that she is poisoning Darnley, but suggests that Bothwell should find 'a more secret way by medicine,' later. Lennox and Moray, again, of all people, did not need to be told, by an annotator, what Mary's possessions and pretensions were. Finally, the lines about poisoning or divorcing Lady Bothwell are not a note explanatory of anything that occurs in Letter II., nor even an annotator's added piece of information; for Lennox cites them directly from the Letter before him, '*She wrote also in her letter*, that the said Bothwell should in no wise fail to give his wife the drink as they had devised'— The Mixture as Before! Thus there seems no basis for the ingenious theory of *marginalia*, supposed to have been cited, instead of the Letter, by Lennox and Moray.

It has again been suggested to me, by a well-known student of the problem of the Casket Letters, that Moray and Lennox are both reporting mere gossip, reverberated rumours, in their descriptions of the mysterious Letter. It is hinted that Lennox heard of the Letters, perhaps from Buchanan, before Lennox left Scotland. In that case Lennox heard of the Letters just two months before they were discovered. He left Scotland on April 23, the Casket was opened on June 21. Buchanan certainly was not Moray's informant : Jhone a Forret carried the news.

As to the idea that Moray and Lennox both report a fortuitous congeries of atoms of gossip,

Moray and Lennox both (1) begin their description with Mary's warning that Darnley's flatteries had almost overcome her.

(2) Both speak to the desirability of speedy performance, but Lennox does not, like Moray, assign this need to the danger of Mary's being won over.

(3) Moray does, and Lennox does not, say that Mary 'will go and fetch' Darnley, which cannot have been part of a letter purporting to be written at Glasgow.

(4) Moray does, and Lennox does not, speak of poisoning Darnley on the road. From a letter of three sheets no two persons will select absolutely the same details.

(5) Moray and Lennox both give the same catalogue, Lennox at more length, of all that Mary sacrifices for Bothwell.

(6) Both Moray and Lennox make Mary talk of the house where the explosion is already arranged : at least Lennox talks of its being 'prepared,' which may merely mean made inhabitable.

(7) Both make her say that the night of Bastian's marriage will be a good opportunity.

(8) Both make Mary advise Bothwell to poison his wife, Moray adding the alternative that he may divorce her.

(9) Lennox does, and Moray does not, mention the phrase 'wishing him then in her arms,' which occurs in Casket Letter II. The fact does not strengthen the case for the authenticity of Letter II.

As to order of sequence in these nine items, they run,

1.	Moray	1.	. .	Lennox	1.
2.	Moray	2.	. .	Lennox	2.
3.	Moray	3. (an error)		Lennox	0.
4.	Moray	4.	. .	Lennox	0.
5.	Moray	8. =	. .	= Lennox	5.
6.	Moray	6.	. .	Lennox	6.
7.	Moray	7.	. .	Lennox	7.
8.	Moray	5. =	. .	= Lennox	8.
9.	Moray	0.	. .	Lennox	9.

Thus, in four out of nine items (Moray 3 being a mere error in reporting), the sequence in Moray's description is the same as the sequence in that of Lennox. In one item Moray gives a fact not in Lennox. In one Lennox gives a fact not in Moray. In the remaining items, Moray and Lennox give the same facts, but that which is fifth in order with Lennox is eighth in order with Moray.

Mathematicians may compute whether these coincidences are due to a mere fortuitous concurrence of atoms of gossip, possessing a common basis in the long Glasgow Letter II., and in the facts of the murder, and accidentally shaken into the same form, and almost the same sequence, in the minds of two different men, *at two different times.*

My faith in fortuitous coincidence is not so strong. I believe that the report of Lennox and the report of Moray, both of them false, as far as regards Letter II., or any letter ever produced, have a common source in a letter at one time held by the Lords, but dropped by them.

The sceptic, however, will doubtless argue, 'We do not know the date of this discourse, in which Lennox describes a letter to very much the same effect as Moray does. May not Lennox have met Moray, in or near London, when Moray was there in July, 1567 ? May not Moray have told Lennox what he told de Silva, and even more copiously? What he told was (by his account) mere third-hand gossip, but perhaps Lennox received it from him as gospel, and sat down at once, and elaborated a long "discourse," in which he recorded as fact Moray's tattle. By this means de Silva and Lennox would offer practically identical accounts of the long letter ; accounts which, indeed, correspond to no known Casket Letter, but err merely because Moray's information was hearsay, casual, and unevidential.' 'Why,' my inquirer goes on, 'do you speak of Lennox and Moray giving their descriptions of the Letter *at two different times* ?'

The answer to the last question may partly be put in the form of another question. Why should Lennox be making a long indictment, of seven folio pages, against Mary, in July, 1567, when Moray was passing through town on his way from France to Scotland ? Mary was then a prisoner in Loch Leven. Lennox, though in poverty, was, on July 16, 1567, accepted as a Joint-Regent by Mary, if Moray did not become Regent, alone.[1] On July 29, 1567, James VI. was crowned, a yearling King, and it was

[1] Throckmorton to Elizabeth, July 18. Bain, ii. 355.

decided that if Moray, who had not yet arrived in
Scotland, refused to be Regent alone, Lennox should
be joined with him and others on a Commission of
Regency.[1] Moray, of course, did not refuse power,
nor did Lennox go to Scotland. But, even if Lennox
had really been made a co-Regent when Moray held
his conversation about the Letter with de Silva, he
would have had, at that moment, no need to draw up
his 'discourse' against Mary. The Lords had
subdued her, had extorted her abdication, and did
not proceed to accuse their prisoner. But, even if
they had meant to try her at this time, that would
not explain Lennox's supposed conduct in then
drawing up against her an indictment, including the
gossip about her Letter, which (on the hypothesis)
he had, at that hour, obtained from Moray, in
London. This can easily be proved: thus. The
document in which Lennox describes the Letter was
never meant for a *Scottish* court of justice. It is
carefully made out *in English*, by an English scribe,
and is elaborately corrected in Lennox's hand, as a
man corrects a proof-sheet. Consequently, this
early 'discourse' of Lennox's, with its description
of the murderous letter, never produced, was
meant, not for a Scottish, but for an English
Court, or meeting of Commissioners. None such
could be held while Mary was a prisoner in Scotland: and no English indictment could then be
made by Lennox. He must have expected the

---

[1] Throckmorton to Elizabeth, July 31, 1567. Bain, ii. 370.

letter he quoted to be produced: which never was done.

Therefore Lennox did not weave this discourse, and describe the mysterious Letter, while Moray was giving de Silva a similar description, at London, in July, 1567. Not till Mary fled into England, nearly a year later, May 15, 1568, not till it was determined to hold an inquiry in England (about June 30, 1568), could Lennox construct an indictment in English, to go before English Commissioners. Consequently his description of the letter was not written at the same time (July, 1567) as Moray described the epistle to de Silva. The exact date when Lennox drew up his first Indictment, including his description of the Letter described by Moray, is unknown. But it contains curious examples of 'the sayings and reports' of Mary's own *suite*, as to words spoken by her in their own ears. Therefore it would seem to have been written *after* June 11, 1568, when Lennox wrote to Scotland, asking his chief clansmen to collect 'the sayings of her servants and their reports.'[1] Again, as late as August 25, 1568, Lennox had not yet received permission from Elizabeth to go to the meeting of the Commission of Inquiry which it was then intended to hold at Richmond. Elizabeth 'flatly denied him,' though later she assented.[2] Thus Lennox's composition of this indictment with its account of the mysterious

[1] *Maitland Miscellany*, vol. iv. part i. p. 119.
[2] Teulet, ii. 255, 256.

epistle, may be provisionally dated between, say, July 1 (when he might have got a letter of information from Scotland in answer to his request for information) and August 25, 1568.

But an opponent, anxious to make the date of Lennox's knowledge of the poisonous letter seem early, may say, 'Probably Lennox, in July, 1567, when Moray was in London, met him. Probably Moray told Lennox what he would not tell Elizabeth. Probably Lennox then wrote down Moray's second-hand hearsay gossip about the letter, kept it, and, later, in 1568, copied it into his discourse to go before English Commissioners. Moray is still his only source, and Moray's source was hearsay gossip. We have, so far, no proof that the letter described by Lennox and Moray ever existed.

To this I reply that we know nothing of communication between Lennox and Moray in July, 1567, but we do know when Lennox began to collect evidence for the 'discourse,' in which this mysterious letter is cited. In June, 1568, Mary complained to Elizabeth that Lady Lennox was hounding Lennox on to prosecute her Mary had somehow got hold of letters of Wood and of Lady Lennox.[1] We also know that, when Lennox first took up his task, he had, in all probability, already seen Scots translations of the Casket Letters as they then existed. We know too that he had now an adviser who should not have allowed him to make a damaging error in his indict-

---

[1] Labanoff ij. 106.

ment, such as quoting a non-existent letter. This adviser was John Wood. After Mary's flight into England (May 16, 1567) Moray had sent, on May 21, his agent, John Wood ('Jhone a Forret'?), to London, where he was dealing with Cecil on June 5, 1568.[1] Now Wood carried with him Scots translations of the Casket Letters, as they then existed. This is certain, for, on June 22, Moray sent to the English Council the information that Wood held these translations, and Moray made the request that the 'judges' in the case might see the Scots versions, and say whether, if the French originals corresponded, they would be reckoned adequate proof of Mary's guilt.[2]

The judges, that is the Commissioners who sat at York in October, apparently did not see Wood's copies : their horrified amazement on seeing them later, at York, is evidence to that. But Lennox, perhaps, did see the Scots versions in Wood's hands. On June 11, from Chiswick, as has been said, Lennox wrote three letters to Scotland ; one to Moray, one to his retainers, the Lairds of Houstoun and Minto, men of his own clan; and one to other retainers, Thomas Crawford, Robert Cunningham, and Stewart of Periven. To Moray he said that of evidence against Mary 'there is sufficiency in her own hand-writ, *by the faith of her letters*, to condemn her.' But he also wanted to collect extraneous evidence, in Scotland.

---

[1] Bain, ii. 423.   [2] *Ibid.* 441, 442.

Here Lennox writes as one who has seen, or been told the contents of, the Casket Letters on which he remarks. And well might he have seen them, for his three despatches of June 11 are 'all written on the same sheets, *and in the same hand*,' as two letters written and sent, on the following day, by John Wood, from Greenwich, to Moray and Lethington. Thus Wood, or his secretary, wrote out all five epistles.[1] Consequently Wood, who had translations of the Casket Letters, was then with Lennox, and was likely to be now and then with him, till the Conference at York in October. On October 3, just before the Conference at York, Lady Lennox tells Cecil that she means to speak to Mr. John Wood, if he is at Court, for he knows who the murderers are.[2] And Wood carried to Lennox, at York, Lady Lennox's despatches.[3] Being allied with Wood, as the Chiswick and Greenwich letters of June 11 prove, and writing to Wood's master, Moray, about Mary's Casket Letters, it is hardly probable that Lennox had not been shown by Wood the Scots versions of the Casket Letters, then in Wood's custody. And when, about this date or later, Lennox composed the long indictment against Mary, and quoted the letter already cited by Moray, it is hardly credible that he described the long poisonous document from mere

---

[1] I do not know where the originals of these five letters now are. They were among the Hamilton Papers, having probably been intercepted by the Hamiltons before they reached Moray, Lethington, Crawford, and the others.

[2] Bain, ii. 514.   [3] *Ibid.* 523, 524.

hearsay, caught from Moray in the previous year.   It is at least as likely, if not much more so, that his description of the long letter was derived from a translation of the letter itself, as it then existed in the hands of Wood.   Is it probable that Wood (who was known to have in his custody the Letters to which Lennox refers, in his epistle to Moray of June 11) could withhold them from the father of the murdered Darnley, a noble who had been selected by the Lords as a co-Regent with Moray, and who was, like himself, a correspondent of Moray and an eager prosecutor of the Queen?   If then Wood did in June, 1568, show to Lennox the Casket Letters as they then existed, when Lennox presently described the long murderous letter, he described what he had seen, namely a *pièce de conviction* which was finally suppressed.   And that it was later than his meeting with Wood, on June 11, 1568, that Lennox prepared his elaborate discourse, is obvious, for what reason had he to compose an indictment before, in June or later, it became clear that Mary's case would be tried in England?

Not till June 8 did Elizabeth send to Moray, bidding him 'impart to her plainly all that which shall be meet to inform her of the truth for their defence in such weighty crimes' as their rebellion against Mary.[1]   Mary, Elizabeth declared, 'is content to commit the ordering of our case to her,' and Moray has consented, through Wood, 'to declare

---

[1] Cal. For. Eliz. viii. 478, 479.   Bain, ii. 426, 427.

to us your whole doings.' Elizabeth therefore asks
for Moray's evidence against Mary. From that date,
June 8, the negotiations for some kind of trial of
Mary went on till October, 1568. In that period,
Lennox must have written the discourse in which he
cites the false letter, and in that period he had the
aid of Wood, in whose hands the Scots translations
were.

The inference that Lennox borrowed his description of a long poisonous epistle from a forged letter,
a very long letter, then in Wood's custody with
the rest, and occupying the place later taken by
Letter II., is natural, and not illogical, but rather
is in congruence with the relations between Wood
and Lennox. The letter described had points in
common with Letter II. (as when Mary wishes
Bothwell in her arms) and with the Casket Sonnets.
It certainly was not a genuine document, and
certainly raises a strong presumption that fraud
was being attempted by Mary's enemies. But we
need not, for that reason, infer that Letter II. is a
forgery. It may be genuine, and may have been in
the hands of Mary's enemies. Yet they may have
tried to improve upon it and make it more explicit,
putting forward to that end the epistle quoted by
Lennox and Moray. If so they later fell back on
Letter II , possibly garbled it, and suppressed their
first version.

Lennox, as we shall see, did not rest on his earlier
form of the indictment, with its description of Mary's

letter about poisoning Darnley and Lady Bothwell, which he originally drew up, say in July–August, 1568. In his letters from Chiswick he asked for all sorts of evidence from Scotland. He got it, and, then, dropping his first indictment (which contained only parts of such matter), he composed a second. That second document was perhaps still unfinished, or imperfect, just before the meeting of Commissioners at York (October 6, 1568).

That the second indictment, about October 1, 1568, was still in the making, I at first inferred from the following passage which occurs in a set of pieces of evidence collected for Lennox, but without date. ' Ferder your h. sall have advertisement of, as I can find, but it is gude that this mater ' (Lennox's construction of a new indictment) ' be not endit quile ' (until) 'your h. *may haif copie of the letter*, quhilk I sall haif at *York*, so sone as I may haif a traist berar ' (a trusty bearer to carry the copy to Lennox). So I read the letter, but Father Pollen, no doubt correctly, in place of ' York ' reads ' your h. ; ' that is, ' Your Honour,' a common phrase. The date yielded by ' York ' therefore vanishes. We can, therefore, only infer that this correspondent, writing not to Lennox, it appears, but to some one, Wood perhaps, engaged in getting up the case, while sending him information for his indictment, advises that it be not finished till receipt of a copy of a certain letter, which is to be sent by a trusty bearer. It may be our Letter II. We can have no certainty. In his new indictment, substi-

tuted for his former discourse, Letter II. is the only
one to which Lennox makes distinct allusion.

He now omits the useful citations of the mysterious
epistle which he had previously used; and, instead,
quotes Letter II. The old passages cited were more
than good enough for Lennox's purpose, but they
are no longer employed by him. There can be no
doubt as to which of his discourses is the earlier and
which the later. That containing the report of Mary's
letter which agrees with Moray's report to de Silva,
lacks the numerous details about Hiegait, Crawford,
Mary's taunts to Darnley, their quarrel at Stirling, and
so forth, and we know that, on June 11, 1568, Lennox
had sent to Scotland asking for all these particulars.
They all duly appear in the second discourse which
contains reference to Letter II. They are all absent
from the discourse which contains the letter about
the scheme for poisoning Darnley and Lady Bothwell.
Therefore that indictment is the earlier: written on
evidence of Darnley's servants, and from 'the sayings
and reports' of Mary's servants.

For what reason should Lennox drop the citations
from the poisonous letter, which he quoted in his
earlier discourse, if such a letter was to be produced
by the Lords? The words were of high value to
his argument. But drop them he did in his later
discourse, and, in place of them, quoted much less
telling lines from Letter II.

All this is explained, if Letter II. was a revised and
less explicit edition of the letter first reported on by

Lennox; or if the letter first quoted was an improved and more vigorous version of a genuine Letter II. Mr. Hosack, when he had only Moray's account of the mysterious letter before him, considered it fatal to the authenticity of Letter II., which he thought a cleverly watered-down version of the mysterious letter, and, like it, a forgery. Mr. Hosack's theory is reinforced by Lennox's longer account of the mysterious epistle. But he overlooked the possibility that Letter II. may not be a diluted copy of the forgery, but a genuine original on which the forgery was based. It may be asked, if the Letter touched on by Lennox and Moray was a forged letter, why was it dropped, and why was another substituted before the meeting of Commissioners at York? As we have only brief condensed reports of the Letter which never was produced, our answer must be incomplete. But Moray's description of the document speaks of ' the house where the explosion was arranged,' before Mary left Edinburgh for Glasgow. Now, according to one confession, taken after the finding of the Casket, namely on December 8, 1567, the explosion was not dreamed of ' till within two days before the murder.'[1] Therefore Mary could not, on reflection, be made to write that the gunpowder plot was arranged before January 21, 1567, for that contradicted the confession, and the confession was put in as evidence.

The proceedings of Mary's accusers, therefore,

---

[1] Bowton's confession. Laing, ii. 256, 257.

must have taken the following line. First, having
certainly got hold of a silver casket of Mary's,
about June 21, 1567, they either added a forgery,
or, perhaps, interpolated, as her Lords said, ' the
most principal and substantious' clauses. They
probably gave copies to du Croc : and they told
Throckmorton that they had not only letters, but
witnesses of Mary's guilt. These witnesses doubtless saw Mary at the murder ' in male apparel,' as
Lennox says some declared that she was. But
these witnesses were never produced. They sent,
probably, by ' Jhone a Forret,' copies to Moray, one
of which, the mysterious letter, in July, 1567, he
partly described to de Silva. In June, 1568, they
sent translated copies into England with Wood.
These were not seen by Sussex, Norfolk, and Sadleyr
(the men who, later, sat as Commissioners at York),
but Wood showed them, or read parts of them, to
Lennox, who cited portions of the mysterious Letter
in his first indictment. But, when Moray, Morton,
Lethington, and the other Commissioners of the
Lords were bound for the Inquiry at York, they
looked over their hand of cards, re-examined their
evidence. They found that the ' long letter' cited
by Moray and Lennox contradicted the confession
of Bowton, and was altogether too large and mythical.
They therefore manufactured a subtler new edition,
or fell back upon a genuine Letter II. If so, they
would warn Lennox, or some one with Lennox, in
framing his new indictment, to wait for their final

choice as to this letter. He did wait, received a copy of it, dropped the first edition of the letter, and interwove the second edition, which may be partly genuine, with his ' discourse.'

This is, at least, a coherent hypothesis. There is, however, another possible hypothesis: admirers of the Regent Moray may declare. Though capable of using his sister's accomplices to accuse his sister, ' the noble and stainless Moray ' was not capable of employing a forged document. On returning to Scotland he found that, in addition to the falsified Letter, there existed the genuine Letter II., really by Mary. Like a conscientious man, he insisted that the falsified Letter should be suppressed, and Letter II. produced.

This amiable theory may be correct. It is ruined, however, if we are right in holding that, when Moray sent Wood into England with Scots versions of the Letters (May, 1568), he included among these a copy of the falsified Letter, which was therefore cited by Lennox.

There is another point of suspicion, suggested by the Lennox Papers. In Glasgow Letter II., Mary, writing late at night, is made to say, ' I cannot sleep as thay do, and as I wald desyre, *that is in zour armes*, my deir lufe.' In the Lennox account of the letter quoted by Moray to de Silva, she ' *wishes him then present in her arms.*' In the Lennox Paper she speaks of Darnley's ' sweet baits,' ' *flattering* and sweet words,' which have ' almost overcome her.' In the

English text of Letter II., Darnley ' used so many kinds
of *flatteries* so coldly and wisely as you would marvel
at.'   His speeches ' would make me but to have pity
on him.'   Finally, in the Lennox version of the unproduced Letter, Mary represents herself as ready to
' abandon her God, put in adventure the loss of her
dowry in France, hazard such titles as she had to the
crown of England, as heir apparent thereof, and also
to the crown of the realm.'   Nothing of this detailed
kind occurs, we have seen, in the Letters, as produced.
Similar sentiments are found, however, in the first and
second Casket Sonnets. ' Is he not in possession of my
body, of my heart which recoils neither from pain,
nor dishonour, nor uncertainty of life, nor offence of
kindred, nor worse woe ?   For him I esteem all my
friends less than nothing. . . . I have hazarded for
him name and conscience ; for him I desire to
renounce the world . . . . in his hands and in his
power I place my son ' (which she did not do), ' my
honour, my life, my realm, my subjects, my own
subject soul.'

It is certainly open, then, to a defender of Mary
to argue that the Letters and Sonnets, as produced
and published, show traces of the ideas and expressions employed in the letter described by Moray,
and by Lennox.   Now that letter, certainly, was
never written by Mary.   It had to be dropped,
for it was inconsistent with a statement as to the
murder put forward by the prosecution ; Bowton's
examination.

In short, the letter cited by Moray, and by Lennox, the long letter from Glasgow, looks like a sketch, later modified, for Letter II., or a forgery based on Letter II., and demonstrates that forgeries were, at some period, being attempted. As the Glasgow Letter (II.), actually produced, also contains (see 'The Internal Evidence') the highly suspicious passage tallying verbally with Crawford's deposition, there is no exaggeration in saying that the document would now carry little weight with a jury. Against all this we must not omit to set the failure to discredit the Letters, when published later, by producing the contemporary copies reported by de Silva to be in the hands of La Forest, or du Croc, as early as July, 1567. But the French Government (if ever it had the copies) was not, as we have said, when Buchanan's 'Detection' was thrust on the courtiers, either certain to compare La Forest's copies and the published Letters critically, or to raise a question over discrepancies, if they existed. In any case neither Charles IX., nor La Mothe Fénelon, in 1571, wrote a word to suggest that they thought the Casket Papers an imposture.

XI

THE LETTERS AT THE CONFERENCE OF YORK

IN tracing the history of the mysterious letter cited by Moray in July, 1567, and by Lennox about July, 1568, we have been obliged to diverge from the chronological order of events. We must return to what occurred publicly, as regards the Letters, after Throckmorton was told of their existence, by Lethington in Scotland in July, 1567. Till May, 1568, Mary remained a prisoner in Loch Leven. For some time after July, 1567, we hear nothing more of the Letters. Elizabeth (August 29) bade Throckmorton tell Mary's party, the Hamiltons, that 'she well allows their proceedings as far as they concern the relief of the Queen.' On August 30, Moray asked Cecil to move Elizabeth 'to continue in her good will of him and his proceedings!'[1] Elizabeth, then, was of both parties: but rather more inclined to that of Mary, despite Throckmorton's report as to Mary's Letters. They are next alluded to by Drury, writing from Berwick on November 29, 1567. 'The writings which comprehended the names and consents

[1] Cal. For. Eliz. viii. 331.

of the chief for the murdering of the King is turned into ashes, the same not unknown to the Queen (Mary) and the same which concerns her part kept to be shown.'[1]

On December 4, the Lords of the Privy Council, 'and other barons and men of judgement,' met in Edinburgh. They were mainly members of the Protestant Left.[2] Their Declaration (to be reported presently) was the result, they tell us, of several days of reasoning and debate. Nor is it surprising that they found themselves in a delicate posture. Some of them had been in the conspiracy; others had signed the request to Bothwell that he would marry the Queen, and had solemnly vowed to defend his quarrel, and maintain his innocence. Yet if they would gain a paper and Parliamentary security for their lives and estates (subject to be attainted and forfeited if ever Mary or her son came to power, and wished to avenge Darnley's murder and the Queen's imprisonment), they must prove that, in imprisoning Mary, they had acted lawfully. This they demonstrated, though ' most loth to do so,' by asking Parliament to approve of all their doings since Darnley's death (which included their promise to defend Bothwell, and their advice to Mary to marry him). And Parliament was

---

[1] Cal. For. Eliz. viii. 363.

[2] Moray, Morton, Glencairn, Errol, Buchan, Home, 'Ruthven, Semple, Glamis, Lindsay, Gray, Graham, Ochiltree (Knox's father-in-law), Innermeith, the treacherous Bishop of Orkney, Sir James Balfour (deeply involved in the murder), Makgill, Lethington, Erskine of Dun, Wishart of Pitarro, Kirkcaldy of Grange, and others of less note.

to approve, because their hostile acts 'was in the said
Queen's own default, in as far as by divers her
private letters, written and subscribed with her own
hand, and sent by her to James, Earl Bothwell, chief
executor of the said horrible murder, as well before
the committing thereof as thereafter, and by her
ungodly and dishonourable proceeding in a private
marriage with him ; . . . it is most certain that she
was privy, art and part, and of the actual device and
deed of the forementioned murder, . . . and therefore justly deserves whatsoever has been attempted
or shall be used toward her for the said cause. . . .'

From the first, it seems, ' all men in their hearts
were fully persuaded of the authors' of the crime.
Bothwell, to be sure, had been acquitted, both
publicly and privately, by his peers and allies.
Moray had invited an English envoy to meet him, at
a dinner where all the other guests were murderers.
People, however, only ' awaited until God should move
the hearts of some to enter in the quarrel of avenging
the same '—which they did by letting Bothwell go
free, and entrapping Mary ! The godly assemblage
then explains how ' God moved the hearts of some.'
The nobles were ' in just fear ' of being ' handled '
like Darnley, ' perceiving the Queen so thrall and
bloody ' (*sic :* probably a miswriting for ' blindly ')
' affectionate to the private appetite of that tyrant,'
Bothwell.

The Council thus gave the lie to their own repeated
averments, that Bothwell caused Mary to wed him by

fear and force. Now she is gracefully spoken of as
'bloody affectionate.'

It will be observed that they here describe Mary's
Letters as 'signed' by herself. The Casket Letters
(in our copies) are unsigned. The originals may
have been signed, they were reported to La Forest to
be signed as late as December, 1568.

On December 15, a Parliament met in Edinburgh.
According to Nau, Mary's secretary, inspired by her,
she had already written from prison a long letter to
Moray. 'She demanded permission to be heard in
this Parliament, either in person or by deputy, thereby to answer the false calumnies which had been
published about her since her imprisonment.' Mary
offered to lay down her crown' ' of free will,' and to
'submit to all the rigour of the laws' which she
desired to be enforced against Darnley's murderers.
None should be condemned unheard. If not heard,
she protested against all the proceedings of the
Parliament.[1]

This may be true: this was Mary's very attitude
when accused at Westminster. Mary made the same
assertion as to this demand of hers to be heard, in her
'Appeal to Christian Princes,' in June, 1568.[2] Not only
had she demanded leave to be present, and act as her
own advocate, but Atholl and Tullibardine, she said,
had admitted the justice of her claim—and just it was.
But neither then, nor at Westminster in December,
1568, was Mary allowed to appear and defend her-

[1] Nau, pp. 71-73.   [2] Teulet, ii. 247.

self. She knew too much, could have proved the guilt of some of her accusers, and would have broken up their party. A Scots Parliament always voted with the dominant faction. The Parliament passed an Act in the sense of the resolution of the Council and assessors. The Letters, however, are now described, in this Act, not as 'signed' or 'subscribed,' but as 'written wholly with her own hand.'[1] No valuable inference can be drawn from the discrepancy.

Nau says not a word about the Letters, but avers that Herries protested that Mary might not have signed her abdication by free will: her signature might even have been forged. He asked leave, with others, to visit her at Loch Leven, but this was refused. 'Following his example, many of the Lords refused to sign the Acts of this Parliament.'[2] It appears that the Letters really were 'produced' in this Parliament, for Mary's Lords say so in their Declaration of September 12, 1568, just before the Commissioners met at York They add that 'there is in no place' (of 'her Majesty's writing') 'mention made, by which her highness might be convict, albeit it were her own handwriting, as it is not.' The Lords add, 'and also the same' (Mary's 'writing') 'is devysit by themselves in some principal and substantious clauses.'[3] This appears to mean that, while the

---

[1] Act in Henderson, 177–185.   [2] Nau, 74, 75.

[3] Goodall, ii. 361. B. M. Titus, c. 12, fol. 157 (*olim* 175). 'And gif it beis allegit, yat hir ma^{tz} wretting producit in pliamēt, sould proiff hir g, culpable. It maybe ansrit yat yāre is na plane mentione maid in it. be ye quhilk hir hienes may be convict Albeit it wer hir awin hand

R

handwriting of the Letters is not Mary's, parts of the substance were really hers, ' principal and sub-stantious clauses ' [1] being introduced by the accusers.

This theory is upheld by Gerdes, and Dr. Sepp, with his hypothesis that the Casket Letters consist of a Diary of Mary's, mingled with letters of Darnley's, and interpolated with ' substantious clauses.' [2]   When the originals were produced in England, none of Mary's party were present to compare them with the Letters shown in the Scottish Parliament.

The Letters are not remarked on again till after Mary's escape from Loch Leven, and flight into England (May 16, 1568), when Moray writes about them on June 22, 1568.

Wood, in May, as we saw, had carried with him into England copies of the Letters ' translated into our language : ' so says Moray, in a letter already cited of June 22, to Elizabeth.   Moray understood that Elizabeth intended to ' take trial ' of Mary's case, ' with great ceremony and solemnities.'   He is ' most loth ' to accuse Mary, though, privately or publicly, his party had done so incessantly, for a whole year. Now he asks that those who are to judge the case shall read the Scots translations of the Letters in Wood's possession (why in Scots, not in the original French ?), and shall say whether, if the French originals coincide, the evidence will be deemed sufficient.[3]

---

wreitt, as it is not And als the same is cuttit (cullit ?) be yame selfis in sum principall & substantious clausis."

[1] Sepp, *Tagebuch*, Munich, 1882.   [2] Bain, ii. 441, 442.
[3] Nau, p. 48.

Whatever we may think of the fairness of this proposal, it is clear that the French texts, genuine or forged, as they then stood, were already in accordance with the Scots texts, to be displayed by Wood. If the mysterious letter was in Wood's hands in Scots, doubtless Moray had a forged French version of it. Any important difference in the French texts, when they came to be shown, would have been fatal. But, apparently, they were not shown at this time to Elizabeth.

It is unnecessary to enter on the complicated negotiations which preceded the meeting of Elizabeth's Commissioners, at York (October, 1568), with Mary's representatives, and with Moray (who carried the Casket with him) and his allies, Buchanan, Wood, Makgill, Lethington, and others. Mary had the best promises from Elizabeth. She claimed the right of confronting her accusers, from the first. If the worst came to the worst, if the Letters were produced, she believed that she had valid evidence of the guilt of Morton and Lethington, at least. In a Lennox Paper, of 1569, we read: 'Whereas the Queen said, when she was in Loch Leven, that she had that in black and white that would cause Lethington to hang by the neck, which Letter, if it be possible, it were very needful to be had.' Nau says that Bothwell, on leaving Mary at Carberry, gave her a band for Darnley's murder, signed by Morton, Lethington, Balfour, and others, ' and told her to take good care of that paper.'

Some such document, implicating Lethington at least, Mary probably possessed ' in black and white.' The fact was known to her accusers, she had warned Lethington as we saw (p. 187), and their knowledge influenced their policy. When Wood wrote to Moray, from Greenwich, on June 12, 1568, as to Scottish Commissioners to meet Elizabeth's, and discuss Mary's case, he said that it was much doubted, in England, whether Lethington should be one of them. To Lethington he said that he had expected Mary to approve of his coming, ' but was then surely informed she had not only written and accused him, and my Lord of Morton as privy to the King's murder, but affirmed she had both their handwritings to testify the same. which I am willed to signify to you, that you may consider thereof. You know her goodwill towards you, and how prompt of spirit she is to invent anything that might tend to your hurt. The rest I remit to your wisdom. . . . . Mr. Secretary ' (Cecil) ' and Sir Nicholas ' (Throckmorton) ' are both direct against your coming here to this trial.' [1] But it was less unsafe for Lethington to come, and perhaps try to make his peace with Mary, than to stay in Scotland. Mary also, in her appeal to all Christian Princes, declares that the handwriting of several of her accusers proves that they are guilty of the crime they lay to her charge. [2] It is fairly certain that she had not the murder band, but something she probably

---

[1] *Maitland Club Miscellany*, iv. pt. i. 120, 121.
[2] Teulet, ii. 248.

did possess. And Nau says that she had told Lethington what she knew on June 16, 1567.

If the Casket Letters were now produced, and if Mary were allowed to defend herself, backed by her own charms of voice and tears, then some, at least, of her accusers would not be listened to by that assemblage of Peers and Ambassadors before which she constantly asked leave to plead, 'in Westminster Hall.' The Casket Letters, produced by men themselves guilty, would in these circumstances be slurred as probable forgeries. Mary would prefer not to come to extremities, but if she did, as Sussex, one of Elizabeth's Commissioners, declared, in the opinion of some ' her proofs would fall out the better.'

This I take to have been Mary's attitude towards the Letters, this was her last line of defence. Indeed the opinion is corroborated by her letter from Bolton to Lesley (October 5, 1567). She says that Knollys has been trying *tirer les vers du nez* (' to extract her secret plans '), a phrase used in Casket Letter II. ' My answer is that I would oppose the truth to their false charges, *and something which they perchance have not yet heard.*' [1] Mr. Froude thinks that Mary trusted to a mere theatrical denial, on the word of a Queen. But I conceive that she had a better policy; and so thought Sussex.

Much earlier, on June 14, 1568, soon after her flight into England, Mary had said to Middlemore, ' If they ' (her accusers) ' will needs come, desire my

[1] Bain, ii. 517.

good sister, the Queen, to write that Lethington and Morton (who be two of the wisest and most able of them to say most against me) may come, and then let me be there in her presence, face to face, to hear their accusations, and to be heard how I can make my own purgation, but I think Lethington would be very loath of that commission.' [1]

Lethington knew Mary's determination. Wood gave him warning, and his knowledge would explain his extraordinary conduct throughout the Conference at York, and later. As has been said, Mary and he were equally able to ' blackmail ' each other. Any quarrel with Moray might, and a quarrel finally did, bring on Lethington the charge of guilt as to Darnley's murder. Once accused (1569), he was driven into Mary's party, for Mary could probably have sealed his doom.

As to what occurred, when, in October, the Commission of Inquiry met at York, we have the evidence of the letters of Elizabeth's Commissioners, Norfolk, Sussex, and Sadleyr. We have also the evidence of one of Mary's Commissioners, Lesley, Bishop of Ross, given on November 6, 1571, when he was prisoner of Elizabeth, in the Tower, for his share in the schemes of the Duke of Norfolk. All confessions are suspicious, and Lesley's alleged gossip against Mary (she poisoned her first husband, murdered Darnley, led Bothwell to Carberry that he might be slain, and would have done for Norfolk !)

---

[1] Bain, ii. 434.

is reported by Dr. Wilson, who heard it![1] 'Lord, what a people are these, what a Queen, and what an ambassador!' cries Wilson, in his letter to Burghley. If Lesley spoke the words attributed to him by Wilson, we can assign scant value to any statement of his whatever: and we assign little or none to Wilson's.

In his confession (1571) he says that, when he visited Mary, at Bolton, about September 18, 1568, she told him that the York Conference was to end in the pardon, by herself, of her accusers : her own restoration being implied. Lesley answered that he was sorry that she had consented to a conference, for her enemies 'would utter all that they could,' rather than apologise. He therefore suggested that she should not accuse them at all, but work for a compromise. Mary said that, from messages of Norfolk to his sister, Lady Scrope, then at Bolton, she deemed him favourable to her, and likely to guide his fellow-commissioners : there was even a rumour of a marriage between Norfolk and herself. Presently, says Lesley, came Robert Melville, ' *before our passing to York,*' bearing letters from Lethington, then at Fast Castle. Lethington hereby (according to Lesley) informed Mary that Moray was determined to speak out, and was bringing the letters, ' whereof he ' (Lethington) ' had recovered the copy, and had caused his wife' (Mary Fleming) ' write them, which he sent to the Queen.' He added that he himself was

[1] Nov. 8, 1571. Murdin, p. 57.

coming merely to serve Mary : *how* she must inform him by Robert Melville. This is Lesley's revelation. The statements are quite in accordance with our theory, that Lethington, now when there was dire risk that the Letters might come out publicly, and that Mary would ruin him in her own defence, did try to curry favour with the Queen : did send her copies of the Letters.

For what it is worth, Lesley's tale to this effect has some shadowy corroboration. At Norfolk's Trial for Treason (1571), Serjeant Barham alleged that Lethington ' stole away the Letters, and kept them one night, and caused his wife to write them out.' *That* story Barham took from Lesley's confession. But he added, from what source we know not, ' Howbeit the same were but copies, translated out of French into Scots : which, when Lethington's wife had written them out, he caused to be sent to the Scottish Queen. She laboured to translate them again into French, as near as she could to the originals wherein she wrote them, but that was not possible to do, but there was some variance in the phrase, by which variance, as God would, the subtlety of that practice came to light.' ' What if all this be true ?   What is this to the matter ? ' asked the Duke.[1]

What indeed ?   Mary had not kept copies of her letters to Bothwell, if she wrote them.   She was short of paper when she wrote Letter II., if she wrote it, and certainly could make no copy : the idea is grotesque.

[1] State Trials, i. 978.

What 'subtlety of practice' could she intend?[1]
Conceivably, if Lethington sent her copies of both
French and Scots (which is denied), she may have
tried whether she could do the Scots into the French
idioms attributed to her, and, if she could not, might
advance the argument that the French was none of
hers. Barham avers that she received no French
copies. But did Lesley say, with truth, that she
received any copies? Here, confession for confession,
that of Robert Melville gives the lie to Lesley's.
Melville (who, years later, had been captured with
Lethington and Kirkcaldy of Grange in the Castle)
was examined at Holyrood, on October 19, 1573.[2]
According to Lesley, Melville rode to Bolton with
Lethington's letters from Fast Castle, *before* the

[1] As to 'the subtlety of that practice,' which puzzled Mr. Froude,
Laing offers a highly ingenious conjecture. Mary was to do the Scots
translations, procured for her by Lethington, into her own French,
omitting the compromising portions. Lethington was next 'privately
to substitute or produce the Queen's transcript instead of the originals,
with the omission of those criminal passages, which might then be
opposed as interpolated in the translation.' But in that case 'some
variance of phrase' by Mary could bring nothing 'to light,' for there
would be no originals to compare. Lethington, while slipping Mary's
new transcript into the Casket (Laing, i. 145, 146), would, of course,
remove the original letters in French, leaving the modified transcript
in their place. 'Variance of phrase' between an original and a translation could prove nothing. Moreover, if Lethington had access to
the French letters, it was not more dangerous for him to destroy them
than to substitute a version which Moray, Morton, Buchanan, and all
concerned could honestly swear to be false. The Bishop of Ross did,
later, manage an ingenious piece of 'palming' letters on Cecil, but, in
the story of 'palming' fresh transcripts into the Casket there is no
consistency. Moreover Melville's word is at least as good as Lesley's,
and Melville denies the truth of Lesley's confession.

[2] British Museum Addit. MSS. 33531, fol. 119, *et seq.* The MS.
is much injured.

meeting of Commissioners at York. But Melville denies this : his account runs thus :

' Inquirit quhat moved him to ryde to the quene in England the tyme that the erll of morey Regent was thair, he not being privie therto ? Answeris it wes to get a discharge of sic thingis as she had gotten from him. And that the Regent wes privie to the same and grantit him licence to follow efter. Bot wald not let him pas in company wt him. *And denys that he past first to bolton bot come first to York.'*

If Melville told truth, then he did not secretly visit Mary before the Conference, and she did not deal then with Lethington, or receive copies of the Casket Letters, or bid any one ' stay these rigorous accusations and travail with the Duke of Norfolk in her favour,' as Lesley confessed.[1] The persons who examined Melville, in 1573, were acquainted with Lesley's confession of 1571, and Melville is de liberately and consciously contradicting the evidence of Lesley. Both confessed when in perilous circum- stances. Which of the two can we believe ?

On Saturday, October 2, Mary's Commissioners arrived in York, but Wood did not ride in from London till October 8.[2] Moray and the other Commissioners of the Lords came in on Sunday, followed, an hour later, by the English negotiators : ' mediators,' Mary calls them. Then began a contest of intrigue and infamy. If we believe

---

[1] Murdin, pp. 52, 53.   [2] Bain, ii. 524.

Melville, he no sooner arrived in York than Moray sent him to Bolton, ' to deal with the Queen as of his awin heid,'—that is, as if the proposal were an unofficial suggestion of his own. He was to propose a compromise : the Lords were not to accuse her, and she was to stay in England with a large allowance, Moray still acting as Regent. ' The Quene did take it verie hardlie at the begyning . . . bot in the end condescendit to it, swa that it come of [part obliterated] the Quene of England's sute.' Melville was then kept going to and from Bolton, till the Commissioners departed to London. On this statement Moray, apparently as soon as the Commissioners met at York, treated with Mary for a compromise in his favour, and Mary assented, though reluctantly.[1]

Turning to the reports of Elizabeth's Commissioners, we find that, on October 4, they met Mary's Commissioners, and deemed their instructions too limited. Mary's men proposed to ask for larger license, and, meanwhile, to proceed. But Herries (Oct. 6) declared that he would ' in no ways say all in this matter that he knew to be true.'[2] Moray and Lethington, already ' though most sorry that it is now come to that point,' said that they must disclose what they knew. Lethington by no means tried to ' mitigate these rigours intended,' as in the letter which Lesley says that he sent to Mary by Melville. He already boasted of what ' they could

---

[1] Addit. MSS. *ut supra*.   [2] Goodall, ii. 111.

an' they would.' Probably Lethington, to use a modern phrase, was 'bluffing.' Nothing could suit him worse than a public disclosure of the letters, laying him open to a *riposte* from Mary if she were allowed to be present, and speak for herself. His game was to threaten disclosure, and even to make it unofficially, so as to frighten Mary into silence, and residence in England, while he kept secretly working for another arrangement with Norfolk, behind the backs of the other English Commissioners.

This was a finesse in which Lethington delighted, but it was a most difficult game to play. His fellows, except Morton, not a nervous man, were less compromised than he, or not compromised at all, and they might break away from him, and offer in spite of him (as they finally did) a public disclosure of the Letters. The other English Commissioners, again, might not take their cue from Norfolk. Above all, Norfolk himself must be allowed to see the Letters, and yet must be induced to overlook or discredit the tale of the guilt of Mary, which they revealed. This was the only part of Lethington's arduous task in which he succeeded, and here he succeeded too well.[1]

On October 6, Norfolk, writing for himself, told Cecil that, from the talk of Mary's enemies, 'the matter I feare wyll fall owte very fowle.'[2] On October 8, Mary's men produced their charges against the Lords. The signers were Lesley, Lord

---

[1] Bain, ii. 518, 519.   [2] *Ibid.* 519.

Livingstone (who certainly knew whether the anecdote about himself, in the Glasgow Letter II., was true or not), Herries (who, in June, had asked Elizabeth what she intended to do if Mary was proved guilty), Cockburn of Skirling, a Hamilton, commendator or lay abbot of Kilwinning, and Lord Boyd.

Lennox, who was present at York,[1] burning for leave to produce his indictment, had asked his retainers to collect evidence against Herries, Fleming, Lord Livingstone, 'and all these then in England,' with Mary. On this head Lennox got no help, except so far as an anecdote, in the Casket Letter II., implied Livingstone's knowledge of Mary's amour with Bothwell. He, therefore, in a paper which we can date about October 4, 1568,[2] suggests 'that the Lord Livingstone may be examined upon his oath of the words between his mistress and him at Glasgow, mentioned in her own letter.' But this very proper step was never taken : nor was Lennox then heard. The words might have been used, but that would not prove Mary's authorship of the letter containing them. They might have been supplied by Lady Reres, after her quarrel with Mary in April–May, 1567. Moray next desired to know—

1. Whether the English Commissioners had authority to pronounce Mary guilty or not guilty. (She had protested (Oct. 7) that she 'was not subject to any judge on earth.')

<hr/>

[1] Bain, ii. 524.　　　[2] Lennox MSS.

2. Whether the Commissioners will promise to give verdict instantly.

3. Whether, if the verdict was 'guilty,' Mary would be handed over to them, or kept prisoner in England.

4. Whether, in that case, Elizabeth would recognise Moray as Regent.

Till these questions were answered (they were sent on to Elizabeth), Moray could not ' enter to the accusation.'[1]   Hitherto they had been 'content rather to hide and conceal than to publish and manifest to the world ' Mary's dishonour.   They had only told all Europe—in an unofficial way.   The English Commissioners waited for Elizabeth's reply. On the 11th October, Moray replied to the charges of Mary, without accusing her of the murder.   He also 'privately,' and unofficially, showed to the English Commissioners some of the Casket Papers. Lethington, Wood (?), Makgill, and Buchanan (in a new suit of black velvet) displayed and interpreted the documents.   They included a warrant of April 19, signed by Mary, authorising the Lords to sign the Ainslie band, advising Bothwell to marry her.[2]   Of this excuse we hear nothing, as far as I have observed, at Westminster.[3]   Calderwood, speaking of Morton's trial in 1581, says that ' he had,' for signing Ainslie's band, ' a warrant from the Queen, which none of the rest had.'[4]   At York, the Lords said that all of them

[1] Bain, ii. 520, 521.   [2] Goodall, ii. 140.
[3] The production is asserted, Goodall, ii. 87.   [4] Calderwood, iii. 556.

had this warrant. 'Before they had this warrant, there was none of them that did, or would, set to their hands, saving only the Earl of Huntly.' Yet they also alleged that they signed 'more for fear than any liking they had of the same.' They alleged that they were coerced by 200 musketeers.[1] Now Kirkcaldy, on April 20, 1567, reports the signing of the Band on the previous day, to Bedford, but says not a word of the harquebus men. They are not mentioned till ten days later.

Lethington kindly explained the reason for Mary's abduction, which certainly needs explanation. A pardon for that, he told the English Lords, would be 'sufficient also for the murder.' The same story is given in the 'Book of Articles,' the formal impeachment of Mary.[2] Presently the English Commissioners were shown 'one horrible and long letter of her own hand, containing foul matter and abominable . . . . with divers fond ballads of her own hand, which letters, ballads, and other writings before specified, were closed in a little coffer of silver and gilt, heretofore given by her to Bothwell.'

After expressing abhorrence, the three Commissioners enclose extracts, partly in Scots.[3] The Com-

[1] For the Ainslie Band, and the signatories, see Bain, ii. 322, and Hay Fleming, p. 446, note 60, for all the accounts.

[2] Hosack, i. 543.

[3] There are two sets of extracts (Goodall, ii. 148-153): one of them is in the Sadleyr Papers, edited by Sir Walter Scott, and in Haynes, p. 480. This is headed 'A brief Note of the chief and principal points of the Queen of Scots Letters written to Bothwell for her consent and

missioners, after seeing the papers unofficially, go on to ask how they are to proceed. Their letter has been a good deal modified, by the authors, in a rather less positive and more sceptical sense than the original, which has been deciphered.[1]

On the same day, Norfolk wrote separately to Pembroke, Leicester, and Cecil. He excused the delays of the Scots : 'they stand for their lives, lands, goods, and they are not ignorant, if they would, for it is every day told them, that, as long as they abstain from touching their Queen's honour, she will make with them what reasonable end they can devise. . . .' In fact, as Melville has told us, he himself was their go-between for the compromise. Norfolk adds that there are two ways, by justice public and condign, 'if the fact shall be thought as detestable and manifest to you, as, for aught we can perceive, it seemeth here to us,' or, if Elizabeth

procurement of the murder of her husband, as far forth as we could by the reading gather.' The other set is in Scots, 'Notes drawin furth of the Quenis letters sent to the Erle Bothwell.' If this were, as Miss Strickland supposed, an abstract made and shown in June–July, it would prove, of course, that Letter II. was then in its present shape, and would destroy my hypothesis. But Cecil endorses it, 'sent October 29.' I think it needless to discuss the notion that Lethington and his companions showed only the Scots texts, and vowed that they were in Mary's handwriting ! They could not conceivably go counter, first to Moray's statement (June 22, 1568) that the Scots versions were only translations. Nor could they, later, produce the Letters in French, and pretend that both they and the Scots texts were in Mary's hand. Doubtless they showed the French (though we are not told that they did), but the English Commissioners, odd as it seems, preferred to send to Elizabeth extracts from the Scots.

[1] Bain, ii. 526–528. See also in Hosack, ii. 496–501, with the obliterated lines restored.

prefer it, 'to make such composition as in so broken a cause may be.'

Norfolk seems in exactly the mind of an honourable man, horrified by Mary's guilt, and anxious for her punishment. He either dissembled, or was a mere weathercock of sentiment, or, presently, he found reason to doubt the authenticity of what he had been shown. Lethington, we saw, showed the letters, unofficially, on October 11. On October 12, Knollys had a talk with Mary. 'When,' asked she, 'will they proceed to their odious accusations, or will they stay and be reconciled to me, or what will my good sister do for me?' Surely an innocent lady would have said, 'Let them do their worst: I shall answer them. A reconciliation with dastardly rebels I refuse.' That was not Mary's posture: 'But,' she said, 'if they will fall to extremities they shall be answered roundly, and at the full, and then are we past all reconciliations.' So wrote Knollys to Norfolk, on October 14.[1] Mary would fall back on her 'something in black and white.'

On October 13, Lesley and Boyd rode to Bolton, says Knollys, and told Mary what Lethington had done: his privy disclosure of her Letters. He himself was doubtless their informant, his plan being to coerce her into a compromise.

Of all things, it now seemed most unlikely that Norfolk would veer round to Mary's side, and desire to marry her. But this instantly occurred, and the

[1] Bain, ii. 529-530.

S

question is, had he seen reason to doubt the authenticity of the letter which so horrified him? Had Lethington told him something on that long ride which they took together, on Saturday, October 16?[1] As shall be shown, in our chapter on the Possible Forgers, this may be what Lethington had done, and over-done. He had shaken Norfolk's belief in the Letter, so much that Norfolk presently forbade Mary to accept a compromise!

The evidence of Lesley is here, as usual, at cross purposes. In his confession (November 6, 1571) he says that Robert Melville took him to Lethington's lodgings, *after* Lethington had secretly shown the Letters. 'We talked almost a whole night.' Lethington said that Norfolk favoured Mary, and wished Moray to drop the charges and arrange a compromise.

Meanwhile in a letter to Mary (after October 16)[2] Lesley first, as in his confession, says that he has conferred with Lethington 'great part of a night.' Lethington had ridden out with Norfolk, on October 16, and learned from him that Elizabeth aimed at delay, and at driving Moray to do his very worst.

---

[1] Bain, ii. 533, 534.

[2] Goodall, ii. 162–170. The dates here are difficult. Lesley certainly rode to Bolton, as Knollys says, on October 13, a Wednesday. (See the English Commissioners to Elizabeth. Goodall, ii. 173. York, October 17.) By October 17, Lesley was again at York (Goodall, ii. 174). Therefore I take it that Lesley's letter to Mary (Bain, ii. 533, 534) is of October 18, or later, and that the 'Saturday' when Norfolk and Lethington rode together, and when Lethington probably shook Norfolk's belief in the authenticity of the Casket Letters, is Saturday, October 16.

When they had produced ' all they can against you,' Elizabeth would hold Mary prisoner, till she could ' show you favour.' Norfolk therefore now advised Mary to feign submission to Elizabeth, who would probably be more kind in two or three months.[1] If so, Lethington's words had not yet their full effect, or Norfolk dissembled.

If we are to believe Sir James Melville, who was at York, Norfolk also conferred with Moray himself, who consulted Lethington and Sir James ; but not the other Commissioners, his allies. His friends advised him to listen to Norfolk. We have Moray's own account of the transaction. In October, 1569, when Norfolk was under the suspicion of Elizabeth, Moray wrote to her with his version of the affair.[2] 'When first in York I was moved to sue familiar conference with the Duke as a mean to procure us expedition.' He found the Duke ' careful to have her schame coverit, hir honour repairit, schew(ed) hir interest to the title of the crown of England. . . . It was convenient she had " ma " (more) children,' who would be friends of Moray, and so on. The guileless Regent dreamed ' of nothing less than that Norfolk had in any way pretended to the said marriage.' But *now* (1569) Moray sees that Norfolk's idea was to make him seem the originator of the marriage.

Meanwhile Robert Melville was still (he says) negotiating between Mary and Moray, on the basis

---

[1] Bain, ii. 533, 534.   [2] *Ibid.* ii. 693.

of Mary's abdication and receipt of a large pension from Scotland. Melville rode to London to act for Mary on October 25.[1] But, before that date, on October 16, Elizabeth wrote to Norfolk as to the demands of Moray made on October 11, and under the influence of what she had now learned from her Commissioners as to the Casket Letters, and, perhaps, of suspicions of Norfolk. Practically, she removed the Conference to London, ordering Norfolk so to manage that Mary should think her restoration was to be arranged.[2] Mary weakly consented to the change of *venue* (October 22). She sent Lesley and Herries to represent her in London.

At this moment, namely (October 22) when Mary consented to the London Conference, it seems that she expected a compromise on the lines discussed between Moray and herself. She would resign the crown, and live affluently in England, while Moray would not produce his accusations, and would exercise the Regency. This course would be fatal to Mary's honour, in the eyes of history, but contemporaries would soon forget all, except that there had been gossip about compromising letters. The arrangement proposed was, then, reluctantly submitted to by Mary, according to Robert Melville. But it occurred to Norfolk that he could hardly marry a woman on whom such a blot rested, or, more probably, that his ambition would gain little by wedding a Queen retired, under a cloud, from her realm. If I am right, he

[1] Bain, ii. 541.   [2] *Ibid.* ii. 533.

had now come, under Lethington's influence, to doubt the authenticity of the Casket Letters.

That he opposed the compromise appears from Robert Melville's deposition. On arriving in London he met Herries, who, rather to his surprise, knew the instructions of Mary to Robert himself. 'The Lord Herries sayand to this deponair that he' (Melville) 'was cum thither with sic commission to deale privelie with the Quene of England, howbeit thair wes mair honest men thair' (than Melville). 'The men that had bene the caus of hir trouble' (Morton and the rest) 'wald be prefarit in credit to thame. This berair (Melville) be the contraire affirmit that the caus of his cumming thair wes to be a witness in caise he should be called upon,' namely to the fact that Mary did not sign her abdication (at Loch Leven) as a free agent. Melville goes on to say that, 'in the tyme quhan it was thocht that course' (the compromise with Murray) 'should have past furthair, thair com a writing from the quene to the Bishop of Ross that the Scotch partie heard the Bishop reid, and partly red him-self, bearing amangis uther purposis that the Duke of Norfolk had send liggynnis' (Liggens, or Lygons his messenger) 'to hir and forbid hir to dimitt hir crown. And sa the Bishop willit the Secretair' (Lethington) 'to lief of that course' (the compromise) 'as a thing the Quene (Mary) was not willing to, without the Duke' (Norfolk) 'gaif hir counsail thairto.' [1]

[1] Addit. MSS. *ut supra.*

Thus it appears that Norfolk prevented Mary from pursuing her compromise (which Lethington was favouring in his own interest) and from abdicating, leaving the Letters unproduced. Lethington had shaken his faith in the authenticity of the Casket Letters. That Mary should have acquiesced in a compromise demonstrates that she dreaded Moray's accusations. That, at a word from Norfolk, she reconsidered and altered her plan, proves that she could, in her opinion, outface her accusers, and indicates that Norfolk now distrusted the genuine character of the Letters. She knew, if not by the copies of her Letters which Lethington did (or did not) send her, at least by Lesley's report of that which Lethington showed the English Commissioners, what her enemies could do. She would carry the war into Africa, accuse her accusers, and, in a dramatic scene in Westminster Hall, before the Peers and the foreign Ambassadors, would rout her enemies. That, if accused, she would not be allowed to be present, and to reply, did not occur to her. Such injustice was previously unknown. That she would be submitting to a judge, or judges, she could overlook, or would, later, protest that she had never done. According to Nau, she had made the same offer to defend herself (as we have seen) to Moray, before the Scots Parliament of December, 1567.

Mary's plan was magnificent. Sussex himself, writing from York, on October 22, saw the force of her tactics.[1] He speaks, as well he might, of ' the inconstancy and subtleness of the people with whom we deal.' Mary must be found guilty, or the matter must be huddled up ' with a show of saving her honour.' ' The first, I think, will hardly be attempted, for two causes : the one for that if her adverse party accuse her of the murder by producing of her letters, she will deny them, and accuse the most of them of manifest consent to the murder, *hardly to be denied* ; so as, upon the trial on both sides, *her proofs will judicially fall out best,* as it is thought.' The other reason for not finding Mary guilty was that, if little James died, the Hamiltons were next heirs. This would not suit Moray, he (like Norfolk) would now wish for more children of Mary's, to keep the Hamiltons out, but, if she were now defamed, there would be a difficulty as to their succession to the crown. So Sussex believed (rightly) that a com- promise was intended, for which Lethington, as he says, had been working at York ,while Robert Melville was also engaged. Sussex then states the compromise in the same terms as Robert Melville did, adding that Moray would probably hand his proofs over to Mary, and clear her by a Parliamentary decree. The Hamiltons had other ideas. ' You will find Lethington wholly bent to composition.' A general routing out of evidence did not suit Lethington.

To Sussex, the one object was to keep Mary in England ; a thing easy if Moray produced his proofs,

[1] His letter is given in full by Hosack, i. 518–522.

and if Elizabeth, 'by virtue of her superiority over
Scotland,' gave a verdict against Mary.   But Sussex
thought that the proofs of Moray 'will not fall out
sufficiently to determine judicially, if she denies her
letters.'

This was the opinion of a cool, unprejudiced, and
well-informed observer.   Mary's guilt could not, he
doubted, be judicially proved.   Moray's party, he
might have added, would have been ruined by an
acknowledgment of English suzerainty.   The one
thing was to prevent the Scots from patching a peace
with Mary.   And, to that end, though Sussex does
not say so, Mary must not be allowed to appear in
her own defence.

On October 30, Elizabeth held a great Council at
Hampton Court.   Mary's Commissioners, and then
those of the Lords, were to have audience of her.
Mary's men were to be told that Elizabeth wished
'certain difficulties resolved.'   To the Lords, she
would say that they should produce their charges :
if they were valid, Elizabeth would protect them, and
detain Mary during their pleasure.   As Mary was
sure to hear of this plan, she was to be removed from
Bolton to Tutbury, which was not done till later.
Various peers were to be added to the English Commission, but not the foreign Ambassadors ; though,
on June 20, the Council reckoned it fair to admit
them.[1]

Mary heard of all this, and of Moray's admission

[1] Goodall, ii. 179–182.

to Elizabeth's presence, from Hepburn of Riccartoun, Bothwell's friend and kinsman (November 21).[1] On November 22, therefore, she wrote to bid her Commissioners break up the Conference, if she, the accused, was denied the freedom to be present, conceded to Moray, the accuser. Nothing could be more correct, but, at the same time, in ' a missive letter ' Mary suggested to her Commissioners that they should again try to compromise, saving her crown and honour.[2] These would not have been saved by the compromise which, according to Robert Melville, Norfolk forbade her to make.

[1] Bain, ii. 551.   [2] Goodall, ii. 182, 186.

XII

THE LETTERS AT WESTMINSTER AND HAMPTON COURT

The Commission opened on November 25 at West-minster, after Elizabeth had protested that she would not 'take upon her to be judge.'[1]

On the 26th Moray put in a written Protestation, as to their reluctance in accusing Mary. They then put in an 'Eik,' or addition, with the formal charge.[2] On the 29th November, the Lords said that this charge might be handed to Mary's Commissioners. Lennox appeared as an accuser, and put in 'A Discourse of the Usage' of Darnley by Mary: the last of his Indictments. It covered three sheets of paper. Mary's men now entered, received Moray's accusation, retired, discussed it, and asked for a delay for consideration. On December 1, they returned. Moray's 'Eik' of accusation had been presented to Mary's Commissioners on November 29. James Melville says that Lethington was not present, had 'a sore heart,' and whispered to Moray that he had shamed himself for ever. The Letters would come

---

[1] Goodall, ii. No. lxvi. 189.
[2] Anderson, iv. 115–121. Goodall, ii. 203–207.

out. Mary would retort. Lethington would be undone. Mary's men might have been expected, as they asked for a delay, to protract it till they could consult their mistress. The wintry weather was evil, the roads were foul, communication was slow, and the injustice to Mary of keeping her at four or five days' distance from her representatives was disgraceful. Instead of consulting her, the Commissioners for Mary met the English on December 1.

They had none of her courage, and Herries had plainly shown to Elizabeth his want of confidence in Mary's innocence. In June he had asked Elizabeth what she meant to do if appearances proved against Mary. And he told Mary that he had done so.[1] He now read a tame speech, inveighing against the accusers, and declaring that, when the cause should be further tried, some of them would be proved guilty of entering into bands for Darnley's murder. Lesley followed, stating that he and his fellows must see Elizabeth, and communicate to her Mary's demand to be heard in person, before Elizabeth, the Peers, and the Ambassadors ; while the accusers must be detained till the end of the cause.[2] On December 3, Lesley and the rest presented these demands to Elizabeth at Hampton Court. The Council later put the request before legal advisers, who replied at length. They answered that even God (though He was fully acquainted with all the circum-

---

[1] Teulet, ii. 237.
[2] Anderson, ii. 125–128. Bain, ii. 562, 563.

stances) did not condemn Adam and Eve unheard. But as to Mary's non-recognition of a mortal judge, that was absurd. If she meant to be heard, she tacitly acknowledged the jurisdiction : which is perfectly true. A door must be open or shut. Thirdly, it was ridiculous to ask Elizabeth to be present, but only as a spectator. Fourthly, it was no less absurd to ask all the nobles to attend a trial which might be long, but they might choose representatives, if Mary desired it, to appear when convenient. Fifthly, it was ridiculous to demand the presence of ambassadors, who would be neither prosecutors, defenders, judges, clerks, nor witnesses : they could only be lookers-on, like other people. That the scene should be London was reasonable, but it might be elsewhere.

There was this addition (*puis est adjouxté*), ' We think this voluntary offer ' (of Mary) 'so important that, in our opinion, all her demands should be granted, without prejudice or contravention to the Queen of England, so that none may be able to say a word against the manner of procedure.' [1]

To myself it appears that the majority of the civilians consulted returned the reply which insists that Mary must be tried with acknowledgment of jurisdiction, if she is to be heard at all, and that the addition, declaring her demands just, is the conclusion of a minority. Mary wanted the pomp and publicity

---

[1] See Hosack, i. 432, 583. The opinions of the Legists are taken from La Mothe, i. 51, 54. December 15, 1568.

of a great trial, which, after all, was to be a mere appeal to public opinion. As Queen of Scots, she could not destroy the fruits of Bannockburn and the wars of Independence, by acknowledging an English sovereign as her Judge and Superior. She could not return to the position of John Balliol under Edward I. She had been beguiled into confiding her cause to Elizabeth, and this was the result.

On December 4, Mary's men, without consulting her, made a fatal error. Before seeing Elizabeth they met Leicester and Cecil, in a room apart, and asked that Elizabeth should be informed of their readiness, even now, to make a compromise, with surety to Moray and his party. Now Mary had declared to Knollys that, if once Moray accused her publicly, they were 'past all reconciliation.' That was the only defensible position, yet her Commissioners, perhaps with her approval, receded from it. Elizabeth seized the opportunity. It was better, she said, and rightly, for her sister's honour, that Mary's accusers should be charged with their audacious defaming of their Queen, and punished for the same, unless they could show 'apparent just causes of such an attempt.' In fact, Elizabeth must see the Letters, or cause them to be seen by her nobles. She could not admit Mary in person while, as at present, there seemed so little to justify the need of her appearance—for the Letters had not yet been shown. When they were shown, it would probably turn out, she said, that Mary need not appear at all.

The unhappy Scottish Commissioners tried to repair a blunder, which clearly arose from their undeniable want of confidence in their cause. The proposal for a compromise, they said, was entirely their own. We remember that, by Norfolk's desire, Mary had already refused a compromise to which she had once consented. She would probably, in the now existing circumstances, have adhered to her resolution.[1]

On December 6, Moray and his party were at Westminster to produce their proofs. But Lesley put in a protest that he must, in that case, withdraw. The English Commissioners declared that, in this protest, Elizabeth's words of December 4 were misrepresented: her words (as to seeing Moray's proofs) having, in fact, been utterly ambiguous. She had first averred that Moray must be punished if he should be unable to show some apparent just causes ' of such an attempt,' and then, at a later stage of the conversation, had 'answered that she meant not to require any proofs.' So runs the report, annotated and endorsed by Cecil.[2] But now the Council were sitting to receive the proofs which Elizabeth had first declared that she would, and then that she would not ask for, while, after vowing that she would not ask for them, she had said that she 'would receive them for her own satisfaction'!

The words of the protest by Mary's Commissioners described all this, and the production of proofs in

---

[1] Goodall, ii. 222–227. But compare her letter of Nov. 22, p. 265, *supra.*   [2] Bain, ii. 565, 566.

Mary's absence, as ‘a preposterous order.’[1] No more preposterous proceedings were ever heard of in history. The English Commissioners, seizing on the words ‘ a preposterous order,’ declined to receive the protest till it should be amended, and at once called on Moray to produce his proofs. Moray then put in the ‘Book of Articles,’ ‘containing certain conjectures,’ a long arraignment of Mary. In the Lennox Papers is a shorter collection of ‘ Probable and Infallyable Conjectures,’ an early form of Buchanan's ‘ Detection.’ The ‘ Book of Articles ’ occupies twenty-six closely printed pages, in Hosack, who first published it, and is written in Scots.[2] The band for Bothwell's marriage is said to have been made at Holyrood, and Mary's signature is declared to have been appended later. This mysterious band seems to have reached Cecil *unofficially*, and is marked ‘ To this the Queen gave consent the night before the marriage,’ May 14 (cf. p. 254). Nothing is noted as to Darnley's conduct in seeking to flee the realm in September, 1566, and this account is given of the well-known scene in which Mary, the Council, and du Croc attempted to extract from him his grievances. ‘ He was rejected and rebuked opinlie in presence of diverse Lords then of her previe counsale, quhill he was constrenit to return

---

[1] Goodall, ii. 229.

[2] In my opinion the book is by George Buchanan, who presents many coincident passages in his *Detection*. On February 25, 1569, one Bishop, an adherent of Mary's, said, under examination, that ‘ there were sundry books in Latin against her, one or both by Mr. George Buchanan,’ books not yet published (Bain, ii. 624). Can the *Book of Articles* have been done into Scots, out of Buchanan's Latin ?

to Streviling.' Though less inaccurate than the
'Detection,' the 'Book of Articles' is a violent *ex
parte* harangue.

Moray also put in the Act of Parliament of
December, 1567. The English heard the 'Book of
Articles' and the Act read aloud, on the night of
December 6. On the 7th,[1] Moray hoped that they
were satisfied. They declined to express an opinion.
Moray retired with his company, and returned
bearing, at last, The Casket. Morton, on oath,
declared that his account of the finding of the Casket
was true, and that the contents had been kept
unaltered. Then a contract of marriage, said to be
in Mary's hand, and signed, but without date, was
produced. The contract speaks of Darnley's death
as a past event, but they 'did suppose' that the deed
was made *before* the murder. They may have based
this suspicion on Casket Letter III. (or VIII.) which,
as we shall show, fits into no *known* part of Mary's
relations with Bothwell. Another contract, said to be
in Huntly's hand, and dated April 5, was next
exhibited. Papers as to Bothwell's Trial were shown,
and those for his divorce. The Glasgow Letter I.
(which in sequence of time ought to be II.) was
displayed in French, and then Letter II.[2] *Neither
letter is stated to have been copied in French from the
French original*, and we have no copies of the

---

[1] When Goodall and Laing wrote (1754, 1804) the Minutes of
December 7 had not been discovered.

[2] Bain, ii. 569, 570.

original French, which, however, certainly existed. Next day (December 8) Moray produced seven other French writings ' in the lyk Romain hand,' which seven writings, ' *being copied,* weare red in Frenche, and a due collation made thereof as neare as could be by reading and inspection, and made to accord with the originals, which the said Erle of Murray required to be redelivered, and did thereupon deliver the copies being collationd, the tenours of which vii wrytinges hereafter follow in ordre, *the first being in manner of a sonnett,* " O Dieux ayez de moy etc." ' Apparently all the sonnets here count as one piece, the other six papers being the Casket Letters III.–VIII.

No French contemporary copies of Letters I. II. have been discovered, as in the cases of III. IV. V. VI. It is notable that while the sonnets, and Letters III. IV. V. VI. VII. VIII. are said to have been copied from the French, this is not said of Letters I. and II. The English versions of I. and II. have been collated with the French, whether copies or the originals. Perhaps no French copies of these have been found, because no copies were ever made : the absence of the copies in French is deplorable.

The next things were the depositions (not the dying confessions, which implicated some of the Lords) of Tala, Bowton, Powrie, and Dalgleish, and other legal documents. It does not appear that Mary's warrant for the signing of the Ainslie band,

T

though exhibited at York, was again produced.[1]   On the 9th the Commissioners read the Casket Papers 'duly translated into English.' They had been translated throughout the night, probably, and very ill translated they were, to judge by the extant copies.[2] Several of the copies are endorsed *in Scots*. Lesley now put in a revised and amended copy of his Protest of December 6. Morton put in a written copy of his Declaration as to the finding of the Casket, and swore to its truth.[3]

Morton's tale is that, as he was dining with Lethington in Edinburgh, on June 19, 1567, four days after Mary's surrender at Carberry, ' a certain man ' secretly informed him that Hepburn, Parson of Auldhamstokes, John Cockburn, brother of Mary's adherent, Cockburn of Skirling, and George Dalgleish, a valet of Bothwell's (and witness, at his divorce, to his adultery), had entered the Castle, then held by Sir James Balfour, who probably betrayed them. Morton sent Archibald Douglas (the blackest traitor of the age) and two other retainers to seize the men. Robert

---

[1] Bain, ii. 571–573. (Cf. pp. 254, 271, *supra*.)

[2] See Appendix E, ' The Translation of the Casket Letters.'

[3] The extant copy is marked as of December viii. That is cancelled, and the date ' Thursday, December 29 ' is given ; the real date being December 9. (Bain, ii. 576, 593, 730, 731.) This Declaration was one of the MSS. of Sir Alexander Malet, bought by the British Museum in 1883. The Fifth Report of the Historical MSS. Commission contains a summary, cited by Bresslau, in *Kassetenbriefen*, pp. 21, 23, 1881. In 1889, Mr. Henderson published a text in his *Casket Letters*. That of Mr. Bain, *ut supra*, is more accurate (ii. 730 *et seq*.). Mr. Henderson substitutes Andrew for the notorious *Archibald* Douglas, and there are other misreadings in the first edition.

Douglas, brother of Archibald, caught Dalgleish in the Potter Row, not far from the Kirk o' Field Gate, with charters of Bothwell's lands. Being carried before Morton, Dalgleish denied that he had any other charge : he was detained, and, on June 20, placed in the Tolbooth. Being put into some torture engine, he asked leave to go with Robert Douglas to the Potter Row, where he revealed the Casket. It was carried to Morton at 8 o'clock at night, and, next day, June 21, was broken open, ' in presence of Atholl, Mar, Glencairn, Morton, Home, Semple, Sanquhar, the Master of Graham, Lethington, Tullibardine, and Archibald Douglas.' The Letters were inspected (*sichtit*) and delivered over to Morton, who had in no respect altered, added to, or subtracted from them.

True or false, and it is probably true, the list of persons present adds nothing to the credibility of Morton's account. The Commissioners of Mary had withdrawn ; there could not be, and there was not, any cross-examination of the men named in Morton's list, as witnesses of the opening of the Casket. Lethington alone, of these, was now present, if indeed he appeared at this sitting, and *his* emotions may be imagined ! The rest might learn, later, that they had been named, from Lethington, after he joined Mary's cause, but it is highly improbable that Lethington wanted to stir this matter again, or gave any information to Home (who was with him in the long siege of the Castle). Sanquhar and Tullibardine, cited by Morton, signed the band for delivering Mary from Loch Leven; so much effect had the 'sichting' of the Casket Letters on *them*.   The story of Morton is probably true, so far: certainly the Lords, about June 21, got the Casket, whatever its contents then were.   But that the contents remained unadded to and unimpaired, and unaltered, is only attested by Morton's oath, and by the necessary silence of Lethington, who, of all those at Westminster, alone was present at the 'sichting,' on June 21, 1567.   But Lethington dared not speak, even if he dared to be present.   If any minute was made of the meeting of June 21, if any inventory of the documents in the Casket was then compiled, Morton produced neither of these indispensable corroborations at Westminster. His peril was perhaps as great as Lethington's, but he was of a different temperament.

The case of the Prosecution is full of examples of such unscientific handling by the cautious Scots, as the omission of minutes of June 21.

Next, on December 9, a written statement by Darnley's servant, Nelson, who survived the explosion, was sworn to by the man himself.   His evidence chiefly bore on the possession of the Keys of Kirk o' Field by Mary's servants, and her economy in using a door for a cover of the ' bath-vat,' and in removing a black velvet bed.   We have dealt with it already (p. 133).

Next was put in Crawford's deposition as to his conversations with Darnley at Glasgow.   This was intended to corroborate Letter II., but, as shall later be shown, it produces the opposite effect.[1] At an unknown date, Cecil received the Itinerary of Mary during the period under examination, which is called ' Cecil's Journal,' and is so drawn up as to destroy Moray's case, if we accept its chronology. We know not on what authority it was compiled, but Lennox, on June 11, had asked his retainers to ascertain some of the dates contained in this ' Journal.'

On December 14[2] Elizabeth added Northumberland and Westmorland to her Commissioners. They not long after rose in arms for Mary's cause. Shrewsbury, Huntingdon, Worcester, and Warwick also met, at Hampton Court. They were to be made to understand the case, and were told to keep it secret. Among the other documents, on December 14, the *originals* of the Casket Letters ' being redd, were duly conferred and compared for the manner of writing and fashion of orthography, with sundry other letters, long time heretofore written and sent by the said Quene of Scots to the Quene's majesty. And next after, there was produced and redd a declaration of the Erle of Morton of the manner of the finding of the said lettres, as the same was exhibited upon his othe, the ix of December. In collation whereof' (of *what?*) ' no difference was found. Of all which letters and writings, the true copies are contained in the memorialls of the actes

---

[1] See ' The Internal Evidence,' pp. 302–313.
[2] Mr. Bain omits December 13 ; see Goodall, ii. 252.

of the sessions of the 7 and 8 of December.' Apparently the ' collation' is intended to refer to the comparison of the Casket Letters with those of Mary to Elizabeth.   Mr. Froude runs the collation into the sentence preceding that about Morton, in one quotation.

The confessions of Tala, Bowton, and Dalgleish were also read, and, ' as night approached' (about 3.30 P.M.), the proceedings ended.[1]

The whole voluminous proceedings at York and Westminster were read through : the ' Book of Articles ' seems to have been read, *after* the Casket Letters were read, but this was not the case.   On a brief December day, the Council had work enough, and yet Mr. Froude writes that the Casket Letters ' were examined long and minutely by each and every of the Lords who were present.' [2]   We hear of no other examination of the handwriting than this : which, as every one can see, from the amount of other work, and the brevity of daylight, must have been very rapid and perfunctory.

There happens to be a recent case in which the reputation of a celebrated lady depended on a question of handwriting.   Madame Blavatsky was accused of having forged the letters, from a mysterious being named Koot Hoomi, which were wont to drift out of metetherial space into the common atmosphere of drawing-rooms.   A number of Koot Hoomi's *later* epistles, with others by Madame Blavatsky, were

---

[1] Bain, ii. 579, 580.   [2] Froude, 1866, iii. 347.

submitted to Mr. Netherclift, the expert, and to Mr. Sims of the British Museum. Neither expert thought that Madame Blavatsky had written the letters attributed to Koot Hoomi. But Dr. Richard Hodgson and Mrs. Sidgwick procured earlier letters by Koot Hoomi and Madame Blavatsky. They found that, in 1878, and 1879, the letter *d*, as written in English, occurred 210 times as against the German *d*, 805 times. But in Madame Blavatsky's earlier hand the English *d* occurred but 15 times, to 2,200 of the German *d*. The lady had, in this and other respects, altered her writing, which therefore varied more and more from the hand of Koot Hoomi. Mr. Netherclift and Mr. Sims yielded to this and other proofs : and a cold world is fairly well convinced that Koot Hoomi did not write his letters. They were written by Madame Blavatsky.[1]

The process of counting thousands of isolated characters, and comparing them, was decidedly not undertaken in the hurried assembly on that short winter day at Hampton Court, when the letters ' were long and minutely examined by each and every of the Lords who were present,' as Mr. Froude says. On the following day (December 15) the ' Book of Articles' was read aloud; though the minute of December 14 would lead us to infer that it was read on that day. The minute states that ' there was produced a writing in manner of Articles

---

[1] Proceedings of Society for Psychical Research, vol. iii. pp. 282, 283, 294.

. . . but, before these were read,' the Casket Letters were studied.   One would imagine that the ' Book of Articles' was read on the same day, after the Casket Letters had been perused.   The deposition of Powrie, the Casket contracts, and other papers followed, and then another deposition of Crawford, which had been put in on December 13.

This deposition is in the Lennox MSS. in the long paper containing the description of the mysterious impossible Letter, which Moray also described, to de Silva.   Crawford now swore that Bowton and Tala, ' at the hour of their death,' confessed, to him, that Mary would never let Bothwell rest till he slew Darnley.   Oddly enough, even Buchanan, or whoever gives the dying confessions of these men, in the ' Detection,' says nothing about their special confession to Crawford.[1]   The object of Crawford's account appears clearly from what the contemporaries, for instance the ' Diurnal,' tell us about the public belief that the confession ' fell out in Mary's favour.'

Hepburne, Daglace, Peuory, to John Hey, mad up the nesse,
Which fowre when they weare put to death the treason did confesse ;
And sayd that Murray, Moreton to, with others of ther rowte
Were guyltie of the murder vyl though nowe they loke full stowte.

---

[1] See Bain, ii. 581, for Crawford ;   the matter of this his *second* deposition, made on Decmber 13, is not given ; we know it from the Lennox Papers.   The *Diurnal* avers that Tala, on the scaffold, accused Huntly, Argyll, Lethington, Balfour, and others of signing the band for the murder, ' whereto the Queen's grace consented.'   Naturally the Queen's accusers did not put the confession about Lethington forward, but if Tala publicly accused Mary, why did they omit the circumstance ?

Yet some perchaunce doo thinke that I speake for affection heare,
Though I would so, thre thousan can hearin trew witness beare
Who present weare as well as I at thexecution tyme
& hard how these in conscience pricte confessed who did the cryme.[1]

A number of Acts and other public papers were then read; 'the whole lying altogether on the council table, were one after another showed, rather " by hap " as they lay on the table than by any choice of their natures, as it might had there been time.' Mr. Henderson argues, as against Hosack, Schiern, and Skelton, that this phrase applies only to the proceedings of December 15, not to the examination of the Casket Letters. This seems more probable, though it might be argued, from the pro-lepsis about reading the ' Book of Articles ' on the 14th, that the minutes of both days were written together, on the second day, and that the hugger-mugger described applies to the work of both days. This is unimportant; every one must see that the examination of handwriting was too hasty to be critical.

The assembled nobles were then told that Eliza-beth did not think she *could* let Mary ' come into her presence,' while unpurged of all these horrible crimes. The Earls all agreed that her Majesty's delicacy of feeling, ' as the case now did stand,' was worthy of her, and so ended the farce.[2]

Mr. Froude, on the authority (apparently) of a Simancas MS., tells us that ' at first only four—

[1] Ballad by *Tom Truth*, in Bain under date of December, 1568.
[2] Goodall, ii. 257–260. Bain, ii. 580, 581.

Cecil, Sadleyr, Leicester, and Bacon—declared themselves convinced.' Lingard quotes a Simancas MS. saying that the nobles 'showed some heart, and checked a little the terrible fury with which Cecil sought to ruin' Mary.[1] Camden (writing under James VI.) says that Sussex, Arundel, Clinton, and Norfolk thought that Mary had a right to be heard in person. But Elizabeth held this advantage : Mary would not acknowledge her as a judge : she must therefore admit Mary to her presence, if she admitted her at all, *not* as a culprit. Elizabeth (who probably forgot Amy Robsart's affair) deemed herself too good and pure to see, not as a prisoner at the Bar, a lady of dubious character. Thus all was well. Mary was firmly discredited (though after all most of the nobles presently approved of her marriage to Norfolk), yet she could not plead her cause in person.

[1] Lingard, vi. 94.

XIII

MARY'S ATTITUDE AFTER THE CONFERENCE

THE haggling was not ended. On December 16, 1568, Elizabeth offered three choices to Lesley : Mary might send a trusty person with orders to make a direct answer ; or answer herself to nobles sent by Elizabeth ; or appoint her Commissioners, or any others, to answer before Elizabeth's Commissioners.[1] Lesley fell back on Elizabeth's promises : and an anecdote about Trajan. On December 23 or 24, Mary's Commissioners received a letter by her written at Bolton on December 19.[2] Mr. Hosack says that 'she commanded them forthwith to charge the Earl of Moray and his accomplices' with Darnley's murder.[3] But that was just what Mary did not do as far as her letter goes, though on December 24, Herries declared that she did.[4] Friends and foes of Mary alike pervert the facts. Mary first said that she had received the 'Eik' in which her accusers lied,

---

[1] Bain, ii. 583.

[2] Another account, by Lesley, but not 'truly nor fully' reported, as Cecil notes, is in Goodall, ii. 260, 261. Compare La Mothe Fénelon, i. 82. Bain, ii. 585.

[3] Hosack, i. 460.　　　　　　　　　　　[4] Goodall, ii. 281.

attributing to her the crimes of which they are guilty.
She glanced scornfully at the charge that *she* intended
to murder her child, whom *they* had striven to destroy in her womb, at Riccio's murder : 'intending to
have slane him and us both.'   She then, before she
answers, asks to see the copies and originals of the
Casket Letters, 'the principal writings, if they have
any produced,' which she as yet knew not.   And
then, if she may see Elizabeth, she will prove her
own innocence and her adversaries' guilt.

Thus she does not by any means bid her friends
forthwith to accuse her foes.   That would have been
absurd, till she had seen the documents brought
against her as proofs.   But, to shorten a long story,
neither at the repeated request of her Commissioners,
nor of La Mothe, who demanded this act of common
justice, would Elizabeth permit Mary to see either
the originals, or even copies, of the Casket Letters.
She promised, and broke her promise.[1]

This incident left Mary with the advantage.   How
can an accused person answer, if not allowed to see
the documents in the case?   We may argue that
Elizabeth refused, because politics drifted into new
directions, and inspired new designs.   But Mary's
defenders can always maintain that she never was
allowed to see the evidence on which she was accused.
From Mary's letter of December 19, or rather from
Lesley's précis of it ('Extract of the principall heidis')
it is plain that she does not bid her Commissioners

---

[1] La Mothe, January 20, 30, 1569, i. 133–162.

accuse anybody, *at the moment.* But, on December 22, Lindsay challenged Herries to battle for having said that Moray, and 'his company here present,' were guilty of Darnley's death. Herries admitted having said that *some* of them were guilty. Lindsay lies in his throat if he avers that Herries spoke of him specially : and, on that quarrel, Herries will fight. And he will fight any of the principals of them if they sign Lindsay's challenge, 'and I shall point them forth and fight with some of the traitors therein.' He communicated the challenge and reply to Leicester.[1] Herries probably hoped to fight Morton and Lethington.

On the 24th, Moray having complained that he and his company were slandered by Mary's Commissioners, Lesley and Herries answered 'that they had special command sent to them from the Queen their Mistress, to lay the said crime to their charge,' and would accuse them. They were appointed to do this on Christmas Day, but only put in an argumentative answer to Moray's 'Eik.' But on January 11, when Elizabeth had absolved both Moray and Mary (a ludicrous conclusion) and was allowing Moray and his company to go home, Cecil said that Moray wished to know whether Herries and Lesley would openly accuse him and his friends, or not. They declared that Mary had bidden them make the charge, and that they had done so, *on the condition* that Mary first received copies of the Casket

[1] Goodall, ii. 272, 273.

documents. As soon as Mary received these, they would name, accuse, and prove the case, against the guilty. They themselves, as private persons, had only hearsay evidence, and would accuse no man. Moray and his party offered to go to Bolton, and be accused   But Mary (as her Commissioners at last understood) would not play her card, her evidence in black and white, till she saw the hand of her adversaries, as was fair, and she was never allowed to see the Casket documents.[1] Mary's Commissioners appear to have blundered as usual. They gave an impression, first that they would accuse unconditionally, next that they sneaked out of the challenge.[2] But, in fact, Mary had definitely made the delivery to her of the Casket Letters, originals or even copies, and her own presence to plead her own cause, the necessary preliminary conditions of producing her own charges and proofs.

Mary's attitude as regards the Casket Papers is

---

[1] Goodall, ii. 307–309.

[2] Lesley, like Herries, had no confidence in Mary's cause. On December 28, 1568, he wrote a curious letter to John Fitzwilliam, at Gray's Inn. Lesley, Herries, and Kilwinning (a Hamilton) had met Norfolk, Leicester, and Cecil privately. The English showed the *Book of Articles*, but refused to give a copy, which seems unfair, as Mary could certainly have picked holes in that indictment. Lesley found the Englishmen 'almost confirmed in favour of our mistress's adversaries.' Norfolk and Cecil 'war sayrest' (most severe), and Norfolk must either have been dissembling, or must have had his doubts about the authenticity of the Casket Letters shaken by comparing them with Mary's handwriting. Lesley asks Fitzwilliam to go to their man of law, 'and bid him put our defences to the presumptions in writ, as was devised before in all events, but we hope for some appointment (compromise), but yet we arm us well.' Mary, however, would not again stoop to compromise. (Bain, ii. 592, 593.)

now, I think, intelligible. There was a moment, as we have seen, during the intrigues at York, when she consented to resign her crown, and let the matter be hushed up. From that position she receded, at Norfolk's desire. The Letters were produced by her adversaries, at Westminster and at Hampton Court. She then occupied at once her last line of defence, as she had originally planned it. If allowed to see the documents put in against her, and to confront her accusers, she would produce evidence in black and white, which would so damage her opponents that her denial of the Letters would be accepted by the foreign ambassadors and the peers of England. ' Her proofs will judicially fall out best as is thought,' Sussex wrote, and he may have known what ' her proofs ' were.

If we accept this as Mary's line, we can account, as has already been hinted, for the extraordinary wrigglings of Lethington. At York, as always, he was foremost to show, or talk of the Casket Papers, *in private*, as a means of extorting a compromise, and hushing up the affair : *publicly*, he was most averse to their production. Whether he had a hand in falsifying the papers we may guess; but he knew that their public exhibition would make Mary desperate, and drive her to exhibit *her* ' proofs.' These would be fatal to himself.

We have said that Mary never forgave Lethington : who had been the best liked of her advisers, and, in his own interests, had ever pretended to wish to

proceed against her ' in dulse manner.'   Why did she
so detest the man who, at least, died in her service ?

The proofs of her detestation are found all
through the MS. of her secretary, Claude Nau,
written after Lethington's death.   They cannot be
explained away, as Sir John Skelton tries to do, by a
theory that the underlings about Mary were jealous
of Lethington.   Nau had not known him, and his
narrative came direct from Mary herself.   It is, of
course, worthless as evidence in her favour, but it is
highly valuable as an index of Mary's own mind,
and of her line of apology *pro vita sua*.

Nau, then, declares (we have told all this, but
may recapitulate it) that the Lords, in the spring of
1567, sent Lethington, and two others, to ask her to
marry Bothwell.   Twice she refused them, objecting
the rumours about Bothwell's guilt.   Twice she
refused, but Lethington pointed out that Bothwell
had been legally cleared, and, after the Parliament
of April, 1567, they signed Ainslie's band.   Yet no
list of the signers contains the name of Lethington,
though, according to Nau, he urged the marriage.
After the marriage, it was Lethington who induced
the Lords to rise against Bothwell, with whom he
was (as we elsewhere learn) on the worst terms.
Lethington it was who brought his friend and kinsman, Atholl, into the rising.   At Carberry Hill,
Mary wished to parley with Lethington and Atholl,
who both excused themselves, as not being in full
agreement with the Lords.   She therefore yielded to

Kirkcaldy; and Bothwell, ere she rode away, gave her the murder band (this can hardly be true), signed by Morton, Lethington, Balfour, and others, bidding her keep it carefully. Entrapped by the Lords, Mary, by Lethington's advice, was imprisoned in the house of the Provost of Edinburgh. Lethington was ' extremely opposed' to her, in her dreadful distress ; he advised imprisonment in Loch Leven; he even, Randolph says, counselled the Lords to slay her, some said to strangle her, while persuading Throckmorton that he was her best friend. Lethington tried to win her favour in her prison, but, having ' no assurance from her,' fled on a false report of her escape. Lethington fought against her at Langside, and Mary knew very well why, though he privately displayed the Casket Letters, he secretly intrigued for her at York. Even his final accession (1569) to her party, and his death in her cause, did not win her forgiveness.

She dated from Carberry Hill her certain knowledge of his guilt in the murder, which she always held in reserve for a favourable opportunity. But, as she neither was allowed to see the Casket Letters, nor to appear in person before the Peers, that opportunity never came.

To conclude this part of the inquiry : Mary's attitude, as regards the Letters, was less that of conscious innocence, than of a player who has strong cards in her hand and awaits the chance of bringing out her trumps.

U

XIV

INTERNAL EVIDENCE OF THE LETTERS

LETTER I

This Letter, usually printed as Letter I., was the first of the Casket Letters which Mary's accusers laid before the Commission of Inquiry at Westminster (December 7, 1568).[1]   It does not follow that the accusers regarded this Letter as first in order of composition.   There exists a contemporary copy of an English translation, hurriedly made from the French ; the handwriting is that of Cecil's clerk. The endorsing is, as usual, by a Scot, and runs, ' Ane short Lettre from Glasco to the Erle Bothwell. Prufes her disdaign against her husband.'   Possibly this Letter, then, was put in *first*, to prove Mary's hatred of Darnley, and so to lead up to Letter II., which distinctly means murder.   If the accusers, however, regarded this piece (Letter I.) as first in order of composition, they did not understand the meaning and drift of the papers which they had seized.[2]

[1] Bain, ii. 570.
[2] In the Cambridge MS. of the Scots translations (C) our Letter II. is placed first.   This MS. is the earliest.

Letter I., so called, must be, in order of composition, a sequel to Letter II. The sequence of events would run as follows : if we reject the chronology as given in 'Cecil's Journal,' a chronological summary handed to Cecil, we know not by whom, and supply the prosecution with a feasible scheme of time. 'Cecil's Journal' makes Mary leave Edinburgh on January 21, stay at Lord Livingstone's house of Callendar (not Callander in Perthshire) till January 23, and then enter Glasgow. If this is right, Letters I. and II. are forgeries, for II. could not, by internal evidence, have been finished before Mary's second night, at least, in Glasgow, which, if she arrived on January 23, would be January 24. Consequently it could not (as in the statement of Paris, the alleged bearer) reach Bothwell the day before his departure for Liddesdale, which 'Cecil's Journal' dates on January 24. Moreover, on the scheme of dates presented in 'Cecil's Journal,' Mary must have written and dispatched Letter I. on the morning of January 25 to Bothwell, whom it could not reach (for he was then making a raid on the Elliots, in Liddesdale), and Mary must, at the same time, have been labouring at the long Letter II. All this, with other necessary inferences from the scheme of dates, is frankly absurd.[1]

The defenders of Mary, like Mr. Hosack, meet

---

[1] It is indubitable that 'Cecil's Journal' was supplied by the prosecution, perhaps from Lennox, who had made close inquiries about the dates.

the Lords on the field of what they regard as the
Lords' own scheme of dates, and easily rout them.
In a court of law this is fair procedure ; in history
we must assume that the Lords, if the Journal represents their ideas, may have erred in their dates.
Now two contemporary townsmen of Edinburgh,
Birrel, and the author of the 'Diurnal of Occurrents,' coincide in making Mary leave Edinburgh on
January 20. Their notes were separately written,
without any possible idea that they might be
appealed to by posterity as evidence in a State
criminal case. The value of their testimony is
discussed in Appendix C, 'The date of Mary's Visit
to Glasgow.'

Provisionally accepting the date of the two
diarists, we find that the Queen left Edinburgh on
January 20, slept at Callendar, and possibly entered
Glasgow on January 21. Drury from Berwick said
that she entered on January 22, which, again, makes
the letter impossible. Let us, however, suppose her
to begin her long epistle, Letter II., at Glasgow on
the night of January 21, finish it in the midnight
hours of January 22, and send it to Bothwell by
Paris (his valet, who had just entered *her* service) on
January 23. Paris, in his declaration of August 10,
1569, avers that he met Bothwell, gave him the
letter, stayed in Edinburgh till next day, again met
Bothwell returning from Kirk o' Field, then received
from him for Mary a letter, a diamond (ring ?), and
a loving message ; he received also a letter from

Lethington, and from both a verbal report that Kirk o' Field was to be Darnley's home. Paris then returned to Glasgow. If Paris, leaving Edinburgh ' after dinner,' say three o'clock, on the 24th, did not reach Glasgow till the following noon, then the whole scheme of time stands out clearly. He left Glasgow on January 23, with the long Letter (II.) which Mary wrote on January 21 and 22. He gave it to Bothwell on the 23rd, received replies ' after dinner ' on the 24th, slept at Callendar or elsewhere on the way, and reached Glasgow about noon on January 25. If, however, Paris reached Glasgow on the day he left Edinburgh (January 24), the scheme breaks down.

If he did not arrive till noon on the 25th, all is clear, and Letter I. falls into its proper place as really Letter II., and is easily intelligible. Its contents run thus : Mary, who left Bothwell on January 21, upbraids him for neglect of herself. She expected news, and an answer to her earlier Letter (II.) dispatched on the 23rd, and has received none. The news she looked for was to tell her what she ought to do. If no news comes, she will, ' according to her commission,' take Darnley to Craigmillar on Monday : she actually did take him on Monday, as far as Callendar. But she is clearly uncertain, when she writes on January 25, as to whether Craigmillar has been finally decided upon. A possible alternative was present to her mind. After describing the amorous Darnley, and her own old complaint, a pain in the side, she says, ' If Paris doth bring back unto me that for which I have sent, it should much amend me.' News of Bothwell, brought by Paris, will help to cure her. She had expected news on the day before, January 24.

Nothing could be more natural. Mary and Bothwell had parted on January 21. She should have heard from him, if he were a punctual and considerate lover, on the 23rd ; at latest Paris should have brought back on the 24th his reply to her long letter, numbered II. but really I. But the morning of ' this Saturday ' (the 25th) has dawned, and brought no news, no answer, no Paris. (That is, if Paris either slept in Edinburgh on the night of the 24th, or somewhere on the long dark moorland road.) Impatient of three days' retarded news, ignorant as to whether Craigmillar is fixed on for Darnley, or not, without a reply to the letter carried to Bothwell by Paris (Letter II.), Mary writes Letter I. on January 25. It is borne by her chamberlain, Beaton, who is going on legal business to Edinburgh. Nothing can be simpler or more easily intelligible.

There remains a point of which much has been made. In the English, but not in the Scots translation, Mary says, ' *I send this present to Lethington*, to be delivered to you by Beaton.' The Scots is ' I send this be Betoun, quha gais ' to his legal business. Nothing about Lethington. On first observing this, I inferred—(a) that Lethington had the reference to himself cut out of the Scots version, as connecting him with the affair. (*b*) I inferred that Lethington could have had no hand in forging the original French (if forging there was), because he never would have allowed his name to appear in such a connection.   Later I observed that several Continental critics had made similar inferences.[1]   But all this is merely one of the many mare's-nests of criticism. For proof of the futility of such deductions see Appendix E, ' The Translation of the Casket Letters.'

On the whole, I am constrained to regard Letter I. as possibly authentic in itself, and as affording a strong presumption that there was an authentic Letter II. Letter I. was written, and sent on a chance opportunity, just because no answer had been received to the Letter wrongly numbered II.   This was a circumstance not likely to be invented.

Letter II

Round this long Letter, of more than 3,000 words, the Marian controversy has raged most fiercely. Believing that they had demonstrated its lack of authenticity, the Queen's defenders have argued that the charges against her must be false.   A criminal charge, supported by evidence deliberately contaminated, falls to the ground.   But we cannot really

---

[1] Bresslau, *Hist. Taschenbuch,* p. 71.   Philippson, *Revue Historique,* Sept., Oct., 1887, p. 31.   M. Philippson suggests that Lethington's name may not have been mentioned in the French, but was inserted (perhaps by Makgill, or other enemy of his, I presume) in the English, to damage the Secretary in the eyes of the English Commissioners.

argue thus : the Queen may have been guilty, even
if her foes perjured themselves on certain points, in
their desire to fortify their case.   Yet the objections to
Letter II. are certainly many and plausible.

1. While the chronology of 'Cecil's Journal'
was accepted, the Letter could not be regarded as
genuine.   We have shown, however, that by rectify-
ing the dates of the accusers, the external chronology
of the Letter can be made to harmonise with real
time.

2. The existence of another long letter, never
produced (the letter cited by Moray and Lennox)
was another source of suspicion.   While we had
only Moray's account of the letter in July 1567, and
while Lennox's version of about the same date in
1568 was still unknown, Mr. Hosack argued thus :
' What is the obvious and necessary inference ?   Is
it not that the forgers, in the first instance, drew up
a letter couched in far stronger terms than that
which they eventually produced ? '   ' Whenever,' says
Robertson, ' a paper is forged with a particular
intention, the eagerness of the forger to establish the
point in view, his solicitude to cut off all doubts and
cavils, and to avoid any appearance of uncertainty,
seldom fail of prompting him to use expressions the
most explicit and full to his purpose.'   ' In writing
this passage, we could well imagine,' says Mr. Hosack,
' that the historian had his eye on the Simancas '
(Moray's) ' description of the Glasgow Letter (II.),
but he never saw it. . . . We must assume that,

upon consideration, the letter described by Moray, which seems to have been the first draft of the forgery, was withdrawn, and another substituted in its place.' [1] This reasoning, of course, is reinforced by the discovery of Lennox's account of the Letter. But Mr. Hosack overlooked a possibility. The Lords may have, originally, after they captured the Casket, forged the Letter spoken of by Moray and Lennox. But they may actually have discovered Letter II., and, on reflection, may have produced *that*, or a garbled form of that, and suppressed the forgery. To Letter II. they *may* have added ' substantious clauses,' but if any of it is genuine, it is compromising.

3. One of the internal difficulties is more apparent than real. It turns on the internal chronology, which seems quite impossible and absurd, and must, it is urged, be the result of treacherous dovetailing. The circumstance that Crawford, a retainer of Lennox, was put forward at the Westminster Commission, in December, 1568, to corroborate part of the Letter makes a real difficulty. He declared that Darnley had reported to him the conversations between himself and the Queen, described by Mary, in Letter II., and that he wrote down Darnley's words ' immediately, at the time,' for the use of Lennox. But Crawford proved too much. His report was, partly, an English translation of the Scots translation of the French of the Letter. Therefore he either took his corroborative evidence from the Letter, or the Letter was in

[1] Hosack, i. 217, 218.

part based on Crawford's report, and therefore was forged.   Bresslau, Cardauns, Philippson, Mr. Hosack, and Sir John Skelton adopted the latter alternative.   The Letter, they say, was forged, in part, on Crawford's report.

4. The contents of the Letter are alien to Mary's character and style : incoherent, chaotic, out of keeping.

We take these objections in the order indicated. First, as to the internal dates of the Letter.   These are certainly impossible.   Is this the result of clumsy dovetailing by a forger ?

There is no date of day of the month or week, but the Letter was clearly begun on the night of Mary's arrival in Glasgow (by our theory, January 21).   Unless it was finished in the night of January 22, and sent off on January 23, it cannot be genuine : cannot have reached Bothwell in time.   We are to suppose that, on sitting down to write, Mary made, first, a list of twelve heads of her discourse, on a separate sheet of paper, and then began her epistle on another sheet.   Through paragraphs 1, 2, 3,[1] she followed the sequence of her notes of heads, and began paragraph 4, ' The King sent for Joachim ' (one of her servants) ' yesternicht, and asked why I lodged not beside him.' [2]

If this means that Mary was in Glasgow on the day before she began writing, the dates cannot be made

---

[1] See the letter in Appendix, ' Casket Letters.'

[2] ' Yesternicht ' is omitted in the English.   See Appendix E, ' Translation of the Casket Letters.'

to harmonise with facts.   For her first night of writing must then be January 22, her second January 23 ; Bothwell, therefore, cannot receive the letter till January 24, on which day he went to Liddesdale, and Paris, the bearer, declared that he gave the letter to Bothwell the day *before* he rode to Liddesdale.

The answer is obvious.   Joachim probably reached Glasgow on the day before Mary's arrival, namely on January 20.   It was usual to send the royal beds, carpets, tapestries, and ' cloth of State ' in front of the travelling prince, to make the rooms ready before he came.   Joachim would arrive with the upholstery a day in advance of Mary.   Therefore, on her first night, January 21, she can speak of what the King said to Joachim ' yesterday.'

The next indication of date is in paragraphs 7, 8. Paragraph 7 ends : ' The morne I wil speik to him upon this point' (part of the affair of Hiegait); paragraph 8 is written on the following day : ' As to the rest of Willie Hiegait's, he ' (Darnley) 'confessit it, bot it was the morne efter my cumming or he did it.' The English is, ' The rest as [to ?] Wille Hiegait [he ?] hath confessed, but it was the next day that he ' (Darnley) ' came hither,' that is, came so far on in his confession.   Paragraph 8, therefore, tells the results of that examination of Darnley, which Mary promised at the end of paragraph 7 to make ' to-morrow.'   We are now in a new day, January 22, at night.

But, while paragraphs 9, 10, 11 (about 500

words) intervene, paragraph 12 opens thus, ' *This is my first journey* ' (day's work) ; ' *I will end to-morrow. I write all, of how little consequence so ever it be, to the end you may take of the whole that shall be best for your purpose. I do here a work that I hate much, but I had begun it this morning.*' [1]

Here, then, after 500 words confessedly written on her *second* night, Mary says that this is her *first* day's work. The natural theory is that here we detect clumsy dovetailing by a forger, who has cut a genuine letter into pieces, and inserted false matter. But another explanation may be suggested. Mary, on her first night, did not really stop at paragraph 7 : ' I will talk to him to-morrow on that point.' *These words happened to come at the foot of her sheet of paper.* She took up another fresh page, and wrote on, 'This is my first journey. . . .' down to ' I had begun it this morning.' Then she stopped and went to bed. Next night (January 22) she took up the same sheet or page as she had written three sentences on, the evening before, but *she took it up on the clean side*, and did not observe her words ' This is my first journey. . . . I had begun it this morning ' till she finished, and turned over the clean side. She then probably ran her pen lightly across the now inappropriate words, written on the previous night, ' This is my first journey,' as she erased lines in her draft for a sonnet in the Bodleian Library.[2] The

---

[1] The last italicised words are in the English translation, not in the Scots.   [2] Hosack, ii. 24.

words, as in the case of the sonnet in the Bodleian, remained perfectly legible, and the translators—not intelligent men—included them in their versions.

The letter should run from paragraph 7, ' I will talk to him to-morrow upon that point ' to paragraph 12, ' This is my first journey . . . . I had begun it this morning.' Then back to paragraph 8, ' As to the rest of Willie Hiegait's,' and so straight on, merely omitting the words written on the previous night, ' This is my first journey, ... but I had begun it this morning.'

Mary's mistake in taking for virgin a piece of paper which really had writing on the verso, must have occurred to most people : certainly it has often occurred to myself.

There is one objection to this theory. In paragraph 25, at the end of the letter, Mary apologises for having written part of a letter on a sheet containing the memoranda, or list of topics, which, as we saw, she began by writing. She says, in Scots, ' Excuse that thing that is scriblit ' (MS. C,[1] ' barbulzeit') ' for I had na paper yesterday quhan I wrait that of ye memoriall.' The English runs, ' Excuse also that I scribbled, for I had yesternight no paper when I took the paper of a memorial.'

Now the part of Mary's letter which is on the same paper as the ' memorial,' or scribbled list of topics, must have been written, not ' yesternight,'

---

[1] Father Pollen kindly lent me collations of this Cambridge MS. translation into Scots, marked by me ' C.'

but 'to-night' (on the night of January 22), unless she is consciously writing in the early morning, after 12 P.M., January 22; in the 'wee sma' hours ayont the twal',' of January 23 : which does not seem probable.

If this however meets the objection indicated, the chronology of the letter is consistent; it is of the night of January 21, and the night of January 22, including some time past midnight. The apparent breaks or 'faults,' then, are not the result of clumsy dove-tailing by a forger, but are the consequence of a mere ordinary accident in Mary's selection of sheets of paper.

We now come to the objections based on Craw-ford's Deposition. Of Letter II., as we have it, para-graph 2, in some degree, and paragraphs 6 (from 'Ye ask me quhat I mene be the crueltie'), 7, 9, 10, and parts of 21 also exist, with, in many places, verbal correspondence in phrase, *in another shape.* The correspondence of phrase, above all in 6, is usually with the *Scots* translation, sometimes, on the other hand, with the *English.* Consequently, as will be seen on comparison of the Scots Letter II. with this other form of part of its contents, these two texts have a common source and cannot be independent.[1] This new form is contained in a Deposition, made on oath

---

[1] See Letter and Crawford's Deposition in Appendix. Mr. Henderson, in his *Casket Letters* (second edition, pp. xxvi, xxvii, 82–84), argues that the interdependence of Crawford's Deposition and of Letter II. 'does not seem to be absolutely proved.' Perhaps no other critic doubts it.

by a gentleman, a retainer of Lennox, named Thomas
Crawford, the very man who met Mary outside
Glasgow (Letter II. 2). He had attended Darnley
in Glasgow, and had received from Darnley, and
written, a verbatim report of his discussions with
Mary. Crawford was therefore brought forward, by
the accusers, on December 9, 1568, before the Commission of Inquiry at Westminster. The object was
to prove that no one alive but Mary could have
written Letter II., because she, and she only, could
know the nature of her private talk with her husband, as reported in Letter II., and, therefore, no one
could have forged the Letter in which that talk was
recorded. Providentially, however, Darnley had informed Crawford about those private talks, and
here was Crawford, to corroborate Letter II.

But it escaped the notice of the accusers that all
the world, or all whom Crawford chose to inform as
to what Darnley told him about these conversations,
might know the details of the talk even better than
Mary herself. For the precise words would fade
from Mary's memory, whereas Crawford, as he swore,
had written them down at once, as reported to him
by Darnley, probably as soon as Mary left his sick-
room. The written copy by Crawford must have
preserved the words with fidelity beyond that of
human memory, and the written words were in the
custody of Crawford, or of Lennox, so long as they
chose to keep the manuscript. This fact is proved
on Crawford's oath. On December 9, 1568, before

the Commissioners, he swore that, when with Darnley, in Glasgow, in January, 1567, 'he was secretly informed by the King of all things which had passed betwixt the said Queen and the King, . . . to the intent that he should report the same to the Earl of Lennox, his Master, and that he did, *immediately at the same time, write the same word by word* as near as he could possibly carry the same away.' He was certain that his report of Mary's words to himself, 'the words now reported in his writing,' 'are the very same words, on his conscience, that were spoken,' while Darnley's reports of Mary's talk (also contained in Crawford's written deposition) are the same in effect, 'though not percase in all parts the very words themselves.' [1]

We do not know whether what Crawford now handed in on December 9, 1568, was an English version of his own written verbatim Scots report done in January, 1567 ; or a copy of it ; or whether he copied it from Letter II., or whether he rewrote it from memory after nearly two years. The last alternative may be dismissed as impossible, owing to the verbal identity of Crawford's report with that in the Scots version of the French Letter attributed to Mary. Another thing is doubtful: whether Lennox, at Chiswick, on June 11, 1568, did or did not possess the report which Crawford wrote for him in January, 1567. Lennox, on June 11, as we saw, wrote to Crawford asking

[1] Goodall, ii. 246.

'what purpose Crawford held with her' (Mary) 'at her coming to the town' of Glasgow. He did not ask what conversation Mary then held with Darnley. Either he had that principal part of Crawford's report, in writing, in his possession, or he knew nothing about it (which, if Crawford told truth, is impossible), or he forgot it, which is next to impossible. All he asked for on June 11 was Crawford's recollection about what passed between himself and Mary ere she entered Glasgow, concerning which Crawford nowhere says that he made any written memorandum. Lennox, then, on June 11, 1568, wanted Crawford's recollections of his own interview with the Queen, either to corroborate Letter II., if it then existed; or for secret purposes of Wood's, who was with him.

It will be observed that Crawford's account of this interview of his with Mary presents some verbal identities with Letter II. And this is notable, for these identities occur where neither Crawford nor the Letter is reporting the speeches on either side. *These* might easily be remembered, for a while, by both parties. But both parties could not be expected to coincide verbally in phrases descriptive of their meeting, and its details. Thus, Crawford, 'I *made my Lord, my Master's humble commendations, with the excuse that he came not to meet her.*' In Letter II. we read '*He made his*' (Lennox's) '*commendations, and excuses unto me, that he came not to meet me.*'

The excuses, in Crawford, are first of Lennox's bad health (*not* in the Letter); next, that he was anxious

x

' because of *the sharp words that she had spoken of him to Robert Cunningham,* his servant,' &c.

In Letter II. this runs: ' considering *the sharp words that I had spoken to Cunningham.*' Crawford next introduces praises of Lennox which are not in the Letter, but, where a speech is reported, he uses the very words of the Scots translation of Letter II., which vary from the words in the English translation.

It follows that, even here, the Letter, in the Scots version, and Crawford's Deposition, have one source. Either Crawford took the Scots translation, and (while keeping certain passages) modified it : or the maker of the Letter borrowed from Crawford's Deposition. In the former case, the sworn corroboration is a perjury : in the latter, the Letter is a forgery.

Crawford has passages which the Letter has not : they are his own reflections. Thus, after reporting Darnley's remark about the English sailors, with whom he denied that he meant to go away (Letter II. 19), Crawford has, what the Letter has not : 'And if he had' (gone away) 'it had not been without cause, seeing how he was used. For he had neither to sustain himself nor his servants, and needed not make further rehearsal thereof, seeing she knew it as well as he.' Is this Crawford's addition or Darnley's speech ? Then there is Crawford's statement that Mary never stayed more than two hours, at a time, with Darnley—long enough, in an infected room of which the windows were never opened. It is here, after the grumble about Mary's brief stay, that Crawford adds, ' She was very pensive, whereat he found fault.'

Now Darnley may have told Crawford (though Crawford does not give this as part of the conversation), ' I was vexed by the Queen's moodiness,' or the like. But it is incredible that Mary herself should also say, in the Letter, just before she mentions going to supper after her first brief interview (*Scots*) ' he fand greit fault that I was pensive ' (Letter II. 5 [1]). To Mary's defenders this phrase appears to be borrowed by the forger of the Letter from Crawford's Deposition; not borrowed by Crawford, out of place and at random (with a skip from Letter II. 5 to Letter II. 19), and then thrust in after his own reflections on the brevity of Mary's visits to Darnley. For Crawford is saying that her visits were not only short, but sulky. On the other hand, in the Letter the writer is made to contrast Darnley's blitheness with her gloom.

Crawford does not report, what the Letter makes Mary report, Darnley's unconcealed knowledge of her relations with Bothwell, at least in the passage, ' It is thocht, and he belevis it to be trew, that I have not the power of myself unto myself, and that because of the refuse I maid of his offeris.'

Crawford ends with his own reply to Darnley, as to Mary's probable intentions : ' I answered I liked

---

[1] The English runs, ' Indeede that he had found faulte with me. . . . .' Mr. Bain notes ' a blank left thus ' (Bain, ii. 723).

it not, because she took him to Craigmillar,' not to
Holyrood. The 'Book of Articles,' we know, declares
that Mary 'from Glasgow, be hir *letteris* and uther-
wise, held Bothwell *continewally* in rememberance of
the said house,' that is, Kirk o' Field. But the Letters
produced do nothing of the kind. Craigmillar, as
we have seen, is dwelt on. In the Deposition the
idea of Darnley's being carried away as a prisoner
is introduced as an original opinion of Crawford's,
expressed privately to Darnley, and necessarily unknown to Mary when she wrote Letter II. But it
occurs thus, in Letter II. 9, after mention of a litter
which Mary had brought for his conveyance, and to
which Darnley, who loved riding of all things, made
objection. 'I trow he belevit that I wald have send
him away Presoner'—a passage *not* in the English
translation. Darnley replied to Crawford's remark
about his being taken as 'a prisoner' that 'he
thought little else himself.' It is reckoned odd that
Mary in the Letter makes him 'think little else himself.' 'I trow he belevit that I wald have send him
away Presoner.'

For these reasons some German defenders of Mary
have decided that the parts of Letter II. which
correspond with Crawford's Deposition must have
been borrowed from that Deposition by a forger of
the Letter. About June, 1568, Lennox, on this
theory, would lend a copy of Crawford's report
(made in January, 1567, at Glasgow) to Wood,
and, on returning to Scotland, Wood might have

the matter of Crawford's report worked into Letter II.

I had myself been partly convinced that this was the correct view. But the existence of Mary's memoranda, and the way in which they influence Letter II., seem to me an almost insuperable proof that part, at least, of Letter II. is genuine. It may, however, be said that the memoranda were genuine, but not compromising, and that the Letter was based, by forgers, on the memoranda (accidentally left lying in her Glasgow room, by Mary) and on Crawford's report, obtained from Lennox. This is not impossible. But the craft of the forger in making Mary, on her second night of writing, find her forgotten memoranda (II. 15), be reminded by them of her last neglected item ('Of Monsieur de Levingstoun '), and then go on (II. 16) to tell the anecdote of Livingstone, never publicly contradicted by him, seems superhuman. I scarcely feel able to believe in a forger so clever. Yet I hesitate to infer that Crawford, when asked to corroborate the statements in the Letter, took his report from the Letter itself, and perjured himself when he said, on oath, that his Deposition was derived from a writing taken down from Darnley's lips 'immediately at the time.'

I should come to this conclusion with regret and with hesitation. It is disagreeable to feel more or less in doubt as to Crawford's honour. We know nothing against Crawford's honour, unless it be that he was cruel to the Hamilton tenantry, and that he

deposed to having received confessions on the scaffold, from Bothwell's accomplices, implicating Mary.[1]
These do not occur in the dying confessions printed in Buchanan's 'Detection,' though Bowton hinted something against Mary, when he was in prison; so that trustworthy work informs us.   Thus Crawford's second Deposition, as to the dying confessions, is certainly rather suspicious.   We know nothing else against the man.   He lived to be a trusted servant of James VI. (but so did the infamous Archibald Douglas); he denounced Lethington of guilt in the murder; he won fame by the capture of Dumbarton Castle.   Yet some are led to suspect that, when asked to corroborate a passage in a letter, he simply took the corroboration, *textually*, from the letter itself. If not the Letter is a forgery.

Mr. Henderson (who does not admit the verbal correspondence of Letter and Deposition) clearly sees no harm in this course. 'It is by no means improbable that Crawford refreshed his recollection by the aid of the Letter, which, in any case, he may have seen before he prepared his statement.'   But he swore that he wrote a statement, from Darnley's lips, 'immediately at the time.'[2]   He said nothing about losing the paper, which he wrote in January, 1567. (Mr. Henderson says it 'had apparently been destroyed'—why 'apparently'?)   But, according to

---

[1] Lennox MSS.

[2] Mr. Frazer-Tytler, who did not enter into the controversy, supposed that Crawford's Deposition was the actual written report, made by him to Lennox in January 1567.   If so, Letter II. is forged.

Mr. Henderson, ' he may have seen the letter before
he prepared his statement. Probably he would have
been ready to have admitted this.' He would have
had an evil encounter with any judge to whom he
admitted that, being called to corroborate part of
a letter, written in French, he copied his corrobo-
rating statement, verbally on the whole, from a Scots
translation of the letter itself! I do not think that
Crawford would have been ' ready to admit ' this un-
conscionable villainy. Yet we must either believe
that he was guilty of it, or that the Letter was
forged.

There is one indication which, for what it is
worth, corroborates the truth of Crawford's oath. He
swore that he had written down Darnley's report of
conversations with Mary ' immediately at the time,'
in order that he, in turn, might report them to
Lennox, ' because the said Earl durst not then, for
displeasure of the Queen, come abroad,' and speak
to Darnley himself. But Crawford never swore, or
said, that he wrote down his own conversation
with Mary. Now, on June 11, 1568, Lennox does
not ask for what Crawford swore that he *wrote*,
much the most important part of his evidence, the
account of Darnley's talks with Mary. Lennox does
not ask for *that*, for what Crawford swore that he
wrote ' immediately at the time.' He merely asks
' what purpois ' (talk) ' Thomas Crawford held with
the Queen at her coming to the town.' This may be
understood to mean that Lennox already held, and so

did not need, Crawford's written account, dictated by
Darnley to him, of the conversations between Mary
and Darnley. For that document, if he had it not,
Lennox would most certainly ask, but ask he did
not. Therefore, it may be argued, Lennox had it all
the while in his portfolio, and therefore, again, parts
of Letter II. are borrowed from Crawford's written
paper of January, 1567.[1]

In that case, we clear Crawford's character for
probity, but we destroy the authenticity of Letter II.[2]
I confess that this last argument, with the fact that
we have no evidence against the character of Crawford, a soldier of extraordinary daring and resource,

[1] Mr. Henderson writes (*Casket Letters*, second edition, p. xxvi) :
' It must be remembered that while Crawford affirms that he supplied
Lennox with notes of the conversation immediately after it took place,
he does not state that the notes were again returned to him by Lennox
in order to enable him to form his deposition.' How else could he get
them, unless he kept a copy? ' It is also absurd to suppose that
Lennox, on June 11, 1568, should have written to Crawford for *notes
which he had already in his own possession.*' But Lennox did not do
that ; he asked, not for Mary's conversation with Darnley, but for
Crawford's with Mary, which Crawford never says that he wrote down
' at the time.' Mr. Henderson goes on to speak of ' the notes having
been lost,' and ' these documents had apparently been destroyed '
(p. 84), of which I see no appearance.

[2] Goodall, ii. 246. *Maitland Club Miscellany*, iv. pt. i. p. 119. It
will be observed that while Crawford swears to having written down
Darnley's report for Lennox ' at the time,' he says that he ' *caused to
be made* ' the writing which he handed in to the Commissioners,
' according to the truth of his knowledge.' Crawford's Deposition
handed in to the Commissioners, in fact, has been ' made,' that is, has
been Anglicised from the Scots ; this is proved by the draft in the Lennox
Papers. This is what Crawford means by saying that he ' caused it to
be made.' There is a corrected draft of the declaration in the Lennox
MSS., but Crawford's original autograph text, ' written with his hand '
(in Scots doubtless), was retained by the Lords (Goodall, ii. 88).

and a country gentleman, not a politician, rather disturbs the balance of probabilities in favour of the theory that he borrowed his Deposition textually from the Letter, and increases the probability that the Letter is a forgery based on the Deposition.[1]

5. The contents of the Letter are said to be incoherent and inconsistent with Mary's style and character. The last objection is worthless. In the Letter she says that she acts ' against her natural '— *contre son naturel*—out of character. As for incoherence, the items of her memoranda are closely followed in sequence, up to paragraph 8, and the interloping part in paragraph 12. The rest, the work of the second night, *is* incoherent, as Mary's moods, if she was guilty, must have been. Information, hatred, remorse, jealousy, and passion are the broken and blended strata of a mind rent by volcanic affections. The results in the Letter are necessarily unlike the style and sentiment of Mary's authentic letters, except in certain very remarkable features.

Either Mary wrote the Letter or a forger wished to give the impression that this occurred. He wanted the world to believe that the Queen, her conscience tortured and her passion overmastering her conscience, could not cease to converse with her lover while paper served her turn. Her moods alternate : now she is resolved and cruel, now sick with horror, but still, sleepless as she is, she must be writing.

[1] The Deposition, in Bain, ii. 313, is given under February, 1567 but this copy of it, being in English, cannot be so early.

Assuredly if this Letter be, in part at least, a forgery, it is a forgery by a master in the science of human nature. We seem to be admitted within the room where alone a light burns through the darkling hours, and to see the tormented Queen who fears her pillow. She writes, ' I would have almaist had pitie of him. . . . He salutes everybody, yea unto the least, and makes pitious caressing unto them, to make them have pitie on hym,' a touching picture. There is a pendant to this picture of Darnley, in Buchanan's ' History.' He is speaking of Mary's studied neglect of Darnley at the time of his son's christening (December, 1566). Darnley, he says, endured all ' not only with patience ; he was seen trying to propitiate her unjust anger in every way, *that humbly, and almost in servile fashion,* he might keep some share in her good graces.' [1] What an etching is this of the man, a little while since so haughty and tyrannous, ' dealing blows where he knew that they would be taken ' ! Again the passage (Letter II. 11) about Mary's heart wherein only Bothwell's ' shot ' can make a breach, does certainly seem (as Laing notes) to refer to a sonnet of Mary's favourite poet, Ronsard.

> Depuis le jour que la première flèche
> De ton bel oëil m'avança la douleur,
> Et que sa blanche et sa noire couleur,
> Forçant ma force, *au cœur me firent brèche.*

---

[1] *Historia*, fol. 213. Yet the Lennox *dossier* represents Darnley as engaged, at this very time, at Stirling, in a bitter and angry quarrel with Mary. He may have been in contradictory moods : Buchanan omits the mood of fury.

As in later letters, the writer now shows jealousy of Bothwell's wife.

The writer again and again recurs to her remorse. ' Remember how, gyf it were not to obey you, I had rather be deid or I dyd it, my heart bleides at it. . . . Alas, I nevir deceivit anybody; but I remit me altogidder to your will.' The voice of conscience ' deepens with the deepening of the night,' a very natural circumstance showing the almost inhuman art of the supposed forger. What ensues is even more remarkable. Throughout, Mary professes absolute submission to Bothwell; she is here, as Sir John Skelton remarks, ' the bond slave and humble minister of Bothwell's ambition.' He argues that she was really ' the last woman in the world who would have prostrated herself in abject submission at the feet of a lover.' [1] But, in a later letter to Norfolk, when she regarded herself as affianced to him, Mary says ' as you please command me, for I will, for all the world, follow your commands. . . .' She promises, in so many words, ' humble submission ' —though, conceivably, she may here mean submission to Elizabeth.[2] Again, ' I will be true and obedient to you, as I have promised.' [3] There are other similar passages in the letters to Norfolk, indicating Mary's idea of submission to a future husband, an attitude which, according to Randolph, she

[1] *Maitland of Lethington*, ii. 337.
[2] Mary to Norfolk, Jan. 31, 1570. Labanoff, iii. 19.
[3] Labanoff, iii. 62.

originally held towards Darnley. These letters to Norfolk, of course, were not dictated by passion. Therefore, under stress of passion or of a passionate caprice, Mary might naturally assume a humility otherwise foreign to her nature. It would be a joy to her to lay herself at her lover's feet: the argument *a priori*, from character, is no disproof of the authenticity of this part of the Letter.

On the whole, these reasons are the strongest for thinking the Letter, in parts, probably genuine. The Lords *may*, conceivably, have added ' some principal and substantious clauses,' such as the advice to Bothwell ' to find out some more secret invention by medicine' (paragraph 20), and they *may* have added the words ' of the ludgeing in Edinburgh ' (Kirk o' Field) to the dubious list of directions which we find at the end of the Scots, but not in the English, version. There is no other reference to Kirk o' Field, though the ' Book of Articles ' says that there were many. And there were many, in the forged letter ! Paris, indeed, confessed that Mary told him that Letter II. was to ask where Darnley should be placed, at Craigmillar or Kirk o' Field. But the evidence of Paris is dubious.

Lennox was very anxious, as was the author of the ' Book of Articles,' to prove that the Kirk o' Field plan was arranged between Bothwell and Mary, before she went to meet Darnley at Glasgow in January, 1567. We have already seen that the ' Book of Articles ' makes Mary and Bothwell ' devise ' this house ' before she raid to Glasgow,' and ' from Glasgow by her letters and otherwise she held him continually in remembrance of the said house.'

The ' Book of Articles' also declares that she ' wrote to Bothwell to see if he might find out *a more secret way by medicine to cut him off*' than the Kirk o' Field plan.   Now this phrase, ' a more secret invention by medicine,' occurs in Letter II. 20, but is instantly followed by ' for he should take medicine and the bath at *Craigmillar :* ' not a word of the house in Edinburgh.

Next, we find Lennox, like the author of the ' Book of Articles,' hankering after, and insisting on, a mention of the ' house in Edinburgh ' in Mary's Letters.   There exists an indictment by Lennox in Scots, no doubt intended to be, as it partly was, later done into English.   The piece describes Moray as present with the English Commissioners, doubtless at York, in October, 1568.   This indictment in Scots is by one who has seen Letter II., or parts of it, for we read ' Of quhilk purpos reported to Heigat she makes mention in hir lettre sent to Boithuile from Glasgow, meaning sen that purpose ' (the plan of arresting Darnley) ' wes reveled that he suld invent *a mare secrete way be medecine to cutt him of*' (the very phrase used in the ' Book of Articles ') ' as alsua puttes the said Boithuil in mynde of the house in Edinburgh, divisit betwix thame for the King hir husband's distructioune, termand thair ungodlie conspiracy " thair affaire." '

Now Mary, in Letter II., does not ' put Bothwell in mind of the house in Edinburgh,' nor does she here use the expression ' their affair,' though in Letter III. she says ' your affair.' In Buchanan's mind (if he was, as I feel convinced, the author of the 'Book of Articles') the forged letter described by Moray and Lennox, with its insistence on Kirk o' Field, was confused with Letter II., in which there is nothing of the sort. The same confusion pervades Lennox's indictment in Scots, perhaps followed by Buchanan. When parts of the Scots indictment are translated into Lennox's last extant English indictment, we no longer hear that Kirk o' Field is mentioned in the Letters, but we *do* read of ' such a house in Edinburgh as she had prepared for him to finish his days in'—which Mary had not done when she wrote Letter II. Consequently the memorandum at the end of Letter II., ' remember zow of the ludge-ing in Edinburgh,' a memorandum *not* in the English translation, may have been added fraudulently to prove the point that Kirk o' Field was, from the first, devised for Darnley's destruction.[1] These passages,

---

[1] The prosecution is in rather an awkward position as to Bothwell's action when he returned to Edinburgh, after leaving Mary at Callendar, which we date January 21, and they date January 23. *Cecil's Journal* says, ' January 23 . . . Erle Huntly and Bothwell returnit *that same nycht* to Edynt [Edinburgh] *and Bothwell lay in the Town.*' The *Book of Articles* has ' Bot boithuell at his cuming to Edinburgh ludgit in the toun, quhair customably he usit to ly at the abbay,' that is, in Holyrood (Hosack, i. 534). The author of the *Book of Articles* clearly knew *Cecil's Journal*; perhaps he wrote it. Yet he makes Mary stay but one night at Callendar; *Cecil's Journal* makes her stay two nights. However, our point is that both sources make Bothwell lie

in any case, prove that the false letter reported by Moray and Lennox haunted the minds of Lennox and Buchanan to the last.

The evidence of Nelson, Darnley's servant,[1] later with Lady Lennox, to the effect that Craigmillar was proposed, but that Darnley rejected it, may be taken either as corroboration of the intention to lodge Darnley at Craigmillar (as is insisted on in Letters I. and II.) or as one of the sources whence Letter II. was fraudulently composed.   On the whole,

in the town, not at Holyrood, on the night of his return from Callendar. His object, they imply, was to visit Kirk o' Field privately, being lodged near it and not in his official rooms. But here they are contradicted by Paris, who says that when he brought Mary's first Glasgow Letter to Bothwell he found him in his chambers *at Holyrood* (Laing, ii. 282).

[1] Nelson, according to Miss Strickland (*Mary Stuart*, ii. 178, 1873), left Edinburgh for England, and was detained by Drury for some months at Berwick. For this Miss Strickland cites Drury to Cecil, Berwick, February 15, 1567, a letter which I am unable to find in the MSS. But the lady is more or less correct, since, on February 15, Mary wrote to Robert Melville, in England, charging him, in very kind terms, to do his best for Anthony Standen, Darnley's friend, who was also going to England (Frazer, *The Lennox*, ii. 7). A reference to Cal. For. Eliz. viii. 193, No. 1029, shows that a letter of Mary to Drury, asking free passage for Standen and four other Englishmen, is really of March 15, not of February 15. Again, a letter of March 8, 1567, from Killigrew, at Edinburgh, to Cecil, proves that 'Standen, Welson, and Guyn, that served the late king, intend to return home when they can get passport' (Bain, ii. 347, No. 479). Now 'Welson' is obviously Nelson. On June 16, Drury allowed Standen to go south (Cal. For. Eliz. viii. 252, No. 1305). Nelson, doubtless, also returned to Lennox. It is odd that Lennox, having these two witnesses, should vary so much, in his first indictment, from the accepted accounts of events at Kirk o' Field. This Anthony Standen is the younger of the two brothers of the same name. The elder was acting for Darnley in France at the time of the murder. He lived to a great age, recounting romances about his adventures.

however, the Craigmillar references in the Letters have an air of authenticity. They were not what the accusers wanted ; they wanted references to Kirk o' Field, and these they amply provided in the Letter about poisoning Lady Bothwell, echoes of which are heard in the 'Book of Articles,' and in Lennox's indictment in Scots.

The letter described by Moray and Lennox, when both, at different dates, were in contact with Wood, was full of references to Kirk o' Field, which are wholly absent in Letters I. and II. The letter known to Moray and Lennox was probably forged in the interval between June 21 and July 8, 1567, when (July 8) the Lords sent 'Jhone a Forret' to Moray. As I shall make it evident that Robert Melville was sent to inform Elizabeth about the capture of the Casket on the very day of the event, the pause of seventeen days before the sending of 'Jhone a Forret' to Moray is very curious. In that time the letter noticed by Moray and Lennox may have been forged to improve the evidence against Mary. At all events its details were orally circulated. But I think that, finding this letter inconsistent, and over-charged, the Lords, in December, 1568, fell back on the authentic, or partially authentic, Letter II., and produced that. My scheme of dates for that Letter need not necessarily be accepted. My theory that Mary made a mistake as to her sheets of paper which caused the confusion of the internal chronology is but a conjecture, and the objection to it I have stated.

The question is one of the most delicately balanced probabilities.   Either Lennox, from January 1567 onwards, possessed the notes which Crawford swore that he wrote concerning Darnley's conversation (in which case much of Letter II. is a forgery based on Crawford), or Crawford, in December 1568, deliberately perjured himself.   The middle course involves the baseless hypothesis that Crawford did take notes ' immediately at the time ; ' but that they were lost or destroyed ; and that he, with dishonest stupidity, copied his deposition from Letter II.   There appears to me to be no hint of the loss or disappearance of the only notes which Crawford swore that he made. Consequently, on either alternative, the conduct of the prosecutors is dishonest.   Dishonesty is again suggested by the mysterious letter which Moray and Lennox cite, and which colours both Lennox's MS. discourses and the ' Book of Articles.'   But, on the other hand, parts of Letter II. seem beyond the power of the Genius of Forgery to produce.   Perhaps the least difficult theory is that Letter II. is in part authentic, in part garbled.

XV

THE SIX MINOR CASKET LETTERS

IF the accusers had authentic evidence in Letters I.
and II., they needed no more to prove Mary's guilt.
But the remaining six Letters bear on points which
they wished to establish, such as Mary's attempt to
make her brother, Lord Robert, assassinate her husband, and her insistence on her own abduction.
There are some difficulties attendant on these Letters.
We take them in order.   First Letter III. (or VIII.).
This Letter, the third in Mr. Henderson's edition, is
the eighth and last in that of Laing.   As the Letter,
forged or genuine, is probably one of the last in the
series, it shall be discussed in its possible historical
place.

LETTER III (IV)

Of this Letter, fortunately, we possess a copy of
the French original.[1]   The accusers connected the
letter with an obscure intrigue woven while Darnley
was at Kirk o' Field.   Lord Robert Stuart, Mary's
half-brother, commendator of Holyrood, is said by
Sir James Melville to have warned Darnley of his
danger.   Darnley repeated this to Mary, but Lord
Robert denied the story.   The 'Book of Articles'

[1] Hatfield MSS. Calendar, i. 376, 377.

alleges that Mary then tried to provoke a fight between her husband and her brother on this point. Buchanan adds that, when Darnley and Lord Robert had their hands on their swords, Mary called in Moray to part them. She hoped that he would 'get the redder's stroke,' and be killed, or, if Darnley fell, that Moray would incur suspicion. As usual Buchanan spoils his own case. If Mary did call in Moray to separate the brawlers, she was obviously innocent, or repented at the last moment. Buchanan's theory is absurd, but his anecdote, of course, may be false. Lennox, in his MSS., says that Moray was present at the quarrel.[1]

The indications of the plot, in the Letter, are so scanty, that the purpose has to be read into them from the alleged facts which the Letter is intended to prove.[2] I translate the copy of the French original.

'I watched later up there' (at Kirk o' Field?) 'than I would have done, had it not been to draw out ['of him,' in Scots] what this bearer will tell you: that I find the best matter to excuse your

[1] Melville, *Memoirs*, 173, 174. Hosack's *Mary*, i. 536 (*The Book of Articles*). Anderson, ii. 18, 19 (*Detection*). *Cecil's Journal*, under date Saturday, February 8, has 'She confronted the King and my lord of Halyrodhouse conforme to hir letter wryttin the nycht before:' that is, this Letter III.

[2] Mr. Hosack makes an error in averring that no letter as to this intrigue was produced at Westminster or later; that the letter was only shown at York in October, 1568. There and then Moray's party '*inferred*, upon a letter of her own hand, that there was another meane of a more cleanly conveyance devised to kill the King' (Goodall, ii. 142; Hosack, i. 409, 410). The letter was that which we are now considering.

affair that could be offered. I have promised him'
(Darnley?) 'to bring him' (Lord Robert?) 'to him'
(Darnley?) 'to-morrow: if you find it good, put
order to it. Now, Sir, I have broken my promise,
for you have commanded me not to send or write.
Yet I do it not to offend you, and if you knew my
dread of giving offence you would not have so many
suspicions against me, which, none the less, I cherish,
as coming from the thing in the world which I most
desire and seek, namely your good grace. Of that
my conduct shall assure me, nor shall I ever despair
thereof, so long as, according to your promise, you
lay bare your heart to me. Otherwise I shall think
that my misfortune, and the fair attitude [1] of those'
(Lady Bothwell) 'who have not the third part of the
loyalty and willing obedience that I bear to you, have
gained over me the advantage won by the second
love of Jason [Creusa or Glauce?] Not that I compare
you *à un si malheureuse*' (*sic*) 'nor myself to one so
pitiless [as Medea] however much you make me a little
like her in what concerns you; or [but?] to preserve
and guard you for her to whom alone you belong,
if one can appropriate what one gains by honourably,
and loyally, and absolutely loving, as I do and will
do all my life, come what pain and misery there may.
In memory whereof and of all the ills that you have
caused me, be mindful of the place near here'

---

[1] The Scots has 'handling.' The Cambridge MS. of the Scots
translation reads 'composing of thame,' from 'le bien composer de
ceux' in the original French.

(Darnley's chamber ?). 'I do not ask you to keep promise with me to-morrow' (the Scots has, wrongly, 'I crave with that ye keepe promise with me the morne,' which Laing justifies by a false conjectural restoration of the French), 'but that we meet' (*que nous truvions = que nous nous trouvions ensemble?*), 'and that you do not listen to any suspicion you may have without letting me know. And I ask no more of God than that you may know what is in my heart which is yours, and that He preserve you at least during my life, which shall be dear to me only while my life and I are dear to you. I am going to bed, and wish you good night. Let me know early to-morrow how you fare, for I shall be anxious. And keep good watch if the bird leave his cage, or without his mate. Like the turtle I shall abide alone, to lament the absence, however short it may be. What I cannot do, my letter [would do?] heartily, if it were not that I fear you are asleep. For I did not dare to write before Joseph' (Joseph Riccio) 'and bastienne (*sic*) and Joachim, who only went away when I began.'

This Letter is, in most parts, entirely unlike the two Glasgow letters in style. They are simple and direct: this is obscure and affected. As Laing had not the transcript of the original French (a transcript probably erroneous in places) before him, his attempts to reconstruct the French are unsuccessful. He is more happy in noting that the phrase *vous m'en dischargeres votre cœur*, occurs twice in Mary's

letters to Elizabeth [1] (*e.g.* August 13, 1568).   But to
' unpack the heart ' is, of course, a natural and
usual expression.   If Darnley is meant by the bird
in the cage, the metaphor is oddly combined with the
comparison (a stock one) of Mary to a turtle dove.
Possibly the phrase ' I do *not* ask that you keep
promise with me to-morrow,' is meant to be understood ' I do not ask you to keep promise except that
we may meet,' as Laing supposes.   But (1) the sense
cannot be got out of the French, (2) it does not help
the interpretation of the accusers if, after all, Mary
is only contriving an excuse for a meeting between
herself and Bothwell.   The obscure passage about
the turtle dove need not be borrowed from Ronsard,
as Laing thinks : it is a commonplace.   The phrase
which I render ' what I cannot do, my letter [would
do] heartily, if it were not that I fear you are asleep,'
the Scots translates ' This letter will do with ane
gude hart, that thing quhilk I cannot do myself gif
it be not that I have feir that ze ar in sleiping.'   The
French is ' ce que je ne puis faire ma lettre de bon
cœur si ce nestoit que je ay peur que soyes endormy.'
Laing, reconstructing the French, says, ' Ce que je
ne saurois faire moi-même ; that is, instigate Lord
Robert to commit the murder.'   The end of the
phrase he takes ' in its figurative sense, *d'un homme
endormi* ; slow, or negligent.'   Thus we are to understand ' what I cannot do, my letter would do heartily

---

[1] Dr. Bresslau notes several such coincidences, but stress cannot
be laid on phrases either usual, or such as a forger might know to be
favourites of Mary's.

—that is excite you to instigate my brother to kill my husband, if I were not afraid that you were slow or negligent.' This is mere nonsense. The writer means, apparently, ' what I cannot do, my letter would gladly do—that is salute you—if I were not afraid that you are already asleep, the night being so far advanced.' She is sorry if her letter arrives to disturb his sleep.

It needs much good will, or rather needs much ill will, to regard this Letter as an inducement to Bothwell to make Lord Robert draw on Darnley. Mary, without Bothwell's help, could have summoned Lord Robert on any pretext, and then set him and Darnley by the ears. The date of Mary's attempt to end Darnley by her brother's sword, Buchanan places ' about three days before the King was slain.' ' Cecil's Journal,' as we saw, places it on February 8. Darnley was murdered after midnight on February 9. Paris said that, to the best of his memory, he carried letters on the Friday night, the 7th, from Mary, at Kirk o' Field, to Bothwell. On Saturday, Mary told her attendants of the quarrel between Darnley and Lord Robert. ' Lord Robert,' she said, ' had good means of killing the King at that moment, for there was then nobody in the chamber to part them but herself.' These are rather suspicious confessions.[1] Moreover, Lennox, in his MSS., says that Moray was present at the incident, and could bear witness at Westminster.

[1] Laing, ii. 286.

The statement of Paris is confused : he carried letters both on Thursday and Friday nights (February 6 and 7), and his declaration about all this affair is involved in contradictions.

According to the confession of Hay of Tala, it was on February 7 that Bothwell arranged the method by gunpowder.   When he had just settled that, Mary, *ex hypothesi*, disturbed him with the letter on the scheme of using Lord Robert and a chance scuffle : an idea suggested to her by what she had extracted, that very night, from Darnley—namely, the warning whispered to him by Lord Robert.   She thinks that, if confronted, they will fight, Darnley will fall, and this will serve ' pour excuser votre affaire,' as the Letter says.   Buchanan adds in his ' History,' that Bothwell was present to kill anybody convenient (fol. 350).   It was a wildly improbable scheme, especially if Mary, as Buchanan says, called in Moray to stop the quarrel, or share the blame, or be killed by Bothwell.

That the Letter, with some others of the set, is written in an odd, affected style, does not yield an argument either to the attack or the defence.   If it is unlikely that Mary practised two opposite kinds of style, it is also unlikely that a forger, or forgers, would venture on attributing to her the practice. To this topic there will be opportunities of returning.

LETTER IV

This Letter merely concerns somebody's distrust of a maid of Mary's.   The maid is about to be married, perhaps to Bastian, but there is nothing said that identifies either the girl, or the recipient of the letter. Its tone, however, is that of almost abjectly affectionate submission, and there is a note of a common end, to which the writer and the recipient are working, *ce à quoy nous tandons tous deux.* If Mary dismisses the maid, she, in revenge, may reveal her scheme. The writer deprecates the suspicions of her correspondent, and all these things mark the epistle as one in this series. As it proves nothing against Mary, beyond affection for somebody, a common aim with him, and fear that the maid may spoil the project, there could be no reason for forging the Letter. A transcript of the original French is in the Record Office.[1] The translators have blundered over an important phrase from ignorance of French.[2]

LETTER V

On the night of April 19, 1567, Bothwell obtained the signatures of many nobles to ' Ainslie's Band,' as it is called, a document urging Mary to marry Bothwell.[3] On Monday, April 21, Mary went to Stirling, to see her child. She was suspected of intending to hand him over to Bothwell. If she meant to do

---

[1] *Mary Queen of Scots,* vol. ii. No. 63.

[2] ' Je m'en deferay au hazard de *la* faire entreprandre : ' the translators, not observing the gender referring to the maid, have blundered.

[3] It appears that they did not officially put in this compromising Ainslie paper. Cecil's copy had only such a list of signers ' as John Read might remember.' His copy says that Mary approved the band on May 14, whereas the Lords allege that she approved before they would sign. Bain, ii. 321, 322. A warrant of approval was shown at York. Bain, ii. 526.

this, her purpose was frustrated. On Wednesday, April 23, she went to Linlithgow, and on Thursday, April 24, was seized by Bothwell, near Edinburgh, and carried to Dunbar. This Letter, if genuine, proves her complicity; and is intended to prove it, if forged. On the face of it, the Letter was written at Stirling. Mary regrets Bothwell's confidence in an unworthy person, Huntly, the brother of his wife. Huntly has visited her, and, instead of bringing news as to how and when the abduction is to managed, has thrown cold water on the plot. He has said that Mary can never marry a married man who abducts her, and that the Lords *se dédiroient*, which the Scots translator renders 'the Lordis wald unsay themselves, and wald deny that they had said.' The reference is to their acquiescence in the Ainslie band of April 19. Mary, as usual, displays jealousy of Bothwell, who has ' two strings to his bow,' herself and his wedded wife. The Letter implies that, for some reason, Mary and Bothwell had not arranged the details of the abduction before they separated. A transcript of the original French is at Hatfield ; the English translation, also at Hatfield, is not from the French, but is a mere Anglicising of the Scots version. Oddly enough the French copy at Hatfield, unlike the rest, is in a Roman hand, such as Mary wrote. The hand resembles that of the copyist of the Casket Sonnets in the Cambridge (Lennox) MSS., and that of Mary Beaton, but it is not Mary Beaton's hand.

LETTER VI

This Letter still deals with the manner of the *enlèvement*. Mary is now reconciled to the idea of trusting Huntly.

She advises Bothwell as to his relations with the Lords. The passage follows :—

' Methinkis that zour services, and the lang amitie, having ye gude will of ye Lordis, do weill deserve ane pardoun, gif above the dewtie of ane subject yow advance yourself, not to constrane me, bot to assure yourself of sic place neir unto me, that uther admonitiounis or forane [foreign] perswasiounis may not let [hinder] me from consenting to that, that ye hope your service sall mak yow ane day to attene ; and to be schort, to mak yourself sure of the Lordis and fre to mary ; and that ye are constranit for your suretie, and to be abill to serve me faithfully, to use ane humbil requeist, joynit to ane importune actioun.

' And to be schort, excuse yourself, and perswade thame the maist ye can, yat ye ar constranit to mak persute aganis zour enemies.'

Now compare Mary's excuses for her marriage, and for Bothwell's conduct, as written in Scots by Lethington, her secretary, in May, 1567, for the Bishop of Dunblane to present to the Court of France.[1] First she tells at much length the tale of Bothwell's ' services, and the lang amitie,' as briefly stated in Letter VI. Later she mentions his ambi-

[1] Labanoff, ii. 32–44.

tion, and ‘practising with ye nobillmen secretly
to make yame his friendis.’ This answers to ‘having
ye gude will of ye Lordis,’ in the Letter. In the
document for the French Court, Mary suggests,
as one of Bothwell’s motives for her abduction,
‘incidentis quhilk mycht occur to frustrat him of
his expectatioun.’ In the Letter he is ‘constrainit
for his suretie,’ to carry her off. Finally, in the
Memorial for the French Court, it is said that
Bothwell ‘ *ceased never till be persuasionis and im-*
portune sute accumpaneit not the less with force,’ he
won Mary’s assent. In Letter VI. she advises him
to allege that he is obliged ‘ *to use ane humble requeist*
joynit to ane importune action.’ Letter VI., in fact,
is almost a succinct *précis*, before the abduction, of
the pleas and excuses which Mary made to the
French Court after her marriage. Could a forger
have accidentally produced this coincidence? One
could : according to Sir John Skelton the letter to
her ambassador ‘is understood to have been drawn
by Maitland.’[1] The letter of excuses to France is a
mere expansion of the excuses that, in the Casket
Letter which we are considering, Mary advises
Bothwell to make to the Lords. Either, then, this
Letter is genuine, or the hypothetical forger had seen,
and borrowed from, the Memorial addressed in May
to the Court of France. This alternative is not
really difficult; for Lethington, as secretary, must
have seen, and may even (as Skelton suggests) have
composed, the Scots letter of excuses carried to

[1] *Maitland of Lethington,* ii. 224.

France by the Bishop of Dunblane, and Lethington
had joined Mary's enemies before they got possession
of the Casket and Letters. Oddly enough, the
letter to the ambassador contains a phrase in Scots
which Lethington had used in writing to Beaton
earlier, Mary 'could not find ane outgait.'[1] No
transcript of the original French, and no English
translation, have been found.

LETTER VII

This Letter purports to follow on another, 'sen
my letter writtin,' and may be of Tuesday, April 22,
as Mary reports that Huntly is anxious about what
he is to do ' after to-morrow.' She speaks of Huntly
as 'your brother-in-law that *was*,' whereas Huntly,
Bothwell not being divorced, was still his brother-in-
law. Huntly is afraid that Mary's people, and especially the Earl of Sutherland, will die rather than let her
be carried off. We do not know, from other sources,
that Sutherland was present. Mary implores Bothwell to bring an overpowering force. No transcript
of the original French, nor any English translation, is
known. Mary must have written two of these letters
(and apparently eleven sonnets also) while ill, anxious,
and busy, on the 22nd, at Stirling, with the third on
the 23rd, either at Stirling or Linlithgow. She could
hardly get answers to anything written as late as
the 22nd, before Bothwell arrived at Haltoun, near
Linlithgow, on the night of April 23.

---

[1] Lethington to Beaton, October 24, 1566; cf. Keith, ii. 542.

LETTER VIII (III IN HENDERSON)

There are differences of opinion as to the date of this curious Letter, and as to its place in the series. The contemporary transcript, made probably for the Commissioners on December 9, 1568, is in the Record Office. I translate the Letter afresh, since it must be read before any inference as to its date and importance can be drawn.

'Sir,—If regret for your absence, the pain caused by your forgetfulness, and by fear of the danger which every one predicts to your beloved person, can console me, I leave it to you to judge; considering the ill fortune which my cruel fate and constant trouble have promised me, in the sequel of sorrows and terrors recent and long passed; all which you well know. But, in spite of all, I will not accuse you either of your scant remembrance or scant care, and still less of your broken promise, or of the coldness of your letters, I being so much your own that what pleases you pleases me. And my thoughts are so eagerly subject to yours that I am fain to suppose that whatsoever comes from you arises not from any of the aforesaid causes, but from such as are just and reasonable, and desired by myself. Which is the final order that you have promised me to take for the safety [1] and honourable service of the sole

---

[1] 'The safety,' 'la seurete.' Mr. Henderson's text has 'la seincte.' The texts in his volume are strangely misleading and incorrect, both in the English of Letter II. and in the copies of the original French.

support of my life, for whom alone I wish to preserve it, and without which I desire only instant death. And to show you how humbly I submit me to your commands, I send you, by Paris, in sign of homage, the ornament ' (her hair) ' of the head, the guide of the other members, thereby signifying that, in investing you with the spoil of what is principal, the rest must be subject to you with the heart's consent. In place of which heart, since I have already abandoned it to you, I send you a sepulchre, of hard stone, painted black, *semé* with tears and bones.[1] I compare it to my heart, which, like it, is graven into a secure tomb or receptacle of your commands, and specially of your name and memory, which are therein enclosed, like my hair in the ring. Never shall they issue forth till death lets you make a trophy of my bones, even as the ring is full of them ' (*i.e.* in enamel), ' in proof that you have made entire conquest of me, and of my heart, to such a point that I leave you my bones in memory of your victory, and of my happy and willing defeat, to be better employed than I deserve. The enamel round the ring is black, to symbolise the constancy of her who sends it. The tears are numberless as are my fears of your displeasure, my tears for your absence, and for my regret not to be yours, to outward view, as I am, without weakness of heart or soul.

[1] This means a ring in black enamel, with representations of tears and bones, doubtless in white : a fantastic mourning ring. Mary left a diamond in black enamel to Bothwell, in June, 1566.

' And reasonably so, were my merits greater than those of the most perfect of women, and such as I desire to be. And I shall take pains to imitate such merits, to be worthily employed under your dominion. Receive this then, my only good, in as kind part as with extreme joy I have received your marriage' (apparently, from what follows, a contract of marriage or a ring of betrothal), ' which never shall leave my bosom till our bodies are publicly wedded, as a token of all that I hope or desire of happiness in this world. Now fearing, my heart, to weary you as much in the reading as I take pleasure in the writing, I shall end, after kissing your hands, with as great love as I pray God (O thou, the only prop of my life !) to make your life long and happy, and to give me your good grace, the only good thing which I desire, and to which I tend. I have shown what I have learned to this bearer, to whom I remit myself, knowing the credit that you give him, as does she who wishes to be ever your humble and obedient loyal wife, and only lover, who for ever vows wholly to you her heart and body changelessly, as to him whom I make possessor of my heart which, you may be assured, will never change till death, for never shall weal or woe estrange it.'

The absurd affectation of style in this Letter, so different from the plain manner of Letters I. and II., may be a poetical effort by Mary, or may be a forger's idea of how a queen in love ought to write. In the latter case, to vary the manner so much from that of the earlier Letters, was a bold experiment and a needless.

Mary, to be brief, sends to Bothwell a symbolic mourning ring, enclosing her hair. It is enamelled in black, with tears and bones. Such a ring is given by a girl to her lover, as a parting token, in the *Cent Nouvelles Nouvelles* (xxvi.), a ring *d'or, esmailée de larmes noires*.[1] She promises always to keep the ' marriage' (that is the contract of marriage, or can it be a ring typical of marriage ?) in her bosom, till the actual wedding in public. Now she had a sentimental habit of wearing love tokens 'in her bosom.' She writes to Norfolk from Coventry (December, 1569), ' I took the diamant from my Lord Boyd, which I shall keep unseene about my neck till I give it agayn to the owner of it and of me both.' [2]

As to the Contract of Marriage (if Mary wore that in her bosom [3]), two alleged contracts were

---

[1] This coincidence was pointed out to me by Mr. Saintsbury.

[2] By the way, she says to Norfolk, in the same Letter, ' I am resolvid that weale nor wo shall never remove me from yow, If yow cast me not away.' Compare the end of this Letter VIII.: 'Till death nor weal nor woe shall estrange me' (jusques à la mort ne changera, *car mal ni bien oncque ne m'estrangera*). Now the forger could not copy a letter not yet written (Labanoff, iii. 5). This conclusion of her epistle is not on the same level as the *customary* conclusion—the prayer that God will give the recipient long life, and to her—something else. *That* formula was usual : ' Je supplie Dieu et de vous donner bonne vie, et longue, et a moy l'eur de votre bonne grasse.' This formula, found in Mary's Letters and in the Casket Letters, also occurs in a note from Marguerite de France to the Duchesse de Montmorency (De Maulde, *Women of the Renaissance*, p. 309). A forger would know, and would insert the stereotyped phrase, if he chose.

[3] On the point of wearing a concealed jewel in her bosom, the

Z

produced for the prosecution. One was a ' contract
or promise of marriage ' by Mary to Bothwell, in the
Italic hand, and in French ; the hand was said to be
Mary's own. It was undated, and a memorandum
in the ' Detection ' says, ' Though some words therein
seme to the contrary, yet is on credible groundes
supposed to have been made and written by her
befoir the death of her husband.' The document
explicitly mentions that ' God has taken ' Darnley.
The document, or jewel, treasured by Mary would,
of course, be Bothwell's solemn promise, or token
of promise, the counterpart of hers to him, published
in Buchanan.[1]

Now there also existed a contract, said to be in
Huntly's hand, and signed by Mary and Bothwell, of
date April 5 (at Seton), 1567. But this contract
speaks of the process of divorce ' intentit ' between
Bothwell and his ' pretensit spouse.' Now that suit,
on April 5, was not yet before the Court (though
some documents had been put in), nor did Lady
Bothwell move in the case till after Mary's abduction.

If Mary kept *this* contract, and if it be correctly
dated, then Letter VIII. is not of January–February,
but of April, 1567.

If Mary regarded herself as now privately married, this pose would explain the phrase ' your
brother-in-law *that was*,' in Letter VIII. But this
is stretching possibilities.

curious may consult the anecdote, ' Queen Mary's Jewels,' in the
author's *Book of Dreams and Ghosts*.

[1] In Laing, ii. 234.

Mr. Hosack has argued that the Letter just translated was really written to Darnley, between whom and Mary some private preliminary ceremony of marriage was said to have passed. In that case the words *par Paris*, ' I send you by Paris, &c.,' are a forged interpolation, as Paris was not in Mary's service till January, 1567. The opening sentence about the danger which, as every one thinks, menaces her correspondent, might refer to Darnley. But the tone of remonstrance against indifference, suspicion, and violated promises, is the tone of almost all the Casket Letters, and does not apply to Darnley—before his public marriage.

As to the ' heart in a ring,' Mary, as Laing notes, had written to Elizabeth ' Je vous envoye mon cœur en bague.' The phrase in the Letter, *seul soutien de ma vie*, also occurs in one of the Casket Sonnets.

To what known or alleged circumstances in Mary's relations with Bothwell can this Letter refer? The alternatives are (1) either to her receipt of Bothwell's answer to Letter II., which Paris (on our scheme of dates) gave to Mary on January 25, at Glasgow; (2) to the moment of her stay at Callendar, where she arrived, with Darnley, on January 27, taking him on January 28 to Linlithgow, whence, on January 29, ' she wraytt to Bothwell.' She had learned at Linlithgow, on January 28, by Hob Ormistoun, that Bothwell was on his way from Liddesdale.[1] Or (3) does the letter refer to Monday, April 21, when she was at

---

[1] *Cecil's Journal.*

Stirling till Wednesday, April 23, when she went to Linlithgow, Bothwell being 'at Haltoun hard by,' and carrying her off on April 24 ? [1]

Taking first (1)—we find Mary acknowledging in this letter the receipt of Bothwell's 'marriage.' If this is a contract, did Bothwell send it in the letter which, according to Paris, he wrote on January 24, accompanying it with a diamond? 'Tell the Queen,' said Bothwell, 'that I send her this diamond, which you are to carry, and that if I had my heart I would send it willingly, but I have it not.' The diamond, a ring probably, might be referred to in Bothwell's letter as a marriage or betrothal ring (French, *union*). In return Mary would send her mourning ring; 'the stone I compare to my heart.'

This looks well, but how could Mary, who, *ex hypothesi*, had just received a ring, a promise or contract of marriage, and a loving message, complain, as she does, of 'the coldness of your letters,' 'your violated promise,' 'your forgetfulness,' 'your want of care for me'? Danger to Bothwell, in Liddesdale, she might fear, but these other complaints are absolutely inconsistent with the theory that Bothwell had just sent a letter, a ring, a promise of marriage, and a loving verbal message. We must therefore dismiss hypothesis 1.

(2) Did Mary send this Letter on January 29 from Linlithgow? She had no neglect to complain of *there*; for, according to her accusers, she was met

[1] *Cecil's Journal.*

by Hob Ormistoun, with a letter or message. Paris says this was at Callendar, where she slept on January 27.[1] In that case Bothwell was yet more prompt. Again, Mary had now no fear of danger to Bothwell's person, as she had just learned that Bothwell had left perilous Liddesdale. Here, once more, there is no room, reason, or ground for her complaints. Again, in the Letter she says that she sends the mourning ring ' by Paris.' But, if we are to believe Paris, she did not do so. He gave her Bothwell's letter, received from Bothwell's messenger, at Callendar, January 27. She answered it at bedtime, gave it to Paris to be given to Bothwell's messenger, enclosing a ring, and the messenger carried ring and letter to Bothwell. She could not write, ' I have sent you by Paris ' the ring, if she did nothing of the sort. Later, according to Paris, she did send him, with the bracelets, from Linlithgow to Edinburgh, where he met Bothwell, just mounting to ride and join Mary and Darnley on their return. The Letter, then, does not fit the circumstances of one written either at Callendar, January 27 (Paris), or at Linlithgow, January 29 (' Cecil's Journal ').

(3) That the ring, and the lamentations, were carried, by Paris, from Linlithgow to the neighbouring house of Haltoun, where Bothwell lay, on the night of April 23, the night before he bore Mary off to Dunbar, is not credible. Nothing indicates her receipt of a

[1] Laing, ii. 285.

token or contract of marriage at that date. The danger to Bothwell was infinitesimal. He was not neglecting Mary, he was close to her, and only waiting for daylight to carry her off. He wrote in reply, Paris says, and verbally promised to meet her, ' on the road, at the bridge.' [1]

To a man who was thus doing his best to please her, a man whom she was to meet next day, Mary could not be writing long, affected complaints and lamentations. She would write, if at all, on details of the business on hand. No ring was carried by Paris, according to his own deposition.

Thus the contents of the Letter do not fit into any recorded or alleged juncture in Mary's relations with Bothwell, after January 21, 1567, when Paris (whom the Letter mentions) first entered her service. Laing places the Letter last in the series, and supposes that the ring and letter were sent from Linlithgow, to Bothwell hard by (at Haltoun), the night before the ' ravishment.' But he does not make it plain that the contents of the Letter are really consistent with its supposed occasion.[2] When was Bothwell absent from Mary, cold, forgetful, and in danger, between the return from Glasgow, and the abduction ? The Letter does not help the case of the prosecution.

We have exhausted the three conceivable alternatives as to the date, occasion, and circumstances of this

---

[1] Laing, ii. 289.

[2] Laing, ii. 325, 326. Laing holds that between April 21 and April 23 Mary wrote Letters V. VI. VII. VIII. and Eleven Sonnets to Bothwell : strange literary activity !

Letter.   Its contents fit none of these dates and occasions.   Mr. Froude adds a fourth alternative. This Letter ' was written just before the marriage ' [1] when Bothwell (whose absence is complained of) was never out of Mary's company.

There is not, in short, an obvious place for this Letter in the recorded circumstances of Mary's history.

[1] Froude, iii. 75, note 1.

XVI

THE CASKET SONNETS

WHEN the 'Detection' of Buchanan was first published, La Mothe Fénelon, French ambassador in England, writing to Charles IX., described the Sonnets as the worst, or most compromising, of all the evidence. They never allude to Darnley, and must have been written after his death.   As is well known, Brantôme says that such of Mary's verses as he had seen were entirely unlike the Casket Sonnets, which are 'too rude and unpolished to be hers.'   Ronsard, he adds, was of the same opinion.   Both men had seen verses written hastily by Mary, and still 'unpolished,' whether by her, or by Ronsard, who may have aided her, as Voltaire aided Frederick the Great.   Both critics were, of course, prejudiced in favour of the beautiful Queen.   Both were good judges, but neither had ever seen 160 lines of sonnet sequence written by her under the stress of a great passion, and amidst the toils of travel, of business, of intense anxiety, all in the space of two days, April 21 to April 23.

That the most fervent and hurried sonneteer should write eleven sonnets in such time and circumstances is hard to believe, but we must allow for

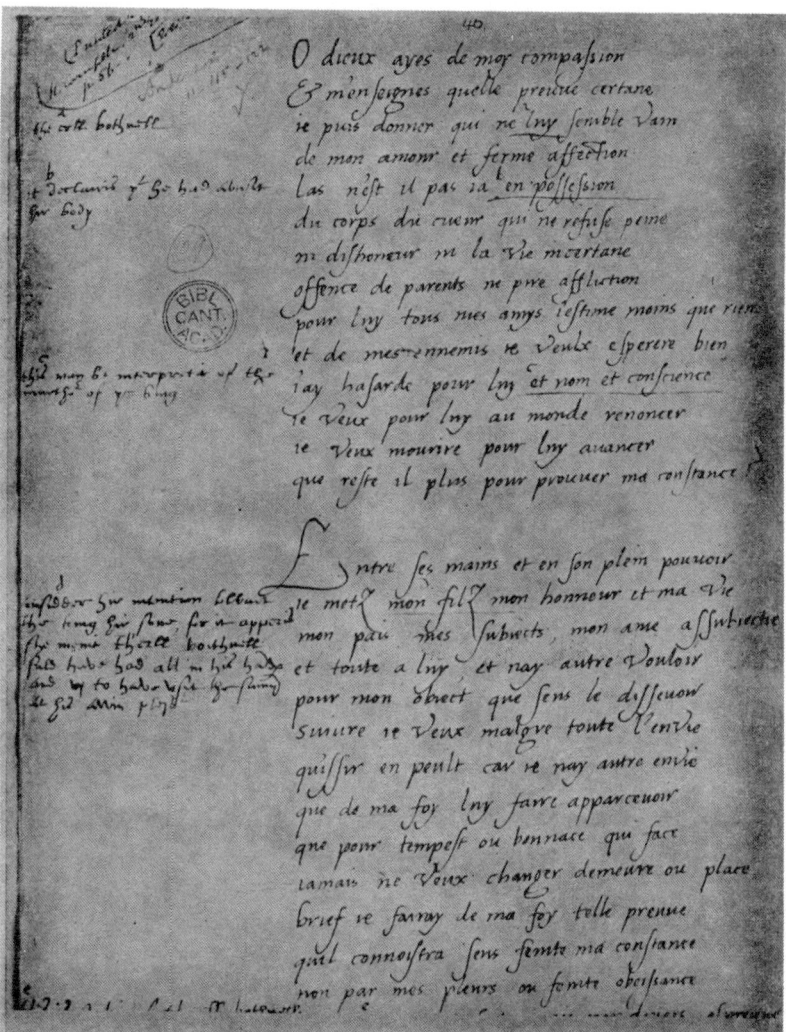

TWO SONNETS FROM THE CAMBRIDGE MS.

The hand somewhat resembles that of Mary in early youth, and that of Mary Beaton.
The copyist is unknown

Mary's sleepless nights, which she may have beguiled by versifying. It is known that a distinguished historian is occupied with a critical edition of these Sonnets. We may await his decision as to their relations with the few surviving poems of the Queen. My own comparison of these does not convince me that the favoured rhymes are especially characteristic of Mary. The topics of the Casket Sonnets, the author's inability to remove the suspicions of the jealous Bothwell ; her protestations of submission ; her record of her sacrifices for him ; her rather mean jealousy of Lady Bothwell, are also the frequent topics of the Casket Letters. The very phrases are occasionally the same : so much so as to suggest the suspicion that the Letters may have been modelled on the Sonnets, or the Sonnets on the Letters. If there be anything in this, the Sonnets are probably the real originals. Nothing is less likely than that a forger would think of such a task as forging verses by Mary : nor do we know any one among her enemies who could have produced the verses even if he had the will. To suspect Buchanan is grotesque. On the theory of a literary contest between Mary and Lady Bothwell for Bothwell's affections, something is to be said in the following chapter. Meanwhile, I am obliged to share the opinion of La Mothe Fénelon, that, as proof of Mary's passion for Bothwell, the Sonnets are stronger evidence than the Letters, and much less open to suspicion than some parts of the Letters.

XVII

CONCLUSIONS AS TO THE LETTERS AND THE POSSIBLE FORGERS

A FEW words must be said as to a now obsolete difficulty, the question as to the language in which the Letters were originally written. That question need not be mooted : it is settled by Mr. Henderson's ' Casket Letters.' The original language of the epistles was French.

I. The epistles shown at Westminster were certainly in French, which was not (except in the first one or two sentences) the French later published by the Huguenots. *That* French was translated from the Latin, which was translated from the Scots, which was translated from the original French. Voluminous linguistic criticisms by Goodall, Hosack, Skelton, and others have ceased, therefore, to be in point.

II. Many phrases, whether as mirrored in the Scots and English translations, or as extant in contemporary copies of the original French, can be paralleled from authentic letters of Mary's. Bresslau proved this easily, but it was no less easily proved that many of the phrases were conventional, and could be paralleled from the correspondence of Catherine de' Medici and other contemporary ladies. A forger would have ample opportunities of knowing Mary's phrasing and orthography. It would be easy for me to write a letter reproducing the phrasing and orthography, which is very distinctive, of Pickle the Spy. No argument against forgery can be based on imitations of peculiarities of phrase and spelling which the hypothetical forger was sure to know and reproduce.

But phrasing and spelling are not to be confounded with tone and style. Now the Letters, in tone, show considerable unity, except at one point. Throughout Mary is urging and spurring an indifferent half-hearted wooer to commit an abominable crime, and another treasonable act, her abduction. Really, to judge from the Letters, we might suppose Bothwell to be almost as indifferent and reluctant as Field-Marshal Keith was, when the Czarina Elizabeth offered him her hand. Keith put his foot down firmly, and refused, but the Bothwell who hesitated was lost. It is Mary who gives him no rest till he carries her off: we must blame Bothwell for not arranging the scheme before parting from Mary in Edinburgh; to be sure, Buchanan declares in his History that the scheme *was* arranged. In short, we become almost sorry for Bothwell, who had a lovely royal bride thrust on him against his will, and only ruined himself out of reluctance to disoblige a lady. It is the old Irish tale of Diarmaid and Grainne over again.

But, on the other hand, Letter II. represents Mary as tortured by remorse and regret. Only to please Bothwell would she act as she does. Her heart bleeds at it. We must suppose that she not only grew accustomed to the situation, but revelled in it, and insisted on an abduction, which even Lethington could only explain by her knowledge of the *apices juris*, the sublimities of Scots law. A pardon for the abduction would, in Scots law, cover the murder.

Such is the chief difference in tone. In style, though the fact seems to have been little if at all noticed, there are two distinct species. There is the simple natural style of Letters I., II., and the rest, and there is the alembicated, tormented, precious, and affected style of Letters VIII. (III.) and IV. Have we any other examples, from Mary's hand, of the obscure affectations of VIII. (III.) and IV.? Letter VIII., while it contains phrases which recur in the Casket 'Sonnets,' is really more contorted and *symboliste* in manner than the verses. These 'fond ballads' contain, not infrequently, the same sentiments as the Letters, whether the Letters be in the direct or in the affected style. Thus, in Letter II., where Lady Bothwell and Mary's jealousy of her are the theme, we read 'Se not hir' (Lady Bothwell) 'quhais feinzeit teiris should not be sa mekle praisit or estemit as the trew and faithful travellis quhilk I

sustene for to merite her place.'   Compare Sonnets
ii. iii. :

> Brief je feray de ma foy telle preuve,
> Qu'il cognoistra sans faulte ma constance,
> Non par mes pleurs ou fainte obeyssance
> Comme autres font, mais par divers espreuve.

In both passages the writer contrasts the 'feigned
tears,' 'feigned obedience' of Bothwell's wife with
her own practical proofs of devotion : in the Sonnet
using 'them' for 'her' as in Letter IV.

A possible, but unexpected explanation of the
extraordinary diversity of the two styles, I proceed
to give. We have briefly discussed the Sonnets, which
(despite the opinion of Ronsard) carry a strong
appearance of authenticity, though whether their
repetitions of the matter and phrasing of the Letters
be in favour of the hypothesis that *both* are authentic
might be argued variously. Now from the Sonnets
it appears that Lady Bothwell was endeavouring to
secure her bridegroom's heart in a rather unlooked-
for manner : namely, by writing to him elaborately
literary love letters in the artificial style of the age
of the Pleiad. As the Sonnets say, she wooes him
' par les escriptz tout fardez de sçavoir.' But Mary
maintains that Lady Bothwell is a mere plagiarist.
Her ingenious letters, treasured by Bothwell, and
the cause of his preference for her, are

> empruntés de quelque autheur luisant !

We have already tried to show that Bothwell was not
the mere 'brave stupid strong-handed Border noble,'

' the rough ignorant moss-trooper,' but a man of taste and culture. If the Sonnets be genuine, there was actually a contest in literary excellence between Bothwell's wife and his royal mistress. This queer rivalry would account for the style of Letter VIII., in which Mary labours to prove to Bothwell, as it were, that she is as capable as his wife of writing a fashionable, contorted, literary style, if she chooses: in poetry, too, if she likes. We naturally feel sorry for a man of action who received, at a moment when decisive action was needful, such an epistle as Letter VIII., and we naturally suppose that he never read it, but tossed it into the Casket with an explosion of profane words. But it is just conceivable that Bothwell had a taste for the ' precious,' and that, to gratify this taste, and eclipse Lady Bothwell, Mary occasionally wrote in the manner of Letter VIII. or quoted Jason, Medea, and Creusa.

This hypothesis, far-fetched as it may seem, at all events is naturally suggested by Sonnet VI. On the other hand, it is difficult to imagine that a dexterous forger would sit down to elaborate, whether from genuine materials or not, anything so much out of keeping with his Letter II. as is his Letter VIII. Yet Letter VIII., as we saw, cannot be connected with any known moment of the intrigue.

While the Letters thus vary in style, in tone of sentiment they are all uniform, except Letter II. We are to believe that the forger deliberately laid down a theory of this strange wooing. The Queen

throughout is much more the pursuer than the
pursued.   Bothwell is cold, careless, breaks promises, is contemptuously negligent, does not write, is
suspicious, prefers his wedded wife to his mistress.
Contemporary gossip averred that this, in fact, was
his attitude.   Thus, after Mary had been sent to
Loch Leven, Lethington told du Croc that ' Bothwell
had written several times to his first wife, Lady
Bothwell, since he lay with the Queen, and in his
letters assured Lady Bothwell that he regarded
her as his wife, and the Queen as his concubine.'
Lethington reported this to Mary herself, who discredited the fact, but Lethington relied on the evidence of Bothwell's letters.[1]   How could he know
anything about them ?   The belief in Bothwell's
preference of his wife was general, and, doubtless,
it may be urged that this explains the line taken by
the forger.

The passion, in the Letters, is all on the side of
Mary.   By her eternal protests of entire submission
she recalls to us at once her eager service to Darnley
in the first days of their marriage, and her constant
promises of implicit obedience to Norfolk.   To
Norfolk, as to Bothwell (we have already shown), she
expresses her hope that ' you will mistrust me no
more.' [2]   ' If you be in the wrong I will submit me to
you for so writing, and ax your pardon thereof.'   She
will beg pardon, even if Norfolk is in the wrong !
Precisely in the same tone does Mary (in Letter

[1] Teulet, ii. 169, 170.   [2] Labanoff, iii. 5.

VIII.), after complaining of Bothwell's forgetfulness, say, 'But in spite of all I will not accuse you, either of your scant remembrance or scant care, and still less of your broken promise, seeing that what pleases you pleases me.'

This woman, whose pride is said to be in contradiction with her submission, as expressed in the Casket Letters, writes even to Elizabeth, 'Je me sousmetray à vos commandemants.' [1] In Letter VIII. Bothwell is congratulated on ' votre victoire et mon agreable perte.' To Elizabeth Mary writes ' Vous aurés fayt une profitable conqueste de moy.'

That any forger should have known Mary so well as to place her, imaginatively, as regarded Bothwell, in the very attitude which we see that, on occasion, she chose later to adopt in fact, as regarded Norfolk, is perhaps beyond belief. It may be urged that she probably, in early days, wrote to Darnley in this very tone, that Darnley's papers would fall into his father's hands, and that Lennox would hand them over as materials to the forger. But 'it is to consider too curiously to consider thus.'

Such are the arguments, for the defence and the attack, which may be drawn from internal evidence of style. To myself this testimony seems rather in favour of the authenticity of considerable and compromising portions of the papers.

Letter VIII. (intended to prove a contract of marriage with Bothwell) remains an enigma to me :

[1] Labanoff, iii. 64.

the three Letters proving Mary's eagerness for the
abduction are not without suspicious traits. The
epistle about bringing Lord Robert to kill Darnley
in a quarrel is involved in the inconsistencies which
we have shown to beset that affair. The note about
the waiting-woman was hardly worth forging, compromising as it is. Letter I. seems to me certainly
authentic, if we adopt the scheme of dates suggested,
and reject that of ' Cecil's Journal,' which appears to
be official, and answers to Lennox's demands for
dates. It may be merely Lennoxian, but no other
scheme of chronology is known to have been put in
by the accusers. Letter I., if our dates are admitted, implies the existence of a letter answering to
Letter II., which I have had to regard as, in some
parts at least, genuine. If forgery and tampering
were attempted (as I think they certainly were in the
letter never produced, but described by Lennox and
Moray, and perhaps in other cases), who was the
criminal ?

My reply will have been anticipated. Whoever
held the pen of the forger, Lethington must have
directed the scheme. This idea, based on we know
not what information, though I shall offer a conjecture, occurred to Elizabeth, as soon as she heard the
first whisper of the existence of the Letters, in June–
July, 1567. On July 21, de Silva mentioned to her
what he had heard—that the Lords held certain
Letters ' proving that the Queen had been cognisant
of the murder of her husband. She told me it was

not true, though Lethington had behaved badly in
the matter.' [1] The person from whom Elizabeth
thus early heard something connecting Lethington,
in an evil way, with the affair must have been Robert
Melville. His position was then peculiar. He was
first accredited to Elizabeth, on June 5, 1567, by
Mary, Bothwell, and Lethington.[2] Melville left
Scotland, for Mary, on June 5, returned to Scotland,
and again rode to London on June 21, as the envoy
of some of her enemies. Now June 21 was the day
of the opening of the Casket, and inspection of its
contents. A meeting of the Privy Council was held
on that day, but Lethington's name is not among
those of the nobles who attended it.[3] The minutes
of the Council say not a word about the Casket,
though the members attending Council were, with
several others, present, so Morton declared, at the
opening of the Casket. Though not at the Council,
Lethington was at the Casket scene, according to
Morton. And on that very day, Lethington wrote a
letter to Cecil, the bearer being Robert Melville, who,
says Lethington, is sent ' on *sudden* dispatch.' [4] Melville, in addition to Lethington's letter, carried a verbal message to Cecil, as the letter proves. We may
glean the nature of the verbal message from the
letter itself.

---

[1] Spanish Calendar, i. 659.   [2] Bain, ii. 329, 330.

[3] Privy Council Register.

[4] Bain, ii. 336. Sir John Skelton did not observe the coincidence
between the opening of the Casket and the ' sudden dispatch ' of
Robert Melville to London. The letter in full is in *Maitland of
Lethington*, ii. 226, 227.

We know that the Lords, in December of the same year, publicly and in Parliament, and with strange logic, declared that the ground of their rising and imprisonment of Mary was her guilt as revealed in letters written by her hand, though these were not discovered when the Lords imprisoned Mary. Now Lethington, in his dispatch to Cecil, carried by Melville the day of the Casket finding, says that the bearer, Mr. Robert Melville, ' can report to you at length the ground of the Lords' so just and honourable cause.' Presently that ' ground ' was declared to be the evidence of the Casket Letters. Melville then would verbally report this new ' ground ' to Cecil and Elizabeth. He was dispatched at that very date for no other reason. The Lords were Melville's employers, but his heart was sore for Mary. Elizabeth, on June 30, tells Mary (Throckmorton carried her letter) that ' your own faithful servant, Robert Melville, used much earnest speech on your behalf.' [1] What Elizabeth knew about Lethington's bad behaviour as to the Letters, and spoke of to de Silva, she must have heard from Robert Melville. She did not, as far as we are aware, mention her knowledge of the subject till de Silva introduced it on July 21, but only from Melville could she learn whatever she did learn about Lethington. Throckmorton, her envoy to Scotland, did not mention the Letters till July 25, four days after Elizabeth spoke to de Silva. ' Jhone

[1] Bain, ii. 339.

A A 2

a Forret,' whom the Lords sent through London on July 8 to bring Moray, was not exactly the man to blame Lethington and discredit the Letters : for he was probably John Wood, later the chief enemy of Mary.

Suspicions of Lethington, later, were not confined to Elizabeth alone. In Mary's instructions to her Commissioners (Sept. 9, 1568) she says, ' There are divers in Scotland, both men and women, that can counterfeit my handwriting, and write the like manner of writing which I use [the ' Roman ' or Italic] as well as myself, *and principally such as are in company with themselves*,' [1] as Lethington then was.

Lesley stated the matter thus : ' There are sundry can counterfeit her handwriting, who have been brought up in her company, of whom there are some assisting themselves' (the Lords) ' as well of other nations as of Scots, as I doubt not both your highness ' (Elizabeth) ' and divers others of your Highness's Court, has seen sundry letters sent here from Scotland, which would not be known from her own handwriting.' [2]

All this is vague, and Mary's reference to *women*, Lesley's reference to those ' brought up in her company,' glance, alas ! at the Queen's Maries. Mary Livingstone, wedded to John Sempil, was not on the best terms with Queen Mary about certain jewels. Mary Fleming was Lethington's wife. Mary Beaton's aunts were at open feud with the Queen. A lady,

---

[1] Goodall, ii. 342, 343. [2] Goodall, ii. 388, 389.

unnamed, was selected as the forger by the author of
' L'Innocence de la Royne d'Escosse ' (1572).

To return to Lethington.   In 1615, Camden,
writing, as it were, under the eye of James VI. and I.,
declared that Lethington ' had privately hinted to
the Commissioners at York, that he had counterfeited
Mary's hand frequently.' [1]   There is nothing incredible, *a priori*, in the story.   Between October 11,
1568 (when Norfolk, having been *privately* shown the
Letters, was blabbing, even to his servant Bannister,
his horror of Letter II.), and October 16, when
Lethington rode out with Norfolk, and the scheme
for his marrying Mary struck deep root, something
may have been said.   Lethington may have told
Norfolk that perhaps the Letters were forged, that he
himself, for amusement, had imitated Mary's hand.
As a fact, the secretaries of two of the foremost of
contemporary statesmen did write to the innumerable
bores who beset well-known persons, in hands hardly
to be distinguished from those of their chiefs.
Norfolk, as Laing says, did acknowledge, at his trial,
that Lethington ' moved him to consider the Queen
as not guilty of the crimes objected.'   Lethington
appears to have succeeded ; possibly by aid of the
obvious argument that, if *he* could imitate Mary's
hand for pastime, others might do it for evil
motives.   Nay, we practically know, and have
shown, that Lethington did succeed in making
Norfolk, to whom, five days before, he had offered

[1] Camden, *Annals*, 143-5.   Laing. i. 226.

the Letters as proofs of Mary's guilt, believe that she had not written them. For, as we have seen, whereas Mary at this time was making a compromise with Moray, Norfolk persuaded her to abandon that course. Thus Lethington, on October 11, 1568, made Norfolk believe in the Letters; on October 16, he made him disbelieve or doubt.

We are not to suppose Lethington so foolish as to confess that he was himself the forger. Even if Lethington did tell Norfolk that he had often imitated Mary's hand, he could not have meant to accuse himself in this case. His son, in 1620, asked Camden for his authority, and we know not that Camden ever replied. He never altered his statement, which meant no more than that, by the argument of his own powers of imitating Mary's handwriting, Lethington kept urging the Duke of Norfolk to doubt her guilt.[1] Lethington's illustration of the ease with which Mary's writing could be imitated is rather, if he used it, a proof that he did *not* hold the pen which may have tampered with the Casket Letters. Our reasons for suspecting him of engaging, though not as penman, in the scheme are :

1. Elizabeth's early suspicion of Lethington, and the probability that Robert Melville, who had just parted from Lethington, inspired that suspicion.

2. The probability, derived from Randolph's letter, already cited, that Lethington had access to

[1] Laing, ii. 224-240.

the Casket before June 21, 1567, but after Mary's capture at Carberry.

3. Of all men Lethington, from his knowledge of Mary's disgust at his desertion, ingratitude, and 'extreme opposition' to her, in her darkest hour, and from his certainty that Mary held, or professed to hold, documentary proof of his own guilt, had most reason to fear her, and desire and scheme her destruction.

4. Kirkcaldy of Grange, on April 20, 1567, months before the Letters were discovered, wrote to Cecil that Mary 'has said that she cares not to lose (a) *France*, (b) *England*, and (c) *her own* country' for Bothwell.[1]

Compare, in the Lennox version of the letter never produced (p. 214)—

(*a*) The loss of her dowry in *France*.

(*b*) Her titles to the crown of *England*.

(*c*) The crown *of her realm*.

Unless this formula of renunciations, *in this sequence*, was a favourite of Mary's, in correspondence and in general conversation, its appearance, in the letter not produced, and in Kirkcaldy's letter written before the Casket was captured, *donne furieusement à penser*.

5. Another curious coincidence between a Casket Letter (VII.) and Mary's instructions to the Bishop of Dunblane, in excuse of her marriage, has already been noticed. We may glance at it again.

---

[1] Bain, ii . 322.

INSTRUCTIONS

LETTER VII.

We thocht his continuance in the awayting upon us . . . had procedit onelie upoun the ackawlegeing of *his dewtie, being our borne subject.*

Gif *abone the dewtie of ane subject* yow advance your self.

The *persuasionis* quhilk oure friendis or his unfriendis *mycht cast out for his hinderence.* . . .

That uther admonitiounis or forane *persuasiounis* may not let me from consenting. . . .

Sa ceased he nevir till be persuasionis and *importune sute, accumpaneit nottheles with force.*

To use *ane humbil requiest joynit to ane importune action.*

The whole scheme of excuse given in Letter VII. is merely expanded into the later Instructions, a piece of eleven pages in length. 'The Instructions are understood to have been drawn by Lethington,' says Sir John Skelton ; certainly Mary did not write them as they stand, for they are in Scots. 'Many things we resolved with ourselves, but never could find ane outgait,' say the Instructions. 'How to be free of him she has no outgait,' writes Maitland to Beaton. If Lethington, as Secretary, penned the Instructions, who penned Letter VII. ?

6. We have already cited Randolph's letter to Kirkcaldy and Lethington, when they had changed sides, and were holding the Castle for the Queen. But we did not quote all of the letter. Lethington, says Randolph, with Grange, is, as Mary herself has said, the chief occasion of all her calamities, by his advice ' to apprehend her, to imprison her ; yea, to have taken presently the life from her.' This follows

a catalogue of Lethington's misdeeds towards Mary, exhaustive, one might think. But it ends, '*with somewhat more that we might say, were it not to grieve you too much herein.*' What 'more' beyond arrest, loss of crown, prison, and threatened loss of life, was left that Lethington could do against Mary? The manipulation of the Casket Letters was left : 'somewhat more that we might say, were it not to grieve you too much herein.'

Randolph had been stirring the story of Lethington's opening the coffer in a green cover, in the autumn of 1570. Charges and counter-charges as to the band for murdering Darnley had been flying about. On January 10, 1571, Cecil darkly writes to Kirkcaldy that of Lethington he 'has heard such things as he dare not believe.'[1] This cannot refer to the declaration, by Paris, that Lethington was in the murder, for *that* news was stale fifteen months earlier.

As to the hand that may have done whatever unfair work was done, we can hope for no certainty. Robert Melville, in 1573, being taken out of the fallen Castle, and examined, stated that ' he thinkis that the lard of Grange ' (Kirkcaldy) ' counterfaitit the Regentis ' (Moray's) 'handwrite, that was sent to Alixr Hume that nycht.' But we do not accuse Kirkcaldy.

There is another possible penman, Morton's jackal,

---

[1] Cal. For. Eliz. ix. 390. Chalmers says, 'he means their participation in Darnley's murder' (ii. 487). But that, from Randolph's point of view, was no offence against Mary, and Kirkcaldy was not one of Darnley's murderers.

a Lord of Session, Archibald Douglas. That political forgery was deemed quite within the province of a Scottish Judge, or Lord of Session, in the age of the Reformation, we learn from his case. A kinsman of Morton, one of Darnley's murderers, and present, according to Morton, at the first opening of the Casket, Archibald was accused by his elder brother, William Douglas of Whittingham, of forging letters from Bishop Lesley to Lennox, the favourite of James VI., and others (1580-1581).[1] Of course a Lord of Session might bear false witness against his brother in the flesh, and on the Bench. But perhaps Archibald himself, a forger of other letters, forged the Casket Letters; he had been in France, and may have known French. All things are conceivable about these Douglases.

It is enough to know that experts in forgery, real or reputed, were among Mary's enemies. But, for what they are worth, the hints which we can still pick up, and have here put together, may raise a kind of presumption that, if falsification there was, the manager was Lethington. 'The master wit of Lethington was there to shape the plot,' said Sir John Skelton, though later he fell back on Morton, with his ' dissolute lawyers and unfrocked priests '— like Archie Douglas.

I do not, it will be observed, profess to be certain,

---

[1] See Hosack, ii. 217, 218. Bowes to Walsingham, March 25, 1581. *Bowes Papers*, 174. Ogilvie to Archibald Beaton. Hosack, ii. 550, 551.

EXAMPLES OF MARY'S HAND

One of these two is, in part, not genuine, but imitated

EXAMPLES OF MARY'S HAND

In one some parts are not genuine, but imitated

The text is Mary to Elizabeth, B. Museum, Calig. C.I. Number 421 in Bain. Calendar II.

p. 659 (1900)

or even strongly inclined to believe, that there was any forgery of Mary's writings, except in the case of the letter never produced. But, if forgery there was, our scraps and hints of evidence point to Lethington as manager of the plot.

As to problems of handwriting, they are notoriously obscure, and the evidence of experts, in courts of justice, is apt to be conflicting. The testimony in the case of Captain Dreyfus cannot yet have been forgotten. In Plates BA, AB the reader will find a genuine letter of Mary to Elizabeth, and a copy in which some of the lines are not her own, but have been imitated for the purpose of showing what can be done in that way. 'The puzzle is' to discover which example is entirely by the Queen, and which is partly in imitation of her hand. In Plate A is an imitation of Mary's hand, as it might have appeared in writing Letter VIII. (Henderson's Letter III.). An imitator as clever as Mr. F. Compton Price (who has kindly supplied these illustrations) would easily have deceived the crowd of Lords who were present at the comparison of the Casket Letters with genuine epistles of Mary to Elizabeth.

Scotland, in that age, was rich in ' fause notaries ' who made a profession of falsification. In the Burgh Records of Edinburgh, just before Mary's fall, we find a surgeon rewarded for healing two false notaries, whose right hands had been chopped off at the wrists. (Also for raising up a dead woman who had been buried for two days.) But these professionals were probably versed only in native forms of handwriting, whereas that of Mary, as of Bothwell, was the new ' Roman ' hand. An example of Mary Beaton's Roman hand is given in Plate C. Probably she had the same writing-master as her Queen, in France, but her hand is much neater and smaller than that of Mary, wearied with her vast correspondence. Probably Mary Beaton, if she chose, could imitate the Queen's hand, especially as that hand was, before the Queen had written so much. The ' Maries ' of Mary Stuart, Mary Beaton, and Mary Flemyng are all very similar. But to a layman, Mary Beaton's hand seems rather akin to that of the copyist of the Sonnets in the Cambridge MSS. (Plate E). The aunts of Mary Beaton, Lady Reres and the Lady of Branxholme, were, after April 1567, on the worst terms with the Queen, railing at her both in talk and in letters. But that Mary Beaton forged the Casket Letters I utterly disbelieve.

Kirkcaldy, whose signature is given, could not have adapted fingers hardened by the sword-hilt to a lady's Roman hand. Maitland of Lethington, whose signature follows Kirkcaldy's, would have found the task less impossible, and, if there is any truth in Camden's anecdote, may perhaps have been able to imitate the Queen's writing. But if any forged letters or portions of letters were exhibited, some unheard-of underling is most likely to have been the actual culprit.

PLATE C

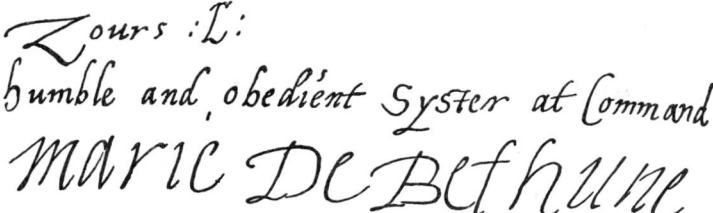

Zours :L:
humble and obedient Syster at Command

MARIC DE BETHUNE

HANDS OF MARY BEATON, KIRKCALDY, LETHINGTON, AND MARY FLEMING

XVIII

LATER HISTORY OF CASKET AND LETTERS

THE best official description of the famous Casket is in the Minutes of the Session of Commissioners at Westminster, on December 7, 1568. It was ' a small gilt coffer, not fully one foot long, being garnished in many places with the Roman (*Italic*) letter F set under a king's crown.' This minute is in the hand of Cecil's clerk, and is corrected by Cecil.[1] The Casket was obviously long in shape, not square, like a coffer decorated with Mary's arms, as Dowager of France, with thistles and other badges, the property of M. Victor Luzarche, and described by him in ' Un Coffret de Bijoux de Marie Stuart ' (Tours, 1868). Possibly the Casket was the *petite boyte d'argent*, which Mary intended to bequeath to Margaret Carwood, if she herself died in childbed in 1566.[2]

The Casket with the Letters was in Morton's hands till shortly before his death in 1681. On November 8, 1582, Bowes, Elizabeth's envoy in Scotland, wrote to Walsingham about the Casket. He had learned from a bastard of Morton's, the Prior (lay) of Pluscarden, that the box was now in the possession of Gowrie,

---

[1] Bain, ii. 569.   [2] Robertson *Inventories*, 124.

son of the Ruthven of Riccio's murder, and himself
engaged in that deed. Gowrie was at this time master
of James's person. Bowes thought that Gowrie
would not easily give up the Casket to Elizabeth,
who desired it.[1]

After trying to get agents to steal the Casket,
Bowes sought to induce Gowrie to give it up, with
promises of 'princely thanks and gratuity.' Gowrie
was not willing to admit the fact of possession, but
Bowes proved that the coffer had reached him through
Sandy Jordan, a servant of the late Earl of Morton.
Gowrie then said that, without the leave of James,
and of the nobles, who had dragged down Mary, he
could not part with the treasure, as the Letters
warranted their action—undertaken before they
knew that such Letters existed! However, Gowrie
promised to look for the Casket, and consider of
the matter. On November 24, Bowes again wrote.
Mary was giving out that the Letters 'were counterfeited by her rebels,' and was trying to procure them,
or have them destroyed. To keep them would
involve danger to Gowrie. Bowes would obtain the
consent of the other lords interested, 'a matter more
easy to promise than to perform;' finally Gowrie
ought to give them to Elizabeth 'for the *secrecy* and
benefit of the cause.' Mary's defenders may urge that
this 'secrecy' is suspicious. Gowrie would think
of it, but he must consult James, which, Bowes said,
'should adventure great danger to the cause.' On

---

[1] *Bowes Correspondence*, 236.

SIDE OF CASKET WITH ARMS OF HAMILTON

RAISED WORK ON ROOF OF CASKET

December 2, Bowes wrote about another interview with Gowrie, who said that the Duke of Lennox (Stewart d'Aubigny, the banished and now dead favourite of James) had sought to get the Letters, and that James knew where they were, and nothing could be done without James's consent.[1]

Gowrie was executed for treason in May, 1584, and of the Casket no more is heard. Goodall, in 1754, supposed that the Earl of Angus got it as Morton's 'heir by tail,' whereas we know that Gowrie succeeded Morton as custodian. In an anonymous writer of about 1660, Goodall found that 'the box and letters were at that time to be seen with the Marquis of Douglas; and it is thought by some they are still in that family, though others say they have since been seen at Hamilton.'[2] In 1810, Malcolm Laing, the historian, corresponded on the subject with Mr. Alexander Young, apparently the factor, or chamberlain, of the Duke of Hamilton. He could hear nothing of the Letters, but appears to have been told about a silver casket at Hamilton, rather less than a foot in length. A reproduction of that casket, by the kindness of the Duke of Hamilton, is given in this book. Laing maintained that, without the F's, crowned as mentioned in Cecil's minute, the casket could not be Mary's Casket. In any case it is a beautiful work of art, of Mary's age, and has been well described by Lady Baillie-Hamilton in 'A Historical

---

[1] Bowes, 265.   [2] Goodall, i. 35, 36.

Relic,' *Macmillan's Magazine*.[1] Lady Baillie-Hamilton,
when staying at Hamilton Palace, asked to be shown
a ring which Mary bequeathed to Lord John Hamilton, created Marquis in 1599. The ring was produced from a silver box, which also contained papers.
One of these, written probably about 1700–1715,
gave the history of the box itself. It was ' bought from
a Papist' by the Marchioness of Douglas, daughter
of George (first Marquis of Huntly). In 1632 this
lady became the second wife of William, first Marquis
of Douglas. Her eldest son married Lady Anne
Hamilton, heiress of James, first Duke of Hamilton,
who later became Duchess of Hamilton in her own
right, her husband (Lord William Douglas, later Earl
of Selkirk) bearing the ducal title. The Marchioness
of Douglas bought the box from a papist at an
unknown date after 1632, the box being sold as
the Casket. The Marchioness ' put her own arms
thereon,' the box having previously borne ' the
Queen's arms.' The Marchioness bequeathed her
plate to her son, Lord John Douglas, who sold it to
a goldsmith. The daughter-in-law of the Marchioness,
namely the Duchess of Hamilton, purchased the box
from the goldsmith, as she had learned from the
Marchioness that it was the historical Casket, and,
by her husband's desire, she effaced the arms of the
Marchioness, and put on her own, as may be seen in
Plate D. Only one key was obtained by the Duchess,
and is shown lying beside the Casket. The lock has

[1] Vol. lxxx. 131, *et seq.*

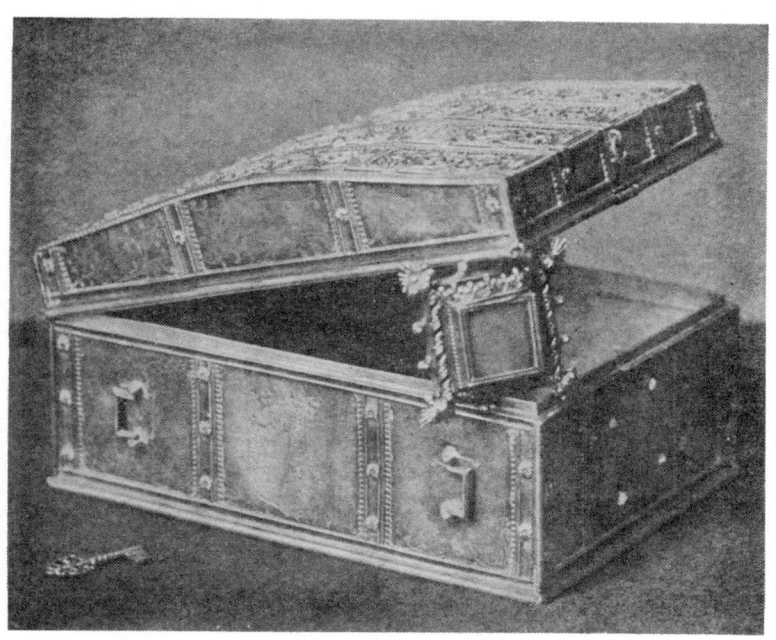

CASKET SHOWING THE LOCK AND KEY

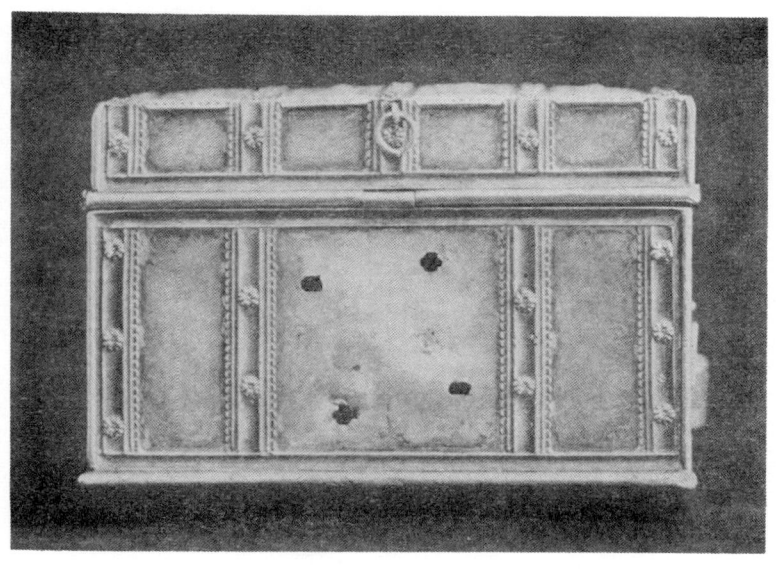

FRONT OF CASKET SHOWING PLACE WHENCE THE LOCK HAS BEEN
'STRICKEN UP'

been, at some time, 'stricken up,' as Morton says that the lock of the Casket was (see Plate E). The box is 'not fully a foot long'; it measures eight inches in length. The scroll-work (Plate E) and bands have been gilded, but the whole piece has not been 'overgilt,' as in Morton's description. That by the English Commissioners at York, 'a little coffer of silver and gilt,' better describes the relic. It is pronounced to be 'French work of the early part of the sixteenth century,' but Lady Baillie-Hamilton observes that the scroll-work closely resembles the tooling on a book of Catherine de' Medici, now in the British Museum.

Is the Hamilton Casket the historical Casket? It has the advantage of a fairly long pedigree in that character, as we have seen. But where are 'the many Roman letters F set under a king's crown,' of Cecil's description, which is almost literally copied in the memorandum added to the English edition of Buchanan's 'Detection'? Buchanan did not insert this memorandum, it is merely borrowed from Cecil's description, a fact of which Lady Baillie-Hamilton was not aware. There is no room on the panel now occupied by the Duchess of Hamilton's arms for *many* crowned F's. Only a cypher of two F's interlaced and crowned could have found space on that panel. Conceivably F's were attached in some way, and later removed, but there is no trace of them. We can hardly suppose that, as in the case of the coffer with a crimson cover, which was sent to

Mary at Loch Leven, the crowned F's were worked
in gold on the covering velvet.   Dr. Sepp, in 1884,
published, in a small pamphlet, the document redis-
covered by Lady Baillie-Hamilton.   He was informed
that there were small crowned F's stamped on the
bottom of the box, but these Lady Baillie-Hamilton
accounts for as ' the mark of a French silversmith,
consisting of a distinctive sign surmounted by a
fleur-de-lis and a crown.'   Thus for lack of any
certainty about the ' many or sundry' crowned F's,
this beautiful piece of work shares in the doubt and
mystery which seem inseparable from Mary Stuart.

APPENDIX A

THE SUPPOSED BODY OF BOTHWELL

MONSIEUR JUSSERAND, the well-known writer on English and Scottish literature, has kindly allowed me to print the following letter on the burial-place of Bothwell, and on the body which is traditionally regarded as his corpse.

Légation de France, à Copenhague, December 26, 1900.

MY DEAR LANG,—Our poor Queen's last scoundrel lies low in a darksome place.

The Faarvejle church is quite isolated on a little emi-

FAARVEJLE CHURCH (ACTUAL STATE).

(1) A side chapel used for burials, now attached to the Zytphen-Adeler family. 'Bothwell' was buried in it, and removed to the vault under the chancel when the Z.-A. family had some time adopted it.
(2) The entrance porch, with a fine oak door ornamented with iron work representing the dragons of 'Drags'-holm.

nence formerly washed by the water of a fiord now dried up (the work of an agricultural company which expected great benefits and lost much money instead). There is no village around ; the houses are scattered rather thinly throughout the country—a very frequent case in Denmark.

This church is, however, the one from which the castle of Dragsholm has ever, ecclesiastically, depended. Castle and church are at some distance : about twenty miles drive.

The castle was formerly a royal one; it was so in Bothwellian times.[1] Little remains of the old building ; it was burnt during the Swedish wars in the seventeenth century ; and rebuilt by the Zytphen-Adeler family (of Dutch origin) ; it still belongs to them.

Only the walls have been preserved ; they are of red brick ; but the actual owner has caused them to be white-washed throughout. The characteristic great tower it used to have in Hepburnian times has been destroyed. Almost no trace of any style is left, and the house, big as it is, is plain enough. The park around it is fine, with plenty of deer, hares, &c. The sea is near at hand and you see it from the walls.

As for the mummy, it lies in an oak coffin now preserved in a vault under the floor of the nave in the Faarvejle church. This vault is under the passage in the middle, near the step leading to the choir. The wooden planks on the floor are removed, a ladder is provided, and you find yourself in a subterranean chamber, with coffins piled on the top of one another, right and left. ' Both-well's ' stands apart on the left ; it is an oak chest ; as it was in a bad state, the present Baron Zytphen-Adeler has caused it to be placed in another one, with a sheet of glass allowing the head to be seen. But he kindly allowed me to see the body complete. The man must have been rather tall, not very ; the hands and feet have

---

[1] Before the Reformation it belonged to the Bishops of Roskilde, and was confiscated from them, Henry VIII.'s fashion.

a very fine and aristocratic appearance ; the mummifying process may have something to do with this appearance ; yet I think some of it came from nature. The head is absolutely hairless ; the face is close shaven ; the skull has no hair. I noticed, however, on the top of it faint traces of reddish-brown hair, but extremely close cropped. Horace Marryat, who saw it in 1859, says (in the same innocent fashion as if he had been performing a pious rite) that he ' severed a lock of his red and silver hair.' If he really did so, he must have severed all that was left. (' Residence in Jutland,' 1860.)

The skin remains ; the nose, very prominent and arched, is complete ; the mouth *very* broad. The jawbone is prominent (partly on account of the drying up of the flesh). The hind part of the skull is broad and deep. The arms are folded on the chest, below which the body is still wrapped in its winding sheet, only the feet emerging from it. The head lies on some white stuff which seems to be silk. All about the body is a quantity of vegetable remains, looking like broken sticks ; they told me it was hops, supposed to have preserving qualities.

As for the authenticity of the relic, there is no absolute proof. It is probable and likely ; not certain. That Bothwell died in Dragsholm and was buried in Faarvejle church is certain. The coffin has no mark, no inscription, no sign whatever allowing identification. But, if not Bothwell, who can this be—for there *it* is ? That careful embalming is not a usual process ; the other people buried in the church either have their names on their coffins or are not of such importance as to justify such a costly process.

A careful burial and no name on the tomb tally rather well with the circumstances : for the man was a great man, the husband of a Queen ; and yet what was to be done with his body ? would he not be sent back to Scotland some day ? what rites should be allowed him ?

Even before his death Bothwell had become, so to say, anonymous; and, to get rid of importunities, the Danish King, Fred. II., had allowed the rumour of his death to be spread several years before it happened.

The question remains an open one. J. J. A. Worsaae believed in the authenticity of the relic. The professor of anatomy, I. Ibsen, has also pronounced in its favour. Others have disagreed. Anatomici certant.

APPENDIX B

THE BURNING OF LYON KING OF ARMS

AMONG the mysteries of Mary's reign, none is more obscure than the burning of Sir William Stewart, the Lyon King at Arms: at St. Andrews, in August, 1569. In 1560, Stewart was Ross Herald, and carried letters between Mary and Elizabeth.[1]   On February 11, 1568, when Moray was Regent, we find Stewart sent on a mission to Denmark. He was to try to obtain the extradition of Bothwell, or, at least, to ask that he might be more strictly guarded.[2]   Now we know that, according to Moray, Bothwell's valet, Paris, did not arrive in Scotland from Denmark till June, 1569, though he was handed over to Captain Clark in October, 1568. Miss Strickland conjectured that Sir William Stewart, now Lyon Herald, brought back Paris from Denmark, learned from him that Mary was innocent, and Moray's associates culpable, and so had to be put out of the way. But the Lyon Herald returned to Scotland without Paris, a year before Paris; for he was in Scotland by July, 1568, and Paris did not land till June, 1569.

On July 20, 1568, Drury informs Cecil that Moray

---

[1] Bain, ii. 250.   [2] Cal. For. Eliz. viii. 413, 414.

'has understanding who has determined to kill him,' and has enlisted a bodyguard of thirty gentlemen. Drury adds—I cite him in his native orthography—

'I send unto your h. herewt. some pease off the woorke that the conjurers that dyd vse theyre develysshe skyle dyd devyse above Edenborogh, the platte whereoff I sente you before paynted.[1] And so ajayne I humbly take my leave.

'Some money they fownde. Will Stwart kyng off herauldee one off the parte players he that they judge schoold be the fynder off the threasure, schoold be the rejente.'

Here Drury speaks of 'conjurers,' who have played some prank involving discovery of a treasure. Stewart was one of the party, but what is meant by 'he that they judge should be finder of the treasure, should be Regent'? There is, apparently, some connection between the treasure hunt and the plot to kill Moray, and Stewart is mixed up with the magic of the treasure hunters. We know that Napier of Merchistoun, inventor of Logarithms, was to assist Logan of Restalrig to find treasure, 'by arts to him known,' at a later date. Probably the divining rod was to be employed, as in a case cited by Scott.

But in 1568, Napier of the Logarithms was only a boy of eighteen.

Returning to the plot to kill Moray: on August 14, 1568, Patrick Hepburn, bastard of the Bishop of Moray, and cousin of Bothwell, was taken in Scone, by Ruthven and Lindsay, brought before Moray at Stirling, and thence taken to Edinburgh. He was examined, revealed the nature of the plot, and gave up the names of his accomplices.[2]

This Patrick Hepburn was parson of Kynmoir by simoniacal arrangement with his father, the Bishop. It

---

[1] This picture seems to be lost.　　　　[2] *Diurnal*, p. 134.

seems possible that Stewart met Bothwell, when he was in Denmark, in the spring of the year, and induced him to arrange a conspiracy with his cousin, Patrick Hepburn. Before Hepburn was taken, the Lyon Herald, on August 2, fled to Dumbarton, where he was safe under the protection of Lord Fleming, then holding Dumbarton Castle for Mary.[1] The Herald 'was suspecte of conspiracy against the life of the Regent, the Earll of Moray.' He lost his place as Lyon King at Arms, and Sir David Lindsay was appointed to the office, held under James V. by his poet namesake. On August 19, Sir William Stewart wrote, from Dumbarton, a letter to a lord, not named. This lord had written to ask Fleming to give up Stewart, who believes that he was instigated by some other. 'For I cannot think that you can be so ingrate as to seek my innocent life and blood, considering that I have so favourably and so oft forewarned you of the great misery that you are like to fall into now, for not following my counsel and admonitions made oft and in due time.' Here we see Stewart claiming foreknowledge of events. 'Desist, I pray you, to seek further my blood, for as I shall answer to the eternal God, I never conspired or consented to the Earl of Moray's death . . . . I fear you not, nor none of that monstrous faction, for, as God is the defender of innocents, so is he.the just and severe punisher of cruel monsters and usurpers, who spare not to execute all kind of cruelty, under the pretext of religion and justice. . . . But there be some of his own secret Council that both directly and indirectly have sought that bloody usurper's life, whom I shall name as occasion shall serve. . . .' Stewart again protests his own innocence, apparently with conviction. He ends ' I pray you be favourable to the Parson of Kenmore' (Patrick Hepburn), 'and with such as have meddled with my apparel, bows, and books,

---

[1] Birrel's *Diary*, p. 17.

to keep all well till meeting, which will be soon God willing. . . .'[1]

This letter shows Stewart as a believer in fore-knowledge of events, as one who hates Moray, 'a bloody usurper,' and as acquainted with a plot against Moray by his intimates. Lethington and Sir James Balfour were more or less at odds with Moray, about this time, but we have no evidence that they conspired to kill him.

How it happened we do not know, but Stewart was captured, despite the protection of Dumbarton Castle. On October 4, 1568, his reception there was one of the charges made, perhaps by John Wood, against Mary's party, 'Lord Fleming refusing his delivery.'[2] At all events, on August 5, 1569, we find Stewart imprisoned in Edinburgh Castle, as also was Paris, who, says Moray, arrived at Leith in June of the year. On August 5, both men were taken to St. Andrews, 'there to be punished according to their demerits.'[3]

On the same day, August 5, 1569, Stewart wrote from the Castle a piteous letter to 'the most merciful Regent.' He declared, as to the conspiracy of 1568, that he only knew of it by public talk. 'The bruit of your Grace's murder was tossed up and down at Edinburgh.' Even if Stewart foreknew and concealed the plot, 'yet till the principal devisers are tried and convicted, I cannot be accused.' Stewart himself first heard of the conspiracy on July 21, 1568, from Patrick Hepburn. The comptroller (Tullibardine) had, on that day, 'purged himself' of the affair at Stirling. Now July 21 was the day after Drury gave his second notice of the treasure-hunt by magic, somehow involving a new regent, in which Stewart was concerned. Stewart cannot be accurate in referring his first hearsay knowledge of the conspiracy to July 21, 1568.

---

[1] Cot. Lib. Calig. B. ix. fol. 272.   Apud Chalmers, i. 441, 442.
[2] Bain, ii. 516.   [3] *Diurnal*, p. 146.

He goes on excusing himself. He could not believe that the persons implicated by Patrick Hepburn ever contemplated the murder of Moray, who knows their names. Moreover, there is some one who predicted many events to Stewart, such as Darnley's murder, the fall of Bothwell, ' the death of Lyon Herald, and my promotion, the Queen's deliverance,' Langside, ' and other predictions which have proved true.' This soothsayer said that Moray was only in danger from ' domestical treason.' Therefore, Stewart disbelieved wholly in Patrick Hepburn's story of a plot, and so did not divulge it. As witness, he cites ' a certain courtier ' to whom he had given the same reason for his scepticism, in the middle of July, 1568. He adds that he thinks it wrong, following St. Paul, to resist ' tyrants and usurpers.' He regarded Moray as a tyrant and usurper, we have seen, in August, 1568. He ends by offering disclosures, privately, and asking for mercy.[1]

On August 15, 1569, ' William Stewart, being convictit for witcherie, was burnt, and the said Paris, convictit for ane of the slayaris of the King, wes hangit in Sanctandrois,' says the ' Diurnal.'

Now, why was Lyon Herald burned ? If there was a conspiracy, in July, 1568, no others suffered for it. It was easy to convict Stewart for ' witchery ' : he confessed to dealings with a soothsayer, and the Kirk was beginning its campaign against witches. But what was the political or personal reason for Moray's cruelty? Had he seen Stewart's letter of August 19, 1568?

As to the soothsayer, he may have been a familiar spirit, but he may also have been the Laird of Merchistoun, Napier, the father of the inventor of Logarithms. One of his prophecies to Stewart dealt with Mary's escape from Loch Leven. And Nau, Mary's secretary, writes, ' The Laird of Merchistoun, who had the reputation of being

[1] Bain, ii. 665.

a great wizard, made bets with several persons, to the amount of 500 crowns, that by the 5th of May, her Majesty would be out of Loch Leven.' [1]

Thus there were two wizard Lairds of Merchistoun, the scientific son (the treasure-hunter for the laird of Restalrig) and his father.

For the rest, the conspiracy against Moray, in July, 1568, and the secret as to the cause of Lyon Herald's death, remain mysterious.[2]

APPENDIX C

THE DATE OF MARY'S VISIT TO GLASGOW

THE question of the possibility that Letter II. may be authentic turns on dates. If the Lords are right in declaring, in 'Cecil's Journal,' that Mary left Edinburgh on January 21, 1567, and arrived in Glasgow on January 23, then the evidence of the Letter is incompatible with that of Paris, and one or both testimonies must be abandoned. They fare no better if we accept the statement of Drury, writing from Berwick, that Mary entered Glasgow on January 22. It is shown in the text that, if we accept the date as given in Birrel's 'Diary,' and also in the 'Diurnal of Occurrents': if we make Mary leave Edinburgh on January 20, and (contrary to Drury and 'Cecil's Journal') make her enter Glasgow on January 21, then the Letter may be brought into harmony with the statement of Paris.

Of course it may be argued that the 'Diurnal' and Birrel's 'Diary' coincide in an error of date. The 'Diary' of Birrel describes itself as extending from 1532 to 1605. One man cannot have kept a daily note of events for

---

[1] Nau, p. 80.

[2] Chalmers's date, as to Stewart's expedition to Denmark, differs from that of Drury.

seventy-three years.   The 'Diary,' in fact, is *not* a daily
record.   There is but one entry for 1561, one for 1562,
one for 1565, ten for 1566, and twenty-four for 1567 ;
up to Mary's surrender at Carberry (June 15).   The
'Diurnal,' for our period, is more copious, and is by a
contemporary, though probably he did not always write his
remarks on the day of the occurrence noted.

From August 19, 1561, to June 15, 1567, the ' Diurnal '
and the 'Diary' record in common twenty-one events,
with date.   In seven of these cases they differ, as to date.
They differ as to the day of Mary's departure from
Edinburgh to Jedburgh, as to the departure of the
ambassadors from Stirling, as to the arrival of Mary
with her infant child in Edinburgh (January, 1567), as to
the return of Mary and Darnley from Glasgow, as to the
day of Darnley's burial, as to the day of opening Parliament, and as to the attack on Borthwick Castle by the
Lords : while the 'Diurnal' makes the explosion at Kirk
o' Field occur at 10 A.M. on February 10, and ends the
Parliament on April 29, which is absurd.   When the
dates are correctly known from other sources, and when
the 'Diary' and the 'Diurnal' coincide as to these dates,
then, of course, we may accept their authority.   But
when, as in the case of Mary's departure from Edinburgh,
and arrival in Glasgow, the 'Diary' and 'Diurnal' oppose 'Cecil's Journal,' and Drury's version, every reader
must estimate the value of their coincidence for himself.   If their date, January 20, is correct, then a letter
may have been written, and sent, and received, and the
facts, so far, are corroborated by Paris's deposition.

The argument of Chalmers, that Mary was at
Edinburgh till January 24, because there are entries as
if of her presence there in the Register of Privy Seal, is
not valid, as such entries were occasionally made in the
absence of the King or Queen.

APPENDIX D

THIS Band, which is constantly cited in all the troubles from 1567 to 1586, is a most mysterious document. We have seen that Mary's secretary, Nau, wilfully or accidentally confuses it with an anti-Darnley band signed by Morton, Moray, and many others, early in October, 1566. We have also seen that Randolph, in 1570, distinguishes between this ' old band' and the band for the murder, which, he says, Lethington and Balfour abstracted from a little coffer in the Castle, covered with green cloth or velvet, immediately after Mary surrendered at Carberry. I have ventured the theory that this carefully covered little coffer may have been the Casket itself.[1] Drury, again, in November, 1568, reports that the band has been burned, while the papers as to Mary are ' kept to be shewn.' But, in Scotland, till Morton's execution in June, 1581, the murder band was believed to be extant : at least Sir James Balfour, if he chose, could give evidence about it. What Mary wished to be believed as to this matter, we have seen in Nau, who wrote under her inspiration between 1575 and 1587. He asserts that Bothwell, ' to ease his conscience ' gave Mary a copy of the band, when he rode away from Carberry (June 15, 1567). He showed Mary the signatures of Morton, Balfour, Lethington, and others. She kept the document, and, when she met Morton on Carberry Hill, told him that he was one of the chief murderers, as she had learned.

---

[1] Such coffers were carefully covered. One had a cover of crimson velvet, with the letter ' F ' in silver and gold work (Maitland Club, *Illustrations of Reigns of Mary and James*). Another coffer, with a cover of purple velvet, is described in a tract by M. Luzarche (Tours, 1868).

He slunk away.[1] Probably Mary did accuse Morton, at
Carberry. When he was executed (June 3, 1581) Sir
John Foster, from Alnwick, sent an account of the trial
to Walsingham. In the evidence against Morton was
'the Queen's confession when she was taken at Carberry
Hill. She said he was the principal man that was the
deed-doer, and the drawer of that purpose.' Morton
certainly was not present, and it is as good as certain
that he did not sign the band. Still, Mary, at Carberry,
charged him with complicity.[2]

We have seen that Mary, ever after Carberry, also
inculpated Lethington, and vowed that she had something
in black and white which would hang him. Something
she probably did possess, but not a band signed also
by Morton. Concerning the murder-band, Hay of Tala,
before execution (January 3, 1567), 'in presence of the
whole people,' named as subscribers 'Bothwell, Huntly,
Argyll, Lethington, Balfour, with divers other nobles.'[3]
Hay saw their signatures, but not that of Morton. 'He
said my Lord Bothwell said to him that he subscribed the
same.' The Black Laird (December 13, 1573), when in
a devout and penitent condition, said that Bothwell had
shown him the contract, 'subscribed by four or five hand-
writes, which, he affirmed to me, was the subscription of
the Earl of Huntly, Argyll, the secretary Maitland, and
Sir James Balfour.' Ormistoun repeated part of the contents : the paper was drawn up by Balfour, a Lord of
Session.[4] (See Introduction, pp. xiii–xviii.)

Morton, we know, was accused of Darnley's death,
and arrested, at the end of December, 1580. Archibald
Douglas was sought for, but escaped into England.
Elizabeth sent Randolph down to save Morton : Hunsdon
was to lead an army over the Border. Every kind of
violence was designed, and forgery was attempted, but

[1] Nau, p. 48.

[2] Tytler, iv. 324, 1864.

[3] *Diurnal*, p. 127.

[4] Laing, ii. 293, 294.

Randolph had to fly to Berwick, at the end of March. Meanwhile the arch traitor, Balfour, had been summoned from France, as an evidence against Morton. But he was not of much use. On January 30, 1581, he wrote from Edinburgh to Mary. He had arrived in Scotland on December 17, 1580, when he found Morton in the height of power. Balfour secretly approached James's new favourite, Stewart d'Aubigny, recently created Earl of Lennox. By giving them information ' *had from your Majesty's self,* and partly by other intelligence which I knew and learned from others,' he gave them grounds for Morton's arrest. But Morton, he says, trusting to the lack of testimony from the absence of Archibald Douglas, boldly ' denies all things promised by him to Bothwell in that matter,' ' except his signature to the band whereof I did send the copy to your Majesty.' Now that was only ' Ainslie's band,' made *after* the murder, on April 19, 1567, to defend Bothwell's quarrel. On an extant copy Randolph has written, ' upon this was grounded thacusation of therle Morton.' [1] This was no hanging matter, and Balfour either had not or would not produce the murder band. He therefore asks Mary for further information : ' all that your Majesty has heard or known thereinto.' [2]

Balfour and Mary corresponded in cypher through Archbishop Beaton, her ambassador in France. On March 18, 1580, she had written to Beaton, ' if possible make Balfour write to me fully about the band which he has seen, with the signatures, for the murder of my late husband, the King, or let him give you a copy in his own hand.' If she really possessed the band which Nau says Bothwell gave her at Carberry, she needed no copy from Balfour. She does not seem to have believed in him and his band. On May 20, 1580, she writes to Beaton : ' I put no faith in what Balfour has sent me, so far, and cannot trust him much having been so wretchedly

[1] Bain, ii. 322.   [2] Laing, ii. 314–318.

betrayed by him,' for Balfour had put Morton on the trail
of the Casket, had sold the Castle, and later, had betrayed
Kirkcaldy and Lethington when they held the Castle
against Morton. However, she sent to Balfour a civil
message, and bade him go on undermining Morton, in
which he succeeded, in the following year. But the
murder-band was never produced. On March 16, 1581,
Randolph described a conference which had passed between him and James VI. ' I spoke again of the *band
in the green box*, containing the names of all the chief
persons consenting to the King's murder, which Sir
James Balfour either hath or can tell of.' Randolph,
who was working for Morton, obviously knew that *he* did
not sign that band : otherwise he would have avoided the
subject.[1]

We have no account of Morton's trial, save what
Foster tells Walsingham. ' The murder of the King was
laid to him by four or five witnesses. The first is the
Lord Bothwell's Testament' (usually thought to be
forged), 'the second, Mr. Archibald Douglas, when he
was his man.' But Douglas, surely, dared not appear in
Court, or in Scotland. Foster clearly means that Archibald's servant, Binning, proved *his* guilt, and that it
reflected on Morton, whose ' man ' Archibald was, in
1567, and later. Next came the charge that Morton
' spoke with ' Bothwell, as he confessed that he did, at
Whittingam, about January 20, 1567, when he says that
he declined to join the plot without Mary's written warrant. How could this be known, except through Mary
or Archibald Douglas ? Possibly his brother, at whose
house the conference was held, may have declared the
matter, as he ' split,' in 1581, on Archibald, and all concerned. ' And then ' Morton was condemned on ' the
consenting to the murder of the King' (how was *that*
proved ?), on Ainslie's band to support Bothwell's quarrel,

[1] Tytler, iv. 323, 1864.

'no person being excepted,' and finally, 'the Queen's confession at Carberry Hill,' when she confessed nothing, but accused Morton.

Mary's conduct, as far as it can be construed, looks as if she knew very little either about Morton or the murder-band. If Bothwell told her anything, what he told her was probably more or less untrue.

APPENDIX E

THE TRANSLATIONS OF THE CASKET LETTERS

THE casual treatment of the Casket Letters by Mary's accusers, and by the English Commissioners, is demonstrated by an inspection of the texts as they now exist. One thing is absolutely certain, the Letters were produced, at Westminster and Hampton Court, in the original French, whether that was forged, or garbled, or authentic. This is demonstrated by the occurrence, in the English translation, of the words 'I have taken the worms out of his nose.' This ugly French phrase for extracting a man's inmost thoughts is used by Mary in an authentic letter.[1] But the Scots version of the passage runs, 'I have drawn all out of him.' Therefore the English translator had a French original before him, *not* the French later published by the Huguenots, where for *tiré les vers du nez*, we find *j'ay sçeu toutes choses de luy*.

Original French letters were therefore produced; the only doubt rests on part of Crawford's deposition, where it verbally agrees with Letter II. But we may here overlook Crawford's part in the affair, merely reminding the reader that the French idioms in that portion of the Letter (Scots version) which most closely resembles his very words, in his deposition, may have come in through

[1] Labanoff, ii. 213.

C C

the process of translating Crawford's Scots into French, and out of French into Scots again, to which we return.

The Casket Letters were produced, in French, on December 7 and 8. On December 9, the English Commissioners read them, 'being duly translated into English.'[1] We are never told that the Scottish Lords prepared and produced the *English* translations. These must have been constructed on December 7 and 8, in a violent hurry. So great was the hurry that Letter VI. was not translated from French at all: the English was merely done, and badly done, out of the Scots. Thus, Scots, 'I am wod;' English, 'I am wood.' As far as this Letter goes, there need have been no original French text.[2] In this case (Letter VI.) the English is the Scots Anglified, word for word. The same easy mode of translating French is used in Letter V.; it is the Scots done word for word into English. In Letters I. and II., M. Philippson makes it pretty clear that the English translator had a copy of the Scots version lying by him, from which he occasionally helped himself to phrases. M. Cardauns, in *Der Sturz der Maria Stuart*, had proved the same point, which every one can verify. Dozens of blunders occur in the English versions, though, now and then, they keep closer to the originals than do the Scots translators.

Of this we give a singular and significant proof. In the Scots of Letter I. the first sentence ends, ' Ze promisit to mak me advertisement of zour newis from tyme to tyme.' The next sentence begins : 'The waiting upon yame.' In the English we read 'at your departure you

---

[1] Bain, ii. 576.

[2] Laing's efforts to detect French idioms lead him to take 'all contrary'—as in

' Mary, Mary,
All contrary,
How does your garden grow ? '—

and ' all goeth ill ' for French too literally translated.

promised to send me newes from you. *Nevertheless I can learn none :*' which is not in the Scots, but is in the published French, ' et toutes fois je n'en puis apprendre.' The *published* French is translated from the Latin, which is translated from the Scots, but each of the French *published* letters opens with a sentence or two from the *original* French : thus the published French, in one of these sentences, keeps what the Scots omits.

Therefore, the Scots translator undeniably, in the first paragraph of Letter I., omitted a clause which was in his French original, and is in the English translation. Consequently, when, in the same short letter, the English has, and the Scots has not, ' *to Ledington, to be delivered to you,*' we cannot, as most critics do, and as Herr Bresslau does, infer that Lethington had that mention of him deliberately excised from the Scots version, as likely to implicate him in the murder. It did not implicate him. Surely a Queen may write to her Secretary of State, on public affairs, even if she is planning a murder with her First Lord of the Admiralty. When the Scots translator omits a harmless clause, by inadvertence, in line 6, he may also, by inadvertence, omit another in line 41.

From these facts it follows that we cannot acquit Lethington of a possible share in the falsification of the Letters, merely because a reference to him, in the original French, existed, and was omitted in the Scots text. He need not have struck out the clause about himself, because the Scots translator, we see, actually omits another clause by sheer inadvertence. In the same way Mr. Henderson's text of the Casket Letters exhibits omissions of important passages, by inadvertence in copying.

Again, we can found no argument on omissions or changes, in the English versions. That text omits (in Letter II.), what we find in the Scots, the word *yesternight*, in the clause ' the King sent for Joachim *yesternight.*'

M. Philippson argues that this was an intentional omission, to hide from the English commissioners the incongruity of the dates. The translators, and probably the commissioners, did not look into things so closely. The English translators made many omissions and other errors, because they were working at top speed, and Cecil's marginal corrections deal with very few of these blunders. On them, therefore, no theory can be based. Nor can any theory be founded on clauses present in the English, but not in the Scots, as in Letter II., Scots, ' I answerit but rudely to the doutis yat wer in his letteris,' to which the English text appends, ' as though there had been a meaning to pursue him.' This, probably, was in the French ; but we must not infer that Lennox had it suppressed, in the Scots, as a reference to what he kept concealed, the rumour of Darnley's intention to seize and crown the child prince. The real fact is that the Scots translator, as we have seen, makes inadvertent omissions.

The English text is sometimes right where the Scots is wrong. Thus, Sir James Hamilton told Mary, as she entered Glasgow, that Lennox sent the Laird of Houstoun to tell him that he (Lennox) ' wald never have belevit that he (Sir James) wald have persewit him, nor zit accompanyit him with the Hamiltounis.' The English has what seems better, ' he,' Lennox, ' wold not have thought that he would have followed and accompany himself with the Hamiltons.' In the end of a paragraph (3), the Scots is gibberish : Scots, ' nevertheless he speikis gude, at the leist his son ' : English (*Henderson*), ' and they so speakith well of them, at least his sonne,' ' and then he speaketh well of them' (Bain). The English then omits (Scots) ' I se na uthir Gentilman bot thay of my company.'

In the next line (Scots) ' The King send for Joachim yesternicht,' the English omits ' yesternicht,' probably by inadvertence. The word has a bearing on the chronology of the Letter, and its omission in the English text may be discounted. It is a peculiarity of that text to write 'he' for 'I,' and a feature of Mary's hand accounts for the error. Where Darnley, in the Scots, says, 'I had rather have passit with yow,' the sentence follows 'I trow he belevit that I wald have send him away Presoner.' This is not in the English, but recurs in the end of Crawford's Deposition, 'I thought that she was carrying him away rather as a prisoner than as a husband.' Probably the sentence, omitted in English, was in the French : whether derived from Crawford's Deposition or not. Presently the English gives a kind of date, not found in the Scots. Scots, 'I am in doing of ane work heir that I hait greitly.' The English adds, *but I had begun it this morning.* Now, to all appearance, she had 'begun it' the night before. How did 'but I had begun it this morning' get into the English ? For the answer see page 300. Even in the first set of Memoranda there are differences : Scots, 'The purpois of Schir James Hamilton.' English, 'The talk of Sir James Hamilton *of the ambassador.*'

There are other mistranslations, and English omissions : the English especially omits the mysterious second set of notes. What appears most distinctly, from this comparison, is the hasty and slovenly manner of the whole inquiry. The English translators had some excuse for their bad work ; the Scots had none for their omissions and misrenderings.

Letter III. (or VIII.) and Letter IV. I have translated, in the body of this book, from the copies of the French originals.

In Letter V. the copy of the French original enables us to clear up the sense. It is a question about a maid or lady in waiting, whom Bothwell, or somebody else, wishes Mary to dismiss. The French is, 'et si vous ne me mondes [mandez] ce soir ce que volles que j'en fasse,

Je mendeferay [m'en deferay] au hazard de *la* fayre
entreprandre ce qui pourroit nuire à ce à quoy nous tandons
tous deus.' The Scots has 'I will red myself of *it*, and
cause *it* to be interprysit and takin in hand, quhilk micht
be hurtful to that quhair unto we baith do tend.' The
English is the Scots, Anglified.

The real sense, of course, is 'if you do not let me
know to-night what step you want me to take, I shall
get rid of *her*, at the risk of making *her* attempt something which might harm our project.' We have no other
known contemporary English translations. Of the four
known, two (I. II.) are made with a frequent glance at
the Scots, two are merely the Scots done into English,
without any reference to the French. Nothing but the
hasty careless manner of the whole inquiry accounts for
these circumstances.

The most curious point connected with the translations
is Crawford's deposition. It was handed in on December 9,
1568. Whoever did it out of Crawford's Scots into English had obviously both the Scots and English versions of
Letter II. before him. Where the deposition is practically
identical with the corresponding passages of Letter II.,
the transcriber of it into English usually followed the
Scots version of Letter II. But there is a corrected draft
in the Lennox MSS. at Cambridge, which proves that the
Angliciser of Crawford's Scots occasionally altered it into
harmony with the English version of Letter II. Thus, in
the first paragraph, the original draft of Crawford in
English has, like the Scots version of Letter II., 'the
rude words that I had spoken to Cunningham.' But, in
the official copy, in English, of Crawford, and in the
Lennox draft of it, 'rude' is changed into '*sharpe* wordes,'
and so on. The part of Crawford which corresponds with
Letter II. is free from obvious literal renderings of the
French idiom, as Mr. Henderson remarks.[1] These abound

[1] *Casket Letters*, pp. 82, 83.

in the English version of the corresponding part of Letter II., but are absent here in the Scots translation. It is, therefore, open to argument that Crawford did make notes of Darnley's and Mary's talk ; that these were done into ' the original French,' and thence retranslated into the Scots (free from French idiom here) and into the English, where traces of French idiom in this passage are frequent.

THE CASKET LETTERS

I PRINT the Scots Texts with one or two variations from C (the Cambridge MS.) and Y (the Yelverton MS.). The English Texts are given, where they are not merely taken direct from the Scots translations ; these and Crawford's Deposition are from MSS. in the Record Office and Hatfield Calendar.

LETTER I

PUBLISHED SCOTS TRANS-LATION	ENGLISH TRANSLATION AT THE RECORD OFFICE
	(State Papers relating to Mary Queen of Scots, vol. ii. No. 62)
IT apeiris, that with zour absence thair is alswa joynit forgetfulnes, seand yat at zour departing ze promysit to mak me advertisement of zour newis from tyme to tyme. The waitting upon yame zesterday causit me to be almaist in sic joy as I will be at zour returning,	IT seemyth that with your absence forgetfulness is joynid consydering that at your departure you promised me to send me newes from you. Neuertheless I can learn none. And yet did I yesterday looke for that that shuld make me meryer then I shall be. I

Published Scots Translation

quhilk ze have delayit langer than zour promeis was.

As to me, howbeit I have na farther newis from zow, according to my commissioun, I bring the Man with me to Craigmillar upon Monounday quhair he will be all Wednisday ; and I will gang to Edinburgh to draw blude of me, gif in the meane tyme I get na newis in ye contrarie fra zow.

He is mair gay than ever ze saw him ; he puttis me in remembrance of all thingis yat may mak me beleve he luifis me. Summa, ze will say yat he makis lufe to me : of ye quhilk I tak sa greit plesure, yat I enter never where he is, bot incontinent I tak ye seiknes of my sair syde, I am sa troubillit with it. Gif Paris bringis me that quhilk I send him for, I traist it sall amend me.

I pray zow, advertise me of zour newis at lenth, and quhat I sall do in cace ze be

English Translation at the Record Office

think you doo the lyke for your returne, prolonging it more than you have promised.

As for me, if I hear no other matter of you, according to my Commission, I bring the man Monday to Cregmillar, where he shall be vpon Wednisdaye. And I go to Edinboroughe to be lett blud, if I haue no word to the contrary.

He is the meryest that euer you sawe, and doth remember vnto me all that he can, to make me beleve that he louith me. To conclude, you wold saye that he makith love to me, wherein I take so muche plesure, that I never com in there, but the payne of my syde doth take me. I have it sore to daye. Yf Paris doth bring back unto me that for which I have sent, it suld muche amend me.

I pray you, send me word from you at large, and what I shall doo if you be not

Published Scots Translation	*English Translation at the Record Office*

returnit quhen I am cum thair; for, in cace ze wirk not wysely, I se that the haill burding of this will fall upon my schoulderis. Provide for all thing, and discourse upon it first with zourself. I send this be Betoun, quha gais to ane Day of Law of the Laird of Balfouris. I will say na further, saifing that I pray zow to send me gude newis of zour voyage. From Glasgow this Setterday in the morning.

returnid, when I shall be there. For if you be not wyse I see assuredly all the wholle burden falling vpon my shoulders. Prouide for all and consyder well first of all. I send this present to Ledinton to be delivered to you by Beton, who goith to one Day a lau of Lord Balfour. I will saye no more vnto you, but that I pray God send me good newes of your voyage.

From Glasco this Saturday morning.

LETTER II

PUBLISHED SCOTS TRANS-LATION	ENGLISH TRANSLATION (State Papers, Mary Queen of Scots, vol. ii. No. 65)

1. Being departit from the place quhair I left my hart, it is esie to be judgeit quhat was my countenance, seeing that I was evin als mekle as ane body without ane hart; quhilk was the Occasioun that quhile Denner tyme I held purpois to na body; nor zit durst ony present thameselfis unto me, judg-

Being gon from the place, where I had left my harte, it may be easily iudged what my Countenance was consydering what the body may without harte, which was cause that till dynner I had used lyttle talk, neyther wold any ~~pson~~ body advance him selfe therunto, thinking that it was not good so to doo.

Published Scots Translation

ing yat it was not gude sa to do.

2. Four myle or I came to the towne, ane gentilman of the Erle of Lennox come and maid his commendatiounis unto me; and excusit him that he came not to meit me, be ressoun he durst not interpryse the same, becaus of the rude wordis that I had spokin to Cuninghame : And he desyrit that he suld come to the inquisitioun of ye matter yat I suspectit him of. This last speiking was of his awin heid, without ony commissioun.

I answerit to him that thair was na recept culd serve aganis feir ; and that he wold not be affrayit, in cace he wer not culpabill ; and that I answerit bot rudely to the doutis yat wer in his letteris. Summa, I maid him hald his toung. The rest wer lang to wryte.

3. Schir James Hammiltoun met me, quha schawit that the uther tyme quhen he hard of my cumming

English Translation

Fowir myles from thence a gentleman of the Erle of Lennox cam and made his commendations and excuses vnto me, that he cam not to meete me, because he durst not enterprise so to doo, consydering the sharp wordes that I had spoken to Conyngham, and that he desyred that I wold com to the inquisition of the facte which I did suspecte him of. This last was of his own head, without commission, and I told him that he had no receipte against feare, and that he had no feare, if he did not feele him self faulty, and that I had also sharply answeared to the doubtes that he made in his letters as though ther had bene a meaning to poursue him. To be short I have made him hold his peace ; for the reste it were to long to tell you. Sir James Hamilton came to meete me, who told me that at another tyme he went his waye when he heard of

Published Scots Translation

he[1] departit away, and send Howstoun, to schaw him, that he wald never have belevit that he wald have persewit him, nor zit accompanyit him with the Hammiltounis. He answerit, that he was only cum bot to see me, and yat he wald nouther accompany Stewart nor Hammiltoun, bot be my commandement. He desyrit that he wald cum and speik with him : He refusit it.

The Laird of Lusse, Howstoun, and Caldwellis sone, with xl. hors or thairabout, come and met me. The Laird of Lusse said, he was chargeit to ane Day of Law be the Kingis father, quhilk suld be this day, aganis his awin hand-writ, quhilk he hes : and zit notwithstanding, knawing of my cumming, it is delayit. He was inquyrit to cum to him, quhilk he refusit, and sweiris that he will indure nathing of him. Never ane of that towne came to speik to me, quhilk causis me think that thay ar his ; and

English Translation

my comming, and that he sent unto him Houstoun, to tell him that he wold not have thought, that he wold have followed and accompany him selfe with the Hamiltons. He answeared that he was not com but to see me ; and that he would not follow Stuard nor Hamilton, but by my commandment. He prayed him to go speake to him ; he refused it.

The Lard Luce, Houstoun and the sonne of Caldwell, and about XLty horse cam to meete me and he told that he was sent to one day a law from the father, which shuld be this daye against the signing of his own hand, which he hathe, and that, knowing of my comming, he hath delayed it, and hath prayed him to go see him, which he hath refused and swearith that he will suffer nothing at his handes. Not one of the towne is ~~to see me~~ come to speake with me, which makith me to think

---

[1] 'He,' that is, Lennox.

Published Scots Translation

neuertheles he speikis gude, at the leist his sone.   I se na uther Gentilman bot thay of my company.

4. The King send for Joachim zisternicht, and askit at him, quhy I ludgeit not besyde him ?   And that he wald ryse the soner gif that wer ; and quhairfoir I come, gif it was for gude appointment ? and gif I had maid my estait, gif I had takin Paris [this berer will tell you sumwhat upon this], and Gilbert to wryte to me ? And yat I wald send Joseph away.   I am abaschit quha hes schawin him sa far ; zea he spak evin of ye mariage of Bastiane.

5. I inquyrit him of his letteris, quhairintill he plenzeit of the crueltie of sum : answerit, that he was astonischit, and that he was sa glaid to se me, that he belevit to die for glaidnes. He fand greit fault that I was pensive.

6. I departit to supper. Yis beirer wil tell yow of my arryuing.   He prayit me to

English Translation

that they be his, and then he speakith well of them at leaste his sonne.

The King sent for Joachim and asked him, why I did not lodge nighe to him, and that he wold ryse sooner and why I cam, whithir it wear for any good appointment, that he[1] cam, and whithir I had not taken Paris and Guilbert to write and that I sent Joseph.   I wonder who hath told him so muche evin of the mariage of Bastian.   This bearer shall tell you more vpon that I asked him of his letters and where he did complayne of the crueltye of some of them. He said that he did dreme, and that he was so glad to see me that he thought he shuld dye.   Indeede that he had found faulte with me. . . .

I went my waye to supper.   This bearer shall tell you of my arryving.   He

---

[1] 'He,' misread for 'I.'

Published Scots Translation

returne : the quhilk I did. He declairit unto me his seiknes, and that he wald mak na testament, bot only leif all thing to me ; and that I was the caus of his maladie, becaus of the regrait that he had that I was sa strange unto him. And thus he said : Ze ask me quhat I mene be the crueltie contenit in my letter ? it is of zow alone that will not accept my offeris and repentance. I confess that I haue failit, bot not into that quhilk I ever denyit ; and siclyke hes failit to sindrie of zour subjectis, quhilk ze haue forgeuin.

I am zoung.

Ze wil say, that ze have forgevin me oft tymes, and zit yat I returne to my faultis. May not ane man of my age, for lacke of counsell, fall twyse or thryse, or inlacke of his promeis, and at last repent himself, and be chastisit be experience ? Gif I may obtene pardoun, I protest I sall never mak fault agane. And I crafit na uther thing, bot yat we may

English Translation

praied me to com agayn, which I did : and he told me his grefe, and that he wold make no testament, but leave all unto me and that I was cause of his sicknes for the sorrow he had, that I was so strange unto him. ' And (said he) you asked what I ment in my letter to speak of cruelty. It was of your cruelty who will not accepte my offres and repentance I avowe that I have done amisse, but not that I have always disauowed ; and so have many other of your subjects don and you have well pardonid them.

I am young.

You will saye that you have also pardoned me many tymes and that I returne to my fault. May not a man of my age for want of counsell, fayle twise or thrise and mysse of promes and at the last repent and rebuke him selfe by his experience ? Yf I may obtayn this pardon I protest I will neuer make faulte agayne. And I ask nothing but that we may be

Published Scots Translation

be at bed and buird togidder as husband and wyfe; and gif ze wil not consent heirunto, I sall never ryse out of yis bed. I pray zow, tell me your resolutioun. God knawis how I am punischit for making my God of zow, and for hauing na uther thocht but on zow; and gif at ony tyme I offend zow, ze ar the caus, becaus quhen ony offendis me, gif, for my refuge, I micht playne unto zow, I wald speik it unto na uther body; bot quhen I heir ony thing, not being familiar with zow, necessitie constranis me to keip it in my breist; and yat causes me to tyne my wit for verray anger.

7. I answerit ay unto him, but that wald be ovir lang to wryte at lenth. I askit quhy he wald pas away in ye *Inglis* schip. He denyis it, and sweiris thairunto; bot he grantis that he spak with the men. Efter this I inquyrit him of the inquisitioun of Hiegait. He

English Translation

at bed and table togiether as husband and wife; and if you will not I will never rise from this bed. I pray you tell me your resolution heerof. God knoweth that I am punished to have made my God of you and had no other mynd but of you. And when I offende you somtyme, you are cause thereof: for if I thought, whan anybody doth any wrong to me, that I might for my refuge make my mone thereof unto you, I wold open it to no other, but when I heare anything being not familiar with you, I must keep it in my mynd ~~makith me out of my wytt~~ and that troublith my wittes for anger.

I did still answair him but that shall be too long. In the end I asked him why he wold go in the English shipp. He doth disavow it and sweareth so, and confessith to have spoken to the men. Afterwards I asked him of the inquisition of Hiegate. He denyed it till

Published Scots Translation

denyit the same, quhill I schew him the verray wordis was spokin. At quhilk tyme he said, that Mynto had advertisit him, that it was said, that sum of the counsell had brocht an letter to me to be subscrivit to put him in Presoun, and to slay him gif he maid resistance. And he askit the same at Mynto himself; quha answerit, that he belevit ye same to be trew. The morne I wil speik to him upon this Point.

8. As to the rest of Willie Hiegait's, he confessit it, bot it was the morne efter my cumming or he did it.

9. He wald verray fane that I suld ludge in his ludgeing. I refusit it, and said to him, that he behovit to be purgeit, and that culd not be done heir. He said to me, I heir say ze have brocht ane lytter with zow; but I had rather have passit with zow. I trow he belevit that I wald have send him away Presoner. I answerit, that I wald tak him with me to Craigmillar, quhair

English Translation

I told him the very wordes, and then he said that Minto sent him word that it was said, that som of the counsayle had brought me a letter to signe to putt him in prison, and to kill him if he did resiste and that he asked this of Minto himself, who said vnto him that he thought it was true. I will talke with him to morrowe vpon that poynte. The rest as Wille Hiegate hath confessed; but it was the next daye that he cam hither.

In the end he desyred much that I shuld lodge in his lodging. I have refused it. I have told him that he must be pourged and that could not be don heere. He said vnto me 'I have hard saye that you have brought the lytter, but I wold rather have gon with yourselfe.' I told him that so I wolde myself bring him to Cragmillar, that the phisicians and I also might cure him

Published Scots Translation

the mediciner and I micht help him, and not be far from my sone. He answerit, that he was reddy quhen I pleisit, sa I wald assure him of his requeist.

He desyris na body to se him. He is angrie quhen I speik of Walcar, and sayis, that he sal pluk the eiris out of his heid and that he leis. For I inquyrit him upon that, and yat he was angrie with sum of the Lordis, and wald threittin thame. He denyis that, and sayis he luifis thame all, and prayis me to give traist to nathing aganis him.

10. As to me, he wald rather give his lyfe or he did ony displesure to me. And efter yis he schew me of sa money lytil flattereis, sa cauldly and sa wysely that ze will abasche thairat. I had almaist forzet that he said, he could not dout of me in yis purpois of Hiegaite's; for he wald never beleif yat I, quha was his proper flesche, wald do him ony evill; alsweill it was schawin that I refusit to subscrive

English Translation

without being farr from my sonne. He said that he was ready when I wolde so as I wolde assure him of his requeste.

He hath no desyre to be seen and waxeth angry when I speake to him of Wallcar and sayth that he will pluck his eares from his head, and that he lyeth; for I asked him before of that, and what cause he had to complayne of some of the lords and to threaten them. He denyeth it, and sayth that he had allready prayed them to think no such matter of him. As for my selfe he wold rather lose his lyfe than doo me the leaste displeasure; and then used so many kindes of flatteryes so coldly and wysely as you wold marvayle at. I had forgotten that he sayde that he could not mistrust me for Hiegate's word, for he could not beleve, that his own flesh (which was myselfe) wold doo him any hurte; and in deed it was sayd that I refused to have him lett

Published Scots Translation

the same ; But as to ony utheris that wald persew him, at leist he suld sell his lyfe deir aneuch ; but he suspectit na body, nor zit wald not ; but wald lufe all yat I lufit.

11. He wald not let me depart from him, bot desyrit yat I suld walk with him. I mak it seme that I beleive that all is trew, and takis heid thairto, and excusit my self for this nicht that I culd not walk. He sayis, that he sleipis not weil. Ze saw him never better, nor speik mair humbler. And gif I had not ane prufe of his hart of waxe, and yat myne wer not of ane dyamont, quhairintill na schot can mak brek, but that quhilk cummis forth of zour hand, I wald have almaist had pietie of him. But feir not, the place sall hald unto the deith. Remember, in re-compence thairof, that ye suffer not zouris to be wyn be that fals race that will travell na les with zow for the same.

English Translation

bludd.[1] But for the others he wold at leaste sell his lyfe deare ynoughe ; but that he did suspecte nobody nor wolde, but wolde love all that I did love.

He wold not lett me go, but wold have me to watche with him. I made as though I thought all to be true and that I wold think vpon it, and have excused myself from sytting up with him this nyght, for he sayth that he sleepith not. You have never heard him speake better nor more humbly ; and if I had not proofe of his hart to be as waxe, and that myne were not as a dyamant, no stroke but comming from your hand could make me but to have pitie of him. But feare not for the place shall contynue till death. Remember also, in recompense therof, not to suffer yours to be won by that false race that wold do no lesse to your selfe.

---

[1] The English translator apparently mistook ' signer ' for ' saigner.'

Published Scots Translation

I beleve thay [1] have bene at schuillis togidder. He hes ever the teir in his eye ; he salutis every body, zea, unto the leist, and makis pieteous caressing unto thame, to mak thame have pietie on him. This day his father bled at the mouth and nose ; ges quhat presage that is. I have not zit sene him, he keipis his chalmer. The king desyris that I suld give him meit with my awin handis ; bot gif na mair traist quhair ze ar, than I sall do heir.

This is my first jornay. I sall end ye same ye morne.

12. I wryte all thingis, howbeit thay be of lytill wecht,to the end that ze may tak the best of all to judge upon. I am in doing of ane work heir that I hait greitly. Have ze not desyre to lauch to se me lie sa weill, at ye leist to dissembill sa weill, and to tell him treuth be-twix handis ? He schawit me almaist all yat is in the name of the Bischop and Sudderland, and zit I have

English Translation

I think they have bene at schoole togither. He hath allwais the teare in the eye. He saluteth every man, even to the meanest, and makith much of them, that they may take pitie of him. His father hath bled this daye at the nose and at the mouth. Gesse what token that is. I have not seene him ; he is in his chamber. The king is so desyrous, that I shuld give him meate with my own hands, but trust you no more there where you are than I doo here.

This is my first journay ; I will end to morrow. I write all, how little conse-quence so ever it be of, to the end that you may take of the wholle, that shall be best *for you to judge.* I doo here a work that I hate muche, *but I had begon it this morning* ; had you not lyst to laugh, to see me so trymly make a lie, at the leaste dissemble, and to mingle truthe therewith ? He hath almost told me all on the bishops behalfe

---

[1] ' They' : Darnley and Lady Bothwell.

Published Scots Translation

never twichit ane word of that ze schawit me ; but allanerly be force, flattering, and to pray him to assure himself of me. And be pleinzeing on the Bischop, I have drawin it all out of him. Ye have hard the rest.

13. We ar couplit with twa fals races ; the devil sinder us, and God knit us togidder for ever, for the maist faithful coupill that ever be unitit. This is my faith, I will die in it.

Excuse I wryte evill, ye may ges ye half of it ; bot I cannot mend it, because I am not weil at eis ; and zit verray glaid to wryte unto zow quhen the rest are sleipand, sen I cannot sleip as thay do, and as I wald desyre, that is in zour armes, my deir lufe, quhome I pray God to preserve from all evill, and send zow repois : I am gangand to seik myne till ye morne, quhen I sall end my Bybill ;

English Translation

and of Sunderland, without touching any word unto him of that which you had told me ; but only by muche flattering him and praying him to assure him selfe of me, and by my complayning of the bishop, *I have taken the worms out* of his nose. You have hard the rest.

We are tyed to by two false races. The *good yeere* untye us from them. God forgive me and God knytt us togither for ever for the most faythfull couple that ever he did knytt together. This is my fayth ; I will dye in it.

Excuse it, yf I write yll ; you must gesse the one halfe. I cannot doo with all, for I am yll at ease, and glad to write unto you when other folkes be a sleepe, seeing that I cannot doo as they doo, according to my desyre, that is betwene your armes my dear lyfe whom I besech God to preserve from all yll, and send you good rest as I go to seeke myne, till to morrow in the morning that will

but I am faschit that it stoppis me to wryte newis of myself unto zow, because it is sa lang.

end my bible. But it greevith me, that it shuld lett me from wryting unto you of newes of myself ~~long the same~~ so much I have to write.

Advertise me quhat ze have deliberat to do in the mater ze knaw upon this point, to ye end that we may understand utheris weill, that nathing thairthrow be spilt.

Send me word what you have determinid heerupon, that we may know the one the others mynde for marryng of any thing.

14. I am irkit, and ganging to sleip, and zit I ceis not to scrible[1] all this paper in sa mekle as restis thairof. Waryit mot this pokische man be that causes me haif sa mekle pane, for without him I suld have an far plesander subject to discourse upon. He is not over mekle deformit, zit he hes ressavit verray mekle. He hes almaist slane me with his braith ; it is worse than zour uncle's ; and zit I cum na neirer unto him, bot in ane chyre at the bed-seit, and he being at the uther end thairof.

I am weary, and am a sleepe, and yet I cannot forbeare scribbling so long as ther is any paper. Cursed be this pocky fellow that troublith me thus muche, for I had a pleasanter matter to discourse vnto you but for him. He is not muche the worse, but he is yll arrayed. I thought I shuld have bene kylled with his breth, for it is worse than your uncle's breth ; and yet I was sett no nearer to him than in a chayr by his bolster, and he lyeth at the furdre syde of the bed.

15. The message of the father in the gait.

The message of the Father by the waye.

[1] ' I cannot ceis to barbulze ' (Y).

Published Scots Translation

The purpois of Schir James Hamilton.

Of that the Laird of Lusse schawit me of the delay.

Of the demandis that he askit at Joachim.

Of my estait.

Of my company.

Of the occasion of my cumming :

And of Joseph.

Item, The purpois that he and I had togidder. Of the desyre that he hes to pleis me, and of his repentence.

Of the interpretatioun of his letter.

Of Willie Hiegaite's mater of his departing.

Of Monsiure de Levingstoun.

16. I had almaist forzet, that Monsiure de Levingstoun said in the Lady Reres eir at supper, that he wald drink to ye folk yat I wist of, gif I wald pledge thame. And efter supper he said to me, quhen I was lenand upon him warming me at the fyre, Ze have fair going to se seik folk, zit ze cannot be sa welcum to thame as

English Translation

The talk of Sir James ~~Hamilton~~ of the ambassador.

That the Lard a Luss hath tolde me of the delaye.

The questions that he asked of Jochim.

Of my state.

Of my companye.

And of the cause of my comming.

And of Joseph.

The talk that he and I haue had, and of his desyre to please me, of his repentance, and of thinterpretation of his letter.

Of Will Hiegate's doinges, and of his departure, and of the L. of Levinston.

I had forgotten of the L. of Levinston, that at supper he sayd softly to the Lady Reres, that he dronk to the persons I knew if I wold pledge them. And after supper he sayd softly to me, when I was leaning vpon him and warming myselfe, 'You may well go and see sick folkes, yet can you not be so welcom vnto them as

Published Scots Translation

ze left sum body this day in regrait, that will never be blyth quhill he se zow agane. I askit at him quha that was. With that he thristit my body, and said, that sum of his folkis had sene zow in fascherie ; ze may ges at the rest.

17. I wrocht this day quhill it was twa houris upon this bracelet, for to put ye key of it within the lock thairof, quhilk is couplit underneth with twa cordounis. I have had sa lytill tyme that it is evill maid ; bot I sall mak ane fairer in the meane tyme. Tak heid that nane that is heir se it, for all the warld will knaw it, becaus for haist it was maid in yair presence.

18. I am now passand to my fascheous purpois. Ze gar me dissemble sa far, that I haif horring thairat ; and ye caus me do almaist the office of a traitores. Remember how gif it wer not to obey zow, I had rather be deid or I did it ; my hart bleidis at it. Summa, he will not cum with me, ex-

English Translation

you have this daye left som body in payne who shall never be meary till he haue seene you agayne.' I asked him who it was ; he tooke me about the body and said ' One of his folkes that hath left you this daye.' Gesse you the rest.

This day I have wrought till two of the clock vpon this bracelet, to putt the keye in the clifte of it, which is tyed with two laces. I have had so little tyme that it is very yll, but I will make a fayrer ; and in the meane tyme take heed that none of those that be heere doo see it, for all the world wold know it, for I have made it in haste in theyr presence.

I go to my tedious talke. You make me dissemble so much that I am afrayde therof with horrour, and you make me almost to play the part of a traytor. Remember that if it weare not for obeyeng I had rather be dead. My heart bleedith for yt. To be shorte, he will not com but with con-

Published Scots Translation

cept upon conditioun that I will promeis to him, that I sall be at bed and buird with him as of befoir, and that I sall leif him na ofter : and doing this upon my word, he will do all thingis that I pleis, and cum with me. Bot he hes prayit me to remane upon him quhil uther morne.

He spak verray braifly at ye beginning, as yis beirer will schaw zow, upon the purpois of the Inglismen, and of his departing : Bot in ye end he returnit agane to his humilitie.[1]

19. He schawit, amangis uther purposis, yat he knew weill aneuch that my brother had schawin me yat thing, quhilk he had spoken in Striviling, of the quhilk he denyis ye ane half, and abone all, yat ever he came in his chalmer. For to mak him traist me, it behovit me to fenze in sum thingis with him : Thairfoir, quhen he requeistit me to promeis unto him, that quhen he was haill we suld have baith

English Translation

dition that I shall promise to be with him as heretofore at bed and borde, and that I shall forsake him no more ; and vpon my word he will doo whatsoever I will, and will com, but he hath prayed me to tarry till after to morrow.

He hath spoken at the fyrst more stoutly, as this bearer shall tell you upon the matter of the Englishmen and of his departure ; but in the end he cometh to his gentlenes agayne.

He hath told me, among other talk, that he knew well, that my brother hath told me at Sterling that which he had said there, wherof he denyed the halfe, and specially that he was in his chamber. But now to make him trust me I must fayne somthing vnto him ; and therfore when he desyred me to promise that when he shuld be well we shuld make but one bed, I told him fayning to believe

[1] ' Humanitie ' (C).

Published Scots Translation

ane bed : I said to him
fenzeingly, and making me
to beleve his [1] promisis, that
gif he changeit not purpois
betwix yis and that tyme, I
wald be content thairwith ;
bot in the meane tyme I
bad him heid that he leit na
body wit thairof, becaus, to
speik amangis our selfis, the
Lordis culd not be offendit
nor will evill thairfoir : Bot
thay wald feir in respect of
the boisting he maid of
thame, that gif ever we
aggreit togidder, he suld
mak thame knaw the lytill
compt thay take of him ;
and that he counsallit me
not to purchas sum of thame
by him.

Thay for this caus wald
be in jelosy, gif at anis,
without thair knawledge, I
suld brek the play set up
in the contrair in thair
presence.

He said verray joyfully,
And think zow thay will
esteme zow the mair of
that ? Bot I am verray
glaid that ze speik to me of
the Lordis ; for I beleve at

English Translation

his faire promises, that if he
did not change his mynd
betwene this tyme and that,
I was contented, so as he
wold saye nothing therof ;
for (to tell it betwen us
two) the Lordis wished no
yll to him, but did feare lest,
consydering the threaten-
inges which he made in
case we did agree together,
he wold make them feel the
small accompte they have
made of him ; and that he
wold persuade me to pour-
sue som of them, and for
this respecte shuld be in
~~by and by~~
jelousy if at one instant,
without their knowledge I
did brake a game made to
the contrary in their presence.

And he said unto me
very pleasant and meary
' Think you that they doo
the more esteem you ther-
fore ? But I am glad that
you talked to me of the

---

[1] His fair promises (C).

Published Scots Translation

this tyme ze desyre that we suld leif togidder in quyetnes : For gif it wer utherwyse, greiter inconvenience micht come to us baith than we ar war of : bot now I will do quhatever ze will do, and will lufe all that ze lufe ; and desyris zow to mak thame lufe in lyke maner : For, sen thay seik not my lyfe, I lufe thame all equallie. Upon yis point this beirer will schaw zow mony small thingis. Becaus I have over mekle to wryte, and it is lait : I give traist unto him upon zour word. Summa, he will ga upon my word to all places.

20. Allace ! I never dissavit ony body : Bot I remit me altogidder to zour will. Send me advertisement quhat I sall do, and quhatsaever thing sall cum thairof, I sall obey zow. Advise to with zourself, gif ze can find out ony mair secreit inventioun be medicine ; for he suld tak medicine and the bath at Craigmillar. He

English Translation

Lordes. I hope that you desyre now that we shall lyve a happy lyfe ; for if it weare otherwise, it could not be but greater inconvenience shuld happen to us both than you think. But I will doo now whatsoever you will have me doo, and will love all those that you shall love so as you make them to love me allso. For so as they seek not my lyfe, I love them all egally.' Therupon I have willed this bearer to tell you many pretty things ; for I have to muche to write, and it is late, and I trust him upon your worde. To be short, he will go any where upon my word.

Alas ! and I never deceived any body ; but I remitt myself wholly to your will. And send me word what I shall doo, and whatsoever happen to me, I will obey you. Think also yf you will not fynd som invention more secret by phisick, for he is to take physick at Cragmillar and the bathes also, and shall

Published Scots Translation

may not cum furth of the hous this lang tyme.

21. Summa, be all that I can leirne, he is in greit suspicioun, and zit notwithstanding, he gevis credit to my word; bot zit not sa far that he will schaw ony thing to me : bot nevertheles, I sall draw it out of him, gif ze will that I avow all unto him. Bot I will never rejoyce to deceive ony body that traistis in me : Zit notwithstanding ze may command me in all thingis. Have na evill opinioun of me for that caus, be ressoun ze ar the occasion of it zourself ; becaus, for my awin particular revenge, I wald not do it to him.

He gevis me sum chekis of yat quhilk I feir, zea, evin in the quick. He sayis this far, yat his faultis wer publeist : bot yair is that committis faultis, that belevis thay will never be spokin of; and zit thay will speik of greit and small. As towart the Lady Reres, he said, I pray God that scho may serve zow for your

English Translation

not com fourth of long tyme.

To be short, for that that I can learn he hath great suspicion, and yet, nevertheles trusteth upon my worde, but not to tell me as yet anything ; howbeit, if you will that I shall avow him, I will know all of him ; but I shall never be willing to beguile one that puttith his trust in me. Nevertheles you may doo all, and doo not estyme me the lesse therfore, for you are the cause therof. For, for my own revenge I wold not doo it.

He giuith me certain charges (and these strong), of that that I fear evin to saye that his faultes be published, but there be that committ some secret faultes and feare not to have them spoken of lowdely, and that ther is speeche of greate and small. And even touching the Lady Reres, he said 'God grant, that she serve

Published Scots Translation

honour : and said, it is thocht, and he belevis it to be trew, that I have not the power of myself into myself, and that becaus of the refuse I maid of his offeris. Summa, for certanetie he suspectis of the thing ze knaw, and of his lyfe. Bot as to the last, how sone yat I spak twa or thre gude wordis unto him, he rejoysis, and is out of dout.

22. I saw him not this evening for to end your bracelet, to the quhilk I can get na lokkis. It is reddy to thame : and zit I feir that it will bring sum malhure, and may be sene gif ze chance to be hurt. Advertise me gif ze will have it, and gif ze will have mair silver, and quhen I sall returne, and how far I may speik. He inragis when he heiris of Lethingtoun, or of zow, or of my brother. Of your brother he speikis nathing.[1] He speikis of the Erle of Argyle. I am in feir quhen I heir him speik ; for he assuris himself yat

English Translation

you to your honour.' And that men may not think, nor he neyther, that myne owne power was not in myselfe, seeing I did refuse his offres. To conclude, for a suerety, he mistrustith vs of that that you know, and for his lyfe. But in the end, after I had spoken two or three good wordes to him, he was very meary and glad.

I have not sene him this night for ending your bracelet, but I can fynde no claspes for yt ; it is ready therunto, and yet I feare least it should bring you yll happ, or that it shuld be known if you were hurte. Send me worde, whether you will have it and more monney, and whan I shall returne, and how farre I may speak. Now as farr as I perceive *I may doo much with you* ; gesse you whithir I shall not be suspected. As for the rest, he is wood when he hears of Ledinton, and of you and my brother. Of your brother

[1] 'Your brother.' Huntly.

Published Scots Translation

he hes not an evill opinioun of him. He speikis nathing of thame that is out, nouther gude nor evill, bot fleis that point. His father keipis his chalmer, I have not sene him.

23. All the Hammiltounis ar heir, that accompanyis me verray honorabilly. All the freindis of the uther convoyis me quhen I gang to se him. He desyris me to come and se him ryse the morne betyme. For to mak schort, this beirer will tell zow the rest. And gif I leirne ony thing heir, I will mak zow memoriall at evin. He will tell zow the occasioun of my remaning. Burne this letter, for it is ovir dangerous, and nathing weill said in it : for I am think-and upon nathing bot fascherie. Gif ze be in Edinburgh at the ressait of it, send me word sone.

English Translation

he sayth nothing, but of the Earl of Arguile he doth ; I am afraide of him to heare him talk, at the least he assurith himselfe that he hath no yll opinion of him. He speakith nothing of those abrode, nether good nor yll, but avoidith speaking of them. His father keepith his chamber; I have not seene him.

All the Hamiltons be heere who accompany me very honestly. All the friendes of the other doo come allwais, when I go to visitt him. He hath sent to me and prayeth me to see him rise to morrow in the morning early. To be short, this bearer shall declare unto you the rest ; and if I shall learne any-thing, I will make every night a memoriall therof. He shall tell you the cause of my staye. Burn this letter, for it is too dangerous, neyther is there anything well said in it, for I think upon nothing but upon greefe if you be at Edin-boroughe.

Published Scots Translation

24. Be not offendit, for I gif not ovir greit credite. Now seing to obey zow, my deir lufe, I spair nouther honour, conscience, hasarde, nor greitnes quhat sumevir tak it, I pray zow, in gude part, and not efter the interpretatioun of zour fals gudebrother, to quhome, I pray zou, gif na credite agains the maist faithful luifer that ever ze had, or ever sall have.

Se not hir, quhais fenzeit teiris suld not be sa mekle praisit nor estemit, as the trew and faithful travellis quhilk I sustene for to merite hir place. For obtening of the quhilk aganis my naturall, I betrayis thame that may impesche me. God forgive me, and God give zow, my only lufe, the hap and prosperitie quhilk your humble and faithful lufe desyris unto zow, quha hopis to be schortly ane uther thing to zow, for the reward of my irksum travellis.

25. It is lait: I desyre never to ceis fra wryting

English Translation

Now if to please you, my deere lyfe, I spare neither honor, conscience, nor hazard, nor greatnes, take it in good part, and not according to the interpretation of your false brother-in-law, to whom I pray you, give no credit against the most faythfull lover that ever you had or shall have.

See not also her whose faynid teares you ought not more to regarde than the true travails which I endure to deserve her place, for obteyning of which, against my own nature, I doo betray those that could lett me. God forgive me and give you, my only frend, the good luck and prosperitie that your humble and faythfull lover doth wisshe vnto you, who hopith shortly to be an other thing vnto you, for the reward of my paynes.

I have not made one worde, and it is very late,

Published Scots Translation

English Translation

unto zou ; zit now, efter the kissing of zour handis, I will end my letter. Excuse my evill wryting, and reid it twyse over. Excuse that thing that is scriblit,[1] for I had na paper zisterday quhen I wrait that of ye memoriall. Remember upon zour lufe, and wryte unto hir, and that verray oft. Lufe me as I sall do zow.

althoughe I shuld never be weary in wryting to you, yet will I end, after kyssing of your handes. Excuse my evill wryting, and read it over twise. Excuse also that [I scribbled], for I had yesternight no paper when took the paper of a memorial. [Pray] remember your frend, and wryte vnto her and often. Love me allw[ais as I shall love you].

Remember zow of the purpois of the Lady Reres.

Of the Inglismen.

Of his mother.

Of the Erle of Argyle.

Of the Erle Bothwell.

Of the ludgeing in Edin-burgh.

LETTER III

ORIGINAL FRENCH VERSION AT HATFIELD

(See Calendar of Hatfield Manuscripts, vol. i. pp. 376–77.)

J'ay veille plus tard la hault que je n'eusse fait si ce neust esté pour tirer ce que ce porteur vous dira que Je treuve la plus belle commoditie pour excuser vostre affaire que se pourroit presenter. Je luy ay promise de le luy mener demain $\wedge$ vous le trouves bon mettes y ordre. Or monsieur j'ay ja rompu ma promesse Car vous ne mavies rien

si

---

[1] 'Scriblit.' Barbulzeit (C).

de comande ∧ vous envoier ni escrire si ne le fais pour vous offencer et si vous scavies la craint que j'en ay vous nauries tant des subçons contrairs que toutesfois je cheris comme procedant de la chose du mond que je desire et cherche le plus c'est votre ∧ grace de laquelle mes
^{bonne}
deportemens m'asseureront et je n'en disesperay Jamais tant que selon vostre promesse vous m'en dischargeres vostre coeur aultrement je penseras que mon malheur et le bien composer de ceux qui n'ont la troisiesme partie de la fidelité ni voluntair obéissance que je vous porte auront gaigné sur moy l'avantage de la seconde amye de Jason. Non que je vous compare a un si malheureuse ni moy a une si impitoiable. Combien que vous men fassies un peu resentir en chose qui vous touschat ou pour vous preserver et garder a celle a qui seulle vous aporteins si lon se peult approprier ce que lon acquiert par bien et loyalment voire uniquement aymer comme je fais et fairay toute ma vie pour pein ou mal qui m'en puisse avenir. En recompence de quoy et des tous les maulx dont vous maves este cause, souvenes vous du lieu icy pres. Je ne demande que vous me tennes promesse de main mais que nous truvions et que nadjousties foy au subçons quaures sans nous en certifier, et Je ne demande a Dieu si non que coignoissies tout ce que je ay au coeur qui est vostre et quil vous preserve de tout mal au moyns durant ma vie qui ne me sera chere qu'autant qu'elle et moy vous serons agreables. Je m'en vois coucher et vous donner le bon soir mandes moy de main comme vous seres porté a bon heur. Car j'enseray en pein et faites bon guet si l'oseau sortira de sa cage ou sens son per comme la tourtre demeurera seulle a se lamenter de l'absence ∧ court quelle soit. Ce que je ne
^{pour}
puis faire ma lettre de bon coeur si ce nestoit que je ay peur que soyes endormy. Car je nay ose escrire devant Joseph et bastienne et Joachim qui ne sont que partir quand J'ay commence.

LETTER IV

ORIGINAL FRENCH VERSION

(In the Record Office State Papers, Mary Queen of Scots, vol. ii. No. 63.)

Mon cueur helas fault il que la follie d'une famme dont vous connoisses asses l'ingratitude vers moy soit cause de vous donner displesir veu que je neusse sceu y remedier sans le scavoir ; et despuis que men suis apersue Je ne vous lay peu dire pour scauoir comment mi guovejernerois car en cela ni aultre chose je ne veulx entreprandre de rien fayre sans en scavoir votre volontay, laquelle je vous suplie me fayre entandre car je la suiuray toute ma vie plus volontiers que vous ne me la declareres, et si vous ne me mandes ce soir ce que volles que jen faise je men deferay au hazard de la fayre entreprandre ce qui pourroit nuire a ce a quoy nous tandons tous deus, et quant elle sera mariee je vous suplie donnes men vne ou ien prandray telles de quoy vous contanteres quant a leur condition mayes de leur langue ou fidelite vers vous ie ne vous en respondray Je vous suplie qune opinion sur aultrui ne nuise en votre endroit a ma constance. Soupsonnes moi may quant je vous en veulx rendre hors de doubte et mesclersir ne le refeuses ma chere vie et permetes que je vous face preuue par mon obeissance de ma fidelite et constance et subjection volontaire, que je prands pour le plus agreable bien que je scaurois resceuoir si vous le voulles accepter, et nen faytes la ceremonie car vous ne me scauriez dauantage outrasger ou donner mortel ennuy.

Letter V

ORIGINAL FRENCH VERSION AT HATFIELD

Monsieur, helas pourquoy est vostre fiance mise en personne si indigne, pour subçonner ce que est entierement vostre. Vous m'avies promise que resouldries tout et que
me
∧ manderies tous les jours ce que j'aurais a faire. Vous nen aves rien fait. Je vous advertise bien de vous garder de vostre faulx beau frere Il est venu vers moy et sens me monstrer rien de vous me dist que ~~vous~~ luy mandies qu'il vous escrive ce qu'auries a dire, et ou, et quant vous me troveres et ce que faires touchant luy et la dessubs m'a preschè que c'estoit une folle entreprinse, et qu'avecques mon honneur Je ne vous pourries Jamaiis espouser, veu qu'estant marié vous m'amenies et que ses gens ne l'endureroient pas et que les seigneurs se dediroient. Somme il est tout contrair. Je luy ay dist qu'estant venue si avant si vous ne vous en retiries de vous mesmes que persuasion
a
ne la mort mesmes ne me fairoient faillir ~~de~~ ma promesse. Quant au lieu vous estes trop negligent (pardonnes moy) de vous en remettre a moy. Choisisses le vous mesmes et me le mandes. Et cependant je suis malade je differeray Quant au propose cest trop tard. Il n'a pas tins a moy que n'ayes pense a heure. Et si vous neussies non plus
pensee
changè de ~~propos~~ depuis mon absence que moy vous
Or
ne series a demander telle resolution. ∧ il ne manque rien de ma part et puis que vostre negligence vous met tous deux au danger d'un faux frere, s'il ne succede bien je ne me releveray Jamais. Il vous envoy ce porteur. Car Je ne ~~m~~'ose me fier a vostre frere de ces lettres ni de la diligence, il vous dira en quelle estat Je suis, et Juges quelle amendement~~e~~ m'a porté ce incertains Nouvelles.

Je voudrois estre morte. Car Je vois tout aller mal. Vous prometties bien autre chose de vostre providence. Mais l'absence peult sur vous, qui aves deux cordes a vostre arc.

Depesches la responce a fin que Je ne faille et ne ∧ ^{vous} fies de ceste entreprinse a vostre frere. Car il la dist, et si y est tout contrair.

Dieu vous doint le bon soir.

LETTER VI

PUBLISHED SCOTS TRANSLATION

Of the place and ye tyme I remit my self to zour brother and to zow. I will follow him, and will faill in nathing of my part. He findis mony difficulteis. I think he dois advertise zow thairof, and quhat he desyris for the handling of himself. As for the handling of myself, I hard it ains weill devysit.

Me thinks that zour services, and the lang amitie, having ye gude will of ye Lordis, do weill deserve ane pardoun, gif abone the dewtie of ane subject yow advance yourself, not to constrane me, bot to asure yourself of sic place neir unto me, that uther admonitiounis or forane perswasiounis may not let me from consenting to that that ye hope your service sall mak yow ane day to attene. And to be schort, to mak yourself sure of the Lordis, and fre to mary ; and that ye are constraint for your suretie, and to be abill to serve me faithfully, to use ane humbil requeist joynit to ane importune actioun.

And to be schort, excuse yourself, and perswade thame the maist ye can, yat ye ar constranit to mak persute aganis zour enemies. Ze sall say aneuch, gif the mater or ground do lyke yow ; and mony fair wordis to Lethingtoun. Gif ye lyke not the deid, send me word, and leif not the blame of all unto me.

Letter VII

scots version

My Lord, sen my letter writtin, zour brother in law yat was, come to me verray sad, and hes askit me my counsel, quhat he suld do efter to morne, becaus thair be mony folkis heir, and amang utheris the Erle of Sudderland, quha-wald rather die, considdering the gude thay have sa laitlie ressavit of me, then suffer me to be caryit away, thay conducting me; and that he feirit thair suld sum troubil happin of it: Of the uther syde, that it suld be said that he wer unthankfull to have betrayit me. I tald him, that he suld have resolvit with zow upon all that, and that he suld avoyde, gif he culd, thay that were maist mistraistit.

He hes resolvit to wryte to zow be my opinioun; for he hes abaschit me to se him sa unresolvit at the neid. I assure myself he will play the part of an honest man : But I have thocht gude to advertise zow of the feir he hes yat he suld be chargeit and accusit of tressoun, to ye end yat' without mistraisting him, ze may be the mair circumspect, and that ze may have ye mair power. For we had zisterday mair than iii. c. hors of his and of Levingstoun's. For the honour of God, be accompanyit rather with mair then les; for that is the principal of my cair.

I go to write my dispatche, and pray God to send us ane happy enterview schortly. I wryte in haist, to the end ye may be advysit in tyme.

LETTER VIII

ORIGINAL FRENCH VERSION

(In the Record Office State Papers, Mary Queen of Scots,
vol. ii. No. 66.)

Monsieur si lenuy de vostre absence celuy de vostre oubli
la crainte du dangier, tant promis d'un chacun a vostre
tant ayme personne peuuent me consoller Je vous en lesse
a juger veu le malheur que mon cruel sort et continuel
malheur mauoient promis a la suite des infortunes et
craintes tant recentes que passes de plus longue main les
quelles vous scaves mais pour tout cela Je me vous accuserai ni de peu de souuenance ni de peu de soigne et
moins encores de vostre promesse violee ou de la froideur
de vos lettres mestant ja tant randue vostre que ce quil
vous plaist mest agreable et sont mes penses tant volon-
terement, aux vostres a subjectes que je veulx presupposer
que tout ce que vient de vous procede non par aulcune des
causes de susdictes ains pour telles qui son justes et raisoin-
ables et telles qui Je desir moy ~~mesme~~ qui est lordre que
maves promis de prendre final pour la seurete et honnor-
able service du seul soubtien de ma vie pour qui seul Je la
veus conserver et sens lequel Je ne desire que breve mort
or pour vous tesmoigner combien humblement sous voz
commandemens Je me soubmets Je vous ay envoie en
signe d'homage par paris lornement du cheif conducteur
des aultres membres inferant que vous investant de sa
despoille de luy qui est principal le rest ne peult que vous
estre subject et avecques le consentement du cueur au
lieu du quel puis que le vous ay Ja lesse Je vous envoie un
sepulcre de pierre dure poinct de noir seme d'larmes et de
ossements, la pierre Je le la compare a mon cueur qui
comme luy est talle en un seur tombeau ou receptacle de
voz commandements et sur tout de vostre nom et memoire

Monsieur   Si lenuy de Vottre absence
celuy de Votre oubli la crainte du
dangier tant promis d'un chacun a
votre tant ayme personne peuuent me
consoller ie vous en lesse a iuier veu le
malheur que mon cruel sort & continuel
malheur mauoient promis a la suite des
infortunes & craintes tant recentes que
passes de plus longue main les quelles
vous scaues mais pour tout cela ie me
vous accuserai ni de peu de souuenance
ni de peu de soigne & moins encores
de votre promesse violee on de la
froideur de vos lettres

MODERN IMITATION OF MARY'S HAND

The text is part of the 'Original French' of Letter VIII. (III.)

The purpose is to show how far Mary's hand can be imitated

qui y sont enclos, comme me cheveulz en la bague pour
Jamais nen sortir que la mort ne vous permet fair trophee
des mes os comme la bague en est remplie en signe que
vous aves fayt entiere conqueste de moy, de mon cueur et
iusque a vous en lesser les os pour memoir de v̅r̅e victoire
et de mon agreable perte et volontiere pour estre mieux
employe que ie ne le merite Lesmail demiron est noir qui
signifie la fermete de celle que lenvoie les larmes sont sans
nombre ausi sont les craintes de vous desplair les pleurs de
vostre absence et de desplaisir de ne pouvoir estre en effect
exterieur vostre comme je suys sans faintise de cueur et
desprit et a bon droit quant mes merites seroint trop plus
grands que de la plus perfayte que Jamais feut et telle que
je desire estre et mettray poine en condition de contrefair
pour dignement estre emploiee soubs vostre domination.
reseues la donc mon seul bien en aussi bonne part, comme
avecques extreme Joie Jay fait vostre mariage, qui jusques
a celuy de nos corps en public ne sortira de mon sein,
comme merque de tout ce que Jay ou espere ni desire de
felicite en ce monde or craignant mon cueuer de vous
ennuyer autant a lire que je me plaire descrir Je finiray
apres vous avoir baise les mains daussi grande affection
que je prie Dieu (O le seul soubtien de ma vie) vous la
donner longue et heureuse et a moy v̅r̅e bonne grace le
seul bien que je desire et a quoy je tends Jay dit a ce porteur ce que Jay apris sur le quel Je me remets sachant, le
credit que luy donnes comme fait celle que vous veult estre
pour Jamais humble et obeisante loyalle femme et seulle
amye qui pour Jamais vous voue entierement le cueur le
corps sans aucun changement comme a celuy que J fait
possesseur du cueur du quel vous pouves tenir seur Jusques
a la mort ne changera car mal ni bien onque ne estrangera.

LETTER IX

THE FRENCH 'SONNETS'

O dieux ayes de moy compassion
E m'enseignes quelle preuue certane
Je puis donner qui ne luy semble vain
De mon amour et ferme affection.
Las n'est il pas ia en possession
Du corps, du cueur qui ne refuse peine
Ny dishonneur, en la vie incertane,
Offence de parents, ne pire affliction ?
Pour luy tous mes amys i'estime moins que rien,
Et de mes ennemis ie veulx esperere bien.
I'ay hazardé pour luy & nom & conscience :
Ie veux pour luy au monde renoncer :
Ie veux mourire pour luy auancer.
Que reste il plus pour prouuer ma constance ?

Entre ses mains & en son plein pouuoir
Je metz mon filz, mon honneur, & ma vie,
Mon pais, mes subjects mon ame assubiectie
Et toute à luy, & n'ay autre vouloir
Pour mon obiect que sens le disseuoir
Suiure ie veux malgré toute l'enuie
Qu'issir en peult, car ie nay autre envie
Que de ma foy, luy faire apparceuoir
Que pour tempest ou bonnace qui face
Iamais ne veux changer demeure ou place.
Brief ie farray de ma foy telle preuue,
Qu'il cognoistra sens feinte ma constance,
Non par mes pleurs ou feinte obeissance,
Come autres ont fait, mais par diuers espreuue.

Elle pour son honneur vous doibt obeissance
Moy vous obeissant i'en puys resseuoir blasme
N'estât, à mon regret, come elle vostre femme.
Et si n'aura pourtant en ce point préeminence
Pour son proffit elle vse de constance,
Car ce n'est peu d'honneur d'estre de voz biens dame
Et moy pour vous aymer i'en puix resseuoir blasme
Et ne luy veux ceder en toute l'obseruance
Elle de vostre mal n'a l'apprehension
Moy ie n'ay nul repos tant ie crains l'apparence
Par l'aduis des parents, elle eut vostre acointance
Moy maugre tous les miens vous port affection
Et de sa loyauté prenes ferme asseurance.

Par vous mon coeur & par vostre alliance
Elle a remis sa maison en honneur
Elle a jouy par vous de la grandeur
Dont tous les siens n'auoyent nul asseurance
De vous mon bien elle à eu la constance,[1]
Et a guagné pour vn temps vostre cueur,
Par vous elle a eu plaisir et bon heur,
Et pour vous a receu honneur & reuerence,
Et n'a perdu sinon la jouissance
D'vn fascheux sot qu'elle aymoit cherement.
Ie ne la plains d'aymer donc ardamment,
Celuy qui n'a en sens, ni en vaillance,
En beauté, en bonté, ni en constance
Point de seconde.   Ie vis en ceste foy.

Quant vous l'aymes, elle vsoit de froideur.
Sy vous souffriez, pour s'amour passion
Qui vient d'aymer de trop d'affection,
Son doil monstroit, la tristesse de coeur

---

[1] Cambridge MS. 'l'acointance.'

N'ayant plesir de vostre grand ardeur
En ses habitz, mon estroit sens fiction
Qu'elle n'auoyt peur qu'imperfection
Peult l'affasser hors de ce loyal coeur.
De vostre mort ie ne vis la peaur
Que meritoit tel mary & seigneur.
Somme de vous elle a eu tout son bien
Et n' a prise ne iamais estimé
Vn si grand heur sinon puis qu'il n'est sien
Et maintenant dist l'auoyr tant aymé.

Et maintenant elle commence à voire
Qu'elle estoit bien de mauuais iugement
De n'estimer l'amour d'vn tel amant
Et vouldroit bien mon amy desseuoir,
Par les escripts tout fardes de scauoir
Qui pour tant n'est en son esprit croissant
Ayns emprunté de quelque auteur eluissant.
A feint tresbien vn enuoy sans l'avoyr
Et toutesfois ses parolles fardez,
Ses pleurs, ses plaints remplis de fictions.
Et ses hautes cris & lamentations
Ont tant guagné que par vous sont guardes.
Ses lettres escriptes ausquells vous donnez foy
Et si l'aymes & croyez plus que moy.

Vous la croyes las trop ie l'appercoy
Et vous doutez de ma ferme constance,
O mon seul bien & mon seul esperance,
Et ne vous peux ie [1] asseurer de ma foy
Vous m'estimes legier je le voy,
Et si n'auez en moy nul asseurance,
Et soubconnes mon coeur sans apparence,
Vous deffiant à trop grande tort de moy.

[1] Cambridge MS. 'je' omitted.

Vous ignores l'amour que ie vous porte
Vous soubçonnez qu'autre amour me transporte,
Vous estimes mes parolles du vent,
Vous depeignes de cire mon las coeur
Vous me penses femme sans iugement,
Et tout cela augmente mon ardeur.

Mon amour croist & plus en plus croistra
Tant que je viuray, et tiendra à grandeur,
Tant seulement d'auoir part en ce coeur
Vers qui en fin mon amour paroitra
Si tres à cler que iamais n'en doutra,
Pour luy ie veux recercher la grandeure,
Et faira tant qu'en vray connoistra,
Que ie n'ay bien, heur, ni contentement,
Qu' a l'obeyr & servir loyamment.
Pour luy iattendz toute bon fortune.
Pour luy ie veux guarder santé & vie
Pour luy tout vertu de suiure i'ay enuie
Et sens changer me trouuera tout vne.

Pour luy aussi ie jete mainte larme.
Premier quand il se fit de ce corps possesseur,
Du quel alors il n'auoyt pas le coeur.
Puis me donna vn autre dure alarme
Quand il versa de son sang maint drasme
Dont de grief il me vint lesser doleur,[1]
Qui me pensa oster la vie, & la frayeur
De[2] perdre las la seule rempar qui m'arme.
Pour luy depuis iay mesprise l'honneur
Ce qui nous peut seul prouoir de bonheur.
Pour luy iay hasarde grandeur[3] & conscience.
Pour luy tous mes parents i'ay quisté, & amys,
Et tous aultres respects sont a part mis.
Brief de vous seul ie cherche l'alliance.

---

[1] Cambridge MS. 'Dont de grief doil me vint ceste dolleur.'
[2] Cambridge MS. 'Per.'   [3] Cambridge MS. 'honneur.'

De vous ie dis seul soubtein de ma vie
Tant seulement ie cherche m'asseurer,
Et si ose de moy tant presumer
De vous guagner maugré toute l'enuie.
Car c'est le seul desir de vostre chere amye,
De vous seruir & loyaument aymer,
Et tous malheurs moins que riens estimer,
Et vostre volunté de la mien suiure.
Vous conoistres avecques obeissance
De mon loyal deuoir n'omettant la science
A quoy i'estudiray pour tousiours vous complaire
Sans aymer rien que vous, soubs la suiection
De qui ie veux sens nulle fiction
Viure & mourir & à ce j'obtempere.

Mon coeur, mon sang, mon ame, & mon soussy,
Las, vous m'aues promes qu'aurois ce plaisir
De deuiser auecques vous à loysir,
Toute la nuit, ou ie languis icy
Ayant le coeur d'extreme peour transie,
Pour voir absent le but de mon desir
Crainte d'oubly vn coup me vient a saisir :
Et l'autrefois ie crains que rendursi
Soit contre moy vostre amiable coeur
Par quelque dit d'un meschant rapporteur.
Un autrefoys ie crains quelque auenture
Qui par chemin deturne mon amant,
Par vn fascheux & nouueau accident
Dieu deturne toute malheureux augure.

Ne vous voyant selon qu'aues promis
I'ay mis la main au papier pour escrire
D'vn different que ie voulou transcrire,
Ie ne scay pas quel sera vostre aduise
Mais ie scay bien qui mieux aymer sçaura
Vous diries bien qui plus y guagnera.

CRAWFORD'S DEPOSITION

(State Papers, Scotland, Elizabeth, vol. xiii. No. 14. Cal. Foreign State Papers, Elizabeth, vol. viii. No. 954, February 1566-7.)

> The Wordes betwixt the Q. and me Thomas Crawforde bye the waye as she came to Glasco to fetche the kinge, when mye L. my Master sent me to showe her the cause whye he came not to mete her him sellfe.

Firste I made my L. mye masters humble cõmendacõns vnto her Mati wᵗʰ thexcuse yᵗ he came not to mete her praing her grace not to thinke it was eathʳ for prowdnesse or yet for not knowinge hys duetye towardes her highnesse, but onelye for want of helyᵉ at yᵉ present, and allso yᵗ he woulde not p̃sume to com in her presence vntille he knewe farder her minde bicause of the sharpe Wordes yᵗ she had spoken of him to Robert Cuninghᵃm hys servant in Sterling. Wherebye he thought he Was in her Maᵗⁱˢ displesvre Notwithstanding he hathe sent hys servantę and frendę to waite vppon her Maᵗⁱ.

She aunswered yᵗ there was no recept against feare.

I aunswered yᵗ mye L. had no feare for anie thinge he knewe in him sellf, but onelye of the colde and vnkinde Wordes she had spoken to hys servant.

She aunswered and said yᵗ he woulde not be a fraide in case he were not culpable.

I aunswered yᵗ I knewe so farr of hys Lordsh. yᵗ he desired nothing more than yᵗ the secretts vf everye creatures harte were writtē in theire face.

She asked me yf I had anie farder com̃ission.

I aunswered no.

Then she com̃aunded me to holde mye peace.

The Wordes y^t I rememb^r were betwixt
the Kinge and the Q. in Glasco when
she took him awaie to Edinbrowghe.

The Kinge for y^t mye L. hys father was then absent
and sicke, bye reason whereof he could not speke wth him
him sellfe, called me vnto him and theise wordes that had
then passed betwixt him and the Quene, he gaue me in re-
membraunce to reporte vnto the said mye Lord hys father.

After theire metinge and shorte speking to geth^r she
asked him of his lr̃es, wherein he complained of the
cruelltye of som.

He aunswered y^t he complained not wthowt cause and
as he beleved, she woulde graunte her sellfe when she
was well advised.

She asked him of hys sicknesse, he answered y^t she
was the cause thereof, and moreover he saide, Ye asked
me What I ment bye the crueltye specified in mye lr̃es, yt
procedeth of yo^w onelye y^t wille not accepte mye offres
and repentaunce, I confesse y^t I haue failed in som thinge,
and yet greater fautes haue bin made to yo^w sundrye
times, wch ye haue forgiuẽ. I am but yonge, and ye will
saye ye haue forgiuẽ me diverse tymes. Maye not a man
of mye age for lacke of Counselle, of wch I am verye
destitute falle twise or thrise, and yet repent and be
chastised bye experience? Yf I haue made anye faile y^t
ye but thinke a faile, howe so ever it be, I crave yor pdone
and protest y^t I shall never faile againe. I desire no oth^r
thinge but y^t we maye be to geath^r as husband and wife.
And yf ye will not consent hereto, I desire never to rise
forthe of thys bed. Therefore I praye yo^w give me an
aunswer here vnto. God knowethe howe I am punished
for makinge mye god of yo^w and for having no oth^r
thowght but on yo^w. And yf at anie tyme I offend yo^w,
ye are the cause, for y^t whẽ anie offendethe me, if for mye
refuge I might open mye minde to yo^w, I woulde speak to

no other, but whē anie thinge ys spokē to me, and ye and I not beinge as husband and wife owght to be, necessite compelleth me to kepe it in my breste and bringethe me in suche melancolye as ye see me in.

She aunswered y^t it semed him she was sorye for hys sicknesse, and she woulde finde remedye therefore so sone as she might.

She asked him Whye he woulde haue passed awaye in Thenglishe shipp.

He aunswered y^t he had spokē w^t thenglishe mā but not of minde to goe awaie w^t him. And if he had, it had not bin wthowt cause consideringe howe he was vsed. For he had neath^r to susteine him sellfe nor hys servante, and nede not make farder rehersalle thereof, seinge she knewe it as well as he.

Then she asked him of the purpose of Hegate, he aunswered y^t it was tolde him.

She required howe and bye whome it was told him.

He aunswered y^t the L. of Minto tolde him y^t a lr̄e was presented to her in Cragmiller made bye her own divise and subscribed by certeine others who desired her to sub-scribe the same, wch she refused to doe. And he said that he woulde never thinke y^t she who was his owne propre fleshe, woulde do him anie hurte, and if anie oth^r woulde do it, theye shuld bye it dere, vnlesse theye took him sleping, albeit he suspected none. So he desired her effectuouslye to beare him companye. For she ever fownde som adoe to drawe her selfe frõ him to her owne lodginge and woulde never abyde w^t him past two howres at once.

She was verye pensiffe. Whereat he fownd faulte he said to her y^t he was adv^{r}tised she had browght a litter w^t her.

She aunswered y^t bicause she vnderstoode he was not hable to ryde on horseback, she brought a litter, y^t he might be caried more softlye.

He aunswered y^t yt was not mete for a sick mā to travelle y^t coulde not sitt on horsebacke and especiallye in so colde weather.

She aunswered y^t she would take him to Cragmiller where she might be w^t him and not farre from her sonne.

He aunswered y^t vppon condicõn he would goe wth her wch was that he and she might be to geath^r at bedde and borde as husband and wife, and y^t she should leaue him no more.   And if she would promise him y^t, vppon her worde he would goe wth her, where she pleised wthowt respecte of anye dang^r eath^r of sicknesse, wherein he was, or otherwise.   But if she would not condescend thereto, he would not goe wth her in anye wise.

She aunswered that her comminge was onelye to that effecte, and if she had not bin minded thereto, she had not com so farre to fetche him, and so she graunted hys desire and p^{o}mised him y^t it shculd be as he had spoken, and therevppon gave him her hand and faithe of her bodye y^t she woulde love him and vse him as her husband.   Notwithstanding before theye coulde com to geath^r he must be purged and clensed of hys sicknesse, wch she truisted woulde be shortlye for she minded to giue him the bathe at Cragmill^r.   Than he said he would doe what soever she would have him doe, and would love all that she loved. She required of him in especialle, whome he loved of the nobilitie and Whome he hated.

He aunswered y^t he hated no mā, and loved all alike well.

She asked him how he liked the Ladye Reresse and if he were angrye wth her.

He aunswered y^t he had litle minde of suche as she was, and wished of God she might serve her to her hono^r.

Then she desired him to kepe to him sellfe the promise betwixt him and her, and to open it to nobodye.   For padventure the Lordes woulde not thinke welle of their suddine agrement, consideringe he and theye were at some wordes before.

He aunswered that he knew no cause whye theye shulde mislike of it, and desired her y^t she would not move anye of thẽ against him even as he woulde stirre none againste her, and y^t theye would worke bothe in one mind, otherwise it might tourne to great^r inconvenience to them bothe.

She aunswered y^t she never sowght anye waie bye him, but he was in fault him sellfe.

He aunswered againe y^t hys faultes were published and y^t there were y^t made great^r faultes than ever he made y^t beleved were vnknownẽ, and yet theye woulde speke of greate and smale.

Farder the Kinge asked me at y^t present time what I thowght of hys voyage. I aunswered y^t I liked it not, bicause she tooke him to Cragmill^r. For if she had desired him wth her sellf or to have had hys companye, she would haue taken him to hys owne howse in Edinbr̃. Where she might more easely visit him, than to travelle two myles owt of the towne to a gentlemãis house. Therefore mye opiniõ was y^t she tooke him awaye more like a prison^r than her husbande.

He aunswered y^t he thowght litle lesse him sellf and feared him sellfe indeid save the confidence, he had in her promise onelye, notwithstandinge he woulde goe wth her, and put him sellfe in her handes, thowghe she showlde cutte hys throate and besowghte God to be iudge vnto them bothe.

Endorsed : ' Thomas Crawfordę deposit.'

INDEX

ABERCAIRNIE, Laird of, Mary's appeal to him on behalf of evicted cottars, 8

'Actio,' the, quoted, on Darnley's murder, 141, 142

'Admonition to the Trew Lordis,' cited, 151

Ainslie's band, purport of, 177, 178 ; defaulters from, 181 ; Morton's stipulation, 254 ; signers of, 329, 330 ; Morton's adhesion to, 383

Alava, Beaton's statement to him about Moray, 210

Alloa, Mary at, 80

'Appeal to Christian Princes,' cited, 240

Argyll, Earl of, disliked by Darnley, 73 ; lodged by Mary in Edinburgh Castle during her labour, 73, 75 ; at Craigmillar, 98 ; Paris's statement as to him and Mary on the night of Darnley's murder, 161 ; in confederation against Bothwell, 181 ; cited, 38

Arran, Earl of, blamed by Bothwell as the cause of the Protestant rebellion, 47 ; feud with Bothwell, 47, 49 ; reconciled to him through Knox, 50 ; discloses to Knox Bothwell's plot to seize Mary, 50 ; apprises Mary of the plot, 51

Atholl, Earl of (member of council), 172 ; confederated against Bothwell, 181 ; cited, 203

BAILLIE HAMILTON, Lady, on the Hamilton casket, 368, 369, 370

Balcanquell, Rev. Walter, receives Morton's confession, 148

Balfour, Sir James, concerned in the murder ' band ' against Darnley, 88, 90, 99 ; gives Bothwell the keys of Mary's room at Kirk o' Field, 163 ; persuaded by Lethington to surrender Edinburgh Castle, 186 ; charged by Mary with complicity in Darnley's murder, 189 ; the Casket in his keeping, 198 ; holds Edinburgh Castle, 274

Ballantyne, Patrick, said to have menaced Mary's life, 38

'Band of assurance for the murder ' of Riccio, 67, 68

Bannatyne (Knox's secretary), his account of the death of the Earl of Huntly, 38

Bannister (Norfolk's servant), Norfolk's statement to him regarding Letter II., 357

Bargany, Laird of, at cards with Archibald Douglas, 32

Barham, Serjeant, asserts that Lethington stole the Casket Letters and that his wife copied them, 248 ; denies that Mary received French copies, 249

Beaton, Archbishop (Mary's ambassador in France), communicates with Mary about Hiegait and Walker, 110, 114 ; affirms

F F